Stream Data Processing: A Quality of Service Perspective

Modeling, Scheduling, Load Shedding, and Complex Event Processing

ADVANCES IN DATABASE SYSTEMS

Volume 36

Series Editors

Ahmed K. Elmagarmid
Purdue University
West Lafayette, IN 47907

Amit P. Sheth
Wright State University
Dayton, Ohio 45435

For other titles published in this series, go to
www.springer.com/series/5573

Stream Data Processing: A Quality of Service Perspective

Modeling, Scheduling, Load Shedding, and Complex Event Processing

by

Sharma Chakravarthy
The University of Texas at Arlington
Arlington, TX, USA

Qingchun Jiang
Oracle Corporation
Redwood Shores, CA, USA

Sharma Chakravarthy
Department of Computer Science
& Engineering
University of Texas at Arlington
Arlington, TX 76019, USA
sharmac@uta.edu

Qingchun Jiang
Oracle Corporation
500 Oracle Parkway
Redwood Shores, CA 94065, USA
dustin.jiang@gmail.com

ISBN: 978-1-4419-4373-6 e-ISBN: 978-0-387-71003-7
DOI: 10.1007/978-0-387-71003-7

Printed on acid-free paper

springer.com

In Loving Memory of my father **Vidwan Chakravarthy Ananthachar** (27th June 1916 to 9th December 2000) who instilled in me an appreciation for learning and a thirst for knowledge

– Sharma Chakravarthy

To my wife **Ailing Wang**, and kids **George and Kevin** for their unconditional love and support

– Qingchun Jiang

Preface

In recent years, a new class of applications has come to the forefront – primarily due to the advancement in our ability to collect data from multitudes of devices, and process them efficiently. These include homeland security applications, sensor/pervasive computing applications, various kinds of monitoring applications, and even traditional applications belonging to financial, computer network management, and telecommunication domains. These applications need to process data continuously (and as long as data is available) from one or more sources. The sequence of data items continuously generated by sources is termed a data stream. Because of the possible never-ending nature of a data stream, the amount of data to be processed is likely to be unbounded. In addition, timely detection of interesting changes or patterns or aggregations over incoming data is critical for many of these applications. Furthermore, the data arrival rates may fluctuate over a period of time and may be bursty at times. For most of these applications, Quality of Service (or QoS) requirements, such as response time, memory usage, and throughput are extremely important. These application requirements make it infeasible to simply load the incoming data streams into a persistent store and process them effectively using currently available database management techniques.

As the currently used data processing paradigm does not fully meet the new requirements of these stream applications, the paradigm shift needed for the effective management of stream data needs to be understood, and new techniques/approaches have to be developed. As stream data is handled by applications in disparate domains, stream data processing can be addressed at different levels and in different contexts: processing of sensor data, pervasive computing, situation monitoring, real-time response, approximate algorithms, on-the-fly mining, complex event processing, or a combination thereof. Although the applications are diverse, some of the fundamental characteristics of stream data and their processing requirements remain common to most applications. Time-critical processing which can be generalized to a QoS requirement is one of the fundamental requirements and forms the thrust of this book. Prior to the advent of stream processing systems as a research area, database management systems (DBMSs) and their variants were used for some of the above applications. Hence, stream processing can also be related to earlier work on main-memory (or in-memory) databases, embedded databases, and real-time transaction processing systems. This book focuses on the QoS aspects of stream processing and concomitant extensions/modifications that are needed in comparison to the features supported by traditional DBMSs.

In this book, we first discuss the characteristics of stream data and its processing requirements to arrive at a paradigm shift, cull out some of the challenges of a data stream processing system (or a DSMS), and propose our solutions to the challenges. We develop an architecture along with the functional components required for processing data streams and meet the requirements of stream applications. After a broad literature survey to provide a bird's-eye view of the research and development efforts in the thrust areas of stream and complex event processing, the book focuses on functionalities of a DSMS from a *QoS* perspective. In other words, techniques and approaches required for guaranteeing QoS requirements are presented and elaborated in this book. This leads us to focus on the topics of: (*a*) continuous query modeling, (*b*) scheduling strategies for improving QoS, (*c*) load shedding to satisfy QoS requirements with minimal deviation in accuracy of results, and (*d*) synergistic integration of stream and complex event processing to satisfy end-to-end QoS requirements. In addition, we analyze a complex, real-life network fault management application in detail to infer the extensions needed for integrating stream and complex event processing. Finally, we describe the design and implementation of a stream processing system and its synergistic integration with an existing Complex Event Processing (CEP) system.

The organization of the book is designed to facilitate reading of groups of chapters depending upon reader's interest. By choosing appropriate chapters, readers of this book can obtain: an overview of the thrust areas (stream and complex event processing), technical details on important issues of focus topics, and insights into the architecture, design, and implementation of stream & CEP systems. The discussions are cross-referenced at the chapter and section level to help the reader.

Objectives

The objective of this book is to provide a comprehensive understanding of stream processing and its relationship with complex event processing. We start with an overview of these areas, a clear understanding of the processing requirements, and challenges leading to a review of the large body of work that exists in these two areas. We then provide a technical discussion of topics from a QoS perspective. This book also introduces readers to a new paradigm, its relevance, importance, and the theoretical underpinnings of the abstractions needed for the new paradigm. The book also addresses the transition of techniques into prototypes along with design and implementation details. The contents of this book have been chosen to highlight the QoS aspects of stream processing. The techniques presented here can be applied to other domains and applications as well. In summary, this book provides the state of the art in the areas of stream and complex event processing, presents technical details on selected topics, and discusses design and implementation of prototypes to make the book useful for a diverse audience.

Intended Audience

What background should one have to appreciate this book and benefit the most? Someone who has an undergraduate or a graduate degree in computer science has that background. Those who have taken a course on or have worked with database management systems can readily relate to the paradigm shift and its details. An understanding of relational databases and mathematical inclination will help the reader in enjoying the technical contents of this book. We provide adequate discussion of related work so that the reader can understand and appreciate the approaches and techniques presented in the book. The discussion of prototypes provides insights into the design and implementation issues of a data stream management system that integrates complex event processing in a seamless manner.

This book would be of interest to: senior undergraduate and graduate students, computer professionals, IT managers, database management system users & administrators, time-critical or event-driven application developers, and developers dealing with publish/subscribe systems.

Acknowledgements

This book owes its existence to a large number of people who have played an active role throughout the development of the work presented in the book. The support from National Science Foundation (NSF) for the `MavHome` project (ITR grant 0121297) at The University of Texas at Arlington (UTA) was instrumental in getting us started on this problem. Qingchun's background in managing network applications and the frustrations he faced in the absence of a data stream processing system provided some of the impetus for this work. Another NSF grant (IIS 0534611) for the integration of stream and event processing helped us continue the work and complete the `MavEStream` prototype.

The following students at UTA enthusiastically worked on the `MavStream` and `MavEStream` prototypes as part of their theses: Altaf Gilani, Satyajeet Sonune, Vamshi Pajjuri, Bala Kumar Kendai, and Vihang Garg. Their contributions to this book are very much appreciated. Raman Adaikkalavan has contributed extensively to the contents of chapters on the integration of events with streams and prototype implementations. We sincerely thank him for his contributions and for his time during the semester on this book. Raman has also edited the entire book, added most of the index, and has improved its technical presentation significantly. It is also our pleasure to thank our colleagues at UTA who were part of the `MavHome` project, especially Diane Cook and Larry Holder.

Proofreading is an arduous and time-consuming task. We were lucky to have several volunteers helping us out on this. We want to thank the following for improving the readability and the quality of presentation of the book: Raman Adaikkalavan, Reuben Brooks, Tejas Chakravarthy, Mohan Kumar, Jonathan Ndede, Roochi Mishra, Charu Puri, and Aditya Telang. Sincere thanks to Aditya Telang for also helping us extensively with figures and references.

Sharma Chakravarthy would like to thank his wife *Shubha* and son *Tejas*, and Qingchun Jiang would like to thank his wife *Ailing* and kids *Kevin* and *George* for their patience, love, encouragement, and support during the preparation of this book.

Last but not least, we would like to thank Ahmed Elmagarmid for suggesting that we consider writing a book on stream processing. This book would not have been possible without the patience, gentle nudging, and timely support of Susan Lagerstrom-Fife and Sharon Palleschi of Springer throughout the preparation of this book. Our sincere thanks to Deborah from Springer author support for resolving several issues on formatting and font usage.

Southlake, Texas
Foster City, California

Sharma Chakravarthy
Qingchun Jiang
November 2008

How to Use the Book

This book can be used in several ways. It can be used as a reference book, but the contents and organization have been successfully used for a graduate course as well. Organization of this book is meant to help readers maximize their benefit based on their interest in the areas of stream and complex event processing.

It is important to read the first three chapters (Introduction, Overview of Data Stream Processing, and DSMS Challenges) as it sets the stage for the rest of the contents of the book. These chapters introduce the problem and characteristics of stream data processing, continuous queries, need for window-based computation, and differences between stream processing & conventional data processing paradigms leading to the challenges arising from the new requirements. The DSMS challenges chapter also includes a concise overview of the material covered in each chapter of the book to provide a sneak peek into what is coming.

The chapter on literature survey (Chapter 4) provides a broad overview of the work carried out in stream and complex event processing along with an exhaustive bibliography. Most of the research systems and some commercial systems are introduced. In addition, detailed discussion of related work in focus topics is provided. The reader can gauge the interest of the research and vendor community on the thrust areas by the number of currently available prototypes and systems. The large number of references provided in the book is meant to help the reader access additional materials as needed. Internet links are also provided, where possible, for theses, technical reports, and home pages of commercial systems.

Each of the next three chapters (Modeling Continuous Queries over Data Streams, Scheduling Strategies for Continuous Queries, and Load Shedding in a DSMS) are fairly technical and self-contained with respect to its topic. These can be read selectively based on the interest of the reader. Each chapter discusses a problem and our proposed solution to that problem. Some of the theoretical aspects can be skipped without sacrificing the understandability of the chapter contents. A concise non-technical summary of these chapters is provided in Chapter 3.

The purpose of Chapter 8 (NFM^i : An Inter-Domain Network Fault Management System) is primarily to analyze a complex, real-life application to cull out the critical requirements beyond stream processing. This chapter brings out the need for integrating complex event processing with stream processing.

Those who are mainly interested in complex event processing can read the first and the fourth chapters to obtain an understanding of CEP development, and continue with Chapters 8 on the need for complex event processing. Chapter 9 analyzes the similarities and differences between the two areas before providing a synergistic, integrated solution. If the design and implementation of systems is of interest, read Chapters 10 and 11 after reading the first four setting-the-stage chapters.

We have summarized the usage of the book into an easy-to-use format, based on the areas of interest, in the Table below.

Areas \ Chapters	1	2	3	4	5	6	7	8	9	10	11	12
Stream Processing (SP)	✔	✔	✔	✔	✔[1]	✔[1]	✔[1]					✔
SP Design & Implementation	✔	✔	✔							✔		✔
Complex Event Processing (CEP)	✔			✔				✔	✔		✔	✔
SP & CEP Integration	✔	✔	✔	✔				✔	✔		✔	✔
SP & CEP	✔	✔	✔	✔	✔	✔	✔	✔	✔	✔	✔	✔

[1] These chapters can be read selectively

Mapping of Areas of Discussion to Chapter Contents

Sharma Chakravarthy continues to use the contents of this book (sans some of the theoretical details) to teach a one-semester graduate course on stream and complex event processing at UTA. Hands-on implementation projects are included to appreciate and apply the concepts taught, and to enhance the course experience. Students implement the same stream and event processing application using different freely available systems to analyze: expressiveness, ease of application development, QoS evaluation, and the ability to handle large data sets. Students discuss their project experience with the rest of the class through an in-class presentation. Most of the stream and complex event processing systems used for the course, such as StreamBase, Aleri, AMiT, Snoop/Sentinel, Coral8, Esper, and RuleCore are available free-of-charge for teaching purposes or as trial/lite/open source versions.

If you are interested in adapting this book for teaching, preliminary slides for the contents of the book can be obtained by sending email to `sharma@cse.uta.edu` with course information.

Contents

List of Figures

List of Tables

List of Algorithms

1

INTRODUCTION

Traditional relational database management systems (DBMSs), consisting of a set of persistent relations, a set of well-defined operations, and highly optimized query processing and transaction management components, have been researched for over thirty years and are used for a wide range of applications. Typically, data processed by a DBMS is less frequently updated, and a snapshot of the database is used for processing queries. Abstractions derived from the applications for which a DBMS [1–10] is intended, such as consistency, concurrency, recovery, and optimization have received a lot of attention.

However, the past two decades have witnessed several classes of applications with additional and/or different set of requirements than those provided by a traditional DBMS. For example, data warehouses have been developed for Online Analytical Processing (OLAP). OLAP requirements have resulted in new techniques for data consolidation from multiple source databases. Furthermore, traditional Online Transactions Processing (OLTP) has been extended to carry out powerful data analysis with flexible aggregation and drill-down capability. As another example, the advent of the Internet has given rise to requirements for supporting eXtended Markup Language (XML) data types and their processing. As a result, DBMSs have successfully accommodated these advances by adding new capabilities to store and process structured, unstructured, and multi-media data types. Similarly, knowledge discovery research has prompted mining of large data sets directly from a relational DBMS using novel mining operators and the Structured Query Language (SQL). The requirements of the above applications have advanced the scope, functionality, and utility of DBMSs.

In recent years, we have witnessed the emergence of another class of data-intensive applications such as sensor data processing, traffic monitoring, and stock trading, that need to process data at a high input-rate. These applications need to process data *continuously* over long periods of time and the data is typically received in the form of a *data stream*. As a result, the amount of data to be processed can be unbounded or never ending. At the same time, these applications need processing capabilities for continuously computing and

S. Chakravarthy and Q. Jiang, *Stream Data Processing: A Quality of Service Perspective*,
Advances in Database Systems 36, DOI: 10.1007/978-0-387-71003-7_1,

aggregating incoming data for identifying interesting changes or patterns in a *timely manner*. Some examples involving processing of data streams are: (*i*) to monitor traffic slowdown or accidents using data sent by each car on the road every few seconds or minutes, (*ii*) to perform program trading based on changes in the stock price of a particular stock relative to other stock prices using data from multiple feeds, and (*iii*) to monitor environmental and security applications for water quality, fire spread, etc. based on data received from sensors. These applications are different from traditional DBMS applications with respect to data arrival rates, update frequency, processing requirements, Quality of Service (QoS) needs, and notification support.

Queries that are processed by a traditional DBMS are termed *ad hoc* queries. They are (typically) specified, optimized, and evaluated *once* over a snapshot of a database. In contrast, queries in a stream processing environment are termed *continuous queries or CQs*. CQs are specified once and evaluated *repeatedly* against new data over a specified life span or as long as there exists data in the stream. They are long-running queries that produce output continuously. The result is also assumed to be a stream possibly with differing rates and schema (as compared to the input). The difference between *ad hoc* queries and *CQs* can be best understood based on their relationship to the data over which they are processed. Different or changing *ad hoc* queries are processed over (relatively) static data in contrast to the same (or static) *CQs* that are processed repeatedly over frequently changing (or dynamic) data.

Traditional DBMSs can be used for stream processing by loading incoming stream data into persistent relations and executing the same *ad hoc* queries over these relations repeatedly. The main problem with this approach is that the storage of stream data, indexing (as needed) and querying will add considerable delay (or latency) in response time that may not be acceptable to many stream applications. The requirement that data needs to be persisted on secondary storage device (that has high latency) before it can be accessed and processed by a DBMS in main memory (that has low latency) is at the core of this mismatch. In addition, the snapshot approach for evaluating stream data may not always be appropriate as the values over an interval are important (e.g., temperature changes) for stream processing applications. Furthermore, the inability to specify quality of service requirements (such as latency or response time) to a DBMS makes its usage less acceptable for stream applications. Finally, conventional query optimization geared towards the minimization of disk accesses (or input/output) may not be the right model for stream data processing applications.

It is clear that applications that process stream data[1] do not readily fit the traditional DBMS model and its processing paradigm since DBMSs were not designed to manage high-frequency updates (in the form of data streams) and to provide continuous computation and output for queries. Hence, the

[1] Data stream and stream data are used interchangeably throughout this book.

techniques developed for DBMSs need to be re-examined to meet the requirements of applications that use stream data. This re-examination has given rise to a paradigm shift along with new approaches and extensions to current techniques for query modeling, optimization, and data processing to meet the requirements of an increasing number of stream-based applications. Systems that have been developed to process data streams to meet the needs of stream-based applications are termed Data Stream Management Systems (DSMSs) in the literature.

1.1 Paradigm Shift

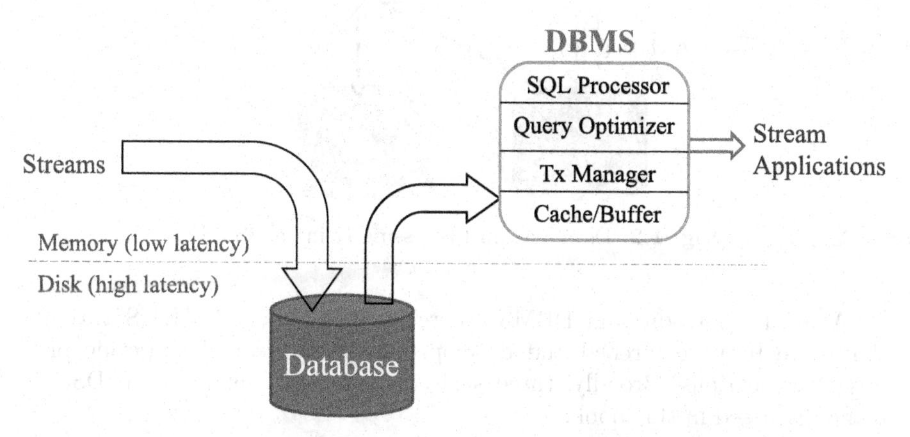

Fig. 1.1. Data Stream Processing Using a DBMS

The basic shift in the paradigm between a DBMS and a DSMS is summarized in Figures 1.1 and 1.2 (adapted from [11]). Figure 1.1 indicates the use of a traditional DBMS for stream processing. Stream data is first persisted in a database and queries are processed over stored data. This approach incurs two I/Os (input/output) for each data item (actually a group/page) processed. And because of high arrival rates of data items coupled with storage and retrieval latency, processing of data items is likely to lag resulting in increased response time for query results. In contrast, Figure 1.2 shows an architecture where the incoming streams are processed *directly* by a DSMS. Hence, I/O is not incurred for any data item thereby decreasing the response time of query results. The data may also be persisted for archival or other purposes (e.g., processing *ad hoc* queries or queries over past data). However, this archiving is done without affecting the computation and performance of continuous queries. It should be noted that, as part of stream processing, data from a DBMS may need to be accessed (e.g., Radio Frequency IDentification

(RFID) applications, click-stream processing applications). This can be done either by efficiently accessing the DBMS or by caching the data required for continuous query processing. Modeling of access to stored relations as part of continuous query processing is addressed in Section 5.3.4 on continuous query modeling.

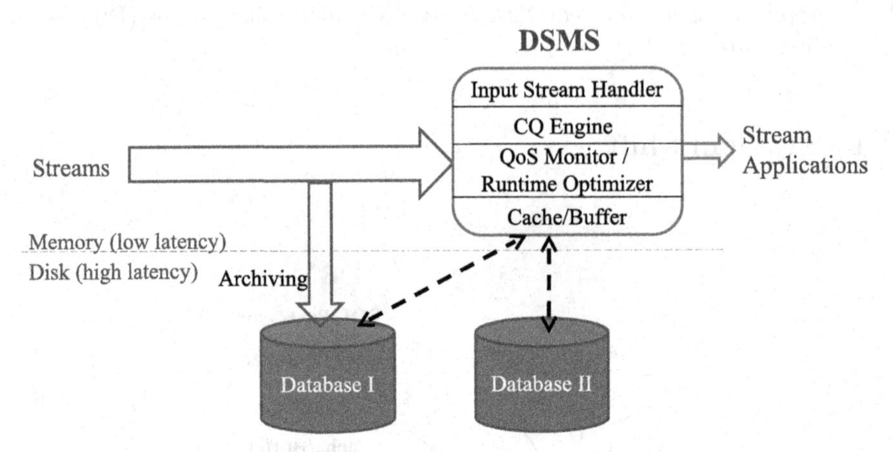

Fig. 1.2. Data Stream Processing Using a DSMS

Apart from traditional DBMSs there are a number of DBMS variants that have been researched and developed over the years for specific purposes/applications. Broadly, three such variants have relevance to DSMSs being discussed in this book:

1. Main memory (or in-memory) DBMSs [12–17]: they cache large amounts of data as well as index in main memory and provide all the functionality of a DBMS including recovery.
2. Embedded DBMSs [18–22]: are used as a component of larger applications with a small footprint and typically include a subset of DBMS functionality.
3. Real-time transaction processing systems (also termed real-time database systems) [23–61]: they satisfy response time requirements of transactions while preserving the transactional properties of a DBMS. They are different from real-time processing or scheduling of tasks with deadlines which do not adhere to transactional requirements.

Without going into additional details, there are fundamental differences between each of the above and a DSMS although some of the goals for the development of the variants were similar. For example, reduction in the footprint and speeding up of main memory query processing were the driving forces behind main-memory and embedded DBMSs. Real-time transaction processing dealt with different types of deadlines (e.g., soft, firm, and hard) associated with database transactions, which are expected to preserve ACID properties (atomicity, consistency, isolation, and durability). The differences among main memory, embedded, and real-time transaction processing systems are often blurred in the literature and product advertisement as some of the features overlap.

1.2 Data Stream Applications

To underscore the ubiquitous nature of data streams in diverse domains and the applications associated with them, we provide a few examples below:

Telecommunication applications: the Call Detail Record (CDR) or Station Message Detail Recording (SMDR) information, and various messages from network elements such as alarm messages, performance messages, and others, fall into the category of stream data. The online billing system requires processing CDR information in real-time in order to generate billing information on the fly. The universal fault management system is required to analyze alarm messages from various sources such as transport networks (e.g., Synchronous Optical NETworking or SONET and Synchronous Digital Hierarchy or SDH), switch networks (e.g., AT&T Class 5 Telephone Electronic Switching System or 5ESS, Nortel Digital Multiplex System or DMS100), signaling systems (e.g., Signaling System #7 or SS7), and intelligent network systems (e.g., 800 service and other value-added systems), in order to locate the primary causes of various faults in real-time. This application is discussed in detail in Chapter 8.

Sensor applications: sensor data monitoring [62, 63] is another group of applications of data stream processing; they are used to monitor various events and conditions using complex filtering and computations over sensor data streams. For example, the highway traffic monitoring and querying (discussed in more detail in Chapters 9 and 11), the smart home at UTA [62, 64], environmental and other types of monitoring are examples of sensor-generated stream processing applications.

Financial applications: the data arising out of stock trading, cash flows, and credit card transactions can be viewed as data streams. The online analysis over these streams includes discovering correlations, identifying trends and outliers (fraud detection), forecasting future values, program trading, etc.

Computer network management applications: the Simple Network Management Protocol (SNMP) data, the routing table information (such as Border Gateway Protocol (BGP) table information), and the network traffic information are representative streams in the network field. All these data arrive rapidly and are usually unbounded in size. Traffic engineering and network security [65] are two representative applications of data stream processing systems in computer network management field.

Homeland security applications: the data from various devices (e.g., scanners, cameras) at an airport security check, border monitoring, or financial transactions can be viewed as data streams used for detecting abnormal behavior through analysis and correlation of incoming data with information from other sources or databases.

Online applications: online banking generates individual transaction streams which need to be analyzed in a timely manner to identify potential fraud. Online auction systems such as ebay [66] generate real-time bid streams and these systems need to update the current bid price and make decisions real-time. Large web sites such as Yahoo [67] and search engines such as Google [68] generate numerous web-clicks and user-queries that need to be analyzed to enable applications such as personalization, load balancing, advertising, etc. on the fly.

Others: other applications include: Healthcare (patient condition monitoring), Global Positioning System (GPS) data processing, supply-chain for large retailers such as Wal-Mart that use Radio Frequency IDentification (RFID) tags.

All of the above applications require some common abstractions that form the core functionality of a DSMS. In the rest of the book, we delve into the details of data stream processing, related literature on stream and complex event processing (as correlation and timely alerting is needed for many stream-based applications), architecture as well as the suite of techniques needed for the success of a DSMS. Continuous query examples in Chapter 2 and the application elaborated in Chapter 8 are drawn from the telecommunication domain.

1.3 Book Organization

The remainder of this book is organized as follows – we begin by providing an overview of data stream processing, important characteristics of streams as well as their applications leading to the architecture of a QoS-aware DSMS in Chapter 2. We discuss the challenges that arise from the QoS requirements of a DSMS in Chapter 3 along with a chapter-by-chapter summary of the rest of the book. We present a broad literature review of stream processing systems and a comparison of work relevant to the topics addressed in this book in Chapter 4. We then present our queueing theory-based continuous query modeling to facilitate system capacity planning and QoS requirements verification in Chapter 5. We develop a number of scheduling strategies along with detailed theoretical and experimental analysis in Chapter 6. In Chapter 7, we present a set of comprehensive QoS delivery mechanisms to handle bursty nature of input data streams in a DSMS.

We present a complex, real-life network management application in Chapter 8. This representative application vividly brings out the need for combining complex event processing with stream data management. Chapter 9 thoroughly analyzes both stream and event processing models to arrive at an architecture for the synergistic integration of the two. In Chapter 10, we discuss the design and implementation of `MavStream`[2] prototype. Integration of `MavStream` with an existing event processing system (Local Event Detector or LED, based on the Snoop event specification language) resulting in the `MavEStream` prototype is discussed in Chapter 11. One of the goals of `MavEStream` is to provide a system that accepts and supports end-to-end application characteristics (e.g., QoS) outlined in Section 2.2. Finally, Chapter 12 concludes with the long-term vision of the applicability of the techniques presented in this book along with research directions in the thrust areas.

[2] The prefix `Mav` for our projects and prototypes comes from the `Mavericks`, the name of UT Arlington's athletic teams (the selection was made in 1971 and predates the Dallas Mavericks choice in 1980).

2

OVERVIEW OF DATA STREAM PROCESSING

Informally, a *data stream* is defined as an unbounded (or never-ending) sequence of *data items* that are usually ordered either explicitly by a timestamp or by the values of one or more *data elements* (e.g., packet sequence identifier in an IP session). It is assumed that the format of a data stream is known in terms of its data elements and their types. Simplistically, a data item of a data stream can be viewed as a tuple[1] of a relation. Correspondingly, a data element of a data item is analogous to an attribute of a relation.

2.1 Data Stream Characteristics

Some characteristics of data streams (e.g., arrival rates of data items, number of attributes, value ranges of attributes, etc.) vary from one another based on the source. However, most data streams share a set of common characteristics that need to be taken into consideration along with their implications for designing a data stream management system. Some of the data stream characteristics and their implications are:

- Data items arrive *continuously* and *sequentially* as a stream and are usually ordered by a timestamp value or other attribute values of the data item. Therefore, data items belonging to the same data stream are usually processed in the order they arrive[2].
- Data streams are usually generated by external sources or other applications and are sent to a Data Stream management System (DSMS). Typically, DSMSs do not have direct access or control over the data sources.

[1] Where it is clear from the context, tuples and data items are used interchangeably throughout the book. Similarly, attributes and data elements are used interchangeably.

[2] It is possible that data items of a stream arrive out of order within a bounded period of time. This issue has been addressed in some systems (e.g., [63]). Most of the discussions in this book assume that the data items arrive in proper order.

S. Chakravarthy and Q. Jiang, *Stream Data Processing: A Quality of Service Perspective*,
Advances in Database Systems 36, DOI: 10.1007/978-0-387-71003-7_2,

- The input characteristics of a data stream are usually not controllable, and are typically unpredictable. The input rate of a data stream ranges from a few bytes per second (for example the readings of a sensor) to a few gigabits per second (such as data traffic over an OC-768 channel at Sprint). Also, the input rate of a data stream can be irregular and at times, bursty in nature. A number of data streams with the so-called self-similar property are highly bursty. Examples of such streams include the local Ethernet traffic streams [69], HTTP traffic flows [70], and Email-messages. Also, the nature of the input does not allow one to easily make multiple passes over a data stream while processing.
- The amount of data in a stream can be very large. For example, the AT&T CDR records are about 1 gigabytes per hour [71] and an OC-768 at Sprint can carry data traffic at speeds as high as 40 gigabits per second. Theoretically, the size of a data stream is potentially unbounded. Therefore, processing requirements may not permit persistence followed by processing. However, the stream (or parts of it) may be persisted, in addition to its processing, for archival or other purposes.
- The data types of attributes in a data stream can be: well-structured data (e.g., temperature readings); semi-structured data (e.g., HTTP log streams, message streams from a circuit switch, complex XML documents); or unstructured data (e.g., Emails, newsfeed).
- Data items in a data stream are not error-free because the data sources are external. Some data items may be corrupted or discarded due to network/transmission problems.

The above characteristics of data streams are very different from those assumed for relations processed by traditional DBMSs and as a result they pose many new challenges in the design of DSMSs (discussed in Chapter 3). One way to understand a DSMS is to think of it as a generalization of a DBMS where certain assumptions are relaxed/modified. For example, relations are no longer persisted, the same tuple/object is not accessed multiple times, and QoS specifications need to be supported. It is possible that the functionality of both a DBMS and a DSMS is needed for an application.

2.2 Data Stream Application Characteristics

The functionality of a DSMS is dictated by the common processing requirements of stream-based applications (listed in Section 1.2). These requirements can be distilled into a set of abstractions that need to be supported by a DSMS. Stream-based application characteristics are summarized below:

- Continuous processing of newly arrived data is necessary for all stream-based applications. This means that a query is long-running (unlike *ad hoc* queries) and needs to be evaluated repeatedly by the system against new data until the query is terminated.

- Many applications can tolerate approximate results as long as other critical (e.g., response time) requirements are satisfied. Approximate results are acceptable when accurate results are either not available or when the system consumes too much of critical resources for computing accurate results. For example, an internet search engine provider such as Google wants to personalize the result pages by inserting related advertisements or recommendations based on a query from user interaction. For each user, a DSMS computes relevant active advertisements and then inserts the top 5 (most relevant) advertisements into the pages shown to the user. During high-load periods, the system may not find the exact top 5 advertisements due to the limited resources and it may be acceptable to provide any 5 related or even less than 5 advertisements.
- Many applications have very specific QoS requirements. Some of the common QoS requirements include: response time (also termed tuple latency), precision, throughput, and allowed memory usage. As these QoS requirements are not independent of each other (e.g., reducing tuple latency typically increases memory requirement), choosing one can affect others dramatically. Hence, there exists trade-offs among these QoS metrics that need to be judiciously balanced by a DSMS based on application needs.
- Usage of available resources (e.g., cpu cycles, memory) to maximize their impact on QoS metrics is critical for stream-based applications. A DSMS needs to incorporate mechanisms for the optimal usage of resources. Tools for capacity planning will also be valuable for designing stream-based applications.
- Finally, Complex Event Processing (CEP), rule processing, and notification are other important requirements of many stream-based applications that detect events or conditions and have to fire rules/triggers/actions in a timely manner when abnormal or user-defined events are detected. For example, by analyzing the temperature and smoke readings from sensors in a smart home environment, a DSMS needs to take a sequence of actions such as dialing 911 for a fire alarm once it detects fire through a combination of temperature and smoke readings within a small geographical area of a building.

It is not possible to satisfy the above requirements of stream-based applications by simply loading the data streams into a state-of-the-art DBMS and processing queries. A DBMS may be useful for providing persistent data management and transaction management support for some stream-based applications. However, it is not designed to provide continuous results. A traditional DBMS has no support for QoS requirements and assumes that all (as well as accurate) results need to be generated for a query. Therefore, a different paradigm to stream processing (shown in Figure 1.2) is used to support the new requirements culled from a large number of emerging stream-based applications.

2.3 Continuous Queries

Continuous queries (CQs) are those that are processed repeatedly against new data to produce new results. They are long-running and produce results continuously. They may also access stored relations in some cases. Continuous queries are typically associated with stream-based applications. Most of the research on DSMS in the literature use the Structured Quer Language (SQL) – a standard for relational DBMSs – with some extensions and modifications to specify the semantics of continuous query processing. Typically, continuous queries consist of relational operators[3] such as `select`, `project`, `join`, and other `aggregation` operators. A logical query plan, analogous to a query tree used in a traditional DBMS, can be generated from the specification of a continuous query. It can then be transformed into a query plan consisting of detailed algorithms used for computing each operator.

Although it makes sense to consider a continuous query as a query plan consisting of operators, the operator and computation semantics are somewhat different from those in a DBMS:

1. All operators in a DSMS compute on data items as they arrive and cannot assume the stream to be finite. This has significant implications for the computation of a number of operators such as `join`, `sort`, and some `aggregation` operators. These operations cannot be completed without processing the entire input data set (or sets) which poses problems due to the unbounded nature of streams. As a result, these operators will `block` and produce no output until the stream ends. Hence, they are termed `blocking` operators. Other relational operators (e.g., `select`, `project`) that work on a single data item at a time do not block computation.

   For an operator to output results continuously (and hopefully smoothly) and not wait until the end of the stream, it is imperative that these `blocking` operators be converted into `non-blocking` ones. The notion of a `window` has been introduced to overcome the `blocking` aspect of a number of operators. Informally, a `window` defines a finite portion of the stream (as a relation) for processing purposes. A `window` specification, added to a continuous query specification, can produce time-varying, finite relations out of a stream.

   As a consequence, algorithms for the `blocking` operators have been modified by imposing a `window` over each input data stream. Several `window`-based algorithms have been proposed to compute `join` over streams [73–76].

---

[3] The operators and continuous query languages supported by stream or CEP systems vary considerably from one another. In this book, we are using relational operators as examples. However, the framework used is independent of the operators and allows for adding new operators. Currently, there is a proposal for making StreamSQL [72] – an extension of SQL – as a standard for real-time stream and complex event processing.

2. Continuous queries are computed using a push or dataflow paradigm in contrast to the traditional pipelined or iterator-based pull paradigm employed by traditional DBMSs. In traditional DBMSs, a query plan is processed by starting the computation at the root operator by obtaining tuples from each of its child operators. Each child operator, in turn, recursively calls on its child operators to get required tuples in order to output computed results to its parent. Leaf nodes can always access data from stored relations.

   However, in a DSMS, the input characteristics of a data stream do not lend themselves for the pull paradigm as the operators would be blocked if there was no input from one of its child operator temporarily. Also, when there are no inputs at one operator, the processing of that operator needs to be suspended and switched to another operator that has inputs. Hence, to accommodate the input nature of data stream processing, a push paradigm is used and the tuples are pushed from leaf operators gradually to the parent operators.
3. Each operator takes one or more streams as input and produces an output stream which can be fed to one or more operators. In addition, each operator may need to buffer tuples during bursty input periods in order not to lose incoming or partially processed data items. Hence, all operators are associated with a main memory queue (or a buffer), which is used to store (not persist) unprocessed or partially processed data items. As a result, the output of an operator is directly sent to the input queues of one or more operators.

Due to the processing differences outlined above, a query plan processed by a DSMS consists of a set of `non-blocking` operators and the queues that connect them. Figure 2.1 contrasts a query plan of a DBMS with that of a DSMS with respect to buffering and processing paradigm. Continuous query processing over data streams can be conceptualized as a data flow diagram as shown in Figure 2.1-(a). In Figure 2.1-(a), a node (e.g., OP1) represents a `non-blocking` operator. While a directed edge (along with the buffer) between two nodes represents the input and output relationship between those two operators. Each leaf node (e.g., OP1) has one or more buffers (depending on the operator type) into which the incoming streams are fed. The root node of the plan (e.g., OP2) produces the results of a CQ and are consumed by an application. The synopsis shown with each node (or operator) corresponds to the resources (primarily main memory) that is needed to hold state information to perform `window`-based computations correctly. For some operators such as `select`, there is no need for a synopsis as no state information need to be maintained; whereas for a `symmetric hash join`, a synopsis is needed. For the `symmetric hash join`, the synopsis consists of the hash tables for the two participating relations for the duration of the `window`.

In contrast, Figure 2.1-(b) represents the widely-used, iterator-based (or pull-based) left-deep tree for processing relational queries. Typically, the intermediate results are pipelined (and not materialized) unless warranted for operations such as sort-merge join and aggregation.

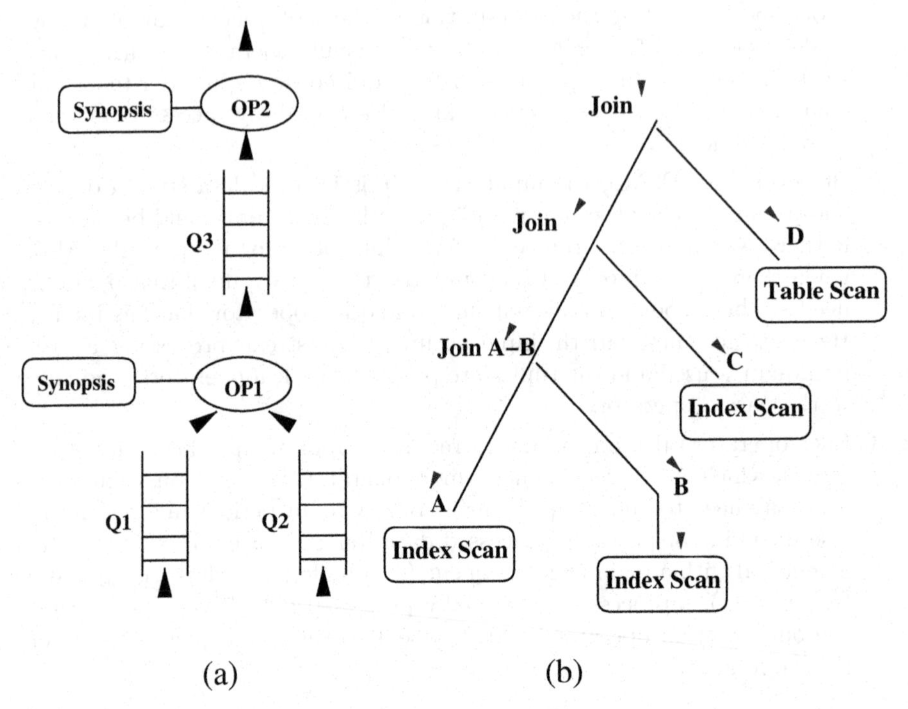

Fig. 2.1. Query Processing in a DSMS Vs. DBMS

2.3.1 Window Specification

As explained earlier, blocking operators are modified to compute in a non-blocking mode by imposing a window. A window is defined as a historical snapshot of a finite portion of a stream at any time point. A window defines the meaningful set of data used by operators to compute their functions. Briefly, two basic types of windows are used widely: time-based (or a physical window) and tuple-based (or a logical window). A time-based window can be simply expressed as [Range N time units, advance M time units] and a tuple-based window can be expressed as [Row N tuples, advance M tuples]. Range specifies the size of the first window. How the window advances to form a new window is specified by the advance component. Absence of advance corresponds to a disjoint window specification. A window can be specified for each data stream used by a query and is applied to all the operators of that query. The window specification can be different for the same stream in different queries. A window is usually specified as a sliding (or rolling) one – either as overlapping or as disjoint (or tumbling) . An overlapping window shares a portion of the current window with the next one whereas a disjoint one does not. The `FROM` clause of SQL is extended to include the `window` specification.

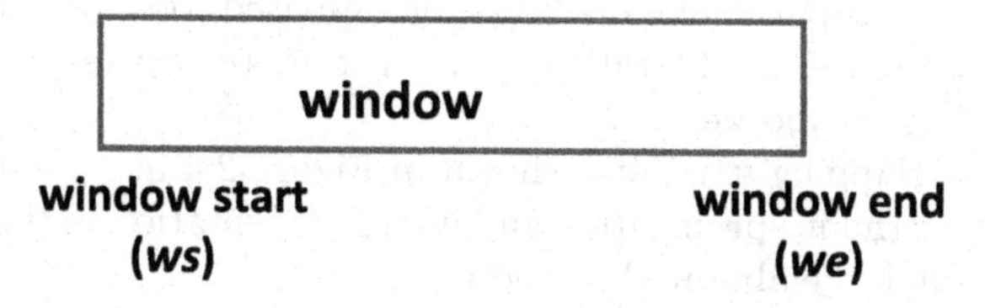

Fig. 2.2. A `Window` With Start and End Boundaries

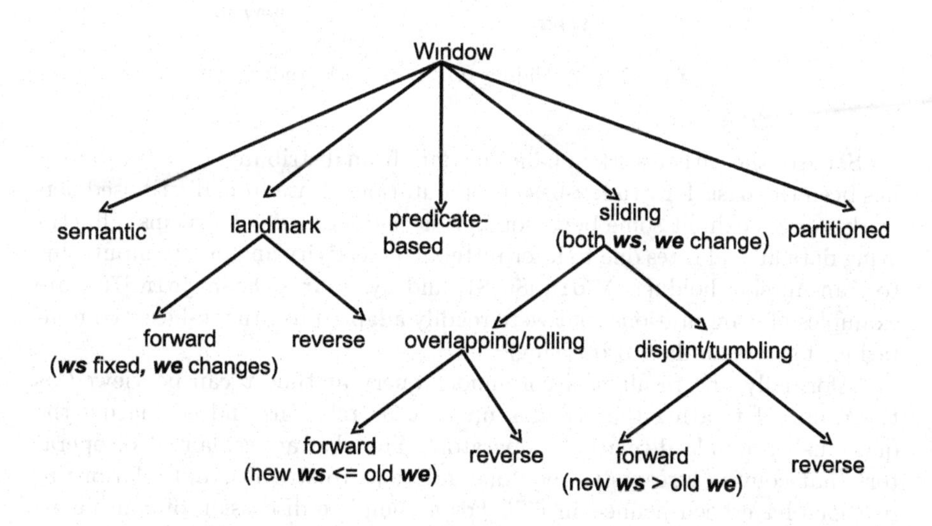

Fig. 2.3. `Window` Types and Their Specification Using Start and End Boundaries

A window is shown in Figure 2.2. The start and end boundaries of a `window` are indicated by the variables `ws` and `we`, respectively. Figure 2.3 depicts different types of `windows` along with how `ws` and `we` are related to consecutive `window` specifications: (*i*) landmark `window` (where the start `ws` of the `window` remains fixed and the end `we` changes), (*ii*) a sliding disjoint or tumbling `window` (where `ws` of next `window` is greater than the `we` of the previous window), (*iii*) a sliding overlapping window (where ws of the next window is less than or equal to the we of the previous window), (*iv*) reverse window types for all of the above where the window boundaries grow/move in the reverse direction over past data items of the stream, and (*v*) other window types such as partitioned [77], predicate-based [78], and semantic [79] have been proposed in the literature. They are more expressive and cannot be specified using ws and we.

A sliding overlapping window is shown in Figure 2.4 along with start and end boundaries. Window specification and its implementation in the MavStream prototype are further elaborated in Section 10.2.

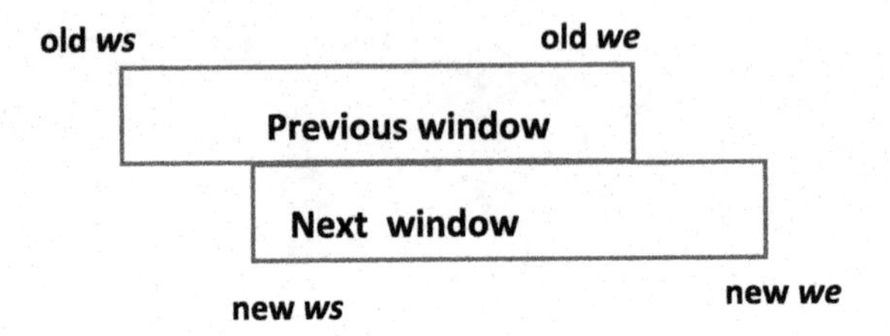

Fig. 2.4. A Sliding (Overlapping) Window

Some of the earlier work in handling data from distributed network sources has been the basis for window-based computations. Data from distributed network sources exhibit some behavior that is characteristic of streams – fluctuating data arrival rates due to intermittent connectivity and bursty inputs due to transmission holdups. XJoin [80, 81] and symmetric hash join [76]) are examples of computations that were readily adapted to window-based computations for stream data processing.

Informally, the result of a continuous query at time t can be viewed as the result of treating the streams up to t as relations and evaluating the query using standard relational operators. The abstract semantics of operators that convert streams to relations, relations to streams, and relations to relations have been defined in [77]. For a complete discussion of continuous query language (CQL) specification and semantics, refer to [72, 77].

2.3.2 Examples of Continuous Queries

Consider the call data record (CDR) streams from circuit switches of a large telecommunication service provider illustrated in Figure 2.5. CDR records are collected for each outgoing or incoming call at a central office. Four fields – *call_ID*, *caller* for outgoing call or *callee* for incoming call, *time*, and *event* (either *START* or *END*) – are extracted from each CDR and sent to a DSMS. Various types of processing can be done over CDR streams using continuous queries. Below are a few sample continuous queries over *Outgoing* and *Incoming* data streams. We assume that the unique call_ID is the same for all switches along the path of a phone call.

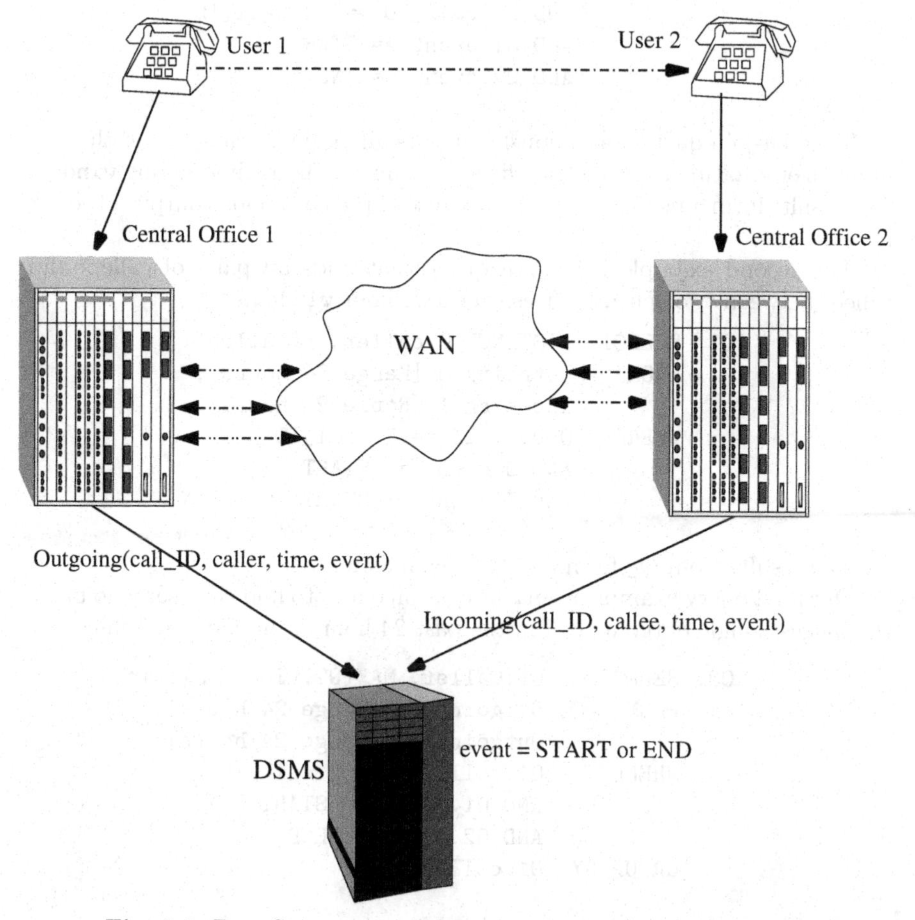

Fig. 2.5. Data Streams in a Telecommunication Service Provider

The first continuous query `Q1` finds all the *outgoing calls* from central office 1 longer than 10 minutes over a 24 hour `window` (assume that no call lasts longer than 24 hours).

```
Q1: SELECT  O1.call_ID, O1.caller
    FROM    Outgoing O1 [Range 24 hours],
            Outgoing O2 [Range 24 hours]
    WHERE   (O2.time - O1.time) > 10 minutes
            AND O1.call_ID == O2.call_ID
            AND O1.event == START
            AND O2.event == END
```

This self-join query continuously outputs all outgoing calls longer than 10 minutes originating from central office 1 within a 24 hour time sliding `window`. The results form a new data stream because of the continuous output of result records.

The second example is a `join` query that finds all pairs of callers and callees between two central offices over a 24 hour `window`.

```
Q2: SELECT  DISTINCT O.caller, I.callee
    FROM    Outgoing O [Range 24 hours],
            Incoming I [Range 24 hours]
    WHERE   O.call_ID == I.call_ID
            AND O.event == START
            AND I.event == START
```

The results from Q_2 form a data stream as well.

Our final query example is an aggregation query to find the user who made the longest single outgoing call in the past 24 hours from a central office.

```
Q3: SELECT    O1.Caller, MAX(O2.time - O1.time)
    FROM      Outgoing O1 [Range 24 hours],
              Outgoing O2 [Range 24 hours]
    WHERE     O1.call_ID == O2.call_ID
              AND O1.event == START
              AND O2.event == END
    GROUP BY  O1.caller
```

2.3.3 QoS Metrics

QoS management is important and critical to the success of a DSMS. The QoS metrics that are considered in this book are:

1. Tuple latency or mean tuple latency: the amount of time or the average amount of time it takes for a tuple or a sequence of tuples to go through processing (including any waits in the buffers) of a query.
2. Memory usage: maximum amount of memory used by the system [4] .

[4] Synopses associated with the operators of a plan are not *usually* counted in the maximum amount of memory used by the system; the amount of memory needed

3. Throughput: the number of tuples that are output per unit of time.
4. Smooth or bursty nature of output streams: whether the tuples are output regularly (smooth) or in a bursty manner. It is better to have a smoother than a bursty throughput.
5. Accuracy of results in terms of error tolerance.

Some or all of the above can be specified with each continuous query. Given the QoS requirements for a continuous query or a set of continuous queries, it is the responsibility of the DSMS to satisfy them or indicate that they cannot be satisfied with the available resources and the current load on the system.

It is important to stress that the QoS metrics are not independent of each other. For example, decrease in average tuple latency is likely to increase the total memory requirement in a DSMS. As another example, decrease in memory usage due to dropping of tuples will reduce the accuracy of results. Because of this tradeoff among QoS metrics, it is important to have a suite of techniques (e.g., scheduling algorithms, load shedding) for optimizing each metric individually and for balancing them as needed.

2.4 Data Stream Management System Architecture

The abstractions needed for supporting data stream characteristics presented in Section 2.1, application characteristics presented in Section 2.2 and continuous query processing needs presented in Section 2.3 need to be incorporated into a data stream management system. In addition, a DSMS needs to compute the results in accordance with QoS specifications. As the resources, such as CPU cycles and main memory size required to process queries over streams, are limited in a DSMS, the ability of the DSMS to optimize resource usage becomes critical.

Based on the requirements discussed in this chapter, we propose an architecture of a QoS-aware DSMS. Figure 2.6 shows the system architecture of our proposed QoS-aware DSMS. This system consists of the following components: `data source manager`, `continuous query processing engine`, `catalog manager`, `scheduler`, `QoS monitor`, and `run-time optimizer`. The `data source manager` accepts continuous data streams and inserts input tuples into corresponding input queues of query plans. The `QoS monitor` monitors various input data stream characteristics that provide useful information for query optimization, scheduling, and QoS management. It also monitors the output QoS values as well. The `continuous query processing engine` is in charge of generating query plans and optimizing them dynamically. It supports both CQs and *ad hoc* queries. The `catalog manager` stores and

for a synopsis associated with an operator is a function of the operator type, specific algorithm used for computing the operator, as well as the `window` size. The input rate fluctuations also has a bearing on the memory needed for the synopsis.

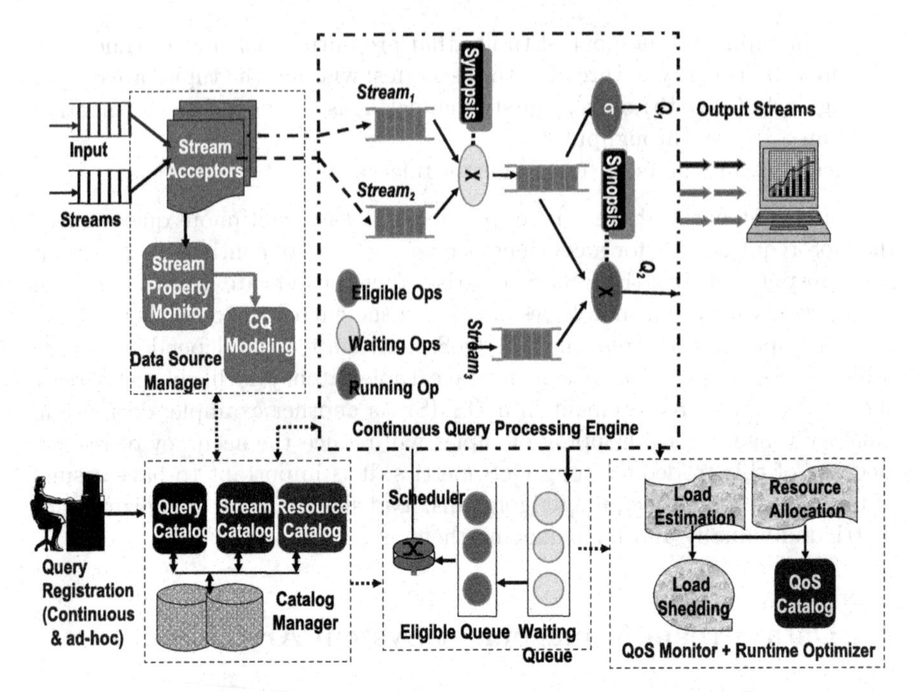

Fig. 2.6. Architecture of the Proposed QoS-Aware DSMS

manages all of the meta data in the system, including stream meta data (e.g., stream name, attributes and their types), detailed query plans, statistics, and resource information. The `scheduler` determines which query or operator or an operator path (a path from a leaf node to a root node of a continuous query plan; defined in Section 5.1.1) executes at any time slot based on the query requirements and measured output values. The `run-time optimizer` receives measured QoS values of output and adjusts scheduling and load shedding to meet the QoS requirements. This is discussed in detail in Section 10.5 on the design and implementation of the `MavStream` prototype.

Due to the fact that most of stream-based applications have specific QoS requirements, the `run-time optimizer` employs a number of QoS delivery mechanisms such as scheduling, load shedding, and admission control to maximize the QoS satisfaction of queries. As many stream-based applications are used for situation monitoring, it is important to have a feedback mechanism as part of the DSMS. The `run-time optimizer` serves that purpose in a DSMS.

2.5 Summary of Chapter 2

In this chapter we have provided an overview of stream processing including stream and application characteristics leading to the architecture of a QoS-aware DSMS. The need for a window was introduced in order to overcome the blocking property of some operators in the context of continuous query processing. We provided a few examples of continuous queries from the telecommunication domain. Finally, we discussed a QoS-aware DSMS architecture to meet the needs of stream processing application requirements.

We conclude this chapter by summarizing the differences between a DBMS and a DSMS using a back-of-the-envelope comparison shown in Table 2.1.

Table 2.1. Back-of-the Envelope Comparison of a DBMS with a DSMS

DBMS	**DSMS**
Persistent relations	Transient streams
One-time (*ad hoc*) queries	Continuous queries
Random (disk) access	Sequential (in-memory) access
Unbounded disk storage	*Bounded* main memory
Snapshot or current state used	Arrival order, window important
Relatively low update frequency	Varying and bursty input rates
No QoS support	QoS support critical
Requires precise results	May tolerate approximate results
Computes all results on a snapshot	Computes window-based results incrementally
Transaction management critical	Transaction management not critical[5]

[5] Data from a traditional DBMS is typically used as read-only data for continuous query processing. If the output of stream processing needs to be stored in a traditional DBMS for sharing, updating, concurrency, and recovery, it is done as any other application of a DBMS. Some of the transactional needs of a typical stream-based application (network fault management system) is discussed in Section 8.5.

3

DSMS CHALLENGES

The characteristics of data streams and the emerging requirements of stream-based applications (as elaborated in Sections 2.1 and 2.2) pose many challenges [82], ranging from theoretical study of data stream algorithms to specification, computation, and expressiveness of continuous query languages to QoS-related issues of a DSMS. The literature review in Chapter 4 summarizes the large body of work that exists in the areas of stream and complex event processing. In this chapter, however, we limit our focus to a few QoS-related problems of stream processing including the relevance of complex event processing for stream-based applications.

3.1 QoS-Related Challenges

In this section, we discuss three primary QoS-related challenges that have received significant attention in the literature, and introduce the challenge of integrating complex event processing with stream processing. The need for complex event processing its functionality is brought out detail in Chapter 8 and the integration issues are addressed in Chapter 9.

3.1.1 Capacity Planning and QoS Verification

The problem of system capacity planning in DSMSs can be informally described as follows: *given a set of CQs with their QoS specifications, what resources – such as CPU cycles, memory size and others – are needed to compute the given CQs and satisfy their QoS requirements?* The converse problem is also equally important. Given a system in terms of available resources (e.g., processing capacity, number of processors, available memory) and a set of CQs with their QoS specifications, will the system be able to satisfy the specified QoS requirements of those CQs? In other words, we would like to verify whether the query results satisfy their predefined QoS requirements. This can be done in two complementary ways: (*i*) modeling continuous query load to

S. Chakravarthy and Q. Jiang, *Stream Data Processing: A Quality of Service Perspective*, Advances in Database Systems 36, DOI: 10.1007/978-0-387-71003-7_3,

estimate the QoS metrics based on conservative input stream and processing characteristics of the system. This can be done for several *what if* scenarios to choose appropriate system capacity to meet the needs of QoS requirements or (*ii*) actually monitor query results at run-time, verify, and make adjustments at run-time using an optimizer to overcome QoS violations. The first approach can be encapsulated into a tool for system capacity planning whereas the second one is usually part of a DSMS for optimizing QoS metrics at run-time. The first approach can also be beneficially employed at run-time by monitoring input stream characteristics and adjusting QoS delivery mechanisms.

To the best of our knowledge, there is no proposed solution for system capacity planning for DSMSs. We address the problem of predicting the QoS metrics of query results by using queuing theory. Specifically, we propose solutions to the problems of predicting the tuple latency of query results and the main memory required to process a set of queries in a DSMS by modeling the query processing system as a network of queuing systems in Chapter 5.

The currently used solution to the QoS verification problem is to continuously monitor the query results at run-time (approach (*ii*) above) and use a run-time optimizer to adjust QoS delivery mechanisms (e.g., scheduling, load shedding) to improve QoS metrics as needed. It is important to understand that this approach incurs some additional overhead at run-time.

If the resources needed for the worst case scenario for processing queries can be verified *before* the system is deployed, it would be cost effective to tweak minor QoS violations by monitoring the output at run-time and adjusting QoS delivery mechanisms to make sure the violations are reverted. This is accomplished by a run-time optimizer that measures the actual QoS values at run-time and adjusts scheduling and load shedding strategies to accommodate bursty situations. A run-time optimizer that can change scheduling for individual queries and apply load shedding selectively is discussed as part of the design and implementation of the `MavStream` system in Section 10.5.

3.1.2 Scheduling Strategies for CQs

A DSMS needs to compute functions over data streams in real-time and in a continuous manner. The problem of resource allocation – scheduling of individual operators of a CQ – arises in a (multiple) continuous query processing system as data items arrive on input streams. Essentially, we need a mechanism to schedule – which query or operator of a query should be scheduled and when – to compute over the newly arrived data items or partially processed data items. In a multiple query processing system, different queries can have different QoS requirements. Some of them may favor a real-time response. Some may prefer accurate results. Others may be interested in a combination of response time and accuracy or may not even care about QoS metrics at all. From a QoS perspective, a DSMS can allocate resources by choosing scheduling strategies based on individual query's QoS requirements. However, the problem is more complicated because:

1. A DSMS may have a limited amount of resources (i.e., CPU cycles and main memory).
2. Different objects (queries or operators) have different processing requirements and different memory release capacities (the amount of memory released when a tuple is processed by an operator).
3. The input pattern of a data stream can be irregular and bursty.

As different operators require different amounts of CPU cycles to process a tuple and release different amounts of memory, scheduling strategies can impact the outcome of query processing. This means a scheduling strategy has significant impact on various performance aspects of a DSMS and hence a DSMS can leverage different strategies to maximize the available physical resources to handle the bursty nature of data streams.

Consider two operators A and B in the system; operator A needs 1 second to process 1 tuple with a size of 2 bytes and outputs 1 tuple with a size of 1 byte (processing rate is 1 tuple/second, and memory release rate is 1 byte/second). However, operator B needs 2 seconds to process 1 tuple with a size of 2 bytes and outputs a tuple with a size of 1 byte (processing rate is 0.5 tuple/second and memory release rate is 0.5 byte/second). If input streams of both operator A and B have an input rate of 1 tuple per second for 5 consecutive seconds and then a pause, a scheduling strategy which schedules A first if there is any tuple waiting at A, then schedules B, requires a maximal memory of 10 bytes (or 5 tuples) that are waiting at B right after the bursty input period. Another strategy which gives B a higher priority than A requires a maximal memory of 14 bytes (5 tuples at A and 2 tuples at B) right after the bursty input period. If the system only has 12 bytes memory in total, the second scheduling strategy is definitely not the best one. Similarly, a scheduling strategy also has a significant impact on overall tuple latency and throughput of a DSMS.

Chapter 6 proposes new scheduling strategies for continuous query processing along with their analysis. The new strategies are also compared with the strategies proposed in the literature. For this problem, the goal is to develop low overhead scheduling strategies for optimizing main memory usage, tuple latency, and their combination. Discussion of other characteristics of scheduling strategies such as starvation, smooth versus bursty output are also included.

3.1.3 Load Shedding and Run-Time Optimization

Scheduling strategies can be used to allocate resources carefully to satisfy the QoS requirements of different queries in a DSMS assuming sufficient total amount of resources. However, a DSMS may be short of resources for processing all registered queries and satisfy their QoS requirements during temporary overload periods due to bursty inputs. For this case, it may be infeasible for a scheduling strategy, no matter how good (or optimal) it is, to satisfy QoS requirements of all registered queries in the system. A natural solution to this problem is to selectively discard some unprocessed or partially processed tuples from the system. It is important to understand that discarding tuples degrade the quality (in terms of accuracy) of query results. However, recall from the characteristics of stream-based applications (Section 2.2) that many of these applications can tolerate approximate results. The process of gradually discarding some tuples from a DSMS with the goal of minimizing errors introduced towards the final results is termed *load shedding.* The load shedding process is necessary and important in a DSMS to deal with the bursty nature of its input data streams.

Issues that arise for the problem of load shedding are: where to discard tuples along the query plan, the choice of tuples to discard and how much to discard, when to discard, and when to stop discarding. This problem is discussed in depth in Chapter 7.

As load shedding is an important mechanism of run-time optimization (in addition to scheduling), details of the run-time optimizer of the `MavStream` prototype are discussed in Section 10.5.

3.1.4 Complex Event and Rule Processing

A monitoring application needs to continuously process stream data in order to detect *interesting events.* These *interesting events* are usually composed to form higher-level events or situations (e.g., fire as a composition of sudden increase in temperature accompanied by smoke within a time interval in a small geographic location) to trigger a sequence of predefined actions once the situation is detected.

A CEP component is not shown as part of the QoS-aware DSMS architecture in Figure 2.6 as a DSMS is not likely to have this component as part of its functionality. DSMSs have little or no support to express events as the outcome of continuous queries and further compose them to form complex events. In contrast, event processing systems that use the Event-Condition-Action (ECA) paradigm have been researched extensively from the situation monitoring viewpoint to detect complex or composite events and to take appropriate actions. Several event specification languages and processing models have been developed, analyzed, and implemented. Researchers have addressed these two topics independently at different periods of time. Many systems claim to be both a stream as well as a complex event processing system further blurring the differences between the two.

In this book, we argue that complex event processing is complementary to stream processing. And the combination of stream and complex event processing is critical for a large number of stream-based applications. The need for complex event processing is further established in Chapter 8 and its integration with a DSMS is addressed in Chapters 9 and 11.

In Chapter 9, we analyze the differences between the two and their roles in monitoring applications. The issues addressed include: (*i*) similarities and differences of these two threads of work, namely the data stream and event processing models, (*ii*) an integrated model that synthesizes the two models by combining their strengths (the sum being greater than its parts), and (*iii*) minimal extensions needed to a DSMS and a CEP system in order to synergistically combine the two.

With an integrated model, and the ability to reason about each system separately, it will become easier to satisfy the end-to-end QoS requirements in the combined system. Some of the work on event processing does not consider large number of events as well as QoS requirements. Hopefully, some of the QoS delivery mechanisms developed for stream processing can also be applied for complex event processing.

3.1.5 Design and Implementation of a DSMS with CEP

Considering the requirements of continuous query processing and the emphasis on QoS, the design of a DSMS needs to address efficient implementation of buffers, operators, scheduling, load shedding, as well as event generation along with complex event and rule processing. Run-time optimization and the ability to change scheduling strategies for the same CQ add further complexity. If the stream data needs to be archived and used for *ad hoc* and historical queries, archiving needs to be done carefully without interfering with the performance of the rest of the system. In stream processing applications, the number of triggers can be large (as a continuous query can give rise to multiple types of events) and the same trigger may be executed a number of times due to continuous nature of computation. Hence triggers need to be managed and executed efficiently. We discuss the design and implementation aspects of a DSMS in Chapter 10 and integration of CEP with a DSMS in Chapter 11.

3.2 Concise Overview of Book Chapters

The `MavHome` project [62, 64] was instrumental in starting our work on stream processing with the goal of building a system to process stream data generated by different types of sensors (a `MavLab` and a `MavPad` were setup for the project). In addition to the initial charter of automating the functionality of `MavHome` through data collection, mining, and inferring the rules for automation, a number of fundamental stream processing issues were identified and pursued. The solutions and algorithms presented in the book are not specific to this project and can be applied to any general purpose stream and complex event processing system.

In the following sections, we provide a sneak preview of the contents of the rest of the chapters of the book.

3.2.1 Literature Review

Literature review is presented in Chapter 4. We provide a brief overview of various projects on stream data processing. We then review the literature to provide a clear understanding of the alternative approaches available for the specific problems addressed in the book. We also contrast our approaches to other relevant work in the literature. We review the literature on complex event processing, progress made in stages over the last two decades, and provide a list of stream and complex event processing systems (prototypes, open source software, and commercial systems).

3.2.2 Continuous Query Modeling

To address this problem, Chapter 5 presents a queueing model to analyze QoS metrics such as tuple latency and memory requirement in DSMSs. We first study the processing characteristics of each operator in a continuous query plan by modeling each operator of a `Select-Project-Join` query (or SPJ query) as a standalone M/G/1[1] queuing system [83, 84]. We study the distribution, average number of tuples, and tuple latency in the queue, under the Poisson arrival of input data streams.

After modeling each operator individually, the entire query processing (or query plan) is modeled as a network of queuing systems with vacation time and setup time. The *vacation time* of an operator is the period of time during which it does not gain CPU cycles, and the *setup time* is the initialization time of an operator before it starts processing the input tuples once it gains the CPU. Under this queuing model, we analyze both memory requirement and tuple latency of tuples in the system under two service disciplines: gated-service discipline and exhaustive-service discipline. Based on our queueing model, we can answer the question of whether a system (defined in terms of resources) can compute a given set of continuous queries with tuple latency requirements over given data streams. In addition, the memory requirement estimation provides useful guideline for buffer allocation of each operator effectively and in addition provides useful information for scheduling as well. The estimation of tuple latency provides critical information about when the outputs violate their predefined QoS requirements, which implicitly determines when the system has to activate appropriate QoS delivery mechanisms to guarantee the predefined QoS requirements.

3.2.3 Scheduling Strategies for CQs

In a DSMS, different scheduling strategies can be employed under different scenarios (i.e., light load periods, heavy load periods) to satisfy the QoS requirements of different queries. It is a challenge to effectively allocate the

[1] Kendall's notation is the standard system used to describe and classify the queueing model that a queueing system corresponds to. M corresponds to the Markovian arrival process (or Poisson arrival process), G corresponds to the general service time distribution, and 1 the number of service channels or servers.

limited resources (CPU cycles, main memory, and so on) to queries at run-time. In Chapter 6, we first present our scheduling model and then propose a family of scheduling strategies for a DSMS.

Specifically, the operator path capacity (PC) scheduling strategy schedules the operator path (a sequence of operators along the path from leaf to root in a query plan, defined in Section 5.1.1) with the biggest processing capacity at any time slot and can achieve the overall minimal tuple latency. In order to decrease its memory requirement, we further propose the segment strategy in which the segment (of an operator path) with the biggest processing capacity is scheduled. Due to the larger processing capacity of the bottom operators in a query plan, the segment can buffer its partially processed tuples in the middle of an operator path. The segment strategy greatly improves the memory requirement by sacrificing a little bit of tuple latency.

The Memory Optimal Segment (MOS) strategy (discussed in Section 6.3.3) employs a segment partition algorithm similar to the one used in the Chain strategy [85] (see section 4.1.2), but minimizes the memory requirement. However, the MOS strategy schedules an operator segment each time, instead of an operator as in the Chain strategy. As a result, the MOS strategy achieves the strictly optimal memory requirement as compared with the near-optimal memory requirement of the Chain strategy. The MOS strategy also achieves better tuple latency and smoother throughput than the Chain strategy.

The Simplified Segment (SS) strategy is a variant of the MOS strategy as it partitions an operator path into at most two segments. The SS strategy preserves the low memory requirement of the MOS strategy and further improves tuple latency. Finally, the threshold strategy is proposed as a combination of the PC strategy and the MOS strategy. It activates the PC strategy to achieve the minimal tuple latency if the memory is not a concern; otherwise, it acts as the MOS strategy in order to decrease the memory requirement. The threshold strategy inherits the properties of both the path capacity strategy and the MOS, which makes it more appropriate for a DSMS.

We further discuss how to extend these strategies to a multiple query processing system in which computations are shared through common subexpressions. All proposed strategies work for multiple continuous queries with computation sharing. The techniques used for extending our strategies to a multiple CQ processing system can also be applied to extend other strategies that only work under a DSMS without computation sharing such as the Chain strategy and others.

Finally, the theoretical results are validated by an implementation using which we evaluate all of the proposed strategies experimentally.

3.2.4 Load Shedding in a DSMS

In order to deal with bursty nature of input data in a DSMS, a framework and techniques for a general load shedding strategy is presented in Chapter 7.

We insert load shedders into query plans and dynamically activate/deactivate built-in shedders based on the estimation of current system load. These shedders can drop tuples in either a randomized manner or employ user-specified application semantics. Specifically, we first address the problem of the physical implementation of a load shedder with the goal of minimizing the overhead introduced by the shedder itself. Our analysis and experiments show that a shedder should be part of the input queue of an operator in order to minimize the load introduced by the shedder and to decrease the memory requirement by discarding tuples before they enter the queue. We then develop a solution for predicting the system load by monitoring the input rates of input streams. The estimated system load implicitly determines when load shedding is needed and how much. The proposed system load estimation technique can be applied to other load shedding techniques proposed in the literature as well. We also develop algorithms to determine the optimal placement of a shedder in a (multiple) continuous query plan in order to maximize load shedding and to minimize the error introduced by discarded tuples during high-input periods. Once we determine how much load needs to be shed and where, we propose a strategy for distributing the total number of tuples to be dropped among all shedders with the goal of minimizing the total relative errors in the query results due to load shedding. Finally, experimental results validate the effectiveness and the efficiency of the proposed load shedding techniques.

3.2.5 NFM^i : A Motivating Application

Chapter 8 analyzes an application from the telecommunication domain to identify the applicability of techniques developed for data stream processing and their advantages as compared to the customized approach currently used by many such applications. In addition, this application vividly brings out the need for complex event and rule processing as part of the general purpose solution. The notion of events as an outcome of a stream computation (termed a `computed event` in this book) is important as they form the "interesting events" of that underlying domain/application. These events need to be composed further for detecting higher-level situations for alerting.

3.2.6 DSMS and Complex Event Processing

In order to extend the expressiveness and applicability of a DSMS by supporting meaningful complex events and their processing, we develop an integrated model that combines the advantages of both stream and event processing models in Chapter 9. Specifically, based on the analysis of the similarities and differences between event and stream processing, we argue that although each one is useful in its own right, their combined expressiveness and computation power is critical for many applications of stream processing. Hence the need for synthesizing the two into a more expressive and powerful model that augments the strength of each. We then suggest enhancements to both the stream- and the event-side to make them suitable for integration.

Essentially, any CQ can generate one or more events by filtering the output in different ways. For example, although the computation of slowing down of a car is the same for any lane, once slowing down of car is determined using a CQ, different events can be generated to signify whether the car was from a high occupancy vehicle (HOV) lane or not using different conditions or masks. These "computed events" are buffered into a complex event processing system to detect composite events and trigger actions. The output of any CQ can also be consumed directly by applications (in addition to generating events). Furthermore, the output of an event (computed, primitive or complex) is a stream and can be fed to another CQ.

With a few additions and enhancements, our integrated model not only supports a larger class of applications, but also makes it easier to reason about end-to-end QoS requirements. None of the enhancements proposed for our integrated model affects the stream processing aspect and can readily be integrated into any data stream management system.

3.2.7 Design and Implementation of Prototypes

We discuss the design and implementation of two prototypes `MavStream` and `MavEStream` in Chapters 10 and 11, respectively. Chapter 10 elaborates on the design and implementation of `MavStream`, a data stream processing engine. Chapter 11 discusses the `MavEStream` system which is an integration of the `MavStream` system with an existing complex event processing system (i.e., the Local Event Detector or LED based on the Snoop event specification language [86–88]) to provide a complete system for stream processing applications.

Finally, Chapter 12 highlights the long-term vision of data reduction coupled with complex event processing to deal with larger class of applications that will demand QoS support. Additional research directions for realizing this vision is also presented as part of the conclusion.

4

LITERATURE REVIEW

The amount of literature on various aspects of stream data processing and complex event processing is overwhelming. We have tried to review as much literature as possible, and specifically those that are relevant to the thrust areas of this book. This chapter starts with a brief review of stream data processing research and continues, in more detail, with related work in the areas of continuous query modeling, scheduling strategies for continuous queries, load shedding, and complex event processing. In addition to the review, we also indicate how our work differs from similar work in the literature. We also list currently available prototypes and systems aimed at stream as well as complex event processing.

4.1 Data Stream Management Systems

4.1.1 Aurora and Borealis

Aurora [63, 89–91] is a system for managing data streams for monitoring applications. Continuous queries in Aurora are specified in terms of a dataflow diagram consisting of boxes and arrows (using a GUI). Tuples flow through a loop-free directed graph of operations (or boxes) for processing. Aurora maintains historical storage as well to answer *ad hoc* queries. It uses SQuAL (Stream Query ALgebra) consisting of several primitive operators for expressing stream processing requirements. Aurora supports continuous queries, views, and *ad hoc* queries using the same conceptual building blocks.

Aurora performs dynamic continuous query optimization on its network (of boxes and arrows) by inserting projections, combining boxes, and reordering boxes of a subnetwork at run-time. An Aurora network is broken into k subnetworks and each is optimized individually. Aurora attempts to maximize QoS for the outputs it produces, especially response time, tuple drops (or load shedding), and the values produced (accuracy of results). Output (or

S. Chakravarthy and Q. Jiang, *Stream Data Processing: A Quality of Service Perspective*, Advances in Database Systems 36, DOI: 10.1007/978-0-387-71003-7_4,

QoS) requirements are accepted as two-dimensional graphs, which are easier to specify, for delay, percentage of tuples delivered, and the output value.

In order to reduce overall processing costs, Aurora uses a two-level scheduling algorithm [92]. The first level determines which continuous queries are executed based on QoS requirements. The second level uses complex train scheduling by exploiting interbox and intrabox nonlinearities. Train scheduling uses the following set of heuristics: (*i*) allow boxes to queue as many tuples as possible without processing, thereby generating long tuple trains, (*ii*) process complete trains at once, thereby exploiting intrabox nonlinearity, and (*iii*) pass tuples to subsequent boxes without having to storing on disk, thereby exploiting interbox nonlinearity. In essence, train scheduling tries to accomplish two goals: (*i*) minimize the number of I/O operations performed per tuple, and (*ii*) minimize the number of box calls made per tuple.

For load shedding [93], Aurora addresses the problems of where, when, and how much load to shed. Both random and semantic drops are supported. Load shedding is treated as an optimization problem and when the capacity of the system is less than the load presented, choices are made for dropping (where and when) and for maximizing the utility of results. Most of the analysis concerning dropping strategies are done statically and are captured in a simple data structure. run-time overhead for load shedding is kept low.

Borealis [94–100] is a second generation system that addresses the problems of distributed operators for stream processing, dynamic revision of query results, dynamic query modification, and flexible and highly-scalable optimization. Load management in distributed stream processing systems is discussed in [101–103].

StreamBase [104], a commercial real-time, stream and complex event processing system, is based on Aurora.

4.1.2 STREAM

Stanford Stream Data Manager (or *STREAM*) [82, 105, 106] is a general-purpose data stream management system that address problems ranging from basic theoretical results to implementing a comprehensive prototype. An algorithm for evaluating conjunctive queries using a bounded amount of memory is presented in [107]. The use of k-constraints to reduce the memory overhead for `select-project-join` (SPJ) queries is discussed in [108].

Continuous Query Language (CQL) is a declarative language developed as an extension of SQL that includes streams and relations and additional constructs for specifying sliding `window` and sampling. CQL has been implemented as part of the STREAM prototype. The denotational semantics of CQL is presented in [109]. An abstract semantics for continuous queries based on formal definitions of streams & relations and the concrete language CQL that instantiates the abstract semantics using SQL is presented in [77, 110].

Chain scheduling strategy [111], an operator scheduling strategy for data stream processing, is near-optimal in minimizing run-time memory usage for any collection of single-stream queries involving `select`, `project`, and foreign-key `join`. However, during bursts in input streams, when there is a buildup of unprocessed tuples, Chain scheduling may lead to high output latency. Babcock at al. [85], study the problem of minimizing maximum run-time memory subject to a constraint on maximum latency and propose a set of heuristics. Experimental evaluation of Chain scheduling and its variants is presented to support analytical conclusions.

Load shedding for aggregate non-`join` queries is discussed by Babcock et al. in [112]. In the paper, Babcock et al. propose a technique involving the introduction of load shedding operators or load shedders at various points in the query plan. Each load shedder is parameterized by a sampling rate p. The load shedder flips a coin for each tuple that passes through it. With probability p, the tuple is passed on to the next operator, and with probability $1-p$, the tuple is discarded. To compensate for the lost tuples caused by the introduction of load shedders, the aggregate values calculated by the system are scaled appropriately to produce unbiased, approximate query answers. The decisions about where to introduce load shedders and how to set the sampling rate for each load shedder are based on statistics about the data streams, including observed stream arrival rates and operator selectivities.

Other issues addressed as part of this project include: adaptive filters for continuous queries over distributed data streams [113], resource sharing in continuous sliding-`window` aggregates [114], resource management and approximate answers in a DSMS [115], and adaptive query caching [116].

The URL `http://infolab.stanford.edu/stream/` provides complete information about the STREAM project.

The commercial stream and complex event processing system Coral8 [117] is based on the STREAM project.

4.1.3 *TelegraphCQ*

TelegraphCQ [118–121] is focused on meeting the challenges that arise in handling large number of continuous queries over high-volume, highly-variable data streams. It grew out of earlier projects on adaptive relational query processing. *TelegraphCQ* is a complete redesign and reimplementation of an earlier project (*Telegraph* [122]) with a sharp focus on shared processing over continuous queries and data streams as compared to the broader focus of *Telegraph* on adaptive dataflow. Eddy [123] and Psoup [124] systems have been extended to develop *TelegraphCQ*.

An *eddy* is a stream query execution mechanism that can continuously reorder operators in a query plan. Each input tuple to an eddy carries its own execution history. This execution history is implemented using two bitmaps. A *done* bitmap records which operators the tuple has already visited and a *ready* bitmap records which operators the tuple can visit next. An eddy routes each tuple to the next operator based on the tuple's execution history and statistics maintained. If the tuple satisfies the predicate of an operator, the operator makes appropriate updates to the two bitmaps and returns the tuple to the eddy. The eddy continues this iteration until the tuple has visited all operators.

Psoup builds on adaptive query processing techniques developed in the *Telegraph* project. It combines the processing of ad-hoc and continuous queries by treating data and queries symmetrically, allowing new queries to be applied to old data and new data to be applied to old queries.

Truviso [125] (earlier Amalgamated Insight) is based on some of the results of *TelegraphCQ*.

4.1.4 `MavStream`

`MavStream` [79, 126–129] has addressed stream processing holistically from a QoS perspective. The `MavHome` project at UTA [62, 64] is a multi-disciplinary project involving machine learning, predicting movements of occupants in a smart space, real-time processing of stream data, and automating the smart space/environment for: security, energy optimization, and assistance by predicting the behavior of occupants.

Starting with the intent of capacity planning and QoS verification (further discussed in Chapter 5), individual relational operators (e.g., `select`, `project`, `join`) initially, and continuous queries later, were modeled using queuing theory. Tuple latency and memory usage are computed using closed-form solutions [130]. Other operators can be modeled using this approach. The approach and the formulation can be used to develop tools to determine the adequacy of resources and for understanding the impact of resources on QoS metrics using *what if* scenarios. This approach has also been used for monitoring input stream characteristics to activate/deactivate load shedding by a run-time optimizer.

The Path Capacity (PC) scheduling strategy [131] (further discussed in Chapter 6) aims to minimize the overall tuple latency in contrast to minimizing the memory requirement. Several variants of the PC strategy have been proposed that can schedule an operator or a an operator path, or something in between. Of the variants proposed, based on their characteristics, the simplified segment strategy and the threshold strategy are better-suited for a DSMS. The optimal properties of the PC and the Memory Optimal Segment (MOS) strategies are established in the context of shared subqueries (in a multiple CQ processing system) as compared with the memory optimal property of the Chain strategy [85, 111] established for queries with no shared subexpressions.

Load shedding [128, 132, 133] addresses the ideal location of load shedders among the alternative options, optimal placement based on weights computed statically (and refined at run-time, if necessary), activation/deactivation of load shedders at run-time and the amount of load to be shed for both random and semantic load shedders.

A DSMS prototype (MavStream) has been designed and implemented [127, 133–139] based on the algorithms and approaches developed in the MavHome project.

Based on the familiarity and study of several applications [79], an integrated architecture is proposed for stream and complex event processing [129]. The goal is to synergistically integrate both stream and complex event processing in order to guarantee end-to-end QoS requirements. To accomplish this goal, a complex event and rule processing system has been integrated into the MavStream [140] prototype.

4.1.5 Others

Gigascope [141, 142] is a lightweight stream database system specialized for network monitoring. Gigascope is a compiled query system. When a user submits a set of queries to Gigascope, the queries are analyzed and optimized, and a set of C and C++ language modules are generated. These are compiled and linked into a run time system, and executed.

StatStream [143] computes a variety of single and multiple stream statistics in one pass with constant time (per input) and bounded memory. The algorithms are highly parallelizable and can handle thousands of streams.

There are also data stream systems that have been developed exclusively for sensor networks and applications such as TinyDB [144, 145] and Cougar [146, 147]. These systems have a slightly different objective, where the focus is on network-related query processing issues such as reducing communication costs, minimizing power consumption, and so on.

Nile [148] extends the query processor engine of an object-relational database management system, Predator [149], to process continuous queries over data streams.

OpenCQ [150], a distributed event-driven continuous query system, uses incremental materialized-views to support continuous query processing for monitoring persistent data streams from a wide-area network. The Niagara system [151] supports continuous queries over large scale of streams by grouping queries based on their signatures for sharing computation.

Continuous queries are also used in *Tribeca* [152, 153] to monitor and analyze network traffic streams by using a dataflow-oriented query language. *Tribeca* uses a procedural query language. Hancock [154] is a domain-specific language created to express computationally efficient signature programs for mining very large amounts of stream data in the telecommunication domain.

Tapestry [155, 156] is an experimental content-based filtering system over email and message streams developed at the Xerox Palo Alto Research Center. *Tapestry* translates filters into continuous queries and processes these continuous queries over an append-only database.

An Expressive Stream Language (ESL) for stream processing has been proposed in [157]. The focus of this work is to extend the power and generality of DSMSs by optimizing and efficiently executing User-Defined Aggregate (UDA) queries.

Ranking to provide top-k answers for *ad hoc* queries over stream updates is discussed in [158]. A survey of data stream management work until 2003 can be found in [159].

4.2 QoS-Related Issues

4.2.1 Continuous Query Modeling for Capacity Planning

System capacity planning and QoS metrics estimation have been extensively studied in the areas of artificial intelligence [160–162] and computer & system performance evaluation [163, 164]. However, there is little work on capacity planning in the context of databases (apart from physical database design, tuning, and benchmarks) mainly due to the absence of QoS support in DBMSs. The bursty input behavior and QoS requirements in DSMSs make estimation of QoS metrics for system capacity planning necessary and important. To the best of our knowledge, system capacity planning and QoS verification issues have been studied for the first time in the context of stream processing in the `MavStream` project.

Although there are a few papers that have studied the performance issues in DSMSs, these papers focus on the study of the various components or operators in a DSMS, rather than the whole system. The performance studies of various components or operators in DSMSs include: Kang et al. [165] investigate various multi-`join` algorithms and their performance in continuous queries over unbounded data streams; Golab et al. [75] analyze incremental multi-way `join` algorithms for sliding `window` over data streams and develop a strategy to find a good join order heuristically; Viglas et al. [166] study maximization of the output rate of a multi-way `join` operator over stream data. The above mentioned papers do not address tuple latency or memory issues for single or a collection of continuous queries.

Our work is also related to a set of papers [76, 81, 167] that address the problems of multiple query optimizations and scheduling. Viglas et al. [167] use input rate-based model instead of the traditional cardinality-based model and try to maximize the output rate. This model does not use scheduling of operators or the buffers commonly assumed for CQ processing in the literature. In terms of system analysis, our work is also related to the memory characterization problem discussed in [168], where the authors characterize the memory requirements of a query for all possible instances of the streams theoretically, and the results provide a way to evaluate a query within bounded memory. We analyze both memory requirements and tuple latency from a different point of view. Furthermore, trade-offs among storage requirements, number of passes, and result accuracy under a stream data model have been studied in [169, 170]. Babcock et al. [171] consider various statistics over a sliding `window` under a data stream model.

Finally, our work is related to a set of papers in the network domain that address the performance study of various queueing systems, congestion control, and avoidance. In the network and telecommunication domain, queueing models used are either multiple-server models [172, 173] along a traffic path from source node to destination or cyclical models within one server [174,175] such as switching strategies (put a packet from input queue to output queue) of ATM switches. Those models are different from our task-driven, queueing model presented in Chapter 5.

4.2.2 Scheduling Strategies for CQs

Various scheduling strategies have been proposed and studied extensively in the computer science literature. The Chain strategy [85, 111] has been proposed with the goal of minimizing the total internal queue size. In contrast, the path capacity (PC) strategy minimizes the tuple latency. Chain strategy schedules operators whereas PC strategy schedules an operator path (defined in Section 5.1.1). We also propose the Memory Optimal Segment (MOS) strategy to minimize the total memory requirement. The MOS strategy uses no more memory than that required by the Chain strategy and we show that the strategy is optimal in terms of total memory requirement in a general DSMS. The proof of optimal memory requirement of Chain strategy is for queries without computation sharing through common subexpressions. The techniques we propose have been extended to multiple CQs with sharing of common subexpressions; and these extensions can be applied to the Chain strategy as well. The Chain-Flush strategy [85] introduces techniques for starvation-free scheduling and QoS satisfaction. These techniques can be applied to all strategies proposed by us in Chapter 6 as well. The Aurora system employs a two-level scheduling approach [92]: the first level handles the scheduling of superboxes which is a set of operators, and the second level decides how to schedule a box within a superbox. This approach uses a heuristic-based strategy to decrease the average tuple latency based on superbox traversal and does not employ optimal scheduling solutions.

In Chapter 6, we propose a suite of scheduling strategies for data stream processing. In contrast to related approaches, we use a different approach and have proved that our PC strategy is optimal in terms of overall tuple latency. Although Aurora's tuple batching – termed train processing – uses a concept similar to the one used in the Chain and our segment strategies, it is heuristics based. Furthermore, we provide a pragmatic scheduling strategy, termed threshold strategy, which has the advantages of both the PC and the MOS strategies.

The rate-based optimization framework proposed by Viglas et al. [167] has the goal of maximizing the throughput of a query. However, the rate-based optimization does not take tuple latency and memory requirement into consideration. Earlier work related to improving the response time of a query includes the dynamic query operator scheduling [176] and the `XJoin` operator of Urban and Franklin [80].

Other works that are closely related to our scheduling work are adaptive query processing [81,123,177,178], which address efficient query plan execution in a dynamic environment by revising the query plan. The novel architecture proposed in Eddy [123] can perhaps efficiently handle bursty input data, in which the scheduling work is done through a router that continuously monitors the system status. However, the large amount of the state information associated with a tuple is likely to limit its scalability; its optimality has not been established.

4.2.3 Load Shedding in a DSMS

The load shedding problem has been studied by the Aurora and STREAM projects. Our work in load shedding shares some of the characteristics of the load shedding techniques proposed in [93]. However, we provide a more general and comprehensive solution. Tatbul et al. [93] propose a load shedding mechanism in Aurora [63, 89–91] to relieve a system from an overloaded situation. Their work provides a solution for determining when to perform load shedding by continuously computing the CPU-cycle time required by each box (operator) or superbox in the system. Once the total CPU-cycles exceed system's capacity, the system begins load shedding. Babcock et al. [112] propose a set of load shedding techniques to non-`join` aggregate queries to guarantee their relative error requirements in a DSMS, rather than for general continuous queries which is the focus of our work. `Window`-aware load shedding techniques for aggregate queries are discussed in [179].

Our solution to the load shedding problem differs from related work in the literature in the following aspects:

1. We identify an optimal physical location (as part of buffer) of a shedder.
2. We compute an optimal placement of a shedder for each operator path.
3. The proposed load shedding techniques in conjunction with scheduling strategies (i.e., earliest deadline first or EDF) or QoS-aware strategies such as PC and Chain-Flush can guarantee QoS requirements of a query.
4. The proposed system load estimation technique explicitly calculates the total load in terms of total system capacity, and does not need to calculate the absolute system capacity as in [93]. Our system capacity estimation technique is useful for other stream processing systems to make decisions on when to activate/deactivate load shedding and how much to shed.
5. The number of shedders and the number of active shedders are minimized in the system.
6. Each shedder has a maximal capacity.

Das et al. [180] study various load shedding strategies for sliding `window join` operator over streaming data under limited resources. They provide the optimal off-line and the best online algorithms for sliding `window joins`. The techniques presented in this book can be used as an alternative approach to determine *in advance* when load shedding should be activated. Since ours is a closed-form solution, it is more useful and has low overhead even when used at run-time as compared with other approaches proposed in the literature.

4.2.4 Design and Implementation of Prototypes

Several DSMS prototypes have been developed [63,106,122,127,151,181], and they focus on the system architecture, CQ execution (i.e., scheduling and various `non-blocking` algorithms), and QoS delivery mechanisms. The main computation over stream data is limited to the set of operators supported by the system and their computation over streaming data.

We discuss some of the functionality and design decisions for implementing a DSMS, and integrating it with complex event processing using `MavStream` and `MavEStream` prototypes in Chapters 10 and 11, respectively.

4.3 Complex Event Processing

Complex event processing has seen a resurgence in the last few years although the need for events, rules, and triggers were realized more than two decades ago. The foundation for complex event processing, in terms of event specification languages, their semantics, event detection algorithms, and integration of event processing with DBMSs as well as standalone applications, has been formed quite some time ago. The advent of stream processing applications have brought to the forefront the criticality of complex event processing and alerts/notifications with renewed requirements.

The saga of complex event processing can be best understood by tracing the periods of development along with the focus of that period. Broadly, three periods can be identified as elaborated below.

4.3.1 Mid- to Late-Eighties: Active Databases

In the mid-to-late eighties, the inability of DBMSs to monitor and trigger alerts and notifications even for conventional applications such as inventory control (e.g., a part needs to be reordered when quantity-on-hand falls below a certain value) prompted the work on automating the above class of applications to reduce or eliminate user intervention. At that time, process control applications had the capability to monitor system state and take appropriate actions. However, most of these systems were custom-developed and optimized for real-time operation and did not use a general framework for the purpose of monitoring and automation. A number of efforts at that time examined a large number of applications from diverse domains such as process control, power distribution, stock trading & portfolio management, and network management, for the use of DBMSs in monitoring applications; the goal was to develop a framework that could be used across several monitoring applications. Timeliness, near real-time response, well-defined semantics, and the ease of management of the system were some of the goals of this research and development.

The early explorers of the events and rule/trigger concept for monitoring were: HiPAC [31,33,182], Postgres [183,184], and ETM [185]. Although all of the above had the same broader goal, their approaches and for addressing the problem were different. HiPAC, perhaps, took the most general approach of incorporating monitoring into a DBMS by assessing the impact on all components of a DBMS: knowledge model (or specification), query optimization, transaction management, and recovery. The separation of an event from condition and action was promoted based on the role of their semantics as compared to other extant approaches. The event component was separated and event operators (disjunction, sequence, and closure) were proposed. Coupling modes between events, conditions, and actions were proposed and their effect analyzed on transaction management. Event-Condition-Action (or ECA) paradigm was proposed as a flexible mechanism for automating a number of diverse functionality in a DBMS such as view materialization, constraint enforcement, situation monitoring, and access control. The Postgres work, on the other hand, concentrated on incorporating triggers into the Postgres framework. Event/trigger mechanism (ETM) explored the notion of active capability in the context of enforcing constraints in design databases using triggers and events. The ECA paradigm was introduced [31, 33, 182] as an expressive way of specifying and separating user intent. Events correspond to *happenings of interest*, conditions correspond to *ascertaining the validity of a state*, and actions correspond to the *outcome of the situation.*

There was eagerness among the DBMS vendors to include the newly proposed monitoring capability into a DBMS. The first commercial DBMS to incorporate triggers was Interbase [186] which developed a DBMS from scratch in the late eighties. The event-action (EA) format was adopted as triggers and is currently used by all commercial DBMSs.

4.3.2 Nineties: Active Object-Oriented Databases

The nineties witnessed an explosion of academic research efforts for incorporating active capability (using the ECA paradigm) into object-oriented, object-relational, and relational DBMSs. A large number of prototypes were developed during this period. Since event component was the least understood part, as compared to conditions and actions (conditions correspond to queries, and actions correspond to transactions), a number of event specification languages were proposed along with semantics and algorithms for composite or complex event detection. Seamless integration of the ECA paradigm into object-oriented and other systems were examined in detail to facilitate its incorporation into commercial DBMSs, legacy systems, and systems where one had access to source code. In addition, various implementation alternatives such as integrated [187], agent-based [188,189], and wrapper-based [190] systems for supporting the ECA paradigm were explored. Rule execution alternatives and their semantics to deal with termination, non-determinism, and confluence were explored [191–198]. Several active rule languages were developed for incorporating them into deductive object-oriented database systems [199–201]. Active rules were integrated into deductive databases as well in a number of ways [202–206]. Denotational semantics for the execution of ECA rules were explored [207]. ECA rules were incorporated into functional database programming languages [208] as well. Parallel event detection in active databases was explored in [209]. The popularity of the area brought out an active database management system manifesto in 1995 [210].

Without differentiating between the event specification languages and the systems that included events and triggers, several event specification languages and systems were developed in the nineties: ACOOD [211], ADAM [212], Alert [213], A-RDL [206], Ariel [214, 215], Chimera [201, 216, 217], COMPOSE [218], EXACT [219], HiPAC [31,33,182], NAOS [220], ODE [221,222], Postgres [223], REACH [224, 225], Rock & Roll [199, 226], SAMOS [227, 228], Sentinel [187,229], SEQ [230], Snoop [86,87], STARBURST [231,232], TriGs [233,234], UBILAB [235], and others [236,237]. A comprehensive description of some of the above systems can be found in [193, 238] and an exhaustive annotated bibliography on active databases up to 1994 can be found in [239].

In addition to the above, there were a number of other projects that used the concept of events – CORBA [240] being one of the earliest. Low level events were being used in network management systems and TIBCO [241] developed an event-based notification system. Furthermore, graphics user interfaces (GUIs) used event-based callbacks and event handlers to carry different computer devices (e.g., keyboard, mouse). Although the notion of events were used in many of the above systems, their semantics, composition, and execution were somewhat different. Other systems that have some notion of events include Weblogic [242], ILOG Jrules [243], and Vitria BusinessWare Automator [244].

Most of the commercial DBMS vendors incorporated triggers into their products. As a consequence of the awareness of events and their utility, SQL3 [245] further refined the specification of triggers and made it a part of the SQL standard. Unfortunately, the trigger capability supported by DBMSs did not get widely used on account of the lack of technical support from the vendors. A detailed study [246] indicated that banks and other targeted users who could really benefit from this feature were not using them because: (*i*) there is not enough support from the vendors on the use of triggers, (*ii*) methodology and guidance for the usage of triggers were not available, and (*iii*) the performance of the DBMS with large number of triggers has not been acceptable to end users. If the performance disadvantage continues, it is unlikely that the trigger mechanism in DBMSs will see a wide use in real-life applications.

In spite of so much interest in triggers and rules, there was no benchmarks (except for Beast [247, 248]) developed for active databases along the lines of TPC suite of benchmarks [249] widely used by DBMSs.

In addition to the above, work continued on distributed event specification, semantics, and detection [209,250–253] as well as other distributed event applications [254]. Sentinel [187] developed a complete global event detector (or GED) that had well-defined semantics and used it for a number of real-life applications. One of them was for monitoring multiple autonomous DBMSs to check on the viability of war- and peace-time plans which depended on weather, intelligence, and availability and fitness of equipment used by the plans. The above information was stored in different databases and updated independently. Changes to these databases generated events that had to be composed outside of these databases to detect the effect on the plan database. A number of tools for managing events and rules as well as their analysis were developed: event/rule visualization [255], debuggers [256], and dynamic rule editors [257, 258].

At the same time, the power and utility of the ECA paradigm on non-database applications was being recognized. Even within the database realm, it was shown that the ECA paradigm can be used not only for monitoring the state of user-defined objects, but also for monitoring system state. This led to the support of multiple transaction models with in a DBMS using rule sets and identifying system-level events [259–261]. These rule sets could be changed at run time programmatically resulting in a different transaction model. In [259, 260], rule sets were defined for interesting system-level events such as *acquire lock*, *release lock* etc. Using the same ECA paradigm internally, transaction models could be changed by users as part of their application. Beyond this, the complex event processing was decoupled from its tight-coupling with DBMSs and was implemented to work with a standalone application [88].

Reactive capability in the form of ECA rules were also shown to be effective for distributed AI tasks such as task sharing [262], result sharing [263], and in general, for cooperative problem solving [264, 265]. Also, the need for combining active and real-time functionality was recognized and explored in [266, 267].

The notion of active capability no longer connotes its usage in the context of databases but has been accepted and recognized as a functionality that can be used for any event-driven, real-life application. Not surprisingly, CEP is finding usage in many event-driven applications (e.g., work flow, access control, information interchange, and more recently in the context of stream processing as elaborated in Chapters 8 and 9).

The first Dagstuhl workshop on active databases was held in 1994 [268] indicating the maturity of this area. Books that discuss active databases and complex event processing include [61, 193, 269, 270].

4.3.3 Beyond 2000: (Distributed) Complex Event Processing

The landscape of active databases and event processing has changed unmistakably as sensors and stream processing have became mainstream. In addition, the breadth of areas and topics that have come to embrace the need for event processing has significantly increased. Distributed event processing [271–273] and event clouds [274] have gained momentum.

IBM's Active Middleware Technology (or AMiT) [275] is a tool that includes both a language and an efficient run-time execution engine, aimed at reducing the complexity of developing event-based applications. AMiT associates computations along with the definition of an event and uses event operators (following the ECA paradigm). AMiT is an example of a system that has tried to incorporate computations into an event specification. The computation part of AMiT resembles CQ processing.

HiFi [276, 277] generates simple events out of receptor data at its *edges* and provides the functionality of complex event processing on these *edges*. HiFi addresses the issue for generating simple events by virtual devices, which interact with heterogeneous sensors to produce application level simple events. Complex event processing can be carried out to correlate these simple events into an application-level event. Although this system is a step in the right direction for the detection of events over sensor data, it does not define and detect events over stream queries. The events detected at *edges* are simple events and cannot be defined over the result of the data processed by a CQ.

Zaniolo et al. [278] enhance the expressive power of SQL over the combination of relation streams and XML streams by introducing new operators (e.g., continuous user-defined aggregates) and supporting sequences queries (e.g., to search for patterns). Aurora [89] explicitly states the need for a supporting a large number of triggers efficiently which earlier DBMSs failed to accomplish. A number of sensor database projects, Cougar [146,147] and TinyDB [144,145] have also tried to integrate event processing with query processing under a sensor database environment. However, the event-driven queries proposed in TinyDB is used to activate queries based on events from underlying operating systems.

CEDR is an event streaming system [279] that tries to integrate event processing, stream processing, and asynchronous messaging technologies. CEDR embraces a temporal stream model to unify the above technologies to further enrich query language features, handle imperfections in event delivery, define correctness guarantees, and define operator semantics.

White et al. [280] take a foundational approach to the event processing problem. A formal framework is presented that distinguishes between standard axioms (common to the design of all event systems) and desirable axioms (not always satisfied, but are useful for achieving high performance). They prove several results including: existence of a unique model up to isomorphism that satisfies the standard axioms and supports associativity; they further show that adding the boundedness condition also results in a unique model. Based on the above, they believe that their model is ideally suited as a temporal model for complex event systems.

Cayuga is a proposed as general purpose, scalable event processing model [281, 282]. Cayuga proposes an algebra for expressing complex event patterns. It is claimed to incorporate several novel system design and implementation issues, focusing on Cayugas query processor, its indexing approach, handling of simultaneous events, and specialized garbage collecting.

SASE [283] is a complex event processing system that performs data to information transformations over real-time streams. It is targeted for filtering data (e.g., in a RFID application) and correlating them for complex pattern detection and transformation to events that provide meaningful, actionable information to end applications. SASE has: designed a complex event language for specifying application logic for such transformation, devised new query processing techniques to efficiently implement the language, and developed a comprehensive system that collects, cleans, and processes RFID data for delivery of relevant, timely information as well as storing necessary data for future querying.

In `MavEStream` [79,128,129,140,284], we have introduced a family of stream modifiers to efficiently compute changes in stream data. These stream modifiers allow a stream processing application to flexibly express and efficiently monitor complicated change patterns. The goal is to process large amounts of high input rate data using CQs to generate event streams that are fed to an event processing system for correlating them as complex events. The `MavEStream` prototype is an integration of `MavStream` and the LED prototype (based on Snoop) to provide a complete and efficient stream and complex event processing system.

In addition to the above, several extensions have been proposed to earlier work on events: interval-based event semantics [285], event generalization & enhanced event consumption modes [286–288], and the use of the event language Snoop in novel applications [289]. The novel applications include role-based access control, expressive pattern searching over text streams & stored documents, and monitoring of web pages for customized changes.

Interest in complex event processing, its criticality as well as its applicability to diverse domains can be inferred from the proliferation of discussions/blogs (almost every vendor in this space has a blog on `http://complexevents.com`), and the new conferences dedicated to the topic of event processing (e.g., Distributed Event-Based Systems or DEBS [290]: `http://debs08.dis.uniroma1.it/`). The application areas for which complex event processing is expected to provide a better and cleaner approach/solution include autonomic computing, Business Activity Monitoring (or BAM), Business Impact Analysis (or BIA), Business Process Management (or BPM), and Event-driven Applications (or EDA).

An Event Processing Technology Society (EPTS) has been established recently (in 2008, `http://www.ep-ts.com/`) [291] whose motto is:

> "To promote understanding and advancement of Event Processing technologies, to assist in the development of Standards to ensure long-term growth, and to provide a cooperative and inclusive environment for communication and learning"

Another web site dedicated to the discussion of event processing is `www.event-based.org`. It is a community portal for discussions on all aspects of event processing and includes a community wiki and an RSS-enabled event calendar [292]:

> "Event-based.org is a community portal that concentrates efforts in event-based computing – scattered across several scientific and professional communities – in one organized point. The portal aims to collect references to research and development initiatives, encourage discussion about practical insights, and report on experiences in event-based computing.
>
> Informally, events represent state transitions of interest to applications, systems, and users. Event-based computing is concerned with abstractions, models, and algorithms for the effective representation, processing, and management of events.
>
> Event-based.org targets researchers and practitioners interested in "everything events", featuring a Link Collection with more than 800 references, an RSS-enabled Event Calendar announcing conferences, symposia, seminars and workshops, a Community Wiki to foster discussion, and a set of archived mailing lists for the dissemination of relevant information."

A recent Dagstuhl seminar on event processing was held in 2007 [293] emphasizing the resurgence of complex event processing. Vendor community participation was substantial (more than 50%) again perhaps underscoring its future potential.

4.4 Commercial and Open Source Stream and CEP Systems

The thrust of complex event processing has certainly moved from databases to a large number of applications in disparate domains as can be seen from the papers in conferences such as DEBS. Service-oriented architectures for event processing, event-driven middleware [294, 295], publish/subscribe systems for event generation and notification, use of XML for specification as well as encapsulating events have become commonplace.

In addition to stream processing prototypes supporting a plethora of event operators for a number of domains, a number of commercial complex event processing systems and in many cases systems which combine stream and complex event processing systems have emerged since 2000.

The following is a partial list of currently available commercial or open source systems related to stream and complex event processing: Aleri [296], Apama [297], AMiT [275, 298], Coral8 [117], Corona Enterprise Suite [299], Esper [300] (open source), GemFire [301], INETCO [302], Oracle CEP [303], RuleCore [304, 305], SENACTIVE [306], SL RTView [307], StreamBase [104], and WestGlobal [308].

A majority of traditional DBMS vendors support complex event processing separately as a separate engine. Stream processing is also included in a number of them. The middleware approach for complex event processing is also becoming popular.

Although there are quite a few systems, currently there is no consensus on a standard query language or semantics. The operators supported for stream and event processing differ considerably from each other and in some cases are based on the target domain. However, most approaches support a graphical Integrated Development Environment (IDE) making it easier to develop applications that include continuous queries and complex events.

StreamSQL [72], based on SQL, has been proposed as a standard query language for stream and complex event processing. A new model that unifies two different SQL extensions (from Oracle and StreamBase) has also been proposed as a standard for Stream processing [309].

5

MODELING CONTINUOUS QUERIES OVER DATA STREAMS

There are two complementary mechanisms to prevent a DSMS system from violating the QoS requirements of continuous queries: (*1*) In order to support the QoS requirements for a set of continuous queries, a mechanism is needed to plan the resources in terms of CPU cycles, main memory, and so on.

(*2*) After a query processing system is deployed, it may experience temporary overload periods due to the irregular and bursty nature of input data streams. To deal with this, QoS delivery mechanisms are needed at run-time for maximizing resource utilization[1].

This chapter focuses on the first mechanism related to QoS management, namely:

1. The system capacity planning problem estimates the system resources, such as CPU cycles, main memory size and others, which are needed to compute the given continuous queries and satisfy their QoS requirements.
2. The QoS metrics estimation problem estimates various QoS metrics of a continuous query in the system based on the current system state (i.e., input rate of a data stream, characteristics of continuous queries, system resources, and so on). Based on the estimation and the difference between the estimated QoS metrics and the required QoS parameters, QoS delivery mechanisms can be activated or deactivated.

In this chapter, we develop a queueing model to study the dynamics of a DSMS given a set of continuous queries over a set of data streams. In this queueing model, we need to know the input rate (or range) of each input stream. This is usually not an issue as various components of DSMSs, such as query optimizer, scheduler, load shedder, need to monitor the input characteristics of data streams for their working. Also approximate rates (or upper bounds) can be used. Therefore, it does not introduce any additional cost to

[1] Of course, moving existing queries to new resources as well as load balancing of new queries are other run-time alternatives to ensure QoS requirements of queries. They are beyond the scope of this book.

S. Chakravarthy and Q. Jiang, *Stream Data Processing: A Quality of Service Perspective*, Advances in Database Systems 36, DOI: 10.1007/978-0-387-71003-7_5,

use our queueing model. DSMSs only needs to monitor the input rate of an input stream periodically and the length of the periods varies as the system load changes.

The rest of the chapter is organized as follows : Section 5.1 provides an overview of our queueing model. We outline the challenges in Section 5.2. In Section 5.3, we discuss how to model an individual operator in a DSMS, and provide tuple latency and memory requirement analysis of an individual operator in detail. We further extend our modeling work to an individual query plan in a general DSMS, and provide a closed-form solution to estimate QoS metrics (i.e., the overall tuple latency and memory requirement) of the output tuples of a query in Section 5.4. Section 5.6 further presents a set of our quantitative experimental results. The conclusion is presented in Section 5.7.

5.1 Continuous Query Processing

Query processing in a DSMS can be handled using either a multiple threads approach or a single thread approach. In a multiple threads approach, each operator runs as a thread, and the operating system (or a DSMS scheduler) determines which thread to run in any time slot. However, it is hard to control the resource management/allocation in this approach, and the context switch cost can be considerably high. In a single thread approach, all the query plans are registered to a single thread. Various strategies can be used for determining allocation of system resources, scheduling of operators, or plans to run. The system behavior in a single thread approach is more controllable, and the context switch cost is minimized. For a single thread approach in a multi-processor architecture, the whole set of query plans is partitioned into subsets; each subset of query plans runs on a particular processor as a single thread. Some sharing and interdependent relationships may exist between any two subsets.

We employ the second approach, which enables us to control the various aspects of the system and to manage QoS requirements associated with each query plan in the best possible way. Furthermore, we have only considered a subset of query plans scheduled on a single processor. A query processing system running on a multi-processor architecture is considered as a set of such independent subsets, where the relationship between any two subsets were ignored in this discussion.

5.1.1 Operator Path

Since the notion of an *operator path* is important for continuous query processing, we introduce it using an abstract query plan shown in Figure 5.1. The edge from node $\mathcal{A}$ to node $\mathcal{B}$ (Figure 5.1-(a)) indicates that the output of operator $\mathcal{A}$ is buffered into the queue $\mathcal{AB}$ that acts as input source of operator $\mathcal{B}$. Each source (input stream) is represented as a special source node, while an application is represented as a root node (both not shown in Figure 5.1) in this data flow diagram. Therefore, the edges originating from source nodes represent the earliest input queues that buffer the external inputs; while the edge terminating at the root node represent final output queue that buffers final query results. In this diagram, each tuple originates from a source node, and then passes through a series of operators until it reaches the root node or is consumed by an intermediate operator. We refer to the path(s) that a tuple travels from a source node to the root node excluding the source node and the root node as an *operator path* (OP) and the bottom node of an OP as its *leaf node*.

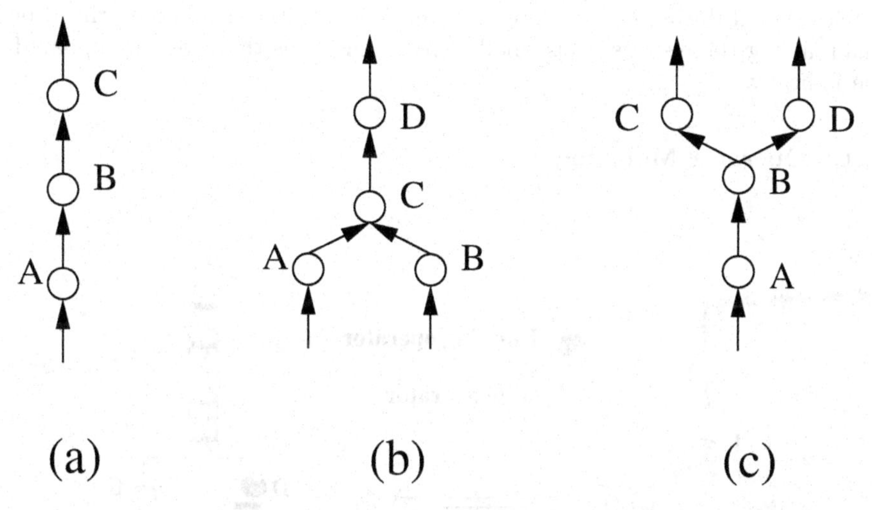

Fig. 5.1. Operator Path

The operator paths can be further classified into two classes in a multiple continuous query processing plan as illustrated in Figure 5.1:

1. Simple operator path: An operator path in which there is no sharing of computation among multiple queries. For example, path *ABC* in Figure 5.1-(a) and paths ACD and BCD in Figure 5.1-(b) are simple operator paths.
2. Complex operator path: If two queries (e.g., with operators A, B, and C and A, B, and D, respectively) share the output of a common subquery (e.g., with operators A and B) as illustrated in Figure 5.1-(c), a complex operator path is formed. For example, there is one complex operator path *ABC/D* in Figure 5.1-(c). In a complex operator path, multiple operators from different queries receive the output of an operator which is the root of a shared computation.

An *operator segment* is defined as a set of connected operators along an operator path. Similar to the operator path, there are simple and complex operator segments in multiple query processing systems. Detailed algorithms are introduced in Section 6.3.3 to partition an operator path into operator segments based on different criteria.

Statistical information such as selectivity, service time[2], and others are maintained for each operator as we maintain statistical information in a DBMS. This information is updated periodically during run-time. The selectivity of an operator can be maintained as a function (i.e., moving average) of the old value of the selectivity and the current ratio of the number of input tuples to the number of output tuples during a schedule. Similarly, the service time of an operator is maintained as a function of the old value of the service time and the current ratio of the total service time to the total number of tuples served during a batch process (i.e., a schedule run). The overhead of maintaining these statistics is small or insignificant as they are only updated periodically.

5.1.2 Operator Modeling

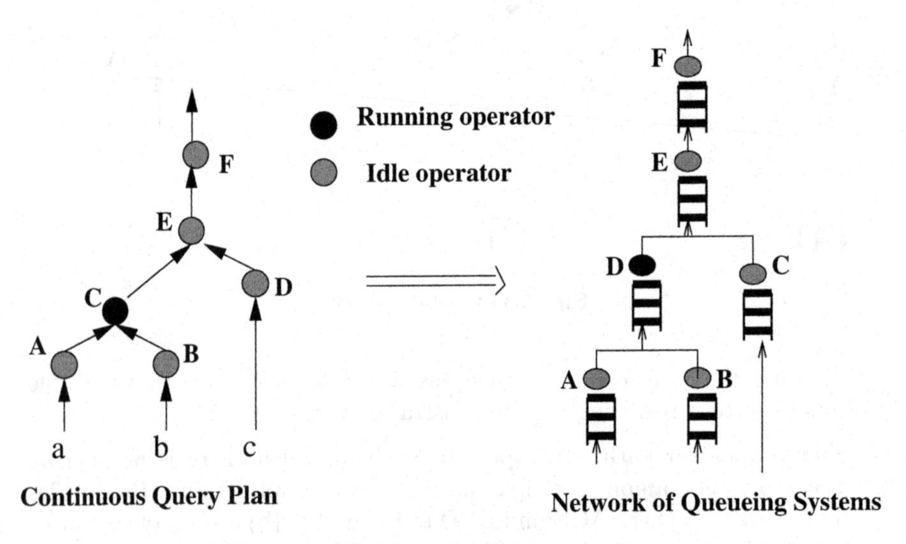

Fig. 5.2. Modeling of a Continuous Query

A queueing system is widely used to model various software and hardware systems [83, 84, 310]. In our approach, each operator in a given query plan is modeled as the service facility of a queueing system [130], and its input buffer(s) are modeled as a logical input queue with different classes of input tuples if it has more than one input stream. The relationship between two

[2] The CPU time needed for an operator to process one tuple.

operators is modeled as a data flow between two queueing systems. Eventually, a query plan is modeled as a network of queueing systems as illustrated in Figure 5.2. A multiple continuous query processing system is modeled as a network of queueing systems, which consists of the network of queueing systems for each query plan.

In this queueing model, we call the queueing system whose inputs are the output of another queueing system the *parent queueing system* of its input queueing systems, and the input queueing systems as its *children queueing systems* . For each external input stream, there exists an *operator path* from the bottom operator to the top operator; we call this path in our queueing network model as a *queueing path.*

Given a subset of query plans scheduled on a processor, at most one operator (in this subset of query plans) is served at any instant of time. Therefore, a scheduling algorithm is necessary to choose an operator to process at each time instant (or time slot), leaving all other operators in the system idle. For an operator in the system, we describe the period when the processor is not available as the *vacation time* of the operator. Furthermore, after the operator gains the processor, it needs some time to setup the environment or to initialize (i.e., context switch, scheduling, and so on); we call this period the *setup time.* Therefore, an operator in a multiple query processing system is further modeled as a queueing system with *vacation time* and *setup time.* The time period when the operator is being served is called its *busy period.*

To summarize, an operator in our queueing model works as follows: once the operator gains the processor, if its input queue is empty, the operator goes to vacation immediately. Otherwise, the processor needs a setup time and then serves a certain number of tuples determined by a specific service discipline using a first-come-first-served order, and the service of a tuple is non-preemptive. When the operator goes to vacation, the processor goes to serve other operators or to handle other tasks during its vacation time and then returns for further service. Thus, each operator is modeled as a queueing system with *vacation time* and *setup time*, and a multiple query processing system is modeled as a network of such queueing systems.

5.1.3 Scheduling and Service Discipline

In our proposed queueing model, the vacation time and busy periods are mainly determined by the scheduling algorithm and the service discipline employed in a DSMS, respectively. The scheduling algorithm determines how often an operator is scheduled statistically and how many other operators or non-query processing tasks can be scheduled between its two consecutive schedules. Once a scheduling algorithm is selected in a DSMS, we are able to find how many other operators or non-query processing tasks are scheduled between its two consecutive schedules, which also implicitly determines how often we schedule an operator. Given a scheduling algorithm, we can analyze the (scheduling) algorithm to find these two items. For example, if the Round

Robin (RR) scheduling algorithm was employed in a DSMS with n operators and each operator was scheduled for 2 (two) time slots once it gains a processor, we know that we will schedule one operator again every $2(n-1)$ time slots. Therefore, the vacation time of each operator in such a DSMS is $2(n-1)$ time slots. However, if a non-deterministic scheduling algorithm (where an object is scheduled based on run-time information in the system), such as operator path [131] or Chain scheduling [85] (both discussed in Chapter 6) is employed, we collect run-time information to statistically determine how many other operators or non-query processing tasks are scheduled between two consecutive schedules of an operator. For example, we can obtain a distribution of the number of operators or tasks scheduled between two consecutive schedules of an operator.

Just as a scheduling algorithm controls the execution order of the operators in a DSMS, a service discipline controls the number of tuples being served when it gains control of the processor. For an overview of various service disciplines, refer to [311, 312]. In general, service disciplines can be categorized into two classes: gated-service and exhaustive-service disciplines. In the case of the gated-service discipline (or GSD), once an operator gains the processor, all tuples waiting in its input queue are served. The tuples which have arrived during the service period are processed in the next round. In the case of exhaustive-service discipline (or ESD), once the operator gets the processor, the processor serves *all waiting* tuples in its input queue as well as the tuples arriving during its service period until its input queue becomes empty. Both service disciplines will be considered in this chapter. Therefore, once the service discipline is employed in a DSMS, given the input characteristics (i.e., input rate) of data streams and the service time of one tuple, we can determine the busy period of an operator.

In summary, the service discipline determines the busy period of an operator and the scheduling algorithm determines the number of operators scheduled between two consecutive schedules of an operator. The service discipline and the scheduling algorithm together determine the length of the vacation time of an operator. In Section 5.4.4, we discuss the computation of the length of the vacation time for an operator in detail.

5.2 Problem Definition

Tuple latency is defined as the number of time units it takes for a tuple from the time it arrives at a leaf node of a continuous query plan to reach the output buffer of the root node (or an application) of that query plan. Therefore, only the output tuples have tuple latency. The tuple latency of a tuple includes the processing of the tuple at each operator along an operator path (see Section 5.1.1) plus the time the tuple spends in buffers or queues along the way. *Mean tuple latency* is defined as an average of tuples latencies for a sequence of tuples or for tuples over a period of time.

Total memory requirement of a continuous query plan at time t is defined as the total main memory units used for processing that query plan at time t. The memory units used for a query at time t is the sum of all queue sizes associated with the query at time t and the memory used for synopsis of each operator, if any. *Maximal memory requirement* of a CQ plan usually refers to the maximum amount of total memory requirement over the duration of processing the CQ plan.

The problem of estimating both tuple latency and the memory requirement of a CQ plan is formally defined as:

Problem Definition 1 *Given a continuous query plan consisting of m operators $\{O_1, O_2, \cdots, O_m\}$ and m queues*[3] *$\{Q_1, Q_2, \cdots, Q_m\}$ over k data streams $\{S_1, S_2, \cdots, S_k\}$, a scheduling algorithm, and a service discipline in a continuous query processing system in a single processor system, determine:*

1. *the total memory units $M(t)$ required by this query in terms of the number of the tuples at time instant t, and*
2. *the tuple latency $R(t)$ at time instant t.*

Both tuple latency and the number of tuples in the above problem are random variables with a continuous parameter (time). It is extremely hard to find the probability distribution function (PDF) for the number of tuples and cumulative distribution function (CDF) for tuple latency in the system. Even if we found them, the overhead to continuously calculate their values would be considerably large. Therefore, we attempt to find approximate mean values of these two performance metrics, which we believe provide sufficient information to manage the QoS requirements of a DSMS. Our experiments show that our approximate solution provides results that are close to what we get from an actual system. Hence, the above problem can be simplified to the following problem that determines mean values.

Problem Definition 2 (Revised Problem) *For the same conditions given in problem 1, determine:*

1. *the total mean memory units $E[M]$ required/consumed by this query in terms of the number of tuples, and*
2. *the mean tuple latency $E[R]$ of tuples from this query.*

Intuitively, the total mean memory size required by this query plan is the sum of the memory required by each operator and the size of queues in the query plan. So $E[M] = \sum_{i=1}^{m} E[Q_i^s] + \sum_{j=1}^{m} E[O_j^s]$, where $E[Q_i^s]$ is the mean number of tuples in the queue Q_i, and $E[O_j^s]$ is the mean number of tuples maintained by the operator O_j in order to compute the operator over a stream. For non-blocking operators such as `select`, `project`[4]; $E[O_j^s] = 0$.

[3] For those operators that have two or more input queues, we consider all its input queues as one logical queue with different kinds of tuples.

[4] Elimination of duplicate tuples is *not* considered here.

For *MAX*, *MIN*; $E[O_j^s] = 1$, which is the biggest or smallest value it has seen so far. For a window-based `symmetric join` operator [76], and window-based `aggregate` operators, $E[O_j^s]$ is a constant[5], which is the number of tuples in its `window`(s) under steady states. Therefore, $\sum_{j=1}^{m} E[O_j^s]$ is a constant $\mathcal{C}$. The total memory is reduced to

$$E[M] = \sum_{i=1}^{m} E[Q_i^s] + \mathcal{C} \tag{5.1}$$

To calculate the total memory consumed by this query, it is sufficient to find the first component of Equation (5.1).

Similarly, the mean tuple latency of an output tuple is the sum of the waiting times at all queues plus the sum of the service times at all operators along its queueing path. The overall tuple latency of a query plan $E[R]$ is the weighted sum of the mean tuple latencies of all queueing paths $E[R_i]$. For a query plan over k data streams, it has k queueing paths or more (e.g., `self-join`). Therefore,

$$\begin{cases} E[R] = \sum_{i=1}^{k} (\varphi_i E[R_i]) \\ E[R_i] = \sum_{i=1}^{\bar{m}} E[W_i] + \sum_{j=1}^{\bar{m}} E[S_j] \end{cases} \tag{5.2}$$

where φ_i is the queueing path weight, which is the ratio of the number of output tuples from that path to the total number of output tuples from that query plan. $E[W_i]$ is the mean waiting time of a tuple in the queue Q_i, and $E[S_j]$ is the mean processing time of a tuple at the operator O_j. Fortunately, both queueing path weight and processing time can be learned during query execution by gathering statistics over a period of time. If we expect these values to change over time, we could collect statistics periodically. As a result, we only need to find a solution for the mean waiting time of a tuple in the queues along its path.

5.2.1 Notations and Assumptions

In this chapter, we use the following notations (variables):

λ: finite mean arrival rate of an external input stream.
U, V, B, S: setup time, vacation time, busy period, and service time distributions, respectively, with their first and second moments $(.)^{(1)}, (.)^{(2)}$, where $(.)$ can be U, V, B, S.
ρ: traffic intensity or utilization with $\rho = \lambda S^{(1)}$.
W: tuple waiting time in the input queue with its first and second moments $W^{(1)}, W^{(2)}$.
C: a cycle that is defined as the period between two successive vacation endings with its first and second moments $C^{(1)}, C^{(2)}$.

[5] Refer to footnote [4] on page 18. Input rate fluctuations can be handled by using a headroom value to allow for bursts.

Q_n^s: queue length at the end of service of the n^{th}customer (tuple).
Q_n^v: queue length at the end of the nth vacation.
$N^{(.)}$: the number of tuples arriving during the period of (.), where (.) can be U, V, B, C.
$A^*(s)$: the Laplace Stieltjes Transformation (LST) of a distribution A with $A^*(s) = E[e^{(-sA)}]$
$A(z)$: the probability generation function (PGF) of a discrete distribution A with $A(z) = E[z^A]$.
μ: the time of an operator taken to process a tuple.

In our queueing model, we make the following assumptions:

1. The arrival times of tuples from an external input form a Poisson process. Although some reports from the network community show that a self-similar traffic model [313] is closer to the real network traffic data than a Poisson model, a Poisson process is still a good approximation for most applications. As most applications over stream data only require approximate results, the results based on a Poisson process provide sufficient information to manage both QoS and resources.
2. The input queue of an operator has an infinite capacity. Therefore, no tuple is discarded.
3. The *setup time* U and selectivity σ of an operator are known or can be learned by collecting run-time statistics in a DSMS periodically.

5.2.2 Stability and Performance Metrics

In order to solve problem 2, we are interested in the mean queue size and the mean tuple latency. In addition, we need mean cycle time, mean service period, and the mean total number of tuples served during a cycle in order to decide vacation time of an operator. To derive these metrics, we need the whole query processing system in a steady state. For both gated- and exhaustive-disciplines, $\rho < 1$ is a necessary and sufficient condition for stability. For readers who interested in stability condition, please refer to [314].

5.3 Modeling Relational Operators

In order to derive a closed form solution for tuple latency and memory requirement of a continuous query in a DSMS, it is useful to identify some characteristics (i.e., waiting time and memory requirement) of individual operators encompassed in a continuous query. In this section, each operator is modeled as a standalone queueing system in order to study its characteristics.

In data management systems, `select`, `project`, and `join` are the most frequently used operators. Once we get the detailed performance metrics of these operators, we will be able to compute the detailed performance metrics of a query, or of an entire query processing system. Some aggregate operators such as `sum` and `average` over a sliding `window` can be modeled in a similar way.

5.3.1 Modeling `Select` and `Project` Operators

Both `select` and `project` are unary operators operating on a single stream processing and have one input and one output queue. The `select` operator works as a filter and evaluates the `select` condition, which can either be a primitive or a composite condition, on each input tuple.

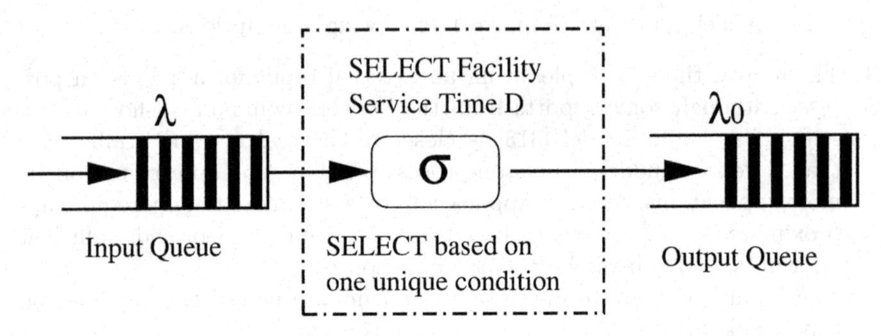

Fig. 5.3. Modeling of `Select` Operator

`Select` Operator with a Primitive Condition

In this case, every tuple is evaluated by one unique condition, and hence the service time for each tuple is a constant. The selection over one primitive condition is modeled as a M/D/1 queuing system as shown in Figure 5.3.

Given a `select` operator that takes $1/\mu$ time to process a tuple over a data stream with a mean input rate λ, the mean and variance of the number of tuples in the select subsystem are respectively,

$$E[\bar{q}] = \rho + \frac{\rho^2}{2(1-\rho)}; \ \textit{Where } \rho = \frac{\lambda}{\mu} \tag{5.3a}$$

$$Var[\bar{q}] = \frac{1}{(1-\rho)^2}(\rho - \frac{3}{2}\rho^2 + \frac{5}{6}\rho^3 - \frac{1}{12}\rho^4) \tag{5.3b}$$

Similarly, the mean and variance of the waiting time W of a tuple (waiting time in the queue plus service time) are respectively,

$$E[W] = \frac{1}{\mu} + \frac{\rho}{2\mu(1-\rho)}; \ \textit{Where } \rho = \frac{\lambda}{\mu} \tag{5.4a}$$

$$Var[W] = \frac{1}{\mu^2(1-\rho)^2}(\frac{\rho}{3} - \frac{\rho^2}{12}) \tag{5.4b}$$

Note that the second component in (5.4a) is the mean waiting time of the tuple in the queue.

`Select` Operator with a Composite Condition

A composite condition consists of several primitive conditions (Conjunctive Normal Form or a conjunction of disjuncts is assumed). In the worst case, the `select` operator needs to evaluate all of the primitive conditions to determine whether a tuple is output or not. On the other hand, it is also possible to make a decision by evaluating just one of the conditions, in the best case scenario. Therefore, the service time is not a constant, and it depends on the selectivity of each condition.

In an optimized query processing system, the first primitive condition has a relatively small selectivity, and the rest have the same order of selectivity. Thereby, only a small portion of tuples are needed to evaluate more than one condition. The service time can be considered as an exponential distribution because every tuple must be evaluated using the first conjunct, and if it is not applicable, the second conjunct will be used and so on. Apparently, the number of tuples to be evaluated by each successive conjunct decreases exponentially.

Corollary 1 *Service time of a* `select` *operator with a composite condition obeys an exponential distribution.*

Proof sketch. Without of loss generality, consider a composite condition consisting of n, where $n \geq 2$, primitive conditions $\sigma_0, \sigma_1, \cdots, \sigma_{n-1}$ and service times for primitive conditions are $1/\mu_0, 1/\mu_1, \cdots, 1/\mu_{n-1}$, respectively. A query processing engine decomposes the composite condition during query optimization phase and processes these primitive conditions in an increasing order of selectivity. Without loss of generality, we assume that $\sigma_0 \leq \sigma_1 \leq \cdots \leq \sigma_{n-1}$. Therefore, σ_0 portion of tuples need a service time of $1/\mu_0$, $(1-\sigma_0)\sigma_1$ (for $n > 2$) portion of tuples need a service time of $(1/\mu_0 + 1/\mu_1)$, $1/\prod_{i=0}^{k-1}(1-\sigma_i)\sigma_k$ (for $1 < k < (n-1)$) portion of tuples need a service time of $\sum_{i=0}^{k} 1/\mu_i$, and $1/\prod_{i=0}^{n-2}(1-\sigma_i)$ portion of tuples need a service time of $\sum_{i=0}^{n-1} 1/\mu_i$. The number of tuples that need more service time decreases exponentially (a factor of $1-\sigma_i$). As a result, we can safely model the service time of an operator with composite condition as an exponential distribution. □

Hence, the `select` operator with a composite condition is modeled as a simple M/M/1 queueing system . For the given situation described in Section 5.3.1, the mean and variance of the number of tuples in the select subsystem with a composite condition are respectively,

$$E[\bar{q}] = \frac{\rho}{1-\rho}; \quad Var[\bar{q}] = \frac{\rho}{(1-\rho)^2} \quad where \ \rho = \frac{\lambda}{\mu} \tag{5.5}$$

The mean and variance of the waiting time are respectively,

$$E[W] = \frac{1}{\mu(1-\rho)}; \quad Var[W] = \frac{1}{\mu^2(1-\rho)^2} \tag{5.6}$$

`project` Operator

A `project` operator extracts a subset of all the attributes of the tuple. In a traditional DBMS, the `project` operator may also be required to eliminate duplicates. Duplicate elimination, however, may not be applicable to a data stream environment because the output of the `project` operator is another data stream. If needed, choosing a non-blocking algorithm for the elimination of duplicates is important[6]. Here, this operator is modeled without taking duplicate elimination into consideration[7], and it works very much like a `select` operator with a primitive condition. Hence it is modeled as a M/D/1 system, where the constant service time is the time for extracting the specified subset of attributes of a tuple. The relative performance metrics for a M/D/1 queueing system as summarized in Section 5.3.1 can be applied.

5.3.2 Modeling `Window`-Based Symmetric Hash `join`

A `window`-based `symmetric hash join` algorithm is based on the architecture where an infinite queue is attached to each data stream as illustrated in Figure 5.4. Let Q_1, Q_2 denote the queues attached to left *data stream 1* and right *data stream 2* respectively, and the output queue Q_O is used to store the results. Typically the size of the reference of a tuple is much smaller than the size of the tuple itself, and hence using references avoids duplicate storage of tuples. Based on this observation, we use a thread to maintain the global tuple pool in a DSMS, including adding new tuples to the pool, passing the reference of the new tuple to the corresponding queue, and deleting an expired tuple and its references in the queues. A tuple expires and is deleted when the difference between its arrival time stamp and current time stamp is greater than the largest time-window required by any operator in the system. For the purpose of this analysis, we define two phases for the above join algorithm: *a transition phase* and *a steady state phase.* The transition phase is defined as the period before the first tuple is removed from the last hash table due to its expiration. After the transition phase, the system enters a steady state phase because the mean of the number of tuples in the system fluctuates slightly around a constant if the input rates obey a Poisson distribution and the `window` size is big enough. Since transition phase is very short in terms of the lifespan of a continuous query, we only analyze the steady state phase.

5.3.3 Steady State Processing Cost

To analyze the computation cost required for processing a new tuple in the steady state, we find that the average number of tuples in each hash table

[6] Duplicate tuples can be eliminated in a non-blocking manner by using a hash table instead of sorting.

[7] If duplicate elimination is performed using the hash table approach, it can still be modeled as a M/D/1 system as explained in Section 5.3.2 for the `window-based hash join`. The service time need to be computed differently.

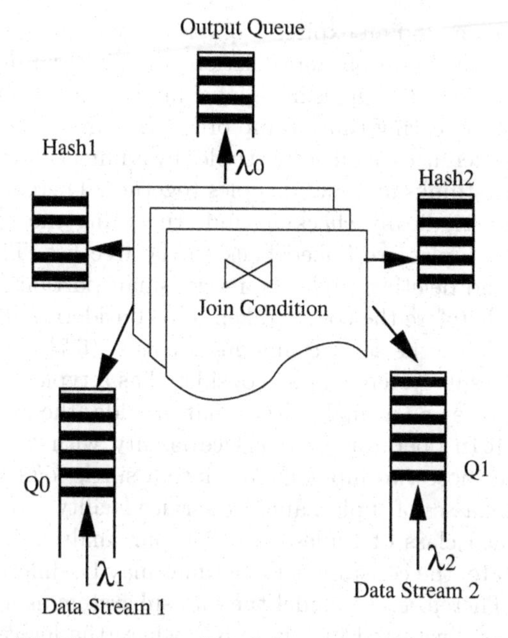

Fig. 5.4. Window-based Symmetric Hash Join

$H_i(n)$ is stable and is given by: $H_i(n) = \lambda_i I_i, i = 1, 2$, where I_i is the predefined time-window for the `join` operator illustrated in Figure 5.4. To process one new tuple from *data stream 1*, the `join` operator needs to do the following operations:

1. Insert the tuple into the hash table $Hash_1$.
2. Hash the tuple into the hash table $Hash_2$ to find the corresponding bucket.
3. Search the corresponding bucket with the join condition.
4. Output the matching tuples to the output queue if any.

Mathematically, the total cost for processing one tuple:

$$D_i = 2C_H + C_O + C_E \left(\frac{H_j(n)}{m_j} \right) \begin{cases} j = 2 \ \textit{if} \ i = 1 \\ j = 1 \ \textit{if} \ i = 2 \end{cases} \tag{5.7}$$

where C_H is the cost of hashing, which is a function call in the system, and it is a constant; C_E is the cost of evaluation of the `join` condition; m_j is the number of buckets in the corresponding hash table. C_O is the cost of output, which is the cost of passing the reference of the matched tuple to the upstream operators or applications for further processing. The output cost is negligible compared to the cost of condition evaluation. Consequently, the total cost D_i of processing a tuple from left data stream is a constant. This holds true for the tuple from data stream 2 as well, though these two costs may be different.

We have not considered the cost of accepting newly arrived tuples and deleting expired tuples, so far. It is useful to take a look at how a new tuple is added to the system and an expired tuple is located and deleted before we model the costs of the addition and deletion. In a general query processing system, it is natural to order tuples in a global buffer along a time axis because tuples arrive in an increasing time-stamp order. In our system, a dirty linked list maintains the references of all active tuples by adding a newly arrived tuple to its head, a free list links all unused tuples together. Therefore, deletion can be done through periodically checking and truncating the tail of the dirty list. Those expired tuples are linked back to the free list. The cost of both accepting tuples and deleting tuples is a very small portion, say $\alpha\%$, of the system load, and therefore the cost is taken into consideration by multiplying a factor of $1/(1-\alpha)$ to the service time in Equation (5.7).

The `hash join` sub-system can be considered as a typical queuing system with two input queues and a single server that provides the join service. First, we consider the `join` operator as a service facility with two input queues. Then, we combine those two input queues into a single logical virtual queue with two different classes of tuples, and the service facility provides a constant service time to each class of tuples based on our analysis in Section 5.3.3. Under a steady state, the constant service times may be different for different classes of tuples. Therefore, we model the join subsystem as a $M/(D_1, D_2)/1$ queueing system as illustrated in Figure 5.5, where the logical virtual input queue has a mean arrival rate $(\lambda_1 + \lambda_2)$, and D_1, D_2 are the service times to process a tuple coming from data streams *1* and *2* respectively.

Steady State Analysis

Based on above queueing system model, the service times are deterministic for each type of tuple. The queueing system is not a simple Markov chain system because the service time does not obey an exponential distribution and satisfy the memoryless property. To fully describe the queue state, we need, not only the number of tuples in the queue, but also the service time for which a tuple has already been in the service facility (or the remaining service time prior to its departure from the join service facility). This two-dimensional state system makes queueing analysis much more complicated than a one-dimensional state system.

The method we present here for finding the mean number of tuples and the mean waiting time in the `join` subsystem is based on an embedded Markov chain approach [315]. The basic idea behind this method is to simplify the description of the state from a two-dimensional description to a one-dimensional description. The usual way is to sample the two-dimensional state information into a special discrete-time point, which explicitly describes the number of tuples in the system, and implicitly contains information about the time spent by a tuple in the join service facility. Usually we select those points at the instant when a tuple in the service facility departs the system. When we specify the number of tuples in the system, we also know that the service time spent for the tuple that just enters the join service facility at that instant is

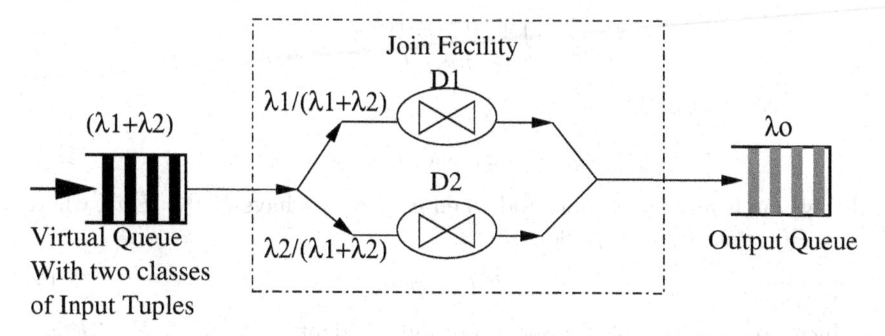

Fig. 5.5. Queueing Model of `Window`-based Symmetric Hash `Join` Operator

zero. By only considering the point when the tuples leave the `join` service facility, the state transitions take place only at these points and form a discrete time space. Fortunately, the solution at these embedded Markov points happens to provide a solution for all points in time as well.

In this section, we define the following random variables.

- C_n represents the nth tuple to enter the system.
- τ_n represents the arrival time of C_n.
- $t_n = \tau_n - \tau_{n-1}$ represents the interarrival time between C_n and C_{n-1}.
- X_n represents the service time for tuple C_n.
- q_n represents the number of tuples left behind by the departure of C_n from the service.
- ν_n represents the number of tuples arrives during service time (of C_n).

THEOREM 1 *Given a window-based* **`hash join`** *system over two data streams with input mean rate λ_1, λ_2, and service times D_1, D_2 for the tuples from left data stream 1 and right data stream 2 respectively, the mean queue size under the steady state is given by:*

$$E[\bar{q}] = \lambda_1 D_1 + \lambda_2 D_2 + \frac{(\lambda_1 + \lambda_2)(\lambda_1 D_1^2 + \lambda_2 D_2^2)}{2(1 - (\lambda_1 D_1 + \lambda_2 D_2))} \tag{5.8}$$

Proof. Considering the time point when C_{n-1} left the system, there are two cases: (*1*) There are no more tuples ($q_n = 0$) in the queue. In this case, the number of tuples in the queue at the time when C_n left the system is the number of tuples arriving during the service period X_n (of C_n); (*2*) There are q_n tuples ($q_n > 0$) in the queue. Therefore, the number of tuples left in the queue is the number of tuples that arrive during the service period of time X_n (of C_n) plus the number of tuples left behind when tuple C_n left the system minus 1. Based on the above analysis,

$$\begin{cases} q_{n+1} = q_n + v_{n+1} - 1 & \text{if } q_n > 0 \\ q_{n+1} = v_{n+1} & \text{if } q_n = 0 \end{cases} \tag{5.9}$$

We define the following step function

$$\delta_k = \begin{cases} 1 & \text{if } k = 1, 2, \cdots \\ 0 & \text{if } k \leq 0 \end{cases} \tag{5.10}$$

we can rewrite (5.9) as

$$q_{n+1} = q_n - \delta_n + v_{n+1} \tag{5.11}$$

If the system is an ergodic one, and when $n \to \infty$, we have $E[\delta] = E[\bar{v}]$, where $E[\delta] = P(\textit{system busy}) = \rho$. So

$$E[\bar{v}] = \rho \tag{5.12}$$

Since random variables v and q are independent, $E[v_n q_n] = E[v_n]E[q_n]$, also $E[q_n \delta_n] = E[q_n]$. Take square and then expectation on both sides of Equation (5.11), when $n \to \infty$, $E[\bar{q}_{n+1}^2] = E[\bar{q}_n^2] + E[\bar{v}_{n+1}^2] + E[\bar{\delta}_n^2] + 2E[\bar{q}_n]E[\bar{v}_{n+1}] - 2E[\bar{q_n}]E[\bar{\delta}_n] - 2E[\bar{v}_{n+1}]E[\bar{\delta}_n]$. Here $E[\bar{\delta}^2] = E[\bar{\delta}]$ because $\delta^2 = \delta$. Then we get

$$E[\bar{q}] = E[\bar{\delta}] + \frac{E[\bar{v}^2] + E[\bar{\delta}]}{2(1 - E[\bar{v}])} \tag{5.13}$$

The only term unknown in Equation (5.13) is $E[\bar{v}^2]$. From the properties of Z-transform, we can get the kth moments easily if we can find the Z-transform function of random variable v. By definition of Z-transform, we have

$$\begin{aligned} V[z] &= \sum_{k=0}^{\infty} P(\bar{v} = k) z^k \\ &= \sum_{k=0}^{\infty} \left(\frac{(\lambda D_1)^k}{k!} e^{-\lambda D1} + \frac{(\lambda D_2)^k}{k!} e^{-\lambda D_2}\right) z^k \\ &= P(D_1) e^{-\lambda D_1 (1-z)} + P(D_2) e^{-\lambda D_2 (1-z)} \end{aligned} \tag{5.14}$$

where $P(D_1) = \frac{\lambda 1}{\lambda_1 + \lambda_2}$ and $P(D_2) = \frac{\lambda 2}{\lambda_1 + \lambda_2}$; taking the first derivative of Equation (5.14), $\frac{dv(z)}{d_z} \|_{z=1} = P(D_1)\lambda D_1 + P(D_2)\lambda D_2 = \lambda_1 D_1 + \lambda_2 D_2 = \rho = E[\bar{v}]$, and taking the second derivative of Equation (5.14), $\frac{d^2 v(z)}{d_z^2} \|_{z=1} = P(D_1)(\lambda D_1)^2 + P(D_2)(\lambda D_2)^2$ We find $E[\bar{v^2}] = \lambda(\lambda_1 D_1^2 + \lambda_2 D_2^2) - E[\bar{v}]$, substituting it into Equation (5.13), which yields

$$E[\bar{q}] = \lambda_1 D_1 + \lambda_2 D_2 + \frac{(\lambda_1 + \lambda_2)(\lambda_1 D_1^2 + \lambda_2 D_2^2)}{2(1 - (\lambda_1 D_1 + \lambda_2 D_2))} \tag{5.15}$$

Remark 1 : *1)* The first part (first two items) of the above equation is the mean number of tuples that arrived during the service time of one tuple. The second part is the mean number of tuples that are left in the queue before the tuple that is in service has entered the service facility.
2) The mean queue size is invariant when both the processing ability and the input rate are increased to k times, namely $\lambda_1' = k\lambda_1, \lambda_2' = k\lambda_2$ and $D_1' = \frac{D_1}{k}, D_2' = \frac{D_2}{k}$. This can be shown by substituting them into Equation (5.8). So the utilization $\rho = \lambda_1 D_1 + \lambda_2 D_2$ is the only factor that affects $E[\bar{q}]$ in the system.

THEOREM 2 *Given a window-based* **hash join** *system described in Theorem 1, the probability distribution of the number of tuples in such a system under the steady state is given by*

$$P(N = k) = (1 - \rho)d_k \tag{5.16}$$

where $d_k = \begin{cases} a_k - \sum_{j=1}^{k} b_j d_{k-j} & \text{if } k = 1, 2, \cdots \\ 1 & \text{if } k = 0 \end{cases}$

$$\begin{aligned} a_k &= \tfrac{c_k}{c_0 k!} - \tfrac{c_{k-1}}{c_0 (k-1)!} & &\text{for } k = 1, 2, \cdots; \\ b_1 &= \tfrac{c_1 - 1}{c_0}; \text{ and } b_k = \tfrac{c_k}{c_0 k!} & &\text{for } k = 2, 3, \cdots; \\ c_k &= \tfrac{\lambda_1}{\lambda} e^{-\lambda D_1} (\lambda D_1)^k + \tfrac{\lambda_2}{\lambda} e^{-\lambda D_2} (\lambda D_2)^k & &\text{for } k = 0, 1, \cdots; \\ \lambda &= \lambda_1 + \lambda_2 \end{aligned}$$

Proof. Take Z-transform on both sides of Equation (5.11),

$$Z^{q_{n+1}} = Z^{q_n - \delta_n + v_{n+1}} \tag{5.17}$$

According to the Z-transform property, the Z-transform of the sum of two random variables equals the product of those two random variables' Z transform.

$$Z^{q_{n+1}} = Z^{q_n - \delta_n} Z^{v_{n+1}} \tag{5.18}$$

Where

$$Z^{q_{n+1}} = \sum_{k=0}^{\infty} P(q_{n+1} = k) Z^{k-1}$$

and

$$Z^{q_n - \delta_n} = P(q_n = 0) + \frac{1}{z} \left(\sum_{k=0}^{\infty} P(q_n = k) z^k - P(q_n = 0)\right)$$

. Since $P(q_n = 0) = 1 - \rho$,

$$Z^{q_n - \delta_n} = 1 - \rho + \frac{1}{z} \left(Z^{q_n} - (1 - \rho)\right) \tag{5.19}$$

We denote the Z-transform of random variable q_n, v_n by Q(z), V(z) respectively, and simplify Equation (5.18),

$$Q(z) = V(z) \frac{(1 - \rho)(1 - z)}{V(z) - z} \tag{5.20}$$

Substituting Equation (5.14) and $\rho = \frac{\lambda_1 D_1 + \lambda_2 D_2}{\lambda}$ into Equation (5.20),

$$Q(z) = \frac{(1 - \rho)\left(1 + \sum_{k=1}^{\infty} \left(\frac{c_k}{c_0 k!} - \frac{c_{k-1}}{c_0 (k-1)!}\right) z^k\right)}{1 + \frac{c_1 - 1}{c_0} z + \sum_{k=2}^{\infty} \frac{z^k}{c_0 k!}} \tag{5.21}$$

where $c_k = \frac{(\lambda D_1)^k}{k!} e^{-\lambda D1} + \frac{(\lambda D_2)^k}{k!} e^{-\lambda D_2}$; Furthermore, we can rewrite Equation (5.21) as

$$Q(z) = (1-\rho)\frac{1+\sum_{k=1}^{\infty} a_k z^k}{1+\sum_{k=1}^{\infty} b_k z^k} = (1-\rho)\sum_{k=1}^{\infty} d_k z^k \tag{5.22}$$

where
$a_k = \frac{c_k}{c_0 k!} - \frac{c_{k-1}}{c_0 (k-1)!}$
$b_1 = \frac{c_1 - 1}{c_0}$; *and* $b_k = \frac{c_k}{c_0 (k-1)!}$
$d_k = \begin{cases} a_k - \sum_{j=1}^{k} b_j d_{k-1} & \text{if } k = 1, 2, \cdots \\ 1 & \text{if } k = 0 \end{cases}$

From Theorem 2, it follows that
$P(N=0) = 1-\rho$
$P(N=1) = (1-\rho)(\frac{1}{\frac{\lambda_1}{\lambda}e^{-\lambda D_1} + \frac{\lambda_2}{\lambda}e^{-\lambda D_2}} - 1)$
$P(N=2) = (1-\rho)(\frac{c_2}{2c_0} - \frac{c_1 + \frac{3}{2}c_0 - 1}{c_0^2})$

Corollary 2 *The variance of the number of tuples in such a join subsystem is given by*

$$Var[\bar{q}] = (1-\rho)\sum_{k=2}^{\infty} k(k-1)d_k + E[\bar{q}] - E[\bar{q}]^2$$

Proof. It follows from Theorem 2 by taking Z-transform, $Q(z) = (1-\rho)\sum_{k=0}^{\infty} d_k z^k$, and then taking the second derivative, $\frac{d^2 Q(z)}{d_z^2}\|_{z=1} = (1-\rho)\sum_{k=2}^{\infty} k(k-1)d_k = E[\bar{q}^2] - E[\bar{q}]$. So the variance of number of tuples in the system $Var[\bar{q}] = E[\bar{q}^2] - E[\bar{q}]^2 = (1-\rho)\sum_{k=2}^{\infty} k(k-1)d_k + E[\bar{q}] - E[\bar{q}]^2$.

THEOREM 3 *Given a window-based hash* `join` *system described in Theorem 1, the mean waiting time of tuples in the join subsystem and in the queue under the steady state are given by, respectively,*

$$W = \frac{\lambda_1 D_1 + \lambda_2 D_2}{\lambda_1 + \lambda_2} + \frac{\lambda_1 D_1^2 + \lambda_2 D_2^2}{2(1-(\lambda_1 D_1 + \lambda_2 D_2))} \tag{5.23a}$$

$$W_q = \frac{\lambda_1 D_1^2 + \lambda_2 D_2^2}{2(1-(\lambda_1 D_1 + \lambda_2 D_2))} \tag{5.23b}$$

Proof. According to Little's result, the waiting time of the tuples in the system is $W = \frac{\bar{N}}{\lambda} = \frac{E[\bar{q}]}{\lambda}$. Substituting Equation (5.8) into the above equation, we get Equation (5.23a). And the second part of Equation (5.23a) is the mean waiting time in the queue.

Remark 2 : *If we increase, at the same time, the processing ability and the input rate k times, as we did earlier, the mean waiting times of the tuples in both the system and the queue decrease to* $1/k$ *of the original mean waiting time. This can be shown by substituting the changed factors into the Equations* (5.23a) *and* (5.23b).

From Remarks 1 and 2, we clearly show that a bigger system with n units processing power and n units input rate is better than n small systems with 1 unit processing power and 1 unit input rate. Although both the bigger system and all small systems require the same amount of memory, the tuple latency in the bigger system is one n^{th} of that in a small system. Therefore, to process data streams, clustering multiple smaller systems into a bigger system is better than multiple standalone small systems.

Corollary 3 *The variance of waiting time of tuples in such a join subsystem is give by*

$$Var(W) = \frac{(1-\rho)}{\lambda^2}\sum_{k=2}^{\infty} k(k-1)d_k - W^2.$$

Proof. From the generalized Little's formula [310], we know $\frac{d^k Q(z)}{d_z^k}\|_{z=1} = \lambda_k^W$, where W_k is the kth moment of the waiting time of tuples in the system. The variance of W, $Var(W) = W_2 - W^2 = \frac{1-\rho}{\lambda^2}\sum_{k=2}^{\infty} k(k-1)d_k - W^2$, where W can be obtained from Equation (5.23a), d_k is given in Equation (5.16).

THEOREM 4 *Given a window-based* `hash join` *system described in Theorem 1, the probability distribution of the waiting time of tuples in the queue under the steady state is given by*

$$W(t) = 1 - (\lambda_1 D_1 + \lambda_2 D_2)e^{(s_0 t)} \tag{5.24}$$

where s_0 is its negative root of Equation (5.29)

Proof. For our $M/(D_1, D_2)/1$ queueing model, we have the Cumulative Distribution Function (CDF) of service time

$$B(s) = \begin{cases} 0 & \textit{if } s < D_1 \\ \frac{\lambda_1}{\lambda_1+\lambda_2} & \textit{if } D_1 \leq s < D_2 \\ 1 & \textit{if } s \geq D_2 \end{cases} \tag{5.25}$$

and its probability density function is
$b(t) = \frac{\lambda_1}{\lambda_1+\lambda_2}\delta(t)(t-D_1) + \frac{\lambda_2}{\lambda_1+\lambda_2}\delta(t)(t-D_2)$
where $\delta(t) = \begin{cases} 1 & t \geq 0 \\ 0 & t < 0 \end{cases}$. Then, computing its LST B*(s)

$$B^*(s) = \frac{\lambda_1}{\lambda_1+\lambda_2}e^{sD_1} + \frac{\lambda_2}{\lambda_1+\lambda_2}e^{sD_2} \tag{5.26}$$

Also, the LST of the interarrival probability distribution function is given by

$$A^*(s) = \frac{\lambda_1+\lambda_2}{(\lambda_1+\lambda_2)+s} \tag{5.27}$$

By substituting Equations (5.26) and (5.27) into the characteristic Equation $A^*(-s)B^*(s) = -1$, defined in Lindley's Equation [310], we have

$$\lambda_1 e^{-sD_1} + \lambda_2 e^{-sD_2} - (\lambda_1 + \lambda_2) + s = 0 \tag{5.28}$$

Obviously, zero is one of its roots. We can also easily find a numerical solution for the above equation by MATLAB or any other mathematical tool. The CDF of the waiting-time for our model

$$W(t) = 1 - (\lambda_1 D_1 + \lambda_2 D_2)e^{(s_0 t)} \tag{5.29}$$

The distribution of the waiting time in the system is the same as that in the queue except we need to add the constant service time D to the above equation.

5.3.4 Handling Bursty Inputs and Disk-Resident Data

The approach presented so far is generally true for any `window`-based `symmetric join` operator, with the only difference being the value of the service time. If a stream data processing system also accesses a stored database, we may need to join the tuples from a data stream with a data set stored on a disk. In this case, the input process may not be a Poisson process; we briefly discuss the impact of more bursty inputs on the performance of these models.

One Relation on Local Disk

If the entire relation on local disks can fit in main memory, we can load all the tuples into memory before we start the join algorithm. There is only one input data stream for this case. The `join` operator works as a single stream processing operator and hence the system can be modeled as a M/D/1 queue with the mean arrival rate λ_1 and constant service time D_1, which is the cost for a tuple from the input stream to join with all tuples in the relation. If all the tuples of the relation on local disks cannot fit in memory, the cost of processing a tuple not only includes those costs listed in Section 5.3.3, but also the extra cost of loading tuples from disks and paging out the probed tuples to the disks. However, the service time is still a constant because for each input tuple from the input stream, the cost of loading tuples from disks and paging out the probed tuples to disks is the same. Therefore, the system can again be modeled as a M/D/1 queue with a larger service time.

Corollary 4 *The mean number of tuples in such a join system when one relation is on local disks is*

$$E[\bar{q}] = \lambda_1 D_1 + \frac{\lambda_1^2 D_1^2}{2(1 - \lambda_1 D_1)}.$$

It follows from (5.8) by setting $D_2 = 0$ and $\lambda_2 = 0$.

Corollary 5 *The mean waiting time of tuples in such a system and in the queue are* $W = D_1 + \frac{\lambda_1 D_1^2}{2(1-\lambda_1 D_1)}$ *and* $\bar{W}_q = \frac{\lambda_1 D_1^2}{2(1-\lambda_1 D_1)}$ *and respectively.*

Similarly, the above results can be derived by setting $D_2 = 0$ and $\lambda_2 = 0$ in Equations (5.23a) and (5.23b).

The queue size in Corollary 4 and the mean waiting time in Corollary 5 have the same forms as the results of a standard M/D/1 presented in Section 5.3.1. This verifies the correctness of our analysis in Section 5.3.3.

Impact of Bursty Inputs

Although many data streams can be approximately modeled as a Poisson input model, many researchers have shown that there is a class of input data streams that are much more bursty than Poisson inputs. This class of input data streams exhibits the so-called *self-similar* [316] property over a wide range of time scale. Partial explanation of this property is that the input data stream itself is a superimposition of many (theoretically, infinite) ON/OFF sub-streams, the distributions of the length of ON/OFF periods are a heavy tailed distribution. The input data streams of a sensor database may demonstrate the *self-similar* property because thousands of sensors send data during ON periods, and then go to OFF (or sleep) mode in order to save energy.

Due to the modeling difficulties of queueing systems fed by self-similar data streams, we do not intend to do an exact analysis. Instead, we highlight here a few key points of the impact of a bursty input data stream on queueing performance. Under steady state:

1. Both the queue size and the tuple latency in the queue have a heavy-tailed distribution, but with a different power. The larger queue size and longer tuple latency do not decrease exponentially as they do in a Poisson model; instead, the tails of the distribution are much longer than those in a standard Poisson model.
2. The more bursty the input data streams are, the longer are both the queue size and tuple latency. The bursty property of the input data streams is mainly dominated by the distribution of the ON periods, not by the departure distribution of the tuples within ON periods.
3. The queueing metrics obtained from a Poisson input process are similar to those obtained from *self-similar* input streams when the system load is not high. However, as the system load increases, the difference based on these two inputs can increase dramatically.

5.4 Modeling Continuous Queries

In the previous section, we analyzed the performance metrics of each operator used in a query plan based on a single-server queueing model. However, in a multiple query processing system, there is only one server (processor) available for all operators in the system. The input process of some operators in a multiple query processing system does not form a Poisson distribution because some operators get their input(s) from the outputs of other operators. Even if the input process of an operator forms a Poisson distribution, its output does not form a Poisson distribution. Therefore, the end-to-end tuple latency or memory requirement of a query plan is not simply the sum of its corresponding parts in those standard queueing systems presented in previous section where each of them requires a dedicated server.

In a multiple-query processing system, some operators have an Exponential service time while others have a deterministic service time or a more general service time. Therefore, all operators with only external inputs in a general DSMS are modeled as an $M/G/1$ queueing system with a vacation time V and a setup time U as we discussed in Section 5.1.2, and those queueing systems form a network of queueing systems. In this queueing network, the queueing system for individual operators can be categorized into three classes based on their inputs, as illustrated in Figure 5.6.

1. Queueing systems with external input(s) (Figure 5.6-(a)). This class has only external input(s) from continuous data streams. Whether it is in a vacation period or in a serving period, the input tuple is inserted into its input queue immediately when it arrives.
2. Queueing systems with internal input(s)(Figure 5.6-(b)). This class of queueing systems only has input(s) from the output of another operator in the system. The arrival time of an input tuple is the departure time of the output process of another operator. Therefore, this class only has inputs during its vacation period, and no input during its setup time and service time.
3. Queueing systems with external and internal input(s) (Figure 5.6-(c)). This class has both internal and external input, and its inputs are a combination of the above two classes.

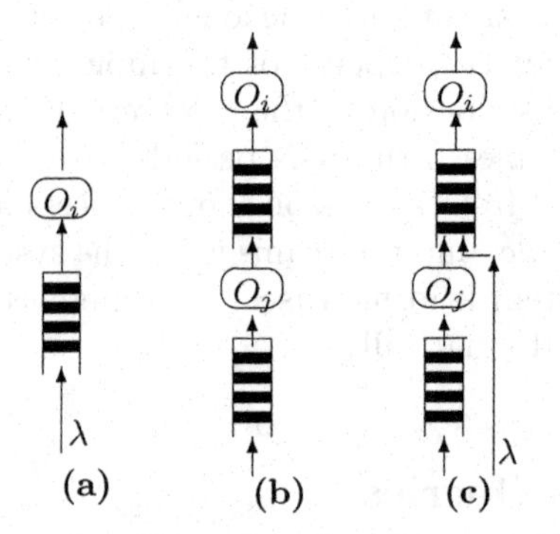

Fig. 5.6. Three Classes of Queueing Models

The above three classes capture all the alternatives possible for a query plan. In the rest of this section, we will derive the mean queue size and the mean waiting time of each class of queueing model under both gated-service and exhaustive-service disciplines. Additionally, to decide the vacation time and the internal input rate(s) of the queueing models, we have to derive the busy period and the total number of tuples served during a cycle as well. We will discuss how to determine vacation period V for each operator in Section 5.4.4.

5.4.1 Modeling Operators with External Input(s)

In the model illustrated in Figure 5.6-(a), each external input has a dedicated thread in the system which accepts input tuples whenever they arrive. The prototype of the queueing model can be a `select` or a `project` or aggregate operator over a continuous data stream, or a `join` operator over one (`self-join`) or two continuous data streams. If the operator has two or more external inputs, we consider the inputs as one logical external input with different class of input tuples and with a mean arrival rate which is the sum of mean arrival input rates of all inputs of the operator.

Exhaustive-Service Discipline

First of all, we need to compute the length of a busy period of an operator under an exhaustive-service discipline. Using that we can derive the number of tuples it served during its busy period, the output rate, and the cycle time.

Corollary 6 *Given a queueing system with external input(s) and its vacation time V, its setup time U, its mean input rate λ, and service time (to serve one tuple) S, the mean busy period at each round this queueing system with an exhaustive-service discipline under the steady state is given by*

$$B^{(1)} = \frac{\rho}{1-\rho}\left((1-q_0)\,U^{(1)} + V^{(1)}\right) \tag{5.30}$$

Proof. Let N be the random variable representing the total number of tuples arrived during vacation and setup time. We have

$$N = \{N^U + N^V\} \parallel_{Q^v>0} \tag{5.31}$$

taking Z transform on both sides

$$N(z) = U^*(\lambda - \lambda z)V^*(\lambda - \lambda z) + q_0(1 - U^*(\lambda - \lambda z)) \tag{5.32}$$

where $q_0 = V^*(\lambda)$ is the probability of an empty queue after one vacation time. Then the busy period B in our $M/G/1$ queueing system with setup time and vacation time consists of N standard busy periods in a standard $M/G/1$ system.

$$B = \sum_{i=1}^{N} \bar{B}_i \tag{5.33}$$

where $\bar{B}_i$ is the standard busy period introduced by i^{th} tuple. Taking LST on both sides of Equation (5.33),

$$\begin{aligned} B^*(s) =& N(\bar{B}^*(s)) \\ =& U^*(\lambda - \lambda \bar{B}^*(s)) V^*(\lambda - \lambda \bar{B}^*(s)) \\ &+ q_0 \left(1 - U^*(\lambda - \lambda \bar{B}^*(s))\right) \end{aligned} \tag{5.34}$$

According to the relationship of the LST of the standard busy period and the LST of service time distribution,

$$S^*(s) = \bar{B}^*(s + \lambda - \lambda S^*(s)) \tag{5.35}$$

From Equation (5.34) and Equation (5.35), we have

$$B^{(1)} = \frac{\rho}{1-\rho} \left((1 - q_0) U^{(1)} + V^{(1)} \right)$$

Remark 3 *By taking the nth derivative from Equation (5.34) and Equation (5.35), we can get the nth moment of the busy period. In this chapter, as we are only interested in mean values, no higher moment is given. The interested reader can take it further.*

Corollary 7 *Given a queueing system with external input(s) described in Corollary 6, its mean cycle time at each round of this queueing system with an exhaustive-service discipline under the steady state is given by*

$$C^{(1)} = \left(\frac{1 - \rho q_0}{1 - \rho} \right) \left(U^{(1)} + \frac{1}{1 - q_0} V^{(1)} \right) \tag{5.36}$$

Proof. A cycle consists of a busy period, a setup period, and one or more vacation periods. It has m vacation periods only if the queue is empty after the first $m-1$ vacations, and there is at least one tuple arrival during the mth vacation period. Therefore

$$C^{(1)} = U^{(1)} + B^{(1)} + E\left[\sum_{m=1}^{\infty} \left(m V^{(1)} P(\mathrm{m}) \right) \right] \tag{5.37}$$

where $P(\mathrm{m})$ is the probability of that a cycle includes m vacations and $P(\mathrm{m}) = (1 - q_0) q_0^{(m-1)}$. The mean length of vacation time $E[\sum_{m=1}^{\infty} (m V^{(1)} P(m))] = \frac{1}{1-q_0} V^{(1)}$. Plugging it into Equation (5.37), we have Equation (5.36).

Corollary 8 *Given a queueing system with external input(s) described in Corollary 6, the mean number of tuples served during each round is given by*

$$N^{C^{(1)}} = \frac{\lambda}{1 - \rho} \left((1 - q_0) U^{(1)} + V^{(1)} \right) \tag{5.38}$$

Proof. The total number of tuples N^C served during one cycle under an exhaustive-service discipline is the total number of tuples N that have arrived during the vacation time and setup time, plus the number of tuples arrived during the busy period. Therefore

$$N^C = \sum_{i=1}^{N} F_i \tag{5.39}$$

where F_i is the total number of tuples introduced by the ith tuple in the input queue during a standard busy period in a standard M/G/1 queue. Taking Z transform on both sides of Equation (5.39), we have

$$\begin{aligned} N^C(z) =& N\left(F(z)\right) \\ =& U^*\left(\lambda - \lambda F(z)\right) V^*\left(\lambda - \lambda F(z)\right) \end{aligned} \tag{5.40}$$

In a standard M/G/1 queue, the Z transform of the number of tuples during a standard busy period has the following relationship with the Z transform of the service time

$$F(z) = zS^*\left(\lambda - \lambda F(z)\right) \tag{5.41}$$

From Equation (5.40) and Equation (5.41), we get Equation (5.38) by taking derivative.

THEOREM 5 *Given a queueing system with external input(s) described in Corollary 6, the mean queue size and mean waiting time of tuples in this queueing system with an exhaustive-service discipline under the steady state are given by, respectively*

$$\begin{aligned} Q^{(1)} =& \rho + \lambda W^{(1)} \\ W_q^{(1)} =& \frac{\lambda S^{(2)}}{2(1-\rho)} + \frac{U^{(2)} + 2U^{(1)}V^{(1)} + V^{(2)} - q_0 U^{(2)}}{2(1-q_0)U^{(1)} + V^{(1)}} \\ W^{(1)} =& S^{(1)} + W_q^{(1)} \end{aligned} \tag{5.42}$$

where $q_0 = V^*(\lambda)$ is the probability of an empty queue after one vacation time.

Proof sketch. According to the decomposition property of M/G/1 queue with vacation time [312], and considering the vacation period termination points, we derive the mean queue size $Q^{(1)}$, and waiting time in the queue and in the queueing system. □

With the increase in system load, we can see that the vacation period increases because the busy periods of other operators in the system increase. As a result, both the waiting time in the queue and the queue size increase.

Gated-Service Discipline

For a gated-service discipline, the processor only serves the tuples that have arrived before the busy period, while the tuples arriving during the busy period will be processed in the next round.

THEOREM 6 *Given a queueing system with external input(s) and its vacation time V, its setup time U, its mean input rate λ, and service time (to serve one tuple) S, the mean queue size and the mean waiting time of tuples in this queueing system with a gated-service discipline under the steady state are given by, respectively*

$$\begin{aligned} Q^{(1)} &= \rho + \lambda W^{(1)} \\ W_q^{(1)} &= \frac{\lambda S^{(2)} + 2U^{(1)} + 2\rho V^{(1)}}{2(1-\rho)} + \\ & \frac{(1-q_0)(U^{(2)} + 2U^{(1)}V^{(1)} + V^{(2)})}{2((1-q_0)U^{(1)} + V^{(1)})} \end{aligned} \tag{5.43}$$

where q_0 has a different value from that under an exhaustive-service discipline, and

$$q_0 = \frac{1}{D} \prod_{j=0}^{\infty} U^*(\lambda - \lambda\eta_j(0)) V^*(\lambda - \lambda\eta_j(0)) \tag{5.44}$$

with denominator

$$D = 1 - V^*(\lambda)(1 - U^*(\lambda)) - \\ \sum_{k=1}^{\infty} (V^*(\lambda - \lambda\eta_k(0))(1 - U^*(\lambda - \lambda\eta_k(0))) \prod_{j=0}^{k-1} U^*(\lambda - \lambda\eta_j(0)) V^*(\lambda - \lambda\eta_j(0))) \tag{5.45}$$

where $\eta_j(0)$ is given recursively by

$$\begin{cases} \eta_0(z) = z \\ \eta_{j+1}(z) = S * (\lambda - \lambda\eta_j(z)) j = 0, 1, \cdots \end{cases}$$

For the moments of the queue length/waiting time, we use the same approach as in [317]. The results are derived by analyzing the departure point of the nth customer in a service period.

Corollary 9 *Given a queueing system with external input(s) described in Theorem 6, its mean busy period at each round in this queueing system with a gated-service discipline under the steady state is given by,*

$$B^{(1)} = \frac{\rho}{1-\rho} \left((1-q_0)U^{(1)} + V^{(1)} \right) \tag{5.46}$$

Proof. The tuples served during a cycle consist of the tuples arrived during last setup period, the tuples arrived during last busy period and the tuples arrived during this vacation period(s). Considering the tuples that are served during busy period, when $n \to \infty$,

$$N^C = (N^U + N^B) \|_{Q^V > 0} + N^V \tag{5.47}$$

Therefore, the busy period is the total service time of those N^C tuples. As a result, we have Equation (5.46).

Although the mean number of tuples under both exhaustive-service and gated-service disciplines are the same, they have different higher moments.

Corollary 10 *Given a queueing system with external input(s) described in Theorem 6, its mean number of tuples served at each round in this queueing system with an gated-service discipline under the steady state is given by,*

$$\begin{aligned} N^{C(1)} &= \lambda(U^{(1)} + \frac{1}{1-q_0}V^{(1)} + B^{(1)}) \\ &= \frac{\lambda(1-\rho q_0)}{1-\rho}\left(U^{(1)} + \frac{1}{1-q_0}V^{(1)}\right) \end{aligned} \tag{5.48}$$

By taking the derivative of both sides of Equation (5.47), we get the above result.

Corollary 11 *Given a queueing system with external input(s) described in Theorem 6, its mean cycle time in this queueing system under a gated-service discipline is the same as under an exhaustive service discipline under the steady state, which is given in Corollary 8.*

Proof sketch. As we mentioned earlier, one cycle includes one busy period, one setup period, and one or more vacation times. The number of vacation times are only related to the q_0. Therefore, the lengths of vacation times under both gated-service and exhaustive-service are the same. This applies to the mean busy period and consequently holds true for the cycle time, while higher moments are different due to the difference in high moments of the busy periods under these two service disciplines. □

5.4.2 Modeling Operators with Internal Input(s)

In this model, queueing systems have only internal input(s), which is(are) the output(s) of processes of its children queueing systems. Therefore, the input process is neither a Poisson process nor a continuous stream. An operator has outputs, if any, only during its busy periods. The number of tuples output from an operator is decided by both the total number of tuples N processed during one cycle and its selectivity σ. For the `select` operator, the selectivity $\sigma \leq 1$; for the `project` operator, $\sigma = 1$[8]. If the operator is a `join` operator, its selectivity may be greater than 1, which is decided by the selectivities of its two `semi-join` operators σ_L, σ_R. We assume that selectivity of an operator is known; otherwise, it can be learned through collecting run-time statistics information in a DSMS.

To derive similar performance metrics as those in Section 5.4.1, we use the following approximate method: consider the operator, such as `select` or `project`, which has only one internal input as illustrated in Figure 5.6-(b).

[8] Under the assumption of not eliminating the duplicates.

In the steady state, we assume that the operator j runs once after its child operator i runs k times, which is called the *weight ratio* of operator i in terms of operator j hereafter. Here, $k \geq 1$ because operator j can only enter its busy period with at least one output tuple from its child operator i. The value k is determined by a scheduling strategy. An example will be given in Section 5.4.4 to demonstrate how to determine k.

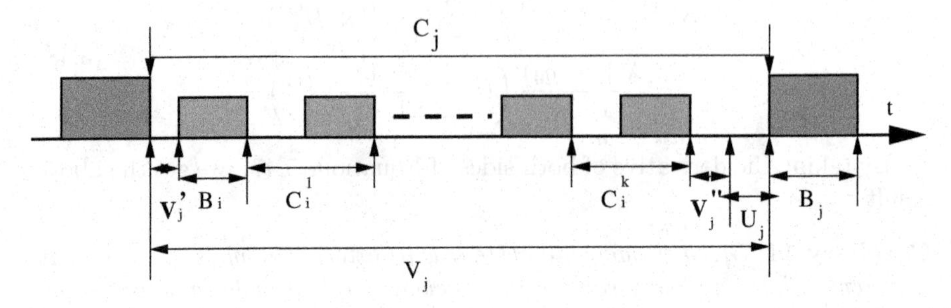

Fig. 5.7. Input Process Of Operator (Internal Input)

For this queueing model, there is no input during its busy periods (since all other operators are idle). Therefore, an exhaustive-service discipline behaves exactly like a gated-service discipline. The input process of the operator j is shown in Figure 5.7. After a busy period is over, the operator j waits for a random period V_j', called *pre-input vacation period* during which time some other operators, if the system does not serve its child operator i immediately after it has served operator j, can be served. It then receives its first batch of inputs from its child operator i during its child operator i's busy period. After waiting another cycle time of its child operator i, it receives another batch of inputs. k rounds later, it waits another random time V_j'' called the *post-input vacation period* during which time some other operators except its child operators can be served; it finally begins its own service cycle, consisting of its own setup time U_j and busy period B_j to serve all the tuples in its input queue. We consider the input of an operator under this model as a discrete batch of inputs and use the following method to approximate the performance metrics.

Corollary 12 *Given a queueing system with internal input(s) and its vacation time V, its setup time U, its mean input rate λ, and a service time (to serve one tuple) S, the mean number of tuples served during one cycle under both gated-service and exhaustive-service discipline is given by:*

For single-input operators,

$$N_j^{C(1)} = k^{(1)} N_i^{C(1)} \sigma_i$$

For two-input operators,

$$N_j^{C(1)} = k_i^{(1)} N_i^{C(1)} \sigma_i + k_{i+1}^{(1)} N_{i+1}^{C(1)} \sigma_{i+1}$$

Proof sketch. The total number of tuples served during a cycle is the sum of k batch inputs. Therefore,

$$N_j^{C(1)} = k^{(1)} N_i^{C(1)} \sigma_i \tag{5.49}$$

where $N_i^{C(1)}$ is the number of tuples at one batch input, which is given in Corollary 8 if the operator i has only external input(s). Otherwise, we have to first compute the number of tuples served during one cycle at its child operator, or its grandchild operator until we reach the bottom operator that only has external input(s).

If the operator j has two internal inputs - one is from its left operator i^{th} and another is from its right child operator $(i+1)^{th}$, the total number of tuples served during a cycle time is the sum of the number of tuples from its left child and from its right child.

$$N_j^{C(1)} = k_i^{(1)} N_i^{C(1)} \sigma_i + k_{i+1}^{(1)} N_{i+1}^{C(1)} \sigma_{i+1} \tag{5.50}$$

where k_i, k_{i+1} are the weight ratios of operator $i, i+1$ in terms of operator j respectively. □

Corollary 13 *Given a queueing system with internal input(s) described in Corollary 12, the mean busy period at each round under both gated-service and exhaustive service disciple is given by*

$$B_j^{(1)} = N_j^{C(1)} S_j^{(1)} \tag{5.51}$$

The busy period is simply the sum of the service times to serve these $N_j^{C(1)}$ tuples.

$$B_j^{(1)} = N_j^{C(1)} S_j^{(1)} \tag{5.52}$$

Corollary 14 *Given a queueing system with internal input(s) described in Corollary 8, the mean cycle time at each round under both gated-service and exhaustive service disciple is given by*

$$C_j^{(1)} = U_j^{(1)} + B_j^{(1)} + \frac{1}{1-q_0} V_j^{(1)}$$

where $q_0 = P(N_j = 0)$.

Clearly, the cycle time in this model has the same form as in the previous model, except that the q_0 and $B_j^{(1)}$ have different values.

THEOREM 7 *Given a queueing system with internal input(s) and its vacation time V, its setup time U, its mean input rate λ, and service time (to serve one tuple) S, the mean waiting time of tuples at this queueing system under both gated-service and exhaustive service disciple is given by*

$$W_q^{(1)} = \frac{kN_i^C\sigma_i - 1}{2} S_j + \frac{(2-\sigma_i)N_i^C - 1}{2} S_i + \frac{(k_i^{(1)} - 1)}{2} C_i^{(1)} + (V_j^{''(1)} + U_j^{(1)}) \tag{5.53}$$

Proof. Considering the pth tuple arrived during the lth batch (busy period of its child operator) shown in Figure 5.7, the waiting time w_l^p of this tuple at operator j consists of:

1. The sum of service times to serve all arrived tuples in first $l-1$ batch inputs, and the first $p-1$ tuples in the l^{th}batch. The number of tuples output from its child operator during each batch $N_i^O = N_i^C \sigma_i$.
2. The time for its child operator i to output(serve) the rest $N_i^C - \frac{p}{\sigma_i}$ tuples in l^{th} batch.
3. $k-l$ cycle periods because the operator j will be served after its child operator i has been served k times.
4. The *post-input vacation period* and itself setup time.

In summary,

$$\begin{aligned} w_l^p &= (l-1)N_i^O S_j + (p-1)S_j + \\ &\quad (N_i^C - \frac{p}{\sigma_i})S_i + (k-l)C_i + V_j^{''} + U_j \end{aligned}$$

The total waiting time W^{total} of all tuples arriving in one cycle time of operator j is $W^{total} = \int_{l=1}^{k} \int_{p=1}^{N_i^C} w_l^p \, d_l d_p$. The mean waiting time of a tuple at the operator j is derived by dividing the total waiting time by the total number of tuples

$$W_q^{(1)} = \frac{kN_i^C\sigma_i - 1}{2} S_j + \frac{(2-\sigma_i)N_i^C - 1}{2} S_i + \frac{(k_i^{(1)} - 1)}{2} C_i^{(1)} + (V_j^{''(1)} + U_j^{(1)}) \tag{5.54}$$

Remark 4

1. *For two internal inputs, the operator j has inputs from both the left child operator i and the right child operator $i+1$. Then we have $W_j^{(1)} = \varphi_i W_j^{i(1)} + \varphi_{i+1} W_j^{i+1(1)}$; where φ_i, φ_{i+1} are the weight of the left input and right input respectively, $\varphi_i = 1 - \varphi_{i+1} = \frac{\sigma_i N_i^{(1)}}{\sigma_i N_i^{(1)} + \sigma_{i+1} N_{i+1}^{(1)}}$.*
2. *The mean tuple latency in above Theorem 7 can be decreased if we decrease the post-input vacation period. This tells us that we need to schedule an operator immediately after its child operators are scheduled in order to decrease the tuple latency in a DSMS.*

Queue size: According to the Little's formula $Q^{(1)} = \lambda_j W_q^{(1)}$, we have the mean queue size $Q^{(1)}$ in a system described in Theorem 7 as follows:

$$Q^{(1)} = \frac{N_j^{(1)}}{C_j^{(1)}} W_j^{(1)} \tag{5.55}$$

5.4.3 Modeling Operators with External and Internal Inputs

In this model, queueing systems have at least one internal input and at least one external input. The internal input is neither a Poisson process nor a continuous stream as explained in Section 5.4.2. The prototype of this queueing model is a `join` operator with two inputs; one is the output of an operator, another is an external data stream. We decompose such a queueing system into two sub-queueing systems: (*a*) the queueing system that only has an internal input, which is modeled in Section 5.4.2; and (*b*) the queueing system that only has an external input, which is modeled in Section 5.4.1. Under both exhaustive-service and gated-service disciplines, the total number of tuples served during one cycle time is the sum of total number of tuples served during one cycle time in each of the decomposed queueing systems, therefore,

$$N_j^{C(1)} = N_j^{'C(1)} + N_j^{''C(1)} \tag{5.56}$$

Since the busy period is the time to serve those $N_j^{C(1)}$, it has the same form as Equation (5.52). Similarly, the cycle time has the same form as in previous two models. The mean waiting time is the weighted sum of the mean waiting times of the tuples from the two sub-models. Again the weight is the ratio of the number of tuples output from a sub-model to the total number of tuples output from the model. The mean queue size can also be derived from mean waiting time through Little's formula.

5.4.4 Scheduling Strategy and Vacation Period

In this section we further discuss how to determine the weight ratio k of an operator in terms of its parent operator, and the lengths of both vacation period V and *post-input vacation period* V'' of an operator given a scheduling strategy.

In a multiple-query processing system, various scheduling strategies have been proposed. They can be broadly classified into two categories: hierarchical scheduling and global scheduling. In hierarchical scheduling, the scheduling is done in a hierarchical way. At the top level, a system only needs to schedule the top-level objects such as a query plan, an operator path [131] and so on. Once a top-level object is scheduled, a lower-level scheduling strategy is employed to schedule the objects within a top-level object such as an operator. In global scheduling, only one scheduling strategy is needed, which schedules all the elementary objects and no composite object that consists of multiple elementary objects can be scheduled. For example, the Chain scheduling algorithm [85,111] employs a global scheduling approach. Here we use the push-up scheduling strategy and the weighted round robin scheduling strategy as examples to show how to derive the vacation periods.

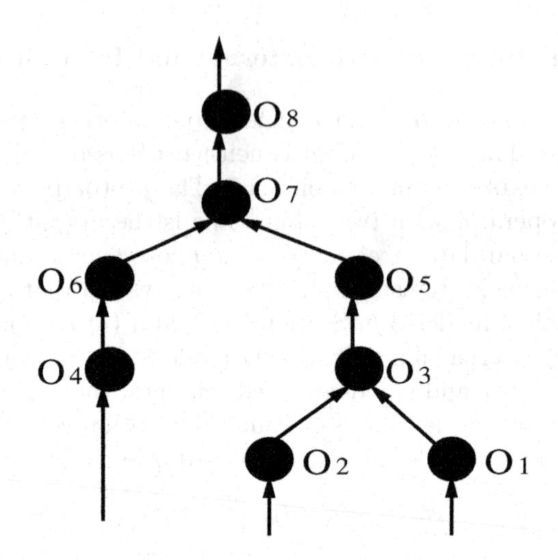

Fig. 5.8. Push-Up Operator Scheduling Strategy

Push-Up Operator Scheduling Strategy

A push-up operator scheduling strategy is a hierarchical scheduling strategy. From Remark 4, we note that the mean tuple latency can be decreased if we can schedule an operator as close as possible to its child operators. Based on this principle, a push-up operator scheduling strategy employs a round robin strategy at the top level to schedule the query plans registered in the system. Therefore, the number of operators scheduled between an operator and its child operators is limited to the number of operators in a query plan. To further limit the number of operators scheduled between the child operators of an operator and the operator itself, it employs a bottom-up approach to schedule all the operators of a query plan during each round. The operators at the bottom are scheduled first, followed by its parent operators. For a query plan with multiple operator paths, the operators at the same level are scheduled from right to left.

For example, the execution order of the operators of the query plan Ψ in Figure 5.8 is $\{O_1, O_2, O_3, O_4, O_5, O_6, O_7, O_8\}$. The weight ratio k is 1 under the scheduling strategy, and the vacation time for the jth operator in the system, which is dedicated to query processing, is

$$V_j^{(1)} = \sum\nolimits_{i=1}^{m} (U_i^{(1)} + B_i^{(1)}) - (U_j^{(1)} + B_j^{(1)}) \tag{5.57}$$

where m is the total number of query plans registered in the system. From Section 5.4, we know that $B_j^{(1)}$ in all cases is a function of $V_j^{(1)}$, and we have m such equations with m unknown variables $V_j^{(1)}; j = 1, 2, \cdots, m$. These m equations are linearly independent, so we can simultaneously solve this set of equations to find $V_j^{(1)}$s. Similarly, the *post-input vacation time* $V_j''^{(1)}$ of an operator can be derived from Equation (5.57), except that m is the total number of operators served during the period between the end point of the last input batch and the starting point to serve its tuples. In some scenarios, a processor has to take α percent[9] of its time to do non-query processing tasks, such as scheduling or system maintenance routines, so we have to multiply the Equation (5.57) by a factor $\frac{1}{1-\alpha}$.

Weighted Round Robin Scheduling Strategy

A weighted round robin scheduling strategy is considered as a global scheduling strategy. The whole query processing system is treated as a pool of individual operators, and a weight is assigned to each operator to decide how often the operator is scheduled in the system compared with other operators. By considering a query processing system with m operators along with their weights[10] $\beta_1, \beta_2, \cdots, \beta_m$ respectively, statistically, we can infer that the operator j, which has its child operator i in the system, will be scheduled once whenever the operator i is scheduled $\frac{\beta_i}{\beta_j}$ times, which is equivalent to the weight ratio k_j of operator j. The mean vacation time of the operator O_j is

$$V_j^{(1)} = \sum_{k=1}^{m} \frac{\beta_k}{\beta_j} (U_i^{(1)} + B_i^{(1)}) - (U_j^{(1)} + B_j^{(1)}) \tag{5.58}$$

There are m equations with m unknown variables, and the same approach used earlier to solve the equations defined by Equation (5.57) can be used here. The approach is also applicable to find *post-input vacation time* $V_j''^{(1)}$ of the operator j.

The above analysis is generally applicable for a large family of scheduling strategies, such as Chain scheduling strategy, Path capacity strategy, round robin Operator strategy, and so on. The weight ratio k can be learned through collecting statistics or through analyzing the scheduling strategy.

---

[9] This may not be negligible. Only if a system is a dedicated query processing system, this α percents is very small and is negligible.

[10] The weight of each operator can be learned from the system through analyzing the scheduling strategy or collecting statistics from an actual system.

5.4.5 Computing Memory Usage and Tuple Latency

Once we find the vacation time and the post-input vacation time of each operator in a query plan, we are able to compute the mean queue size of each queue, and the mean tuple latency of each queueing path of each query execution plan in the system. Substituting these values into Equation (5.1) and Equation (5.2), the total memory requirement and the mean tuple latency of a query plan are obtained.

5.5 Intuitive Observations

We elaborate on a few intuitive observations gleaned from the modeling of operators and continuous queries below.

5.5.1 Tuple Latency

There are two ways to decrease the tuple latency in a DSMS without changing the configuration of the system:

1. *Clustering* n *(*$n > 1$*) small systems into one larger system.*
2. *Decreasing the number of operators scheduled between the child operators of an operator and the operator itself.*

Although it cannot decrease the memory requirement by clustering n smaller systems into one bigger system for stream processing, the mean tuple latency in the bigger system is only one n_{th} of that in small systems as shown in Remark 2. Remark 4 shows that the mean tuple latency decreases as the post-input vacation time decreases. One way to decrease post-input vacation time is to decrease the number of operators scheduled between the child operators of an operator and the operator itself.

5.5.2 Service Discipline

By using an exhaustive-service discipline, the query can achieve a better tuple latency than using a gated-service discipline under the non-null vacation queue situations.

From our analysis of both the exhaustive-service discipline and the gated-service discipline in Section 5.4.2, we found that the queueing system has the same cycle time and the same number of tuples on average are served for these two service disciplines, but the tuple latencies under these disciplines are different. Under the non-null vacation queue situation[11] where $q_0 = 0$, the

[11] In a moderately loaded continuous query processing system, the probability that the input queue of an operator is empty after it returns from vacation is very small, and can be ignored.

mean tuple latency of an operator under the exhaustive-service discipline is $\frac{U^{(1)}+\rho V^{(1)}}{1-\rho}$ less than that under the gated service discipline. As it is a positive value, the difference increases dramatically when the system load increases or its vacation time increases.

Similarly, a service discipline in which the larger number of tuples is processed in busy period, the lower tuple latency will be. It also means that for a n-limited service discipline, a limit of processing 100 tuples in its busy period introduces a better tuple latency than a limit of processing 50 tuples in each busy period. In general, an exhaustive-service discipline is better than any kind of gated-service discipline such as n-limited service discipline in terms of mean tuple latency. However, in some cases, an exhaustive-service discipline may introduce a longer cycle time, which causes a long vacation time for some query plans. To solve this problem, we need to assign a weight to each query, and a n-limited service discipline is used for a query plan that has a long cycle time. Although the tuple latencies of the other query plans decrease, the mean tuple latency of the query plan with long cycle time increases.

5.5.3 Scheduling Algorithms

The hierarchical scheduling approach with a push-up operator strategy is better than any global scheduling approach under exhaustive- or gated-service discipline.

Consider the ith query plan in a total of m query plans processing system. The total service time of all query plans except the ith query plan is S during the steady state, and the total service time of all the operators in i^{th} query plan is S_i. In general, $S \gg S_i$. If a hierarchical scheduling approach (a query plan, or an operator path is treated as a schedulable object) with a push-up operator strategy is used, the implication is that no operator from other query plans is interleaved with any operator in i^{th} query plan: (a) If the operator k has only one child operator, it is scheduled right after its child operator j is served. Therefore the *post-input vacation time* of the operator k is zero. (b) If an operator has two child operators, the *post-input vacation time* of one of its sub queueing system is not zero because only one operator can be scheduled at one time. However, the *post-input vacation time* is *minimized*.

If a global scheduling approach (that is, an operator is a schedulable object) is used, it is highly possible that some operators, say p operators, are served between the service periods of two consecutive operators j, k of a queueing path of the ith query plan. Consequently, the *post-input vacation time* of the operator k is the total service time of those p operators, which is larger than zero or at least equals to the service time of one of its child operators for an operator with two children. The vacation times under these two service disciplines are the same.

From Equation (5.2), we can conclude that the overall tuple latency of the ith query plan is larger under the global scheduling approach than under the hierarchical scheduling approach with a push-up operator scheduling strategy.

In general, any operator path or query plan based scheduling strategy can achieve a better tuple latency than any scheduling strategy which uses an operator as a schedulable object. The concept of PC (or path capacity) strategy discussed in Chapter 6 is based on this observation.

Starvation is an issue that needs to be addressed when using certain scheduling algorithms. A discussion on starvation can be found in Sections 6.3.2 and 6.3.6.

5.5.4 Choice of Query Plans

Among all the different implementations of a general query, the query plan that has a minimal total service time is better than the one that has minimal peak memory requirement but longer total service time in a multiple query processing system.

If a query plan with a longer service time but minimal peak memory requirement is chosen, all the other query plans in the system will have a longer vacation time due to its longer service time. The longer vacation time causes a longer tuple latency and increases the backlog of the tuples of all query plans registered in the system. The total increase of the backlog of all the query plans in the system may be significantly larger than the memory size it saves.

5.5.5 Input Rate

Linear increase of all the input rates in a query processing system can decrease the overall performance of the system dramatically (faster than a linear decrease).

From Section 5.4, we know that with a linear increase in input rate of a queueing path, the service times of all the operators along that path increase linearly, which causes the vacation time of all the other query plans in the system to increase. As a result, the service times of those operator paths increase due to a higher number of tuples arriving during their vacation periods. Consequently, the vacation time of the queueing path that increased its input rate rises, which causes its service time to rise further. Therefore, the overall tuple latency increases with a rate faster than linear, and the same is true for the queue size.

Similarly, the above statement holds for both selectivity and the number of query plans (system load) as well. Linearly increasing these factors causes the overall performance of the query processing system to decrease at a speed faster than the linear speed. Our experiments in the following section clearly testify to these observations.

5.6 Experimental Validation

We conducted several sets of experiments to validate our theoretical analysis of both relational operators and continuous queries presented in this chapter. We present a few representative results – one for operator validation and the other for multiple query validation. All experiments were run on an alpha-based dual-processor computer with an OFS1 (Tru Unix) V5.1 operating system, and 2GB RAM. We were able to keep the tuples within the predefined `window` completely in main memory. Also there are no other user applications in the system when performing these experiments.

Input Data Streams

All data streams used in our experiments are synthetic network traffic data streams and consist of 7-field tuples (along with their data types):
(int sequenceId, int hostAdd, int networkAdd, int portNumber, int packSize, int protocolId, int serviceType).

Once a tuple enters our system, a stream identifier, an arrival time-stamp, a departure time-stamp, and expired time-stamp are added for each tuple and the reference of the tuple is passed to the input queues of operators in the system for further processing. The arrival time stamp is the time of the tuple entering the system; the departure time-stamp is assigned when the tuple is output from the system; and the expired time stamp is assigned when the tuple enters the system based on the largest time `window` of all queries registered in the system.

The input data streams that we used are either a bursty data stream generated from a Poisson distribution or a more bursty stream that has so called self-similarity property. Each data stream has a different mean input rate.

The input data streams with self-similarity property are highly bursty streams, which we believe resembles the situation in real-world applications. Each input stream is a super imposition of 64 or 128 flows. Each flow alternates ON/OFF periods, and it only sends tuples during its ON periods. The tuple inter-arrival time follows an exponential distribution during its ON periods. The lengths of both the ON and the OFF periods are generated from a Pareto distribution that has a probability mass function $P(x) = ab^a x^{-(a+1)}, x \geq b$. We use $a = 1.4$ for the ON period and $a = 1.2$ for the OFF period. For more detailed information about self-similar traffic, please refer to [316]. In our experiments for validating query plans, we use 5 such self-similar input data streams with different mean input rates.

Operators and Query Plans for Experiments

The operator used in validating our operator models is a `symmetric hash join` operator. All of our queries used for validating query plan models are

CQs consisting of `select`, `project`, and `symmetric hash join` operators. To be more consistent with a real application, we run 16 actual CQs with 116 operators over 5 different data streams in our system. The selectivity of each operator is widely distributed ranging from 0 to 1. Both the selectivity and the processing capacity of each operator are determined by collecting statistical information periodically during run time.

Tuple latency is measured by computing the difference between the arrival time stamp and the departure time stamp from either a queue for validating operator models or the DSMS system for validating query plan models. A large `window` size in our experiments is used in order to accurately measure tuple latency of a tuple in a DSMS. In OFS and most of current operating systems, the finest level of time unit is 10^{-3} seconds or higher. If the actual tuple latency is less than one 10^{-3} seconds due to a small `window` size (also means small service time), the underlying operating system provide us nothing to measure the tuple latency and we will get a 0 ms as tuple latency. However, this limitation does not affect our analysis and validation of our analysis.

5.6.1 Validation of Operator Models

We present our first set of experiments to verify the theoretical analysis of `hash-join` operators presented in this chapter. In this set of experiments, the delay of a tuple, shown in tables and figures, is equivalent to the delay of tuples in the queue. We have conducted a wide range of experiments by varying the processing rates, `window` sizes, and input rates.

Same `window` Size for Two Streams

This set of experiments measures the mean and CDF of the waiting time of a tuple in the queue under the same data stream input rates, and the mean number of tuples in the queue. In this case, we used two stream generators that send tuples to the system using the Poisson distribution with the same mean value. The `window` sizes for two data streams are one million tuples (about 10000 seconds), and the processing rates for both data streams are 209.4 tuples per second. The results presented here are obtained from the log file by deleting the first 2M records because the first 2M records are logged during the transition phase.

Table 5.1 shows that the mean queue sizes from our experiments are very close to the theoretical results obtained from the second part of the Equation (5.8) in Section 5.3.3. The mean delays are a little larger than the results calculated from Equation (5.23b) because of the overhead associated with the recording of the departure time, and passing the reference to the `hash join` facility after dequeueing from the input queue. Figure 5.9 shows that the CDF of tuple latency in the queue is very close to our analysis results that were obtained from Equation (5.24). The 3 digit numbers in the legend represent the total input rates (number of tuples per second), and the graphs with a

Table 5.1. Delay & Queue Size (Same `Window` Size)

Item	Exp1	Exp2
Input Rate(#/sec)	100	100
Utilization	0.9551	0.8595
Mean Delay(Theory)	0.05080	0.01257
Mean Delay(Exp)	0.05867	0.01539
Mean QueueSize(Theory)	10.6380	2.6313
Mean QueueSize(Exp)	10.6385	2.9399

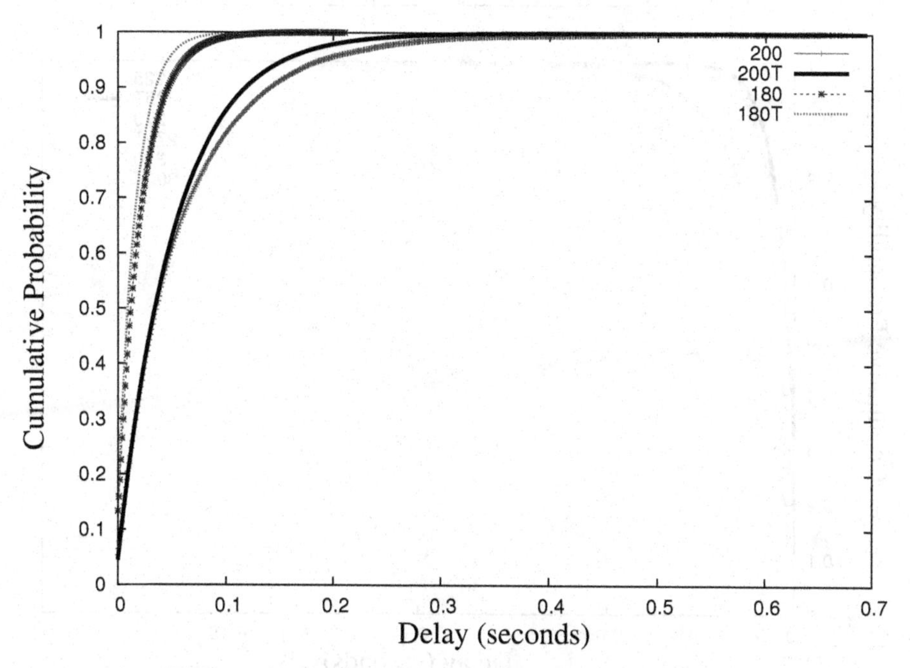

Fig. 5.9. CDF of Delay In Queue (Same `Window` Size)

3 digit number following a letter 'T' represent the results of our theoretical analysis; otherwise they represent our experimental results.

Different `window` Size for Two Streams

The following sets of experiments are done with different `window` sizes. We have 0.8 million tuples in hash table 1, and 0.4 million tuples in hash table 2. So the service time for a tuple that comes from the right stream is twice of the service time for a tuple that comes from the left stream. Specifically, the processing rates are 440 tuples and 220 tuples per second for left stream and right stream respectively.

Table 5.2 shows that the mean queue size as well as the mean delay is decreasing when the system utilization decreases. Also, the mean delay de-

Table 5.2. Delay & Queue Size (Different `Window` Size)

Item	Exp1	Exp2	Exp3
Input Rate1(#/sec)	200	180	150
Input Rate2(#/sec)	100	90	75
Utilization	0.9091	0.8182	0.6812
Mean Delay(Theory)	0.01549	0.06276	0.00249
Mean Delay(Exp)	0.01931	0.00781	0.00291
Mean QueueSize(Theory)	5.1130	2.0710	0.8217
Mean QueueSize(Exp)	5.3817	2.1054	0.8438

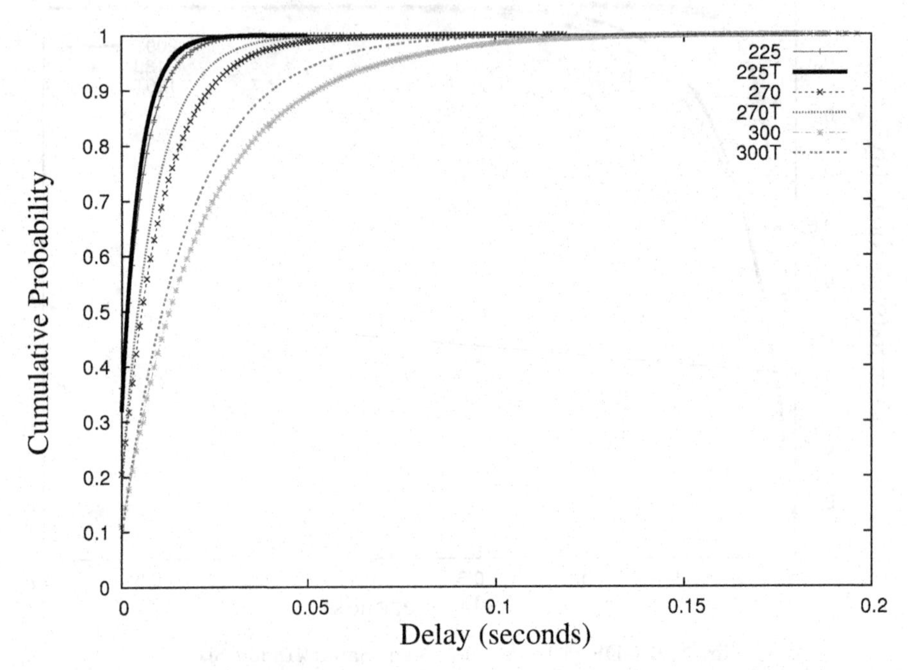

Fig. 5.10. CDF of Delay In Queue (Different `Window` Size)

creases when the service decreases with the same utilization. This indicates that we can either increase the processing capability of the system or decrease the input rates in order to achieve a better tuple latency. In our experiments, the longest delay of a tuple in the input queue can be more than 7 seconds if the utilization is very high and the service time is as low as 1/400 second. Another observation is that the delay of a tuple in the system primarily depends on the waiting time in the input queue if the utilization is high, and it depends on the service time of one tuple in the service facility under low utilization. Figure 5.10 shows the CDF of delay of tuples in the input queue under different `window` sizes as well as different input rates. The results show that there is a small probability for a tuple to wait in queue for as long as

10 times the mean waiting time. So it may not be difficult to meet the tuple latency for most tuples, but it is hard to achieve a 99% or higher confidence interval.

From our analysis and experimental results, we believe that to design a data stream processing system - especially for those that have a response time requirement - accurate estimation of the waiting time in the queue and service time is very important to determine the computational capability and the system capacity. The numbers of tuples in the input queue and in the service facility are negligible in terms of the number of tuples in the hash table, and the memory size mainly depends on the sliding time-`window` size.

5.6.2 Validation of Continuous Query Plan Models

In this set of experiments, we run an actual continuous query processing system, which consists of 16 actual queries with 116 operators over 5 different data streams on a dual-processor Alpha machine, where one processor is used exclusively for query processing and another is used for collecting data. Each experiment is started with a 3 hours transition phase[12], following a parameter collection phase in which we collect the various parameters for each operator such as processing rate, selectivity, setup time, weight ratio and so on. After that, the experiment enters a normal query processing phase which lasts about 5 to 8 hours. The results shown in this section are the mean values of various performance metrics we measured under a gated-service discipline. The results under an exhaustive-service discipline are slightly less than those under a gated-service discipline in terms of overall tuple latency of the whole query processing system. However, it does not give the system any choice to determine how many tuples it serves in each round. In most query processing system, we have to control the service time allocated to each query or operator, therefore, a gated-based service discipline is employed in most of continuous query processing system, and the results under an exhaustive-based service discipline have a similar tendency as those under a gate-based service discipline presented in this section. All results reported in this section are collected from our target query plan illustrated in Figure 5.11, one of the 16 CQs are active in the system. The results for other query plans show comparable results similar to those from our target query plan. From Little's formula, the number of tuples in a queueing system has a linear relationship with the mean tuple latency. Therefore, we only need to validate the tuple latency. The related parameters about this query plan are listed in Table 5.3.

[12] During a transition phase, the number of tuples in the window increases until the window is full, which causes the service time of a tuple to increase. As a result, processing rate is decreasing as there is increase in the number of tuples in its buffers.

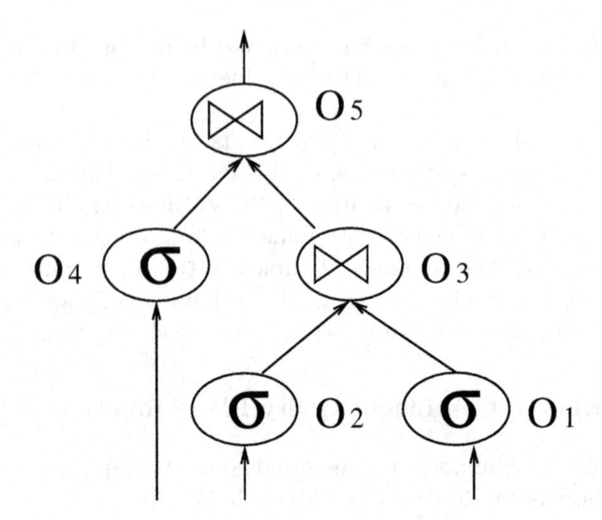

Fig. 5.11. Target Query Plan

Table 5.3. Parameters for Target Query Plan

Operator name	Processing rate(#/s)	Left selectivity	Right selectivity	Setup time
O_5	5894.1	0.308514	0.307712	7.4224E-4
O_4	28461.9	0.36534	-	1.1502E-5
O_3	5285.81	0.30703	0.300177	6.9477E-4
O_2	21861	0.487534	-	1.9599E-5
O_1	41684.7	0.24288	-	4.8044E-5

Scheduling Approaches

Our first group of experimental results not only confirms our analytical results but also compares the performance of two different scheduling approaches in a multiple query processing system. The results presented in Table 5.4 are for a hierarchical scheduling strategy where we schedule all the queries in the system in a round-robin manner, and a push-up strategy is employed to schedule the operators of a chosen query plan. The results presented in Table 5.5 are for a global scheduling strategy in which we schedule one operator from our target query plan, and then schedule operators from 3 other query plans. Both Table 5.4 and Table 5.5 present the theoretical results for our target query plan and the two sets of experimental results that we chosen from a set of experiments under different scheduling strategies. One (Exp A) represents the best results that we obtained and the other (Exp B) represents the worst results. The theoretical results are derived by solving 116 linear equations that we get from Section 5.4.4.

The system load in the experiments presented in both tables are about 90% of its maximal capacity. First, these results show that our experimental results are very close to our theoretical results because the difference is less than $\frac{0.00016}{0.1527} = 0.1\%$ in the best case, and no more than $\frac{0.04093}{0.19204} = 21.3\%$ in the worst case under a hierarchical scheduling strategy. The difference, under a global scheduling strategy, is less than $\frac{0.038356}{0.285155} = 13.5\%$ in the worst case. The average difference for all our experiments is less than 9.5%. When system load is less than 85% of its maximal capacity, the differences from these experiments are much better and are less than 3%. Second, the overall tuple latency in a hierarchical scheduling strategy is much less than that in a global scheduling strategy though the service times of one cycle under both strategies are same (they process the same number of tuples). The reason is that the operators in our target query plan are scheduled in an interleaved manner, which causes all operators in our target query plan to have a much larger post-input vacation time. However, the tuple latency for other query plans should be the same because all the other query plans are scheduled in a hierarchical scheduling strategy. Therefore, a hierarchical scheduling strategy is generally better than any kind of global scheduling strategy in which operators are scheduled in an interleaved manner.

Table 5.4. Tuple Latency (in seconds) Under Hierarchical Scheduling Strategy

Op. Name	O_1	O_2	$O_3(10^{-3})$	O_4	$O_5(10^{-3})$	Query Plan Latency(s)
Theoretical	0.14690	0.147114	2.3277	0.146988	2.64285	**0.15111**
Exp. A	0.14868	0.149151	2.4561	0.14665	2.5963	**0.15127**
Diff	0.00178	0.002037	0.1284	-0.000338	0.1284	**0.00016**
Exp. B	0.18849	0.188792	3.18175	0.186408	3.2960	**0.19204**
Diff	0.0019	0.041678	0.85405	0.03942	0.65315	**0.04093**

Table 5.5. Tuple Latency (in seconds) Under Global Scheduling Strategy

Op. Name	O_1	O_2	O_3	O_4	O_5	Query Plan Latency(s)
Theoretical	0.147114	0.146114	0.079383	0.14690	0.075269	**0.246832**
Exp. A	0.152936	0.149876	0.083768	0.15308	0.076646	**0.257601**
Diff	0.005822	0.003762	0.004385	0.00618	0.001377	**0.010769**
Exp. B	0.169569	0.162786	0.092675	0.169223	0.084885	**0.285188**
Diff	0.022455	0.016672	0.013292	0.02233	0.009616	**0.038356**

System Load

This group of experimental results shows how system load impacts the overall performance of a query plan. The system load can be increased by either increasing the number of queries in the system or increasing input rates of data streams. In this set of experiments, we increase our system load by increasing mean input rates of all data streams. The maximal capacity of the system is to process 485 tuples/per second on average. The system load is considered as $\frac{total\_input\_rates}{maximal\_capacity}$. From Figure 5.12, we can see that the tuple latency of our target query plan increases slowly when system load is small. However, when system load reaches 95% of its maximal capacity (around 460 tuples/second), the tuple latency increases sharply as the increase in input rates of all data streams. As the system load approaches to 1, the tuple latency increases dramatically.

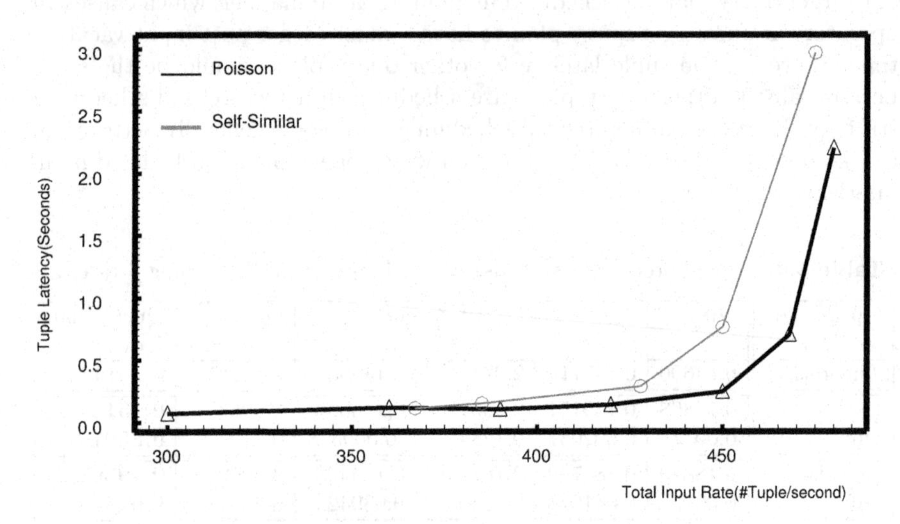

Fig. 5.12. Tuple Latency Vs. System Load

Bursty Input Data

These experiments are conducted to show how bursty input streams impact the system performance (tuple latency). The bursty input streams we used are self-similar input streams. In this set of experiments, we use 5 self-similar input data streams with different mean input rates. The results in Figure 5.12 show that the difference between the tuple latencies from our Poisson input streams and the tuple latencies for self-similar input streams are very small when the system load (measured by input rates) is not too high (less than 95% of its maximal capacity). The results shown here are mean values. However, the maximal tuple latency and the variance of the tuple latency from self-similar inputs are much higher than those from our Poisson input streams. Only when the system load is close to its maximal capacity, the tuple latency that we get from our Poisson model is optimistic for a highly bursty input such as a self-similar input.

5.7 Summary of Chapter 5

In this chapter, we addressed the problem of predicting QoS metrics of continuous queries in a general DSMS. These QoS metrics provide fundamental quantitative information and basis for a DSMS to manage, control, and deliver its QoS requirements. For example, the predicted QoS metrics can be used to assist a DSMS to determine when to activate or deactivate different QoS delivery mechanisms. Also the model and results presented in this chapter are general and are useful for any DSMSs. Although our modeling and analysis work are based on relational operators in a DSMS, our approach can be extended to any user-defined operators as long as we can learn the processing capacity and selectivity of those user-defined operators. We can always learn these parameters through run-time statistics.

By modeling individual operators on a dedicated server, we analyzed, in detail, the mean number of tuples, the mean waiting time of tuples in the queue and the distribution of the number of tuples, the distribution of waiting time of tuples at that operator. Furthermore, by modeling a general `select-project-join` query over streaming data using a queueing network, we analyzed both memory requirement and tuple latency in the system under both gated- and exhaustive-service disciplines. We further discussed how the scheduling strategy, system load, operator selectivity, and input rates impact the performance of a general query processing system. The experiments based on our implementation of a query processing system clearly validate the accuracy and effectiveness of our analysis.

Finally, the results obtained in this chapter can be encapsulated in a tool to analyze the characteristics of the load (CQs, input rates, selectivities, scheduling strategy, etc) with respect to the QoS metrics. As DSMSs are used in many mission-critical applications, the ability to estimate the resources as well as play with "what-if" scenarios is extremely important. We believe that the theory presented in this chapter forms the basis for such a tool.

5.7 Summary of Chapter

6

SCHEDULING STRATEGIES FOR CQs

In this chapter, we focus on run-time resource allocation problem of stream data processing. Scheduling, a mechanism for the allocation of CPU cycles, determines the order in which operators or operator paths are scheduled at each time slot in a multiple-CQ processing system. The irregular and bursty input characteristics of data streams and the near real-time response requirements from stream-based applications further entail DSMSs to carefully allocate the limited resources in the system. Improper resource allocation can cause DSMSs to fail in handling temporary bursty data streams and in providing timely responses. As we will show in this chapter, improper resource allocation can cause delayed responses which may not be acceptable to many applications. Improper allocation of resources can also cause steep increase in maximal memory needed by the system and may even exceed physical memory available in the system resulting in system failures. However, these failures can be avoided with proper resource allocation mechanisms in place and proper capacity planning (as discussed in Chapter 5). The long-running characteristic of CQs and the unbounded nature of inputs further makes the resource allocation a run-time problem as decisions may have to be changed during the course of execution of a CQ. In short, it is clear that a resource allocation mechanism is critical to the success of a DSMS.

The scheduling problem in a DSMS is also a complicated one. First, it has significant impact on the performance metrics of the system, such as tuple latency, maximal memory requirement, and system throughput. We will define these performance metrics in Section 6.1.2 below. Second, although the resources such as memory size and CPU speed are fixed, scheduling can be highly dynamic (changing over a period of time) based on the observed performance metric values. Third, various predefined QoS requirements for a query add additional constraints to an already complex problem. Finally, the problem is a complicated one because the problem of finding the schedule that only minimizes the memory required is NP-complete as shown in [85]. Additionally, a desirable scheduling strategy in a DSMS should be able to: (*i*) achieve the maximal performance using bounded amount of resources;

S. Chakravarthy and Q. Jiang, *Stream Data Processing: A Quality of Service Perspective*, Advances in Database Systems 36, DOI: 10.1007/978-0-387-71003-7_6,

(*ii*) be aware of the unexpected overload situations, and take corresponding actions in a timely manner; (*iii*) guarantee user- or application-specified QoS requirements for a query, if any; and (*iv*) be implemented easily, and run efficiently with a low overhead.

A single scheduling strategy is not likely to satisfy all of the above mentioned performance metrics, as there are trade-offs among these performance metrics and the usage of limited resources. Although a large number of scheduling strategies exist in the literature for a broad range of needs, specific strategies have also been proposed for minimizing the maximal memory requirements in a DSMS. For stream applications, tuple latency is another important measure that is used in Quality of Service (QoS) specifications. In this chapter, we develop the following scheduling strategies:

1. the *Path Capacity* (PC) strategy to achieve the best overall tuple latency;
2. the *Segment* strategy to achieve lower maximal memory requirement than the PC strategy and better overall tuple latency than all operator-based strategies, such as an operator-level Round Robin strategy, the Chain strategy [85], and others;
3. the *Memory Optimal Segment* (MOS) strategy, which achieves the optimal memory requirement and further improves the maximal memory requirement of the Chain strategy, which has a near-optimal memory requirement;
4. the *Simplified Segment* (SS) strategy, which requires slightly more memory but much smaller tuple latency than the segment strategy;
5. the *Threshold* strategy, which is a hybrid of PC and MOS strategies.

The above strategies provide a reasonable overall performance although they do not meet all the desirable properties.

The rest of the chapter is organized as follows. Section 6.1 provides detailed discussion of our scheduling model, and a summary of notations used in this chapter and the rest of the book. Section 6.2 introduces some preliminary scheduling strategies and shows the impact of a scheduling strategy on performance (i.e., maximal memory requirement, tuple latency, throughput, and so on) of a DSMS. In Section 6.3, we first propose the PC strategy, and then compare the PC strategy with the Chain strategy. We then discuss the segment strategy, its variants (the MOS strategy and the SS strategy), and conclude with the threshold strategy. Finally, we discuss CQ plan characteristics and strategies for avoiding starvation. Section 6.4 presents our quantitative experimental results, detailed analysis, and comparison with theoretical results. We summarize our scheduling work in Section 6.5.

6.1 Scheduling Model and Terminology

In a DSMS, a CQ plan is decomposed into a set of operators (as in a traditional DBMS) such as `project`, `select`, `join`, and other aggregate operators and a sequence of these operators form operator paths or segments (defined in Section 5.1.1). Detailed algorithms are introduced in Section 6.3.3 to partition an operator path into operator segments based on different criteria.

6.1.1 Scheduling Model

A multiple-CQ processing system consists of (*i*) a set of schedulable objects, which can be query plans, operator paths, operator segments, operators, and others, (*ii*) a scheduling function, and (*iii*) a set of job executors (i.e., processors/processes/threads), illustrated in Figure 6.1, from a scheduling point of view.

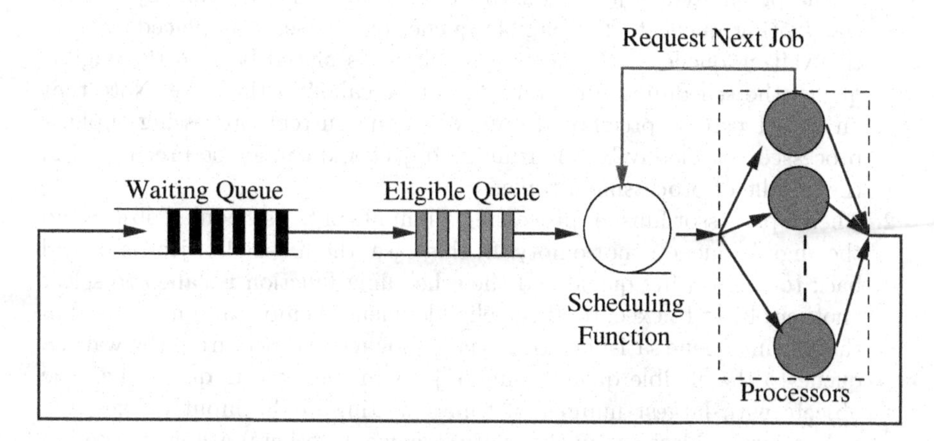

Fig. 6.1. Scheduling Model

In order to minimize the overhead introduced by scheduling itself, we employ an event-driven and preemptible scheduling model. In this scheduling model, we try to minimize the frequency of calls to the scheduling function. Although the cost of calling the scheduling function is small, frequent calls of the scheduling function can introduce considerable overhead in a DSMS. This is because: (*1*) the total cost of frequent calls to the scheduling function can be high; (*2*) the context switching cost can also be high. (*3*) the cost introduced by instruction cache miss, for example, if an operator only processes one tuple each time it is invoked, many instruction cache misses will occur, which results in high context-switching overhead [318, 319].

A schedulable object is initially in the waiting queue and is moved to the eligible queue only when some events occur. Examples of such events are: the number of waiting tuples in the input queues of an object exceeds a predefined threshold value, an object in the waiting queue has been waiting longer than a predefined threshold value, the eligible queue is empty and one processor is idle, and others.

A scheduling function only schedules objects in the eligible queue and is called to determine next executable job when either of the following events occurs:

1. when a new eligible object is inserted into the eligible queue from the waiting queue. In this case, the scheduling function selects one object to execute among all objects in the eligible queue and the running objects, such that the selected object has the lowest property (i.e., priority, processing capacity, and others). If the selected object is the current running one, no change is made; otherwise, the running object is preempted and the selected object is scheduled. The preempted object is placed back in the eligible queue only if the unprocessed tuples left in the input queue of the preempted object satisfies the criteria of moving an object from the waiting queue to the eligible queue; otherwise, it is placed back in the waiting queue. If the preempted object is placed back in the eligible queue, the scheduling function will not be called in this case. Note that an object can be preempted only when the current processing tuple is processed completely by the running object and cannot be preempted in the middle of processing a tuple.
2. when a processor finishes processing all inputs of the scheduled object and the eligible queue is not empty. In this case, the finished object is placed back to the waiting queue and the scheduling function is called to select another object to execute. If the eligible queue is empty and no objects in the waiting queue satisfy the criteria of moving an object from the waiting queue to the eligible queue, some objects in the waiting queue (i.e., the objects with largest number of tuples waiting in the input queues, the objects with oldest age in the waiting queue, or others) are moved to the eligible queue directly without checking moving criteria.

Even in a multiple processor architecture, we assume that no two or more processors call the scheduling function to request the next executable object at the same instant. If this is the case, we process them serially in an arbitrary order (this can be done through a lock mechanism or interlocked hardware instructions).

Once an operator within the scheduled object is scheduled, the tuples waiting in its input queues can be processed in a different order. There is a need for another scheduling strategy to determine which tuple is processed first. We refer this scheduling strategy within an operator as `operator-inner-scheduling strategy`. If the operator is computed over a tuple-based `window`, the operator-inner-scheduling strategy does not affect the amount of memory needed to maintain synopsis of an operator in order to compute the operator correctly. However, if the operator is computed over a time-based `window` or semantic `window`, the operator-inner-scheduling strategy does affect the amount of memory needed for synopsis.

For a two- or multiple-way `join` operator, the different order to process the input queues can cause different memory requirements for the maintenance of synopsis. For example, considering a `join` operator over a 5-minute sliding `window` over streams A and B. Suppose there is a burst of tuples that arrive on stream B. Then the synopsis of B that is needed to compute the join with A will be large, until those A tuples that arrive 5 minutes after the burst have been processed by the `join` operator. An operator-inner-scheduling strategy that chooses to schedule A's tuples before B's tuples as early as possible will free up memory from B's synopsis as early as possible, whereas a strategy that schedules B's tuples before A's tuples will result in the large synopsis of B staying around for a longer period of time, which possibly causes a larger maximal memory requirement in the system.

In our model, we employ a First In First Out (FIFO) scheduling strategy for operator-inner-scheduling[1] since we would like to preserve the order of tuples during the processing. For an object with one input stream, this is straightforward. For objects with two or more input streams, in our theoretical model, we maintain one input queue with different classes of tuples and tuples from different input streams are placed in the input queue based on their arrival time stamps. When the object is scheduled, the tuples in its input queue are processed based on their orders in the queue and the time stamp of an output tuple is the time stamp of the tuple from the input queue, not the tuple from synopsis.

Based on our FIFO operator-inner-scheduling strategy and the same assumption in [85], we can assume that the run-time state or synopsis information stored by each operator is fixed in size and, therefore, the variable portion of the maximal memory requirement is derived from the sizes of the input queues to operators. We also assume that the root node (note that the root node represents an application as explained in Section 5.1.1) consumes its inputs immediately after they enter queues. Therefore, there is no tuple waiting in the input queues of the root node, and the root node is simply treated as a sink in our formulation.

6.1.2 Notations

For the purpose of our analysis, we use the following notations.

- *Maximal memory requirement:* the maximal amount of memory consumed by the tuples waiting in the input queues of all operators at any time instant in the system. The memory requirement in this chapter means the maximal memory requirement unless specified otherwise.
- *Tuple latency:* the length of time an output tuple stays in the CQ processing system after it enters the system. The tuple latency for an output tuple that only passes through unary operators is straightforward. As mentioned earlier, a `join` or a multi-way operator is computed by getting

[1] How different operator-inner- scheduling strategy affect the maximal memory requirement and other metrics is beyond the scope of this book.

a tuple from its input queue and then computing the result with the stored synopsis information. The arrival time stamp of an output tuple for such an operator is derived as the arrival time stamp of the tuple from the input queue. Since we maintain a virtual queue for a `join`- or multi- way `join` and employ a FIFO scheduling strategy for the operator-inner-scheduling strategy, the time stamp of the tuple from the queue is also the latest time stamp compared with those in the stored synopsis. The tuple latency is computed as the difference between the departure time stamp of an output tuple and its arrival time stamp. Although different systems may use different ways to compute the tuple latency, the scheduling strategies proposed in this book do not depend on the way of computing tuple latency. The overall tuple latency is the weighted average of the tuple latency of all output tuples in the system. The tuple latency in this chapter means the overall tuple latency unless specified otherwise.

- *Throughput:* the number of result tuples output from the query processing system per time unit.
- *Operator processing capacity* $C^P_{O_i}$: the number of tuples that can be processed within one time unit at operator O_i. Inversely, the operator service time is the number of time units needed to process one tuple at this operator. A `join` or `k-way operator` is considered as two or k semi-operators. Each of them has its own processing capacity, selectivity, and memory release capacity.
- *Operator selectivity* σ_i: it is the same as in a DBMS except that the selectivity of a `join` operator is considered as two `semi-join` selectivities.
- *Operator memory release capacity* $C^M_{O_i}$: the number (or amount) of memory units such as bytes, pages that can be released within one time unit by operator O_i.

$$C^M_{O_i} = C^P_{O_i}(InputTupleSize - T_i\sigma_i) \tag{6.1}$$

where T_i is the size of the tuple output from operator O_i; the input tuple size from each input stream of a `join` or `k-way` operator is considered as the input tuple size of its corresponding semi-operator.

- *Operator path processing capacity* $C^P_{P_i}$: the number of tuples that can be processed within one time unit by the operator path P_i. Therefore, the operator path processing capacity depends not only on the processing capacity of individual operator along the operator path, but also on the selectivity of these operators and the number of operators in the path. For a simple operator path P_i with k operators, its processing capacity can be derived from the processing capacities of the operators that are along its path, as follows:

$$C^P_{P_i} = \frac{1}{\frac{1}{C^P_{O_1}} + \frac{\sigma_1}{C^P_{O_2}} + \frac{\sigma_1\sigma_2}{C^P_{O_3}} + \cdots + \frac{\prod_{j=1}^{k-1}\sigma_j}{C^P_{O_k}}} \tag{6.2}$$

where $O_l, 1 \leq l \leq k$ is the lth operator along P_i starting from the leaf node. The denominator in Equation (6.2) is the total service time for the path P_i to serve one tuple. The general item $(\prod_{j=1}^{h}\sigma_j)/C^P_{O_{h+1}}$ is the service time at the $(h+1)^{th}$ operator to serve the output part of the tuple from the hth operator along the path, where $1 \leq h \leq k-1$.

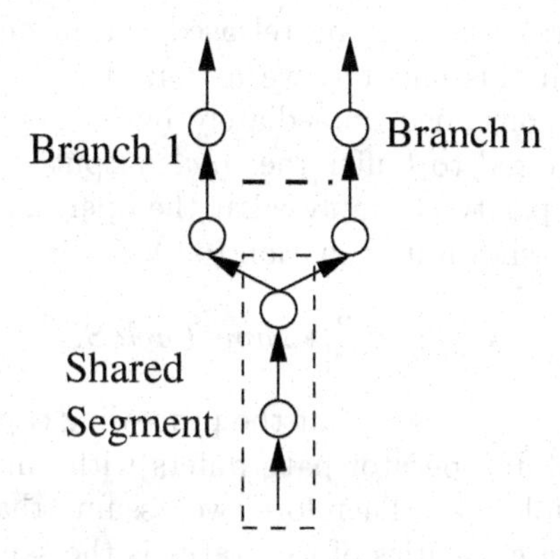

Fig. 6.2. A Complex Operator Path/Segment

For a complex operator path P_i with k operators along its shared segment and with m branches with m_k operators along its branches as illustrated in Figure 6.2, its processing capacity can be derived from the processing capacity of the shared segment and the processing capacities of its m branches. The processing capacity of the branch B_i with i_k operators and its sharing segment can be computed from Equation (6.2) by considering each of them as a simple path as follows:

$$C^B_i = \frac{1}{\frac{1}{C^P_{O_1}} + \frac{\sigma_1}{C^P_{O_2}} + \frac{\sigma_1\sigma_2}{C^P_{O_3}} + \cdots + \frac{\prod_{j=1}^{i_k-1}\sigma_j}{C^P_{O_{i_k}}}} \tag{6.3}$$

Therefore, the processing capacity of the complex operator path P_i is derived as follows:

$$C^P_{P_i} = \frac{1}{\frac{1}{C^{SharingSegment}} + \left(\prod_{j=1}^{k-1}\sigma_j\right) * \sum_{i=1}^{i<=m}\frac{1}{C^B_i}} \tag{6.4}$$

In the above equation, the $\frac{1}{C^{SharingSegment}}$ part is the total processing time needed by the sharing segment to process one input tuple and the part $\left(\prod_{j=1}^{k-1} \sigma_j\right) * \frac{1}{C_i^B}$ is the total processing time needed by branch B_i to process what the sharing segment outputs by processing one input tuple. Recursively, for a complex operator path with branches that have their own sub-branches, we first compute the processing capacity of any sub-branch, and then compute the processing capacity of each branch as Equation (6.4) by considering each branch as a complex operator path, and finally compute the processing capacity of the complex operator path as Equation (6.4).

- *Path memory release capacity* $C_{P_i}^M$: the number of memory units (or amount of memory) that can be released within one time unit by the path P_i. Again, in this chapter, we assume that all the output tuples from a query are consumed immediately by its applications. Therefore, no memory is required to buffer the *final* output results and hence the memory release capacity is simply what the operator path consumes per time unit, which is shown in Equation (6.5).

$$C_{P_i}^M = C_{P_i}^P * InputTupleSize \tag{6.5}$$

From Equation (6.5), we know that the processing capacity and the memory release capacity of an operator path differs with only a constant factor, which is the input tuple size. Therefore, we assume that the partial order between the processing capacities of two paths is the same as the partial order between their memory release capacities. We believe that this assumption is reasonable under a data stream processing environment. For instance, a CQ processing system that is used to analyze Internet traffic has the same tuple input size, where the tuples are the header of the Internet IP packets. Although the sizes of all input tuples from some applications may not be exactly the same, their differences are not large enough to change the relative partial orders of their operator paths. Hereafter, we use the path capacity to refer to both the processing capacity and the memory release capacity.

- *Segment Processing Capacity* $C_{S_i}^P$: the number of tuples that can be processed within one time unit by the operator segment S_i. And the processing capacity of a simple segment or a complex segment, illustrated in Figure 6.2, has the same definition as that given in Equations (6.2) and (6.4) respectively.
- *Segment Memory Release Capacity* $C_{S_i}^M$: the number of memory units that can be released within one time unit by the segment S_i. For a simple segment, its memory release capacity $C_{S_i}^M$ is defined as:

$$C_{S_i}^M = C_{S_i}^P \left(InputTupleSize - S_o * \prod_{i=1}^{k} \sigma_i\right) \tag{6.6}$$

where S_o is the size of the output tuple from segment S_i. Note that the size of the tuple takes into account the size change of a tuple (e.g., due to

`project, join`) and not the number of tuples which is based on selectvities. Hence the need for the product term. For the last segment, the size of the output tuple is zero because of the assumption that the output can be consumed by its applications immediately.
For a complex operator segment S_i with k operators along its shared segment and with m branches with m_k operators along its branches as illustrated in Figure 6.2, its memory release capacity is derived as:

$$C^M_{S_i} = C^P_{S_i}\left(InputTupleSize - \left(\prod_{i=1}^{k}\sigma_i\right) * \sum_{j=1}^{j<=m}\left(S^j_o * \prod_{i=j_1}^{i<=j_k}\sigma_i\right)\right) \tag{6.7}$$

In above Equation (6.7), the item $\left(\prod_{i=1}^{k}\sigma_i\right)$ is the portion of one tuple output by the shared segment with m operators in Figure 6.2 by processing one input tuple; the item $\left(S^j_o * \prod_{i=j_1}^{i<=j_k}\sigma_i\right)$ is the total output size output by the jth branch by processing one tuple waiting at the beginning of the branch. Therefore, the product of these two items is the total size output by each branch by processing one input tuple. Similarly, the memory release capacity of a complex segment that has its own sub-branches can be computed recursively.

6.2 Impact of Scheduling Strategies on QoS

A DSMS has multiple input streams and if the input rate of each stream is trackable (i.e., it is known as to how many tuples will be arriving in future time slots), we can find an optimal scheduling strategy that can achieve the best performance with respect to a metric[2] by using the minimal resources. However, in most cases, the input of a data stream is unpredictable, and highly bursty, which makes it hard, or even impossible to find such a feasible, optimal scheduling strategy. In practice, heuristics-based or near-optimal strategies are used. And these strategies have different impact on the performance and the usage of the system resources. The Chain strategy [85] is a near optimal scheduling strategy in terms of total internal queue size.

In the rest of this section, we use the FIFO strategy described below and the Chain strategy to illustrate the impact of a strategy on the internal queue size (memory requirement), tuple latency, and throughput of a CQ processing system.

FIFO Strategy: *Tuples are processed in the order of their arrivals. Once a tuple is scheduled, it is processed by the operators along its operator path until it is consumed by an intermediate operator or output to the root node. Then the next oldest tuple is scheduled.*

[2] We mean tuple latency, memory requirement, or throughput in this chapter.

Chain Strategy: *At any time, consider all tuples that are currently in the system; of these, schedule a single time unit for the tuples in the input queues of those operators that lies on the segment with the steepest slope in its lowest envelope simulation. If there are multiple such tuples, select the tuple which has the earliest arrival time.*

The slope of a segment in the Chain strategy is the ratio of the time it spends to process one tuple to the memory size changed of that tuple. The tuple in the Chain strategy refers to a batch of tuples, instead of an individual tuple. For further details, refer to [85].

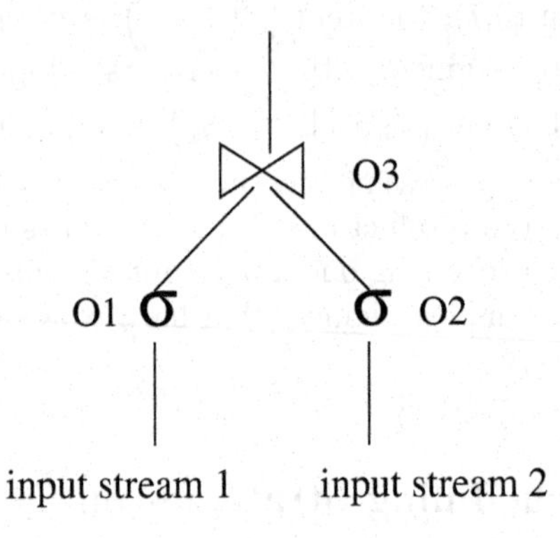

Fig. 6.3. A Query Execution Plan

Let us consider a simple query plan illustrated in Figure 6.3, which is a common query plan that contains both `select` and `join` operators. The processing capacity and selectivity of the operators are listed in Table 6.1. The input streams are assumed to be highly bursty in order to accurately model stream query processing systems. Table 6.2 shows the total internal queue size, tuple latency, and throughput of the query plan under both the FIFO strategy and the Chain strategy for the given input patterns.

Table 6.1. Operator Properties

Operator Id	1	2	3
Selectivity	0.2	0.2	0.8
Processing capacity	1	1	0.2

Table 6.2. Performance (F:FIFO, C:Chain)

Time	Input		Queue Size		Tuple Latency		Throughput	
	1	2	F	C	F	C	F	C
1	1	0	1.0	1.0	-	-	0	0
2	0	1	1.2	1.2	-	-	0.0	0
3	1	1	3.0	2.4	2	-	0.16	0
4	0	0	2.2	1.6	-	-	0	0
5	0	0	2.0	0.8	3	-	0.16	0
6	0	0	1.2	0.6	-	5	0	0.16
7	0	0	1.0	0.4	4	5	0.16	0.16
8	0	0	0.2	0.2	-	5	0	0.16
9	0	0	0	0	6	6	0.16	0.16
10	1	0	1.0	1.0	-	-	0	0

The table clearly shows that the Chain strategy performs much better than the FIFO strategy for the total internal queue size (see values under column Queue Size). However, it performs much worse than the FIFO strategy in terms of tuple latency (see values under column Tuple Latency) and produces a more bursty and irregular throughput than the FIFO (see values and the periodicity of output under column Throughput). Clearly, the FIFO strategy maintains its entire backlog of unprocessed tuples at the beginning of each operator path. It does not take the inherent properties of operators, such as selectivity, processing rate into consideration which causes the total internal queue size to be larger under the FIFO strategy than under the Chain strategy. In contrast, as the Chain strategy pushes the tuples from the bottom, it inherits the bursty property of the input streams. If the input streams are highly bursty in nature, the output of the CQ processing system under the Chain strategy demonstrates highly bursty property too, but the bursty input property in its output is partially determined by the selectivity of the operators and the system load. Therefore, FIFO has a smoother throughput and a better tuple latency than the Chain strategy.

Chain strategy pushes tuples as far as possible to reduce the memory requirement. On the other hand, FIFO gives preference to early arrivals no matter what. Both do not consider the processing capacity of a path to push tuples faster towards the output to reduce tuple latency. Based on these observations, we develop the PC strategy which considers tuple latency and throughput as its primary priorities and the total internal queue size as its secondary priority.

6.3 Novel Scheduling Strategies for CQs

In this section, we first present the PC strategy, and then provide a thorough comparison with the Chain strategy. To overcome the non-optimal memory requirement of the PC strategy and to preserve its minimization of tuple latency property, we further propose the segment strategy and its variants – the MOS strategy and the SS strategy. Finally, we discuss the threshold strategy, which is a hybrid of the PC strategy and the MOS strategy.

6.3.1 Path Capacity Strategy

From Section 6.2, we observe that the FIFO strategy has two promising properties: reasonable tuple latency and throughput. However, it does not consider the characteristics of an operator path such as processing capacity and memory release capacity. Also as it schedules one operator each time, the scheduling overhead is considerably high. This motivates us to develop the PC strategy which improves upon the high memory requirement of the FIFO strategy, and has better tuple latency and smoother throughput than the FIFO strategy.

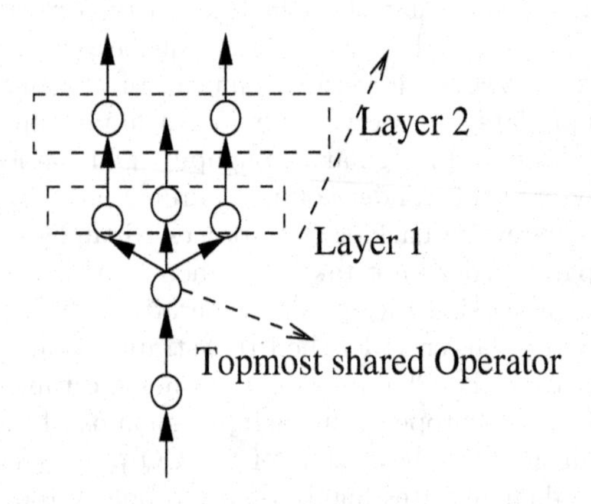

Fig. 6.4. Bottom-up Scheduling Strategy

Path Capacity Strategy: *At any time instant, consider all the operator paths that have input tuples waiting in their queues in the system, schedule a single time unit for the operator path with largest processing capacity to serve until its input queue is empty or there exists an operator path which has a non-null input queue and a larger processing capacity than the currently scheduled one. If there are multiple such paths, select the one with the largest processing capacity. If there are multiple paths with the largest processing capacity, select one arbitrarily*[3]*. The following bottom-up operator scheduling strategy is used to schedule the operators of the chosen path.*

[3] Due to the high cost of keeping track of the oldest tuple in the queues, we do not schedule the operator path with the oldest tuple in its input queue when there exists multiple operator paths with the largest processing capacity.

Bottom-up operator scheduling strategy

Once an operator path is chosen, a bottom-up approach[4] is employed to schedule all the operators along the chosen path. For a simple operator path, the order of operators scheduled by this bottom-up scheduling strategy is straightforward. For a complex operator path in a multiple query processing system, illustrated in Figure 6.4, the order of the operators along the sharing segment of the complex OP is scheduled bottom-up. For the operators along the branches of the complex OP, the operators are categorized into layers based on their distances to the topmost shared operator as also illustrated in Figure 6.4. The operators on a lower layer are scheduled earlier than those in a higher layer. For the operators in the same layer, the operator with largest processing capacity (note not the path) is scheduled first and an arbitrary one is scheduled if two operators have the same processing capacity.

Once an OP is scheduled, it will finish processing all tuples in its input queue or be preempted by another OP with larger capacity. The PC strategy is a *static* priority scheduling strategy. The processing capacity of an operator path is used to define its scheduling priority. Because the processing capacity of an operator is completely determined by the operators along its path, their selectivity, and the processing capacity of each individual operator in the path, the priority of an operator path does not change over time until we revise the selectivity of operators. Therefore, the scheduling cost is minimized and can be negligible. Most importantly, the PC strategy has the following two optimal properties that are critical for a multiple CQ processing system.

Theorem 6.1. *The path capacity strategy is an optimal one in terms of the total tuple latency or the average tuple latency among all scheduling strategies.*

Proof. First, an operator path-based scheduling strategy is a strategy where operator path is the finest schedulable object. In the previous Chapter 5.5.3, we showed that if the operators of two query plans or operator paths are scheduled in an interleaved manner, the overall tuple latency becomes worse. For example, operator path-based round robin strategy has a better tuple latency than the ones that do not use an operator path as a scheduling unit. The operators of two operator paths under the path-based strategy are never scheduled in an interleaved manner. Therefore, the PC strategy (which is an operator path-based strategy) has a better tuple latency than any non-path based scheduling strategy.

Second, the PC strategy has a minimized tuple latency among all path based scheduling strategies. At any time instant, consider k operator paths $p_1, p_2, \cdots, p_k$, which have $N_i \geq 1, i = 1, 2, 3, \cdots, k$ tuples in their input queues in the system, with their capacities $C_1, C_2, \cdots, C_k$ respectively. Without loss of generality, we assume that $C_1 \geq C_2 \geq \cdots \geq C_k$. The PC strategy has

[4] This book only discusses bottom-up scheduling strategies. It is possible to consider other strategies (e.g., pipelined) as well for this model.

a schedule of $p_1, p_2, \cdots, p_k$, that is to serve the N_1 tuples of operator path p_1, following the N_2 tuples of operator path p_2 , and so on. In the simplest case where $N_i = 1, i = 1, 2, 3, \cdots, k$, the total tuple latency $T = k\frac{1}{C_1} + (k-1)\frac{1}{C_2} + \cdots + (k-g+1)\frac{1}{C_g} + \cdots + (k-h+1)\frac{1}{C_h} + \cdots + \frac{1}{C_k}$, where $(k-i)\frac{1}{C_i}, i = 0, 1, \cdots, k-1$ is the total waiting time of all the tuples in the system due to processing the tuple at operator O_i. If we switch any two tuples (two paths), say g, h, where $g < h$, in the PC strategy, then the total tuple latency $T' = k\frac{1}{C_1} + (k-1)\frac{1}{C_2} + \cdots + (k-g+1)\frac{1}{C_h} + \cdots + (k-h+1)\frac{1}{C_g} + \cdots + \frac{1}{C_k}$. The difference of two tuple latency$\Delta = T - T' = (h-g)\left(\frac{1}{C_g} - \frac{1}{C_h}\right) \leq 0$ because of $g < h$ and $C_g \geq C_h$. Similarly, for the general case, by switching any two tuples in two input queues of these k operator paths, we still have $\Delta \leq 0$. Therefore, any other scheduling strategy causes at least the same total tuple latency or mean delay as the PC strategy causes.

Theorem 6.2. *Any other path-based scheduling strategy requires at least as much memory as that required by the PC strategy at any time instant in the system.*

Proof. At any time instant, the PC strategy schedules the tuples waiting in the input queue of the operator path which has the largest capacity among all the paths with non-empty input queues in the system. Within one time unit, the path scheduled by the PC strategy consumes the maximal number of tuples because it has the largest capacity. Any other path-based scheduling strategy (for example, path-based round robin) which does not schedule the tuples waiting in the input queue of the operator path with the largest capacity at that time instant consumes less number of tuples. Therefore, any other path based scheduling strategy requires at least the same amount of memory required by the PC strategy.

Theorem 6.1 clearly shows that the PC strategy is the optimal one in terms of total tuple latency and it performs much better than the FIFO strategy and the Chain strategy for tuple latency. Theorem 6.2 shows that the PC strategy performs better than any other path-based strategy, but not as well as the Chain strategy in terms of the memory requirement.

6.3.2 Analysis of CQ Scheduling Strategies

Both the PC strategy and the Chain strategy have their optimal properties as well as shortcomings. In this section, we present a comprehensive comparison and show how these two scheduling strategies impact the various performance metrics of a CQ processing system. A quantitative experimental study for these two scheduling strategies will be presented in Section 6.4.

Tuple Latency and Throughput

The PC strategy can achieve the optimal tuple latency as compared to any other scheduling strategy and it also has a much smoother output rate than other strategies. The main reason for the large tuple latency in the Chain strategy is that the leaf nodes usually have a much larger capacity than other nodes of a query plan, which causes the Chain strategy gradually to push all the tuples from the leaf nodes toward the root node, and a large number of tuples are buffered along an operator path. This situation becomes even worse during a temporary overload period in which the input rates temporarily exceed the processing capacity of the system. All the computational resources are allocated to these operators at the bottom of a query plan during the bursty input periods[5] and there is almost no throughput from the system. On the other hand, the throughput is surprisingly high immediately after the highly bursty period because there are not too many tuples waiting at leaf nodes, and most of the computation resources is available for the operators in the upper part of the query plans where a large number of partially processed tuples wait. As a result, the Chain strategy not only has a high tuple latency, but also a bursty output rate if the input streams are bursty. The bursty output rates may negate part of its saved memory because the consumed rates of applications cannot keep up with the bursty output rates, which causes portion of the results to backlog in the query processing system for a while.

Memory requirement

Both strategies have an optimal property in terms of the memory requirement. But the optimal property of the PC strategy is a relative one among all path-based scheduling strategies, whereas the near optimal property of the Chain strategy is a global optimal property. Under non-overload conditions, the amount of memory required by these two strategies is similar, and there are not too many tuples buffered in the queues. However, during bursty input periods, the Chain strategy performs better than the PC strategy because the PC strategy buffers the unprocessed tuples at the beginning of an operator path.

Starvation

Both strategies have the starvation problem in which some operators or operator paths may never be served because both of them depend on a set of static priorities. Under heavy load situations, the Chain strategy spends most of its computation resources on the bottom-side operators of an operator path; as

[5] For input streams that exhibit self similar property, bursty periods are relatively long.

most of operators in the upper-side of an operator path (closer to the root) have lesser capacity, they are likely to starve. On the other hand, as the PC strategy spends most of its computation resources on the operator paths with a larger path processing capacity, the operator paths with less capacity are likely to starve. One significant difference is that during heavy load situations, the Chain strategy has very small or even no throughput at all, whereas the PC strategy still has reasonable throughput. The starvation problem in the Chain has been resolved in its improved version, called Chain-Flush strategy [85], by introducing possible larger maximal memory requirement and larger overhead. The technique introduced in the Chain-Flush can be applied to the PC strategy as well as to any other strategy with the starvation problem. In addition, we also propose techniques to overcome the starvation problem, which are discussed in Section 6.3.6.

Scheduling Overhead

Clearly, both strategies have very small scheduling overhead because both are static priority strategies. But the scheduling overhead incurred by the PC strategy is less than that incurred by the Chain strategy because the number of operator paths in a system is less than the number of operators. In our query processing model, the number of OPs is equal to the number of input data streams (to be precise, the number of leaf nodes as the same stream may have to be input to two or more queries when sharing is not possible). Although the cost of scheduling one operator or operator path is very small, the cost to process one tuple is even smaller than that. Therefore, the number of tuples served by each schedule has significant impact on the performance of a CQ processing system as we discussed in Section 6.1.1.

To overcome the overhead introduced by scheduling itself, a number of techniques are proposed in the literature and can be applied to the scheduling strategies proposed in this book: (*1*) Considering a tuple as a fixed memory unit such as page, rather than an individual tuple as proposed in [85]; (*2*) An event-driven scheduling model as we discussed in Section 6.1.1 can be used, instead of making a scheduling decision at every time unit. In addition, we are studying a non-preemptive scheduling model to further decrease the need of making a scheduling decision and to increase the number of tuples processed once an operator is invoked. In this non-preempted scheduling model, an object is eligible to be scheduled/invoked only when the number of tuples exceeds a predefined minimal value, say its processing capacity. Once the object is scheduled/invoked, the object cannot be preempted until all jobs (input tuples) have been processed or the time units used have exceeded a predefined maximal number of time units. In a real-life application, we can either use an exhaustive service discipline [130,320] or a gated service discipline in order to further decrease the overall scheduling overhead.

Context Switching Overhead

When each operator is implemented as a single thread, the context switching cost incurred by a scheduling algorithm can be considerably high. The performance of the system will degrade dramatically as the number of operators increases. It is beneficial to implement the entire query processing as a single thread or as a few threads over a multiple-processor system to keep the switching overload low. Indeed, we have implemented the whole query processing system as a single thread, and hence the cost of switching from one operator path to another is just a function call, which is quite low in a modern processor architecture. As a batch of tuples, rather than one tuple, is scheduled for each scheduling round, the cost of making a function call is negligible as compared with the cost of processing a batch of tuples.

6.3.3 Segment Strategy and Its Variants

Although the PC strategy has optimal memory requirement among all path-based scheduling strategies, it still buffers all unprocessed tuples at the beginning of an operator path. In a CQ processing system with a shortage of main memory, a trade-off exists between the tuple latency and the total internal queue size. Therefore, we have developed the segment strategy which has a much smaller total internal queue size requirement as compared to the PC strategy, and a smaller tuple latency than the Chain strategy. Furthermore, we introduce two variants of the segment strategy: the MOS strategy, which achieves the strict minimization of maximal memory requirement by theoretically comparing with the near-optimal memory requirement property of the Chain strategy, and the SS strategy (a special case of the segment strategy) which further improves tuple latency with a slightly larger memory requirement than the segment strategy.

The segment strategy and its variants employ an idea that allows us to improve upon the PC strategy in terms of maximal memory requirement. Operator scheduling and path scheduling can be seen as two extremes of the spectrum, whereas segment strategies cover the points in between. Instead of buffering the unprocessed tuples at the beginning of an operator path, we partition an operator path into a few segments, so that some partially processed tuples can be buffered at the beginning of a segment. This allows the system to take advantage of the lower selectivity and fast service rate of bottom side operators of a query execution plan. The processing capacity and the memory release capacity for a segment are defined in Section 6.1.2.

The segment strategy employs the same scheduling model as the PC strategy. It schedules an operator segment, rather than an operator path as the case of the PC strategy.

Segment Scheduling Strategy: *At any time instant, consider all the operator segments that have input tuples waiting in their input queues. Schedule* *a single time unit for the operator segment that has the maximal memory release capacity to serve until its input queue is empty or there exists another operator segment that has a non-null input queue and a larger memory release capacity than the currently scheduled one. If there are multiple such segments, select the one with the largest memory release capacity. If there are multiple segments with the largest memory release capacity, select one arbitrarily. The bottom-up operator scheduling strategy (described earlier) is used to schedule the operators of the chosen segment.*

The key component of the segment strategy and its variants is the algorithm to partition an operator path into segments. We propose three algorithms to partition an OP into segments. These algorithms work for both simple operator paths and complex operator paths. We discuss the details of our segment construction algorithms when we present our segment strategy and its variants in the following subsections.

Segment Strategy

The segment strategy, also termed greedy segment strategy, is a static priority driven strategy and it employs the following greedy segment construction algorithm to partition an OP into segments.

The segment construction algorithm shown in Algorithm 1 consists of two main steps. First, it partitions an operator path into a few segments in the first 14 lines of the algorithm. Second, it prunes the global segment link list, which is initially empty, due to the `join` or multiple-way operators and the sharing of two or more query plans and then adds the new segments into the list.

For each operator path in the system, we repeat the following procedure: Consider an operator path with m operators $O_1, O_2, \cdots, O_m$ from leaf to root. Starting from O_1, a segment of the operator path is defined as a set of consecutive operators $\{O_k, O_{k+1}, \cdots, O_{k+i}\}$ where $k \geq 1$, such that $\forall j, k \leq j < k+i, C^M_{O_j} \leq C^M_{O_{j+1}}$. Once such a segment is constructed, we start the construction procedure again from O_{k+i+1} until all the operators along the operator path have been processed. In the pruning procedure, a new segment is added to the segment link list only if: (*i*) any of its subsets has already been in the list, then we remove all its subsets from the segment list and then add the new segment into the list; (*ii*) none of its supersets has been in the list, then we add it to the list; otherwise, the new segment is discarded.

For a simple operator path, the above greedy segment construction algorithm works in a straightforward manner. However, for a complex operator path with branches, as shown in Figure 6.2, the algorithm cannot be applied directly due to the branches of the operator path. In the bottom-up operator scheduling strategy, proposed as an internal scheduling strategy within the PC strategy, the operators in the shared segment of a complex operator path is scheduled from bottom. The operators along the branches are scheduled

Algorithm 1: Greedy Segment Construction Algorithm

```
   INPUT: the operator path p, the global operator segment link GSL
   OUTPUT: the updated global operator segment link
   /*p consists of a list of operator references along the path from left to root */
 1 tempListS ← NULL;
 2 seg ← NULL;
 3 while p ≠ NULL do
 4     if seg == NULL then append p->operator to seg else
 5         if the processing capacity of p->operator is no less than that of the
           last operator of the segment seg then append p->operator to seg;
 6         else
 7             add seg to tempListS;
 8             seg ← NULL;
 9             append p->operator to seg
10         end
11     end
12     p ← p->next
13 end
14 if seg ≠ NULL then add seg to tempListS;
   /*the pruning procedure;                                                  */
15 foreach segment s in tempListS do
16     needAdd ← TRUE;
17     foreach segment s0 in global segment list GSL do
18         if s is a subset of s0 or s == s0 then
           /*no need to add s to the global segment list; continue to process
              next segment in tempList                                       */
19         needAdd ← FALSE;
20         break;
21         else
22             if s is a superset of s0 then delete s0 from GSL;
23         end
24     end
25     if (needAdd == TRUE) then add segment s to GSL
26 end
```

from a low layer to a high layer and for the operators in the same layer, those with larger processing capacity are scheduled first. Based on their execution order, we transform a complex operator path into a simple operator path, then apply the above algorithm to partition a complex operator path into segments.

The order in which we partition an operator path does not matter because the final segment list is the same for a given query plan, and the order of a segment in the segment list does not affect its priority. We only need to execute the above algorithm once in order to construct the segment list. Later on, when a new query plan is registered with the system, we need to execute the algorithm for all operator paths of the newly registered query plan. When a query plan is unregistered from the system, we need to delete all the segments belonging to that query plan. In a multiple query processing system, as one segment may be shared by two or more query plans, we have to add a *count* field to each operator of a segment to indicate how many query plans are using it. Once a segment is deleted from the system, we decrease the value in the *count* field by one for each operator that belongs to the segment. When the *count* value of an operator reaches zero, it is deleted from the segment.

Since CQ plans in a stream processing system are long-running queries, the number of queries that will be registered with a system or unregistered from a system is not likely to be too large (typically no more than a few per hour). Therefore, the cost of the algorithm has very little impact on system performance.

The segment strategy shares the same operator segment concept used by the Chain strategy [85] and the Train strategy [92] in Aurora. However, it is unclear from the literature how a segment (superbox) is constructed in [92]. On the other hand, the segment strategy is different from the Chain strategy in that: (*i*) the segments used in these two strategies are different. The segments used in the Chain strategy have steepest slope in its lower envelope, while the segments used in the segment strategy consist of consecutive operators that have an increasing memory release capacity. Therefore, the Chain strategy can achieve the near optimal internal queue size requirement, while the segment strategy has a slightly larger internal queue size requirement, but it achieves better tuple latency, (*ii*) it clusters a set of operators as a scheduling unit, and hence there are no partially processed tuples buffered in the middle of an operator segment at the end of each time unit as in the Chain strategy, and (*iii*) it has a smaller scheduling overhead than the Chain strategy. The Chain strategy is an operator-based strategy where all the operators along a segment have the same priority, while the segment strategy is a segment- based strategy. In a general query processing system, as the number of segments is less than the number of operators, the scheduling overhead is lower for the segment strategy.

The MOS Segment Strategy

In order to achieve the optimal memory requirement, we propose the MOS strategy, which achieves the optimal memory requirement by employing the memory-optimal segment construction algorithms illustrated in Algorithm 2 for a simple operator path and Algorithm 3 for a complex operator path.

For a simple operator path, the Algorithm 2 partitions a simple OP into segments by finding the segment with the largest memory release capacity among all possible segments that begin with the leaf operator of an OP or the remaining of an OP.

For a complex operator path, the greedy segment construction algorithm cannot achieve the optimal memory requirement. Instead, we introduced the Algorithm 3 to partition a complex operator path into segments. There are

Algorithm 2: Memory-Optimal Segment Construction Algorithm For a Simple Operator Path

```
   INPUT: the simple operator path p, the global operator segment link GSL
   OUTPUT: the updated global operator segment link
1  tempListS ← NULL;
2  seg ← NULL;
3  startOpOfSeg ← p->operator;
4  endOpOfSeg ← NULL;
5  while startOpOfSeg ≠ NULL do
6  |  potentialEndOp ← startOpOfSeg;
7  |  maxCapacity ← 0;
8  |  while potentialEndOp ≠ NULL do
9  |  |  form the segment seg by all operators from startOpOfSeg to
   |  |  potentialEndOp;
10 |  |  tempCapacity ← compute the memory release capacity of the
   |  |  segment seg;
11 |  |  if maxCapacity ≤ tempCapacity then
12 |  |  |  maxCapacity ← tempCapacity ;
13 |  |  |  endOpOfSeg ← potentialEndOp;
14 |  |  end
15 |  |  potentialEndOp ← potentialEndOp->next;
16 |  end
17 |  form the segment seg by all operators from startOpOfSeg to
   |  endOpOfSeg;
18 |  add seg to tempListS;
19 |  startOpOfSeg ← endOpOfSeg->next;
20 end
   /*the pruning procedure is the same as in the Algorithm 1;                */
```

three main steps in this algorithm: (*1*) transform a complex operator path into a list of possible simple operator paths; (*2*) apply Algorithm 2 to each simple operator path constructed in the first step and then select the segment with the largest memory release capacity; (*3*) for the remaining part of the complex operator path (excluding those in the segment constructed in second step), recursively apply step 1 and 2 until there is no operator left.

The first step is to transform a complex operator path to a list of possible simple paths (Line 3 in Algorithm 3). The main idea behind this step is to enumerate all possible execution orders of the operators along a complex operator path, but preserving orders of operators along each simple path. An operator A that takes direct or indirect outputs of another operator B cannot be scheduled before B is scheduled. For example, the operators along the shared segment must be scheduled according to their order along the segment, and the operators along a branch must be scheduled according to their order along the branch too, but not necessarily in a consecutively order; operators from other branches can be scheduled between two operators. For example, for the complex operator illustrated in Figure 6.5-a, we list some possible execution orders in Figure 6.5-b. The second step is to find the segment with the largest memory release capacity among all segments from all possible simple operator paths constructed in the first step (from Line 4 to Line 26 in Algorithm 3). Note that only the first segment (Line 7 to Line 21 in Algorithm 3) is constructed from a simple path because the second one has less memory release capacity than the first one; If it is not, we can reconstruct the first segment by combining the first and the second segment into a new segment which must have a bigger memory release capacity than the first one. The third step is to repeat step 2 for the remaining part of the simple operator path that is used in step 2.

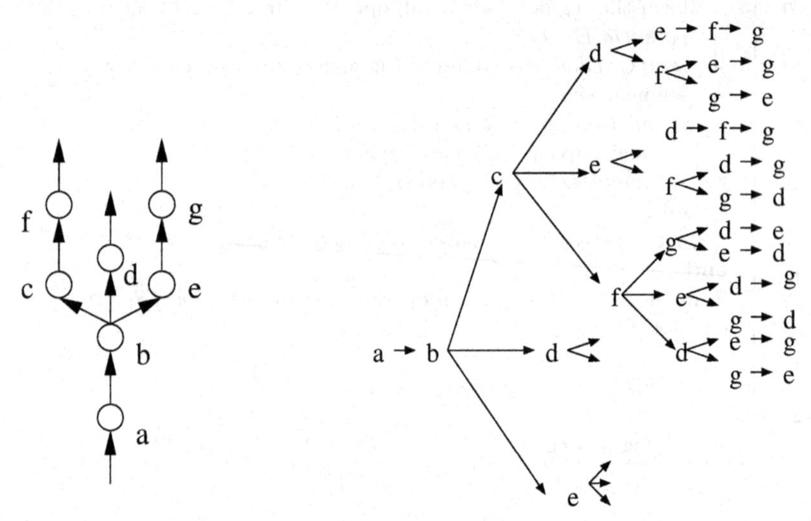

a : Example of a complex operator path
b : Partial execution orders

Fig. 6.5. Example of Complex MOS Construction

The difference between the MOS segment construction algorithms and the Greedy segment construction algorithm lies in the way segments are constructed. The segments constructed by the Algorithm 1 (greedy) consist of consecutive operators as long as the memory release capacity of an operator in the segment is not larger than that of its next operator. On the other hand, the segments constructed by the Algorithm 2 (memory-optimal) consist of a list of consecutive operators as long as the memory release capacity of the segment formed by the list of operators is not less than that of any segment formed by the first operator in the list to each upstream operator along the *operator path*, instead of *operator segment.* An example is shown in Figure 6.6 in which the Algorithm 1 partitions the path into 2 segments, which are *ABC*

Algorithm 3: Memory-Optimal Segment Construction Algorithm For a Complex Operator Path

```
    INPUT: the complex operator path p, the global operator segment link GSL
    OUTPUT: the updated global operator segment link GSL
 1  TempList ← NULL;
 2  while p ≠ NULL do
        /*STEP ONE: emulatePossibleSimpleOperatorPaths(p) list all possible
          execution orders of the operators along the complex operator path p
          and those execution orders do not violate their order along the path. */
 3      EmulationListE ← EmulatePossibleSimpleOperatorPaths(p);
        /*STEP TWO: find the segment with the largest memory release
          capacity among all segments from any simple path in EmulationListE.
          */
 4      OptimalSegS ← NULL;
 5      SimplePath ← NULL;
 6      foreach SP in EmulationListE do
            /*find the segment with the largest memory release capacity among
              all segments starting from the first operator of the simple path SP.
              */
 7          seg ← NULL;
 8          startOpOfSeg ← SP->operator;
 9          endOpOfSeg ← NULL;
10          potentialEndOp ← startOpOfSeg;
11          maxCapacity ← 0;
12          while potentialEndOp ≠ NULL do
13              form the segment seg by all operators from startOpOfSeg to
                potentialEndOp;
14              tempCapacity ← compute the memory release capacity of the
                segment seg;
15              if maxCapacity ≤ tempCapacity then
16                  maxCapacity ← tempCapacity ;
17                  endOpOfSeg ← potentialEndOp;
18              end
19              potentialEndOp ← potentialEndOp->next;
20          end
21          form the segment seg by all operators from startOpOfSeg to
            endOpOfSeg;
            /*Select the segment with the largest memory release capacity and
              the simple path to which it belongs;                              */
22          if (OptimalSeg == NULL) OR (OptimalSeg->processingCapacity
            < seg->processingCapacity) then
23              optimalSeg = seg;
24              SimplePath = SP;
25          end
26      end
        /*STEP THREE: remove all operators on the seg from the SimplePath
          and repeat STEP ONE and STEP TWO;                                     */
27      TempList ← {TempList + optimalSeg};
28      p ← {SimplePath - seg};
29  end
    /*STEP FOUR: add all segments in TempList to global list GSL by starting
      the pruning procedure in the Algorithm 1;                                 */
```

and DE; while the Algorithm 2 partitions the path into 1 segment, which is $ABCDE$.

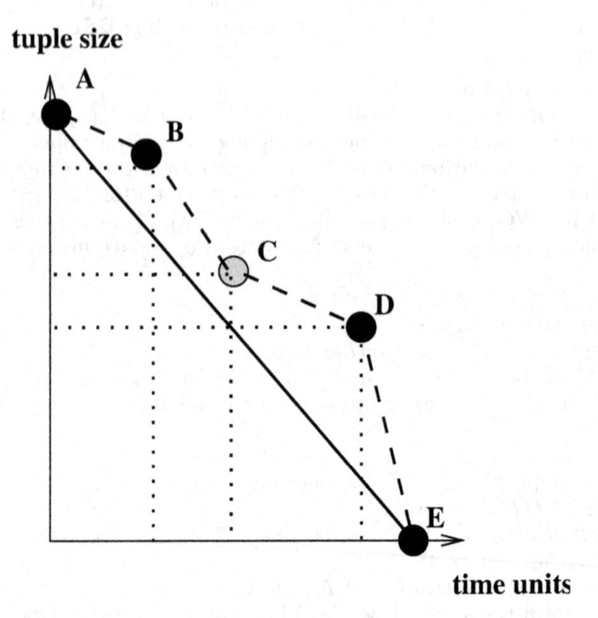

Fig. 6.6. Example of Segmentation

In our segment strategy, the memory requirement (internal queue size) of the query processing is minimized by using the segments constructed by Algorithms 2 and 3. The segment strategy that employs the MOS construction algorithms is termed as MOS strategy. The MOS strategy has a number of advantages over the Chain strategy although both use the similar algorithm to construct the segments in the system (Note: the progress chart construction in the Chain strategy is only for simple operator paths. We extend it to the complex operator paths in this book). First, it works under both single query (no shared computation) and multiple query (with shared computation) processing systems. Second, it theoretically achieves the strictly optimal memory requirement, instead of the near optimal memory requirement as in the Chain strategy. Third, it achieves better tuple latency and smoother throughput than the Chain strategy. Finally, it has lower overhead than the Chain strategy. We discuss these advantages in detail in the rest of this chapter.

Theorem 6.3. *The MOS strategy minimizes the memory requirement of a CQ processing system with multiple queries. It achieves the optimal memory requirement.*

Proof. We assume that there exists an optimal algorithm ALG_{opt}, which always schedules the object that could be an operator, an operator segment, an operator path or a bigger schedulable object (i.e., a query plan) to minimize the memory requirement in the system at any time point. Considering each of these cases: an operator, an operator segment, an operator path or bigger object, we prove the memory required by the MOS strategy is no more than that required by the ALG_{opt}.

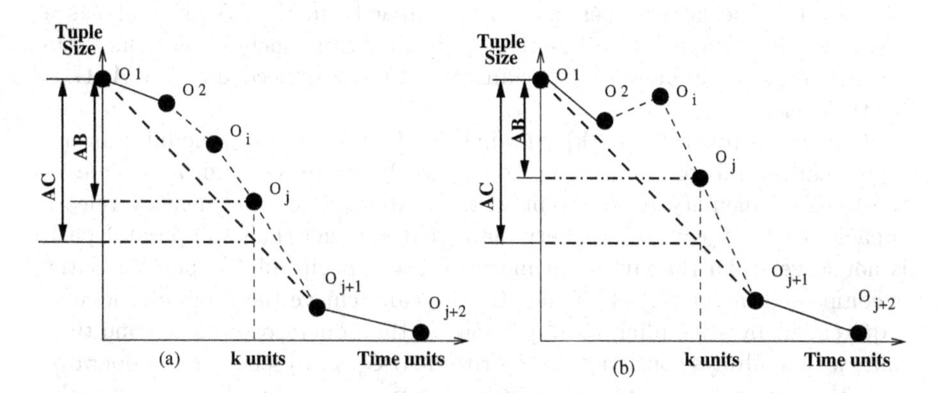

Fig. 6.7. Two Cases For The Memory Release Capacity Of The Operator O_i

Case one (operator): at time slot t_i, the ALG_{opt} schedules an operator for one time unit and achieves the minimal memory requirement so far. Without loss of generality, we can assume that the operator is O_i along a k-operator segment $\mathcal{S}_k$, which consists of $< O_1, O_2, \cdots, O_i, O_{i+1}, \cdots, O_k >$. There are two subcases: one is shown in Figure 6.7-a where the memory release capacity of the operator O_i is not larger than that of the segment $\mathcal{S}_k$; another is shown in Figure 6.7-b where the memory release capacity of the operator O_i is larger than that of the segment $\mathcal{S}_k$. For either case, the inputs of the operator O_i are the outputs of the operator O_{i-1}. Therefore, the ALG_{opt} must have scheduled the operators from O_1 to O_{i-1} along that segment at least once so far in order to be able to schedule the operator O_i. At each time, when the ALG_{opt} schedules one of these operator, we have an algorithm ALG_{seg} to schedule the segment $\mathcal{S}_j$ once. The segment $\mathcal{S}_j$ consists of the operators $< O_1, O_2, \cdots, O_j >$ along the segment $\mathcal{S}_k$ and its the memory release capacity is not less than that of the segment consisting of $< O_1, O_2, \cdots, O_i >$. In the worst case, we have a segment consisting of $< O_1, O_2, \cdots, O_i >$. The total amount of memory released by ALG_{opt} is AB shown in Figure 6.7. The amount of memory released by ALG_{seg} is AC shown in Figure 6.7. It clearly shows that the amount of memory released by ALG_{seg} is not less than that released by ALG_{opt}. According to the definition of MOS strategy, we know that MOS always schedules the segment with the largest memory release capacity. Therefore, the amount of memory released at each time unit by MOS strategy is not less than that released by ALG_{seg}. In general, the amount of memory released by the MOS strategy is not less than that released by ALG_{opt} if it schedules an operator at any time slot in the system. In other words, the MOS strategy requires no larger amount of memory than the ALG_{opt}.

Case two (segment): at any time slot, if the ALG_{opt} schedules the operator segment S_{opt} for one time unit and achieves the minimal memory requirement in the system, the amount of memory required by S_{opt} within one time unit is its memory release capacity $C^M_{S_{opt}}$. Since the segment scheduled by MOS strategy has the largest memory release capacity in the system and has a memory release capacity no less than $C^M_{S_{opt}}$. We can conclude that the MOS strategy requires no more than the amount of memory needed by the ALG_{opt} for this case.

Case three (operator path): at time slot t_i, the ALG_{opt} schedules an operator path or a bigger object (i.e., query pan) for one time unit and achieves the minimal memory requirement in the system. Since the memory release capacity of an object (i.e., a query plan) that is larger than an operator path is not larger than the largest memory release capacity of all operator paths encompassed in the object, if the ALG_{opt} can achieve the minimal memory requirement by scheduling an object bigger than operator path for one time unit, we can always construct an algorithm ALG_{path} to schedule the operator path that has the largest memory release capacity among all operator paths encompassed in the object for one time unit. The amount of memory required by ALG_{path} is no less than that released by ALG_{opt}. Similarly, the memory release capacity of an operator path is not larger than the largest memory release capacity of all segments encompassed that operator path. If ALG_{path} can achieve the minimal memory requirement by scheduling an operator path one time unit in the system, we could construct an algorithm $ALG_{s\bar{e}g}$ to schedule the segment with the largest memory release capacity among all segments encompassed in that operator path. The memory required by $ALGs\bar{e}g$ is not more than that required by ALG_{path}. Since the MOS strategy schedules the segment with the largest memory release capacity the system, the memory release capacity of the segment scheduled by the MOS strategy is no less than that of the segment scheduled by $ALG_{s\bar{e}g}$. Therefore, the memory required by the MOS strategy is no more than that required by ALG_{opt} for this case.

In conclusion, the MOS strategy requires no more memory than that required by the ALG_{opt} for any of the cases. It is an optimal strategy in terms of memory requirement.

The advantages of the MOS strategy as compared to the Chain strategy are due to the following facts:

- The segment construction algorithms used in MOS strategy not only work for query processing systems with simple operator paths, but they also work for multiple query processing systems with computation sharing (i.e., sharing sub-common expressions giving rise to complex operator paths) where one input tuple can output multiple tuples for different paths. However, the progress chart in the Chain strategy only works for query plans without any computation sharing (i.e, only for simple paths). Our segment construction algorithm for a complex operator path can also be applied to extend the progress chart in the Chain strategy to work in a multiple query processing system. The proof of minimization of memory requirement in [85] is only for the query plans without `join` or multi-way operators and without computation sharing through sub-common expression. In this chapter, we proved that the MOS strategy minimizes the memory requirement for a multiple CQ processing system with general query plans.

- There are tuples buffered in the middle of the segment for the Chain strategy and no tuples are buffered in the middle of a segment for the MOS strategy. That is the reason for the Chain to be a near optimal strategy in terms of memory requirement and the MOS strategy to be an optimal one. Although both of them partition an operator path into a set of segments, the Chain assigns the same priority to all the operators in that segment and then it schedules operators based on priority. For operators with the same priority, it schedules the operator with the oldest tuples, which also cause higher overhead due to the bookkeeping needed to track the oldest tuple. The MOS strategy, on the other hand, schedules the whole segment as one object and for segments with the same priority, the MOS strategy schedules one arbitrarily. At any time instant, the Chain schedules the operator with the highest priority for one time unit (or one tuple) while the MOS strategy schedules the operator segment on which the operator scheduled by the Chain lies, one time unit (or one tuple).
- The MOS strategy preserves the order of the operators with the same priority by placing them along a segment. Therefore, no other operators can be scheduled in an interleaved manner with those operators along one segment. The Chain strategy may schedule the operators of these segments in an interleaved manner if two or more segments in the system have the same priority (memory release capacity) and the tuples with these segments have the same age. This, in turn, would cause longer overall tuple latency. For example, given two segments $ABCD$ and $EFGH$, the Chain strategy may schedule those operators in the order $AEBFCGDH$ (one of the interleavings), while MOS strategy schedules operators in order of segment $ABCD$ and segment $EFGH$ or vice versa. In either case, the MOS strategy achieves a better tuple latency than the Chain strategy and the same or better memory requirement.
- As we discussed earlier, the PC strategy has a smoother throughput than the Chain strategy. For the same reason, the MOS strategy has a smoother throughput than the Chain strategy, but is a little bit more bursty in throughput as compared to the PC strategy because the MOS strategy buffers some partial processed tuples in the middle of an operator path.
- The MOS strategy has a lower overhead than the Chain strategy. This is because (*i*) the number of segments in the system is less than the number of operators; (*ii*) for the operators with the same priority, the Chain strategy needs to keep track of the ages of the tuples. Due to the highly

dynamic input characteristics of data streams and the frequent calls to the scheduling function, the overhead can be high even though the number of operators with the same priority is small. The MOS strategy schedules the segments with the same priority arbitrarily, and it does not have this overhead.

Simplified Segment Strategy

The (greedy) segment strategy and the MOS strategy decrease the memory requirement as compared to the PC strategy, but they still cause longer tuple latency than the PC strategy because they partition one operator path into multiple segments. Chapter 5 shows that the overall tuple latency of the tuples from an operator path increases significantly if other operators are scheduled in an interleaved manner with the operators along the operator path. In order to decrease the interleaving of the operators of two segments, we propose the SS strategy by partitioning an OP into at most two segments.

The SS strategy differs from the segment strategy and the MOS strategy in that it employs a simplified MOS segment construction algorithm. In a practical multiple CQ processing system, we observe that: *i*) the number of segments constructed may not be significantly less than the number of operators presented in the query processing system and *ii*) the leaf nodes are the operators that have faster processing capacities and less selectivity in the system; all the other operators in a query plan have a much slower processing rate than the leaf nodes. Based on these observations, we partition an operator path into at most two segments, rather than a few segments. The first segment includes the leaf node and its consecutive operators that come from the operator path by using the MOS construction algorithm (Algorithm 2). The remaining operators along that operator path, if any, forms the second segment.

Although the memory requirement of the SS strategy is slightly larger than the segment strategy because the first segment of an operator path releases the maximum amount of memory that can be released by the operator path, it has the following advantages: (*i*) the tuple latency decreases significantly because the number of times a tuple is buffered along an operator path is at most two, (*ii*) the scheduling overhead significantly decreases as well due to the decrease in the number of segments, and finally (*iii*) it is less sensitive to the selectivity and service time of an operator because there exists at most two segments for an operator path.

6.3.4 Hybrid Threshold Scheduling Strategy

The threshold strategy is a dynamic strategy and is a hybrid of the PC strategy and the MOS strategy. The intuition behind it is that the PC strategy is used to minimize the tuple latency when the memory is not a bottleneck; otherwise, the MOS strategy is used to decrease the total memory requirement. Therefore, this one combines the properties of these two strategies.

Threshold Strategy: *Given a CQ processing system with a maximal available queue memory*[6] $\mathcal{M}$, *the maximal threshold* $\mathcal{T}_{max}$ *and the minimal threshold* $\mathcal{T}_{min}$, *where* $\mathcal{T}_{min} < \mathcal{T}_{max} < \mathcal{M}$, *at any time instant, when the current total queue memory consumed* $\mathcal{M}_c \geq \mathcal{T}_{max}$, *the system enters its memory saving mode in which the MOS strategy is employed. The system transits from the memory saving mode to the normal mode in which the PC strategy is employed when* $\mathcal{M}_c \leq \mathcal{T}_{min}$.

The values of the maximal threshold $\mathcal{T}_{max}$ and the minimal threshold $\mathcal{T}_{min}$ mainly depend on the load of the system and the length of the bursty periods; and they can be obtained heuristically or experimentally. Given that the mean total queue memory consumed by a CQ processing system is $\bar{\mathcal{M}}$ memory units, we define the values of these threshold parameters in our system as

$$\begin{cases} \mathcal{T}_{max} = min\left(\frac{1+\alpha}{2}\mathcal{M}, \beta\mathcal{M}\right); \; \alpha = \frac{\bar{\mathcal{M}}}{\mathcal{M}} \\ \mathcal{T}_{min} = min\left(\bar{\mathcal{M}}, \beta\mathcal{T}_{max}\right); \quad 0.5 < \beta < 1 \end{cases} \tag{6.8}$$

In Equation (6.8), β is a safety factor that guarantees a minimal memory buffer zone between the normal mode and the saving mode, which prevents a system from frequently oscillating between the memory saving mode and the normal mode. A smaller value of β causes a longer tuple latency. Therefore, its value is recommended to be in the range of 0.5 to 1.0. α is used to adjust the threshold values as the system load changes. The mean total queue size increases as the system load increases, which causes α to increase. When α approaches 1, the $\frac{1+\alpha}{2}\mathcal{M}$ factor approaches the maximal available queue memory $\mathcal{M}$. That is why we need $\beta\mathcal{M}$ to guarantee that there is a minimal buffer between the $\mathcal{T}_{max}$ and $\mathcal{M}$. We use $\beta = 0.9$ in our system. Our experiments show these parameters work well in general.

In a practical system, we have to monitor the current queue memory in order to determine when to switch the mode. But the cost to this is small because:

1. each queue in our system maintains its current queue size and the tuple size, and the current queue memory is the sum of the memory used by each queue;
2. instead of computing the current queue memory by the end of each time, we compute it by the end of each time interval. The length of time interval is dynamically determined based on current queue memory. If the current total queue memory size is far away from the total available memory size, a longer time interval is used. Otherwise, a shorter interval is used.

[6] The queue memory here refers to the memory available for input queues, not including the memory consumed for maintaining the state information (synopsis) of an operator.

Therefore, the overall overhead incurred by the threshold strategy has very little impact on the system performance. As the mean load of the system increases, the period for which the system stays under the memory saving mode increases and the overall tuple latency becomes worse. When there is no more memory available for the internal queues under the memory saving mode, load shedding techniques have to be used to relieve the system from suffering from a shortage of memory. Load shedding will be discussed in detail in Chapter 7.

6.3.5 CQ Plan Characteristics

In this section, we briefly discuss how different execution plans of a CQ impact the performance of a system under the proposed scheduling strategies. A logical CQ can be implemented as different physical query plans. Based on our analysis of the scheduling strategies, we find that the following points are helpful for choosing the right physical execution plan in order to improve the system performance.

Push `Select` and `Project` Operators Down

Both the PC and the segment strategy can benefit from the lower selectivity of a leaf operator and from the earlier `project` operator. From Equation (6.2), we know that: (*i*) the lower selectivity of a leaf operator dramatically increases the processing capacity and the memory release capacity of an operator path or segment; (*ii*) the down-side `project` operators can decrease the output size of the tuples earlier and the released memory can be quickly reused. Therefore, both tuple latency and memory requirements of an operator path or segment can be optimized by pushing the selection and the `project` as far down as possible in a physical query plan.

Make the Operator Path Short

The processing capacity of an operator path or segment depends not only on the selectivity of the individual operator, but also on the number of the operators. Making an operator path short may not increase the processing capacity of an operator path or segment because the service time of an individual operator may increase. For example, by incorporating a `project` operator into a `select` operator, we can shorten the operator path without increasing the processing rate of the path. However, the number of times an output tuple is buffered decreases, which can decrease the tuple latency and the scheduling overhead of a scheduling strategy as well. In addition, fewer number of operators in a path makes it much easier to control or estimate the tuple latency.

6.3.6 Starvation-Free Scheduling

All the scheduling strategies discussed so far are priority driven strategies. Under an overloaded system some paths/segments may have to wait for a longer period to be scheduled or even not scheduled at all theoretically. To overcome the starvation problem, we discuses two simple solutions here. The solutions we present here are applicable to all strategies discussed in this chapter. Furthermore, an operator path and an operator segment are used interchangeably in this subsection.

Periodically Schedule the Path With the Oldest Tuple in its Input Queue

A straightforward solution to the starvation problem is to periodically schedule the path with the oldest tuple in its input queues in our proposed strategies. The length of the period to schedule the oldest operator path depends on the load of a system and the QoS requirement of its applications.

Dynamic Priority

Another solution is to change the priority of the strategies periodically. The total waiting queue size and the age of the oldest tuple of an operator path characterize its activities, such as the mean input rate, schedule frequency, and so on. In order to avoid the starvation problem, we consider the total waiting queue size and age of the oldest tuple as two additional factors of the priority of an operator path. And we define the priority factor f_i of the operator path i as:

$$f_i = \tau_i Q_i$$

where τ_i is the normalized waiting time of the oldest tuple in the input queue of the path i; Q_i is the normalized total current queue size of that operator path. Therefore, the new capacity of an operator path $\hat{C}_i^P = C_i^P f_i$. Evidently, as the age increases, the queue size increases as well, which makes the priority factor f_i increase exponentially. During a highly bursty input period, its priority factor increases too. Eventually, the oldest path will be scheduled.

Although the above solutions can solve the starvation or long waiting problem due to the temporary overload (the overall input rate of the system is greater than its overall processing rate), they cannot reduce the system load. Once the load of a system is beyond the maximal capacity it can handle, load shedding [93, 126, 132] or sampling techniques have to be used to relieve the load, which is beyond the capability of a scheduling strategy. However, a run-time optimizer needs to be aware as to when these techniques need to be used.

6.4 Experimental Validation

We have implemented the proposed scheduling strategies as part of the prototype of a QoS-aware DSMS [127, 130]. In this section, we discuss the results of various experiments that we have conducted in order to compare the performance of these scheduling strategies.

6.4.1 Setup

We begin with a brief description of our experimental setup. The scheduling strategies we have implemented include: the PC strategy, the Chain strategy, the MOS strategy, the SS strategy, the Threshold strategy, and various round-robin strategies. We use the following data streams and CQs in our experiments. The scheduling model used for the experiments is the model discussed in Section 6.1.1. An object is moved from the waiting queue to the eligible queue if the number of waiting tuples exceeds a threshold value which is the number of operators in that object times 100.

We only need the strategies that do a better job during high-load situations in the system. A strategy that can do a much better job during light load periods is not very useful if it cannot do a better job during high load or bursty periods. Therefore, the performance reported in this chapter is the performance of each strategy from the same periods and during those periods, the system is overloaded at least for a period of time.

Input Data Streams

The input data streams we used are highly bursty streams and the input rate of each stream is controlled by a global bursty factor and a local bursty factor. Since we are interested in the behavior of the strategy during heavy load periods, we don't present results for normal or light load periods. Therefore, only the performance data during the heavy load periods are reported and compared.

The global burst factor is a 3-phase period. Each stream is generated by repeating the 3-phase period with an increasing standard mean rate. Each phase lasts about 20 minutes. In the first phase, the mean input rate is 2 times of the standard mean rate. In the second phase, the standard mean rate is used. In the last phase, a much lower input rate is used, which is one quarter of the standard mean rate. In order to test how strategies react to the overload situations, we continuously increase, by 5 percent or so, the standard mean input rate each time when we repeat the 3-phase pattern until the system is overloaded (When the maximal memory requirement is larger than 2M bytes, we regard the system as overloaded).

The local burst factor is a so-called self-similarity factor. Given the mean input rate of each phase of each period, at each time unit (second in this book), the input rate is controlled by the so called self-similarity property of each stream. This self-similarity property is due to each input stream being a superposition of 64 or 128 flows. Each flow alternates ON/OFF periods, and it only sends tuples during its ON periods. The tuple inter-arrival time follows an exponential distribution during its ON periods. The lengths of both the ON and the OFF periods are generated from a Pareto distribution which has a probability mass function $P(x) = ab^a x^{-(a+1)}, x \geq b$. We use $a = 1.4$ for the ON period and $a = 1.2$ for the OFF period. For more detailed information about self-similar traffic, please refer to [316]. In our experiment, we use 5 such self-similar input data streams with different mean input rates.

Query Plans for the Experiment

All of our queries are CQs that consist of `select`, `project`, and `symmetric hash join` operators. To be more close to a real application, we ran 16 actual CQs with 116 operators over 5 different data streams in our system. The selectivity of each operator is widely distributed ranging from 0 to 1. Both the selectivity and the processing capacity of each operator can be determined by collecting statistical information periodically during run time. The details of the list of queries and their properties can be found in [128].

The prototype is implemented in C++, and all the experiments were run on a dedicated dual processor Alpha machine with 2GB of RAM. One of the processors was used to collect experiment results while the other processor was used for query processing.

6.4.2 Evaluation of Scheduling Strategies

Due to the fact that the CQs are also long-running queries and that the scheduling strategies demonstrate different performance during different system load periods, we ran each experiment for more than 24 hours (including the statistics collection period), and each experiment consists of multiple phases. In each phase, we intentionally increased the average input rates of data streams in order to study and validate the performance characteristics of a scheduling strategy under different system loads. We only present a portion of our experimental results (from a few phases), rather than a full range of results due to limited space. For threshold strategy, we set the maximal threshold $\mathcal{T}_{max}$ to 10M bytes, which means it employs the PC strategy when its total queue size is less than 10Mbytes. Otherwise, it employs the MOS strategy to decrease total queue size requirement.

Tuple Latency

The tuple latency of an output tuple is computed by taking the difference of its arrival timestamp and its departure timestamp when it leaves the query processing system. We presented two sets of our experiments for the proposed scheduling strategies in Figure 6.8 and Figure 6.9 respectively. The tuple latencies shown in both figures are the average tuple latency of all output tuples within every 1 second.

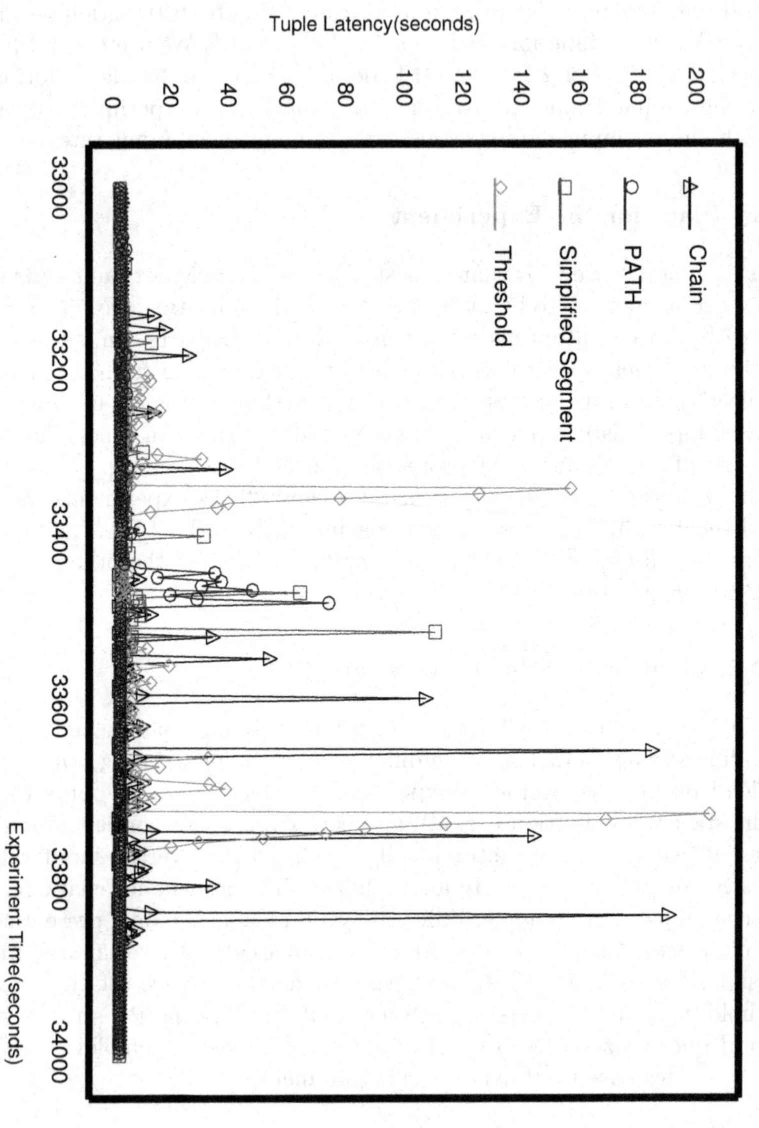

Fig. 6.8. Tuple Latency Vs. Time

From the results in Figure 6.8, we observe that the overall tuple latency is much better under the PC strategy than under the SS strategy and the Chain strategy. The Chain strategy performs worst among them. Furthermore, the overall tuple latency increases as the system load increases, but the difference among them becomes much sharper as the system load increases. The threshold strategy has a tuple latency as good as the PC strategy when total queue size is less than 10M bytes (i.e., from 33200 to 33300 along the X-axis). However it performs as bad as the MOS strategy during heavy bursty periods (i.e., from 33600 to 33800 along the X-axis). It is worth noting that during light load periods (i.e., the first 200 seconds in Figure 6.8, which is from 33000 to 33200 along X-axis), all of them have a reasonable tuple latency except that the Chain strategy has a few spikes. When the system load increases, the tuple latency increases sharply during the highly bursty input periods for both the SS strategy and the Chain strategy. As we explained earlier, the high tuple latency under the Chain strategy and the SS strategy contributes to their buffered tuples in the middle of an operator path. The SS strategy performs better than the Chain strategy because it buffers a tuple less number of times along an operator path than the Chain strategy.

The tuple latency shown in Figure 6.9 further confirms the conclusions that we derived from the first set of experiments: the PC strategy achieves a much better tuple latency than the Chain strategy. The figure also shows that the MOS strategy achieves a better tuple latency than the Chain strategy, but a longer tuple latency than the PC strategy. This is due to the fact that MOS is a kind of segment strategy.

Throughput

The total throughput of a CQ processing system under any scheduling strategy should be the same because it should output the same number of output tuples, no matter what scheduling strategy it employs. However, the output patterns are likely to be dramatically different under different scheduling strategies. Figures 6.10 and 6.11 show the output patterns under different strategies. In order to clearly show the difference, we use the logarithm scale along Y-axis in Figure 6.11.

In Figure 6.10, the PC strategy and the SS strategy have a much smoother output rate than the Chain strategy, and the threshold strategy has the characteristics of both the PC strategy and the MOS strategy. The PC strategy performs best among them in terms of the smoothness of output. The output rate under all four strategies increases as the input rates increase when the system load is moderate, which is the first 300 seconds in Figure 6.10 from 33000 to 33300 along X-axis, and their output patterns do not differ with each other too much. After the system enters the high load periods, the PC strategy and the SS strategy have a much smoother throughput than the other two during the high bursty input periods which are the periods of the 10400 second to 11000 second and from the 12400 second to 12800 second along X-axis. In contrast, the Chain strategy has a very low throughput, even no throughput during heavy load periods. On the other hand, it has a surprisingly high throughput immediately when system load decreases. Its highest

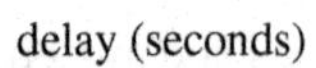
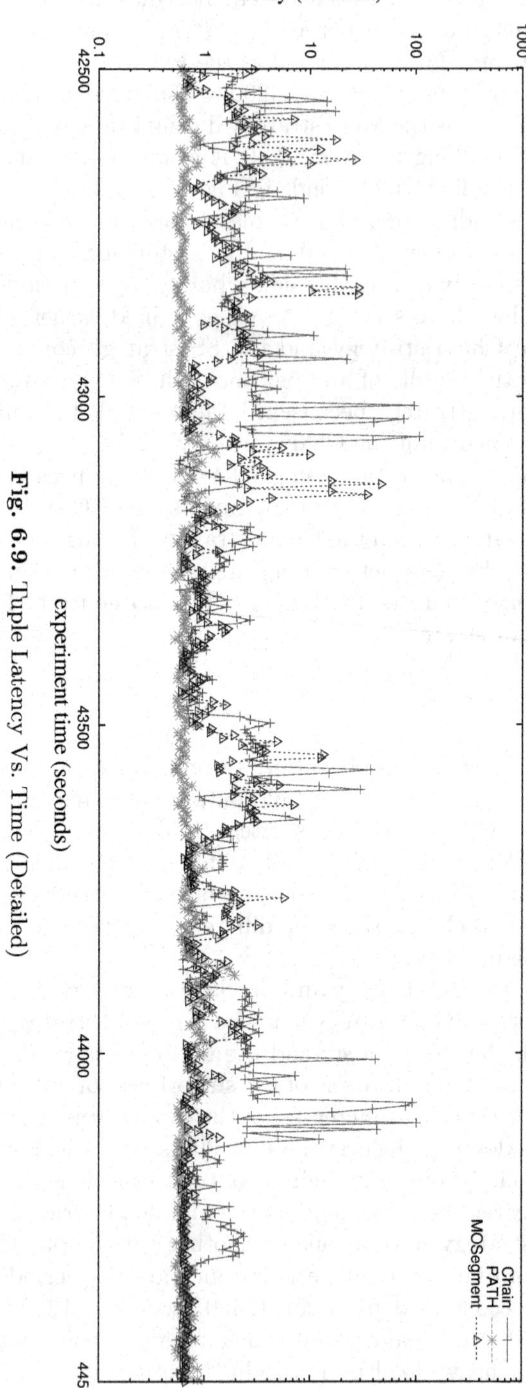

Fig. 6.9. Tuple Latency Vs. Time (Detailed)

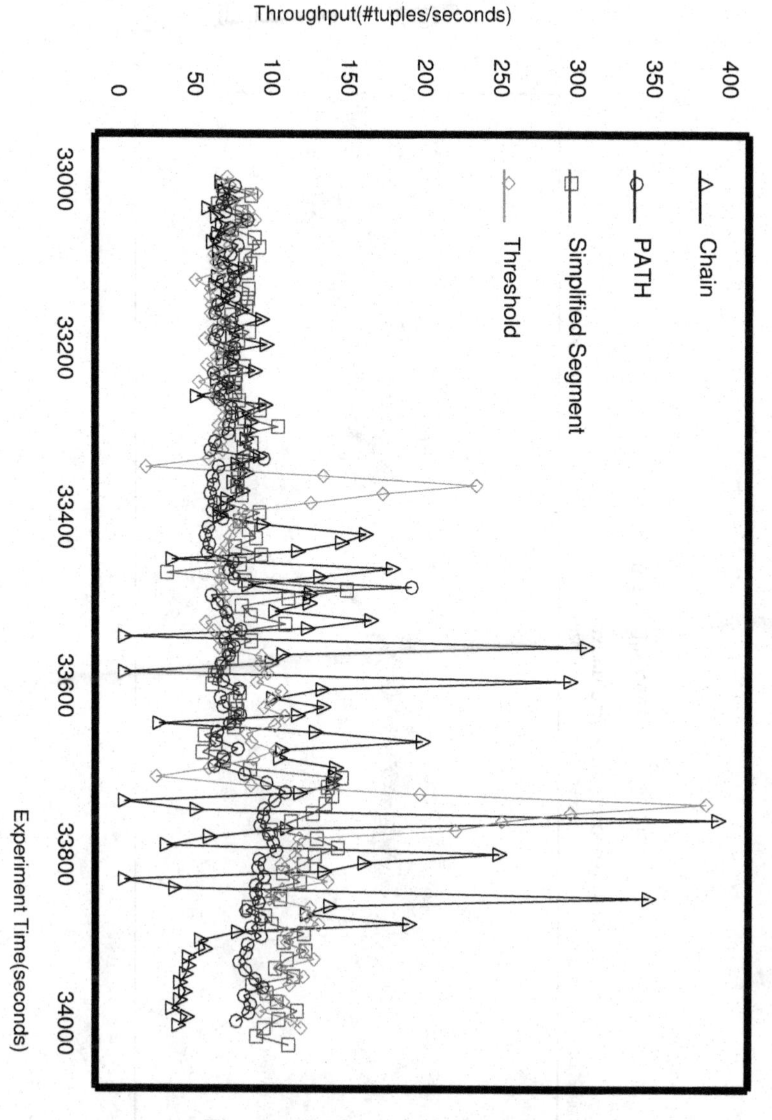

Fig. 6.10. Throughput Vs. Time

output rate is almost 4 times its average output rate. The situation becomes worse when the system load or the length of the highly bursty input periods increases. This highly bursty output rate is not desirable because of the amount of partial results that have to be buffered in the system temporarily, which consumes unnecessary memory.

The throughput patterns shown in Figure 6.11 further confirm that the PC strategy has a much smoother throughput pattern than the Chain strategy.

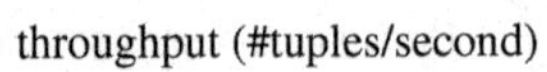

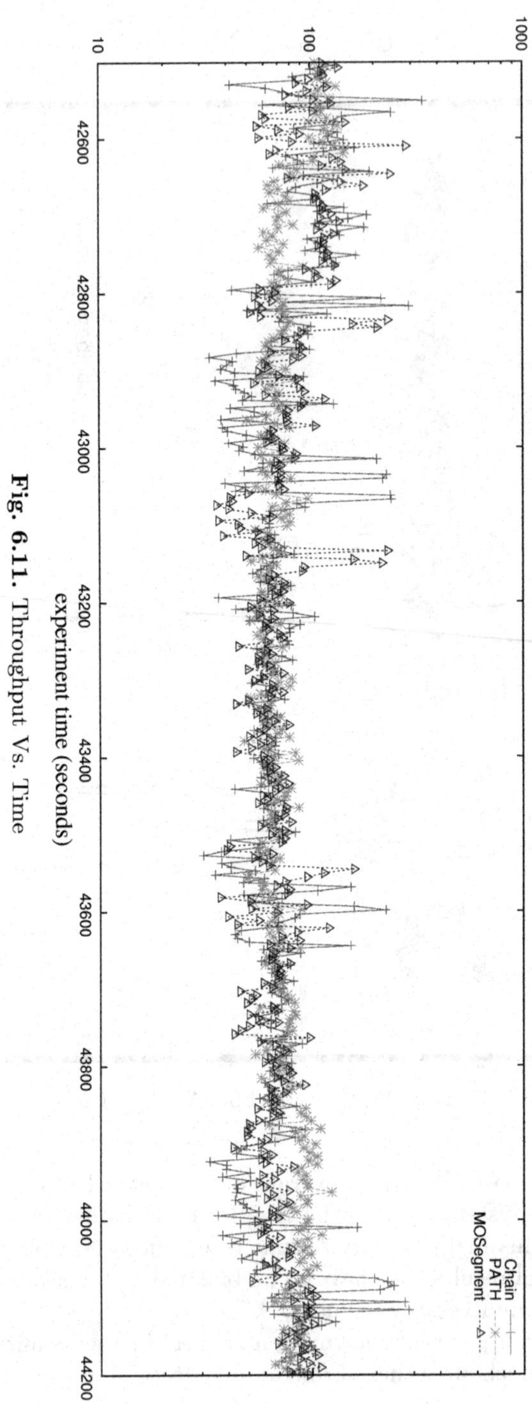

Fig. 6.11. Throughput Vs. Time

The figure also shows that the MOS strategy has a smoother throughput than the Chain strategy during the high load periods. During the low load periods, all strategies have similar throughput patterns.

Memory Requirement

We study the total memory requirement of a CQ processing system under different scheduling strategies for the same input pattern. The amount of memory consumed by the query processing system is measured by calculating the memory consumed by all input queues every one second. The memory consumed by each input queue is the total number of tuples waiting in the queue times the size of the tuple. The amount of memory consumed by the scheduling strategies proposed in this chapter is presented in Figures 6.12 and 6.13. The Y-axis in Figure 6.13 is the logarithm of the amount of memory consumed by the query processing system.

From the results presented in Figure 6.12, we observe that the Chain strategy performs better than the others. The Chain strategy and the SS strategy can absorb the extra memory requirement during the bursty input periods when system load is not high. Although the PC strategy has the capability to absorb the temporary high bursty input, its ability is much less than the other two strategies. The reason, as we mentioned earlier, is that the leaf nodes have a much larger memory release capacity than the other nodes of a query plan and that the memory release capacity of an operator path is much less than that of a leaf node. As the system load or the length of a bursty period increases, the PC strategy requires much more memory to temporarily buffer the unprocessed tuples than the other two strategies. The SS strategy requires a little bit more memory than the Chain strategy during the highly bursty periods. This is because it only takes benefit of the larger memory release capacities of the leaf nodes that are major part of the operators with a larger memory release capacity in a CQ processing system, but not all of them behave like the Chain strategy. The threshold strategy has a similar memory requirement as the PC strategy during the first 300 seconds in Figure 6.12, which is from 33000 to 33300 in X-axis. It then switches to the Chain strategy and maintains its total memory requirement around 10M bytes, which is similar to the Chain strategy.

From the results shown in Figure 6.13, we can see that the MOS strategy has a smaller memory requirement than the Chain strategy and the PC strategy has the largest memory requirement. This is due to that (*i*) the MOS strategy does not buffer tuples in the middle of a segment, which is unavoidable for the Chain strategy; (*ii*) the overhead introduced by MOS strategy is smaller than the Chain strategy. The PC strategy requires much more memory than the MOS and Chain strategy because it does not take advantage of the higher memory release capacity of the operators at the bottom side of an operator path.

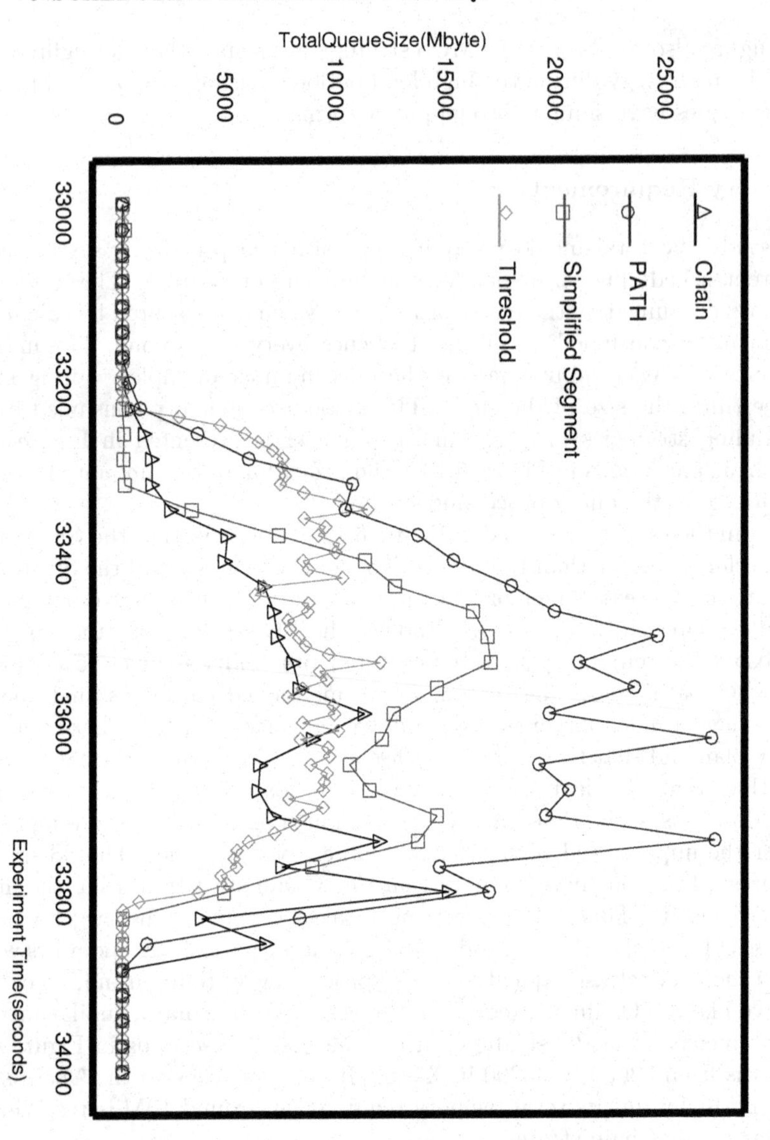

Fig. 6.12. Total Memory Requirement Vs. Time

As can be seen from the above evaluation, the analytical behavior is matched by the experimental results. The behavior of various CQ scheduling strategies proposed is as expected confirming our theoretical analysis.

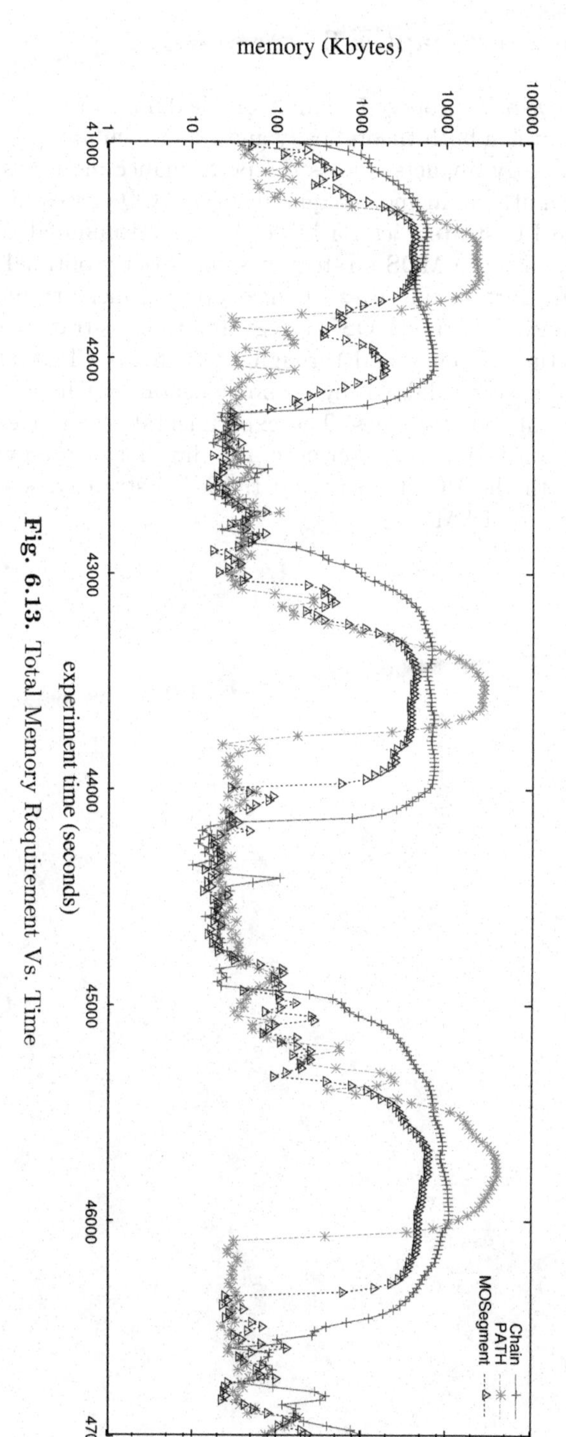

Fig. 6.13. Total Memory Requirement Vs. Time

6.5 Summary of Chapter 6

In this chapter, we have proposed a family of scheduling strategies for a DSMS and investigated them both theoretically and experimentally. We showed how a scheduling strategy impacts/affects the performance metrics such as tuple latency, throughput, and memory requirement of a CQ processing system. We proved that the PC strategy can achieve the overall minimal tuple latency. We also proved that the MOS strategy has the strictly optimal memory requirement, which further improves the near optimal memory requirement of the Chain strategy. Both the MOS strategy and the SS strategy demonstrate a much better tuple latency and throughput than the Chain strategy. The theoretical results were validated by an implementation where we performed experiments on all the strategies. The experimental results clearly validate our theoretical conclusions. Furthermore, the threshold strategy inherits the properties of both the PC strategy and the MOS strategy, which makes it more applicable to a DSMS.

7

LOAD SHEDDING IN DATA STREAM MANAGEMENT SYSTEMS

In this chapter, we focus on a fundamental problem that is central to a DSMS. Namely, we investigate the problem of `load shedding` during temporary overload periods. This problem is not an issue in a traditional DBMS since:

- its queries are one-time queries;
- its data sources, although large, are static in nature;
- there is no support for QoS requirements for query processing.

In contrast, multiple CQs in a DSMS are active simultaneously for a long period of time. Theoretically, a CQ can be active in the system forever. The input rates of input streams are uncontrollable and highly dynamic in many stream-based applications. This highly dynamic input rate can prevent the system from keeping up with the tuple processing rate during high input rate periods. As a result, a large amount of unprocessed or partially processed tuples can be backlogged in the system, and tuple latency can increase without bound. Due to the predefined QoS requirements of a CQ, the query results that violate their QoS requirements may become useless or even cause major problems. Therefore, we need to limit the number of tuples buffered in the system so that all final query results satisfy their predefined QoS requirements. A feasible and viable solution to limit the number of buffered tuples in the system is to gracefully drop a portion of its unprocessed or partially processed tuples during high input periods, thereby relieving system load, and making it feasible to satisfy predefined QoS requirements. This process of gracefully dropping tuples is called `load shedding`. It should be pointed out that the accuracy of final query results is degraded due to loss of tuples in a load shedding process. Fortunately, many stream-based applications can tolerate some inaccuracy (i.e., approximate instead of precise results) in final query results if we are able to guarantee an upper bound on the inaccuracy. Generally speaking, `load shedding` is the mechanism for preventing final query results from violating predefined QoS requirements by discarding a portion of unprocessed or partially processed tuples. The predefined QoS requirements considered in this chapter mainly include the Maximal Tolerable Tuple Latency (MTTL)

S. Chakravarthy and Q. Jiang, *Stream Data Processing: A Quality of Service Perspective*, Advances in Database Systems 36, DOI: 10.1007/978-0-387-71003-7_7,

and the Maximal Tolerable Relative Error (MTRE) of a CQ in its final query results.

In this chapter, we propose a framework and a set of techniques [126, 128, 132] for a general load shedding strategy by dynamically activating `load shedders` in query plans or deactivating active load shedders based on the estimation of current system load. These load shedders drop tuples in either a randomized manner or using user-specified application semantics. Specifically,

1. We exploit the optimal physical implementation of shedders in DSMSs with a goal of minimizing computation overhead and memory-consumption of a shedder.
2. We develop techniques to estimate system load to implicitly determine when load shedding is needed and how much needs to be shed.
3. We develop algorithms to compute the optimal placement of a load shedder in a query plan.
4. We also develop algorithms that determine how to distribute the total number of tuples (in terms of percentage) to be dropped among all load shedders with the goal of minimizing the total relative errors in the final query results due to load shedding.
5. Finally, we perform extensive experiments to validate the effectiveness and the efficiency of proposed load shedding techniques.

The rest of the chapter is organized as follows. Section 7.1 provides a formal definition of the load shedding problem. Section 7.2 discusses the detailed physical implementation of shedders. Section 7.3 describes our load estimation and load shedding algorithms. Section 7.4 presents a prototype implementation and the experimental results. Section 7.5 summarizes the chapter.

7.1 The Load Shedding Problem

In a multiple query processing system over streaming data, various scheduling strategies have been proposed either to minimize the maximum memory requirements [111, 131] and tuple latency [131] or to maximize the throughput [167]. A scheduling strategy can improve the usage of the limited resources in such a system. However, it can never improve the maximal computational capacity of a system, which is inherently determined by its fixed amount of resources such as CPU cycles, size of RAM, and so on. When the total load of active queries in a system exceeds the maximal computational capacity of the system, the query processing system has to either temporarily backlog some unprocessed or partial processed tuples that cannot be processed immediately in queues (or buffers) or discard them immediately. However, if the tuples are temporarily backlogged in queues, this causes a longer tuple latency, which is theoretically unbounded (as the queue size can grow indefinitely). Depending upon applications, this longer tuple latency may be unacceptable. Fortunately, most of these applications can tolerate approximate results. Therefore, discarding extra tuples in the system is a natural choice to avoid a longer tuple latency.

Our focus is to address how to limit the number of tuples that can be backlogged in the system to satisfy both tuple latency and approximation requirements of final query results based on predefined QoS specifications. We call this scenario in which the system has to discard the tuples in order to prevent the system from violating the predefined QoS requirements of its queries as `query processing congestion`, a problem very similar to the concept of `network congestion` used by the network community. The network congestion problem has been extensively researched in the computer network fields and the techniques proposed to deal with this problem can be classified into two categories: (*a*) `congestion avoidance` techniques [321], which are used to prevent the system from entering a congestion situation and (*b*) `congestion control` techniques [322,323], which are used to bring a system back from a congestion situation once the system enters the congestion situation. These two techniques are complementary and usually used together.

In this chapter, we present a general approach to `query processing congestion avoidance` problem for a DSMS to prevent the system from entering query processing congestion through dynamic activation of load shedders. This approach is different from those query congestion control techniques, which drop tuples only after they find the predefined QoS requirements have been violated through monitoring final query results. Specifically, we formulate the load shedding problem as follows:

Problem 7.1. Given a multiple query processing system with k active queries $\mathcal{Q} = \{Q_1, Q_2, \cdots, Q_k\}$ over n streams $\mathcal{I} = \{I_1, I_2, \cdots, I_n\}$, and each query with its predefined QoS requirement specified in terms of its maximal tolerable tuple latency and its maximal tolerable relative error of query results, the load shedding problem is to guarantee minimal computation resources, which make it possible to satisfy all predefined QoS requirements in the system by gracefully dropping some tuples, and at the same time, minimizing the relative errors in the system introduced by dropping tuples.

The load shedding problem is an optimization problem, and consists of three sub problems, namely:

1. how to efficiently and effectively estimate the current system load, which implicitly determines when we need to do load shedding in order to avoid a query processing congestion. It also implicitly determines how much load we have to shed in order not to violate the predefined QoS requirements in the system;
2. how to find the best position for a potential load shedder that we need to insert into queries so that the introduced relative error in final query results can be minimized and at the same time the load saved can be maximized by discarding one tuple;

3. how to find an optimal allocation strategy for allocating the total shedding load among all non-active load shedders with a goal of minimizing the overall relative errors among all queries.

Additionally, the problem of how to implement shedders so that the overhead introduced by the shedders themselves is minimized is also very important in order to minimize the impact of the load shedding process on system performance. We will first discuss the characteristics of a shedder and then present our algorithms for the subproblems of the load shedding problem.

7.2 Integrating Load Shedders

The main task of a load shedder is to shed load by discarding a number of tuples from the system. However, this process has a significant impact on both system performance and accuracy of final query results. It affects system performance mainly because: (*a*) the system load is very high when a system activates the load shedding mechanism. Any additional overhead introduced at this time affects both tuple latency and peak memory requirement, and (*b*) the actual load is shed through a number of load shedders collaboratively. The total load (or overhead) introduced by the load shedders can be substantial. By decreasing the overhead introduced by load shedders themselves, it is not only possible to increase effective system usage, but also improve the accuracy of final query results (less number of tuples will be discarded). Also different tuples may have different contribution to the final query results. More errors in final query results are introduced if more important (or contributing more to the error) tuples are discarded. Therefore, it is desirable for a load shedder to shed as few tuples as possible which in turn reduces the errors in final query results. In the following section, we discuss how a load shedder can achieve this desirable property. We will discuss how a load shedder can benefit from its placement along an operator path to achieve its desirable property in Section 7.3.2.

Currently, a load shedder is considered as a `drop` operator in many DSMSs. It is inserted into the current query operator network and deleted from the network dynamically according to the system load. This case is illustrated in Figure 7.1-a and 7.1-c. In case (a), the drop operator is considered a normal operator, its functionality is to determine whether to drop a tuple or not; its input queue is used to buffer its inputs because of bursty input modes in data streams. In this case, for each input tuple, we have to make a function call to determine whether to drop it or not. First, the total cost of hundreds (or thousands) of such function calls is likely to be high although the cost of each function call in itself is very small in current operating systems. Second, the extra memory required by its input queue increases the peak memory requirement. Finally, the scheduling cost increases as well because of the increase in the number of operators. In case (c), the drop operator is considered as

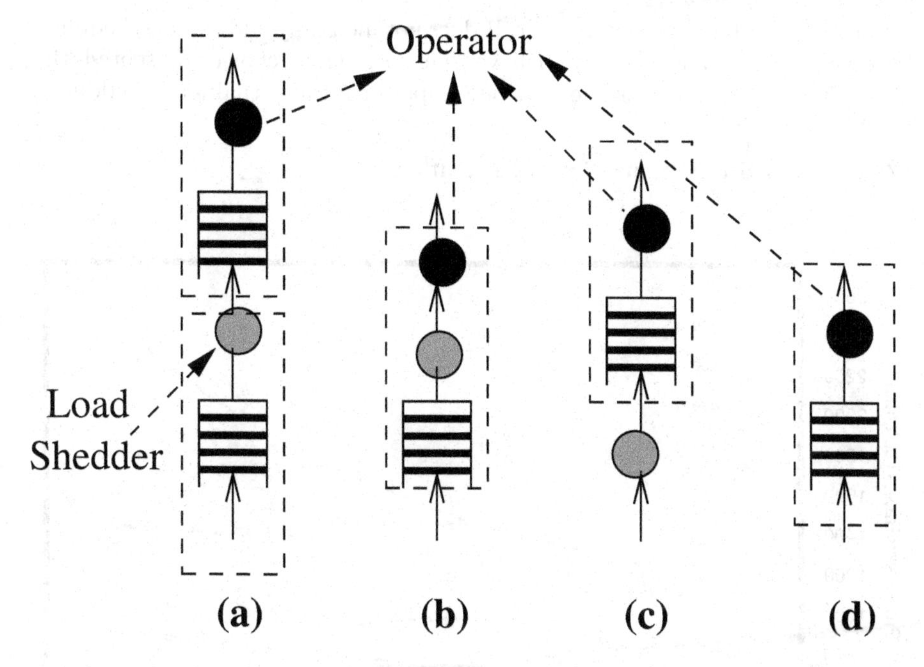

Fig. 7.1. Load Shedders

a special operator. Since it does not have its own input queue, it cannot be scheduled as a normal object. It has to process its inputs whenever the inputs arrive, which means it has to be run as a thread. Although it does not require any extra memory, its processing cost increases due to the context switch cost of a thread. Therefore, it may not be a good choice to shed load by inserting a drop operator into the query network dynamically.

We consider shedding as one of the functions of a normal operator in the system. There are two places where we can incorporate the shedding function into a normal operator: the operator and its input queue, illustrated in Figures 7.1-b and 7.1-d respectively. In Figure 7.1-b, the shedding function determines whether the input tuple needs to be passed to its operator. In this case, the processing cost is the same as that of case (a) and case (c). However, it does not introduce any additional overhead cost for scheduling because it is considered as part of a normal operator. On the other hand, a tuple is shed before its processing and is queued in the buffer prior to that. The time spent in the buffer prior to it being discarded will unnecessarily increase the memory requirements. In Figure 7.1-d, the shedding function is incorporated into its input queue. When its input queue receives a tuple, it accepts it only when the tuple passes the shedding function and the load shedding function is enabled. This case decreases the processing cost by incorporating the shedding function as part of enqueue function of its input queue. It also decreases the peak memory requirement because it discards the tuples immediately if those tuples will not be processed further. It does not incur any additional scheduling overhead either. Therefore, we believe that, of the four choices presented, the last case (Figure 7.1-d) is the best one to perform the actual load shedding.

7.2.1 Load Shedder as Part of a Buffer

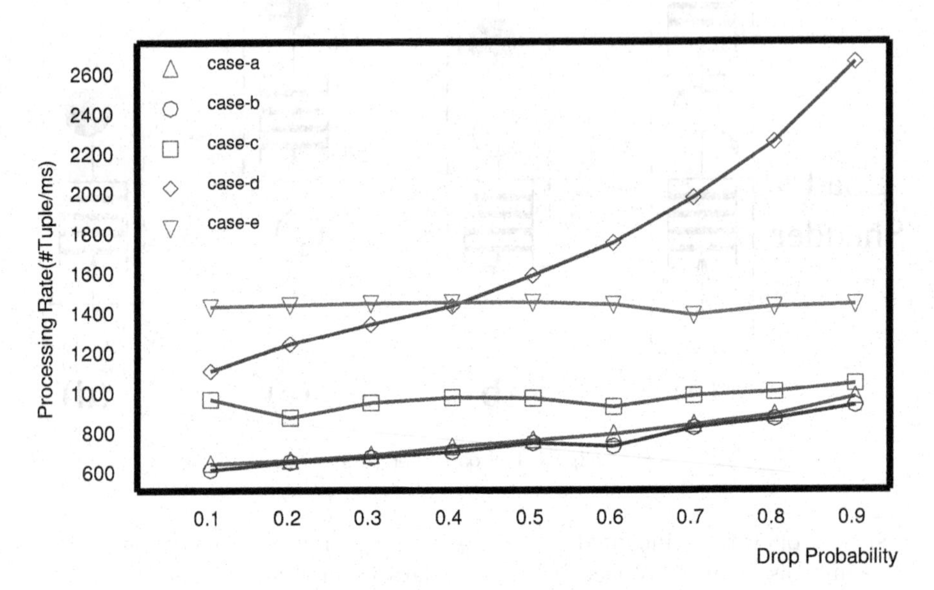

Fig. 7.2. Cost of Load Shedders

As the incorporation of shedding function into a CQ plan has big impact on the overall performance of the DSMS, experiments were conducted to compare the cost of four different load shedders presented above. Figure 7.2 shows the processing rate of a `select` operator with and without a load shedder as the drop probability of the shedder increases. Case-{a,b,c,d} in Figure 7.2 corresponds to the `select` operator with four (a,b,c,d) different implementation of a shedder discussed earlier in Figure 7.1. Case-e corresponds to the cost of the `select` operator *without a load shedder.*

The processing rate is the number of tuples consumed by both shedder and `select` operator per millisecond. This graph clearly shows that case-d performs much better than all the other cases. As drop probability of the shedder increases, the processing rate in case-d increases much faster than other cases. This is mainly because of the lower cost of discarding a tuple in this case as compared to the others. The processing rate of case-e remains flat because it does not shed load. All other cases (a, b, and c) indicate that the cost of the shedder is much higher than the cost of of a `select` operator. Although this experiment was performed for the `select` operator, it is easy to see that the overhead incurred by the cases is independent of the computation and only depends on the where the load shedding function is included.

7.2.2 Types of Load Shedders

A load shedder can introduce less error in final query results by discarding less important tuples. Two kinds of load shedders are proposed in the literature [93]: *random shedders* and *semantic shedders.* A random shedder is implemented as a p `gate` function; for a tuple, it generates a random value $\acute{p}$. The tuple passes to the next operator if $\acute{p} \geq p$; otherwise, it is discarded. A semantic shedder discards tuples that are less important to final query results. For example, in a continuous query for detecting fire alarm over a temperature stream, the lower values in that temperature stream are less important than higher values. It is natural to drop lower values first in order to get less errors in final query results. A semantic shedder acts functionally as a `select` operator, which drops less important tuples based on a condition that has selectivity of $1 - p$ in order to drop p percent of its tuples. A discarded tuple by a semantic shedder introduces less error in final query results. However, it requires specific information from a query and its application domain in order to determine the relative importance of a tuple in a stream.

We propose four kinds of semantic shedders over a numerical attribute in our system:

1. *Smallest-first shedder* that discards tuples with smallest values first;
2. *Largest-first shedder* that discards the tuples with largest values first;
3. *Center-first shedder* that discards the tuples nearest to a user-specified center;
4. *Outlier-first shedder* that discards the tuples that are farthest away from a user-specified center.

When users submit queries, they can specify different load shedders based on their application needs.

In our load shedding system, we support both kinds of shedders (random and semantic). If a semantic shedder is applicable, we assume that there exists a function between the selectivity of the shedder and the relative error in the final query results. For all the other cases, we assume that all tuples in the same data stream have equal importance to the accuracy of the final results of a query.

7.3 Load Shedding Framework

The query processing congestion avoidance techniques that we propose consist of two components: `system load estimation` and `load shedding`. The *system load estimation* component is used to estimate the actual computation load based on current input rates of data streams and characteristics of active continuous queries registered in the system. This estimated load is used to determine when to activate the load shedding mechanism and how much load to shed once it detects a query processing congestion. The *load shedding* component is used to execute the actual load shedding, which includes computing the optimal placement/location of load shedders in order to minimize the error introduced, and how to allocate and distribute the total load shedding requirement among non-active load shedders. The system load estimation component proposed is independent of the load shedding component, and can be used in conjunction with any load shedding approaches (e.g., the load shedding techniques proposed for aggregation queries [112]).

7.3.1 Prediction of Query Processing Congestion

Consider a general query processing system with m active queries in the system over n data streams (denoted by $I_1, I_2, \cdots, I_n$). Each query Q_i has its predefined QoS requirements specified by its maximal tolerable tuple latency L_i and its maximal tolerable relative error E_i in final query results. The actual computation load of such a system at a time instant is completely determined by the input characteristics of its data streams and the characteristics of the queries (operators of queries) at that time instant in the system. Let us assume that we know[1] the current input rates v_i of input stream I_i. Then we can estimate its actual computation load for such a given query processing system as follows.

Without loss of generality, m active queries in the system can be further decomposed into k operator paths[2] $\mathcal{P} = \{p_1, p_2, \cdots, p_k\}$. To prevent a query from violating its predefined QoS requirements (i.e., L_i and E_i), we have to guarantee that the output results from each of its operator paths do not violate its QoS requirements. Therefore, we push the QoS requirements of a query down to each operator path that is encompassed in this query. As a result, each operator path has QoS requirements for the final results from this path. These QoS requirements are the same as those of its query. For operator path p_i, the query processing system has to process all the tuples that arrived during the last L_i time units in order not to violate the MTTL L_i no matter what the scheduling strategy is. It may schedule the operators along the path multiple times within that L_i time units, or schedule some operators of that path more often than others, but the age[3] of the oldest unprocessed or partially processed tuple left in the queues along that operator path must be less than L_i. Therefore, without considering the cost of scheduling, its minimal

[1] Actually, we can measure them directly, which will be discussed in Section 7.3.1.
[2] In this chapter, an operator path means a simple operator path and a complex operator path is partitioned into multiple simple operator paths. Each simple path is defined as a unique path from the leaf node to the root node.
[3] The age of a tuple is defined as the elapsed time after it enters the query processing system.

computation time T_i required for the operator path to process all the tuples arrived within L_i time units is

$$T_i = \frac{\int_{t-L_i}^{t} v_k(t)d_t}{C_i}; \qquad 1 \leq i \leq k \tag{7.1}$$

where $v_k(t)$ is the input rate of its input stream at time instant t, and C_i is the processing capacity of the operator path, as defined in Equation (6.2). The Equation (7.1) gives the minimal absolute computation time units the operator path p_i requires to be within its MTTL. Furthermore, the percentage of computation time units ϕ_i it requires is,

$$\phi_i = \frac{T_i}{L_i} \tag{7.2}$$

Equation (7.2) shows that the query processing system has to spend at least ϕ_i portion of its CPU cycles to process the tuples along the operator path p_i within every MTTL time units in order to guarantee that the query results do not violate its MTTL L_i.

Without considering shared-segments among operator paths in the system, the total percentage of computation time units Φ for a query processing system with k operator paths is:

$$\Phi = \sum_{i=1}^{k} \phi_i \tag{7.3}$$

by plugging Equation (7.1) and Equation (7.2) into Equation (7.3), it is easy to see that

$$\Phi = \sum_{i=1}^{k} \frac{\int_{t-L_i}^{t} v_k(t)d_t}{C_i L_i} \tag{7.4}$$

Due to the fact that the MTTL of a query ranges over no more than a few seconds, we can expect that the input rate during a MTTL period of time can be captured by its mean input rate. Then Equation (7.3) can be approximated as:

$$\Phi \approx \sum_{i=1}^{k} \frac{\bar{v}_k L_i}{C_i L_i} = \sum_{i=1}^{k} \frac{\bar{v}_k}{C_i} \tag{7.5}$$

where $\bar{v}_k$ is the mean input rate of the input stream of the operator path p_k within a period of time of its MTTL. It is also worth noting that the length of MTTL of an operator path does not have a direct relationship with the minimal percentage of computation time units it requires in order not to violate its MTTL requirements. Therefore, when two or more operator paths share a shared-segment, we do not need to deal with the problem of which MTTLs we have to use to compute the minimal percentage of computation time units it requires.

If the estimated total percentage of computation time units is greater than 1.0, the system will definitely experience a query processing congestion and the tuple latencies of some or all query results will be longer than those specified in their predefined QoS requirements. In order to avoid such a query processing congestion, we have to drop some tuples so that the total percentage of computation load is always less than 1.0. The total load Δ we have to shed is given as follows:

$$\Delta = \begin{cases} \Phi - 1.0 & ; \quad if\ \Phi > 1.0 \\ 0 & ; \quad if\ \Phi \leq 1.0 \end{cases} \tag{7.6}$$

For example, if the estimated total percentage of computation time units requires $\Phi = 1.25$, this means the system is short of 25% of computation time units. We have to shed enough tuples so that we can release at least 25% of computation time units in order to avoid a query processing congestion.

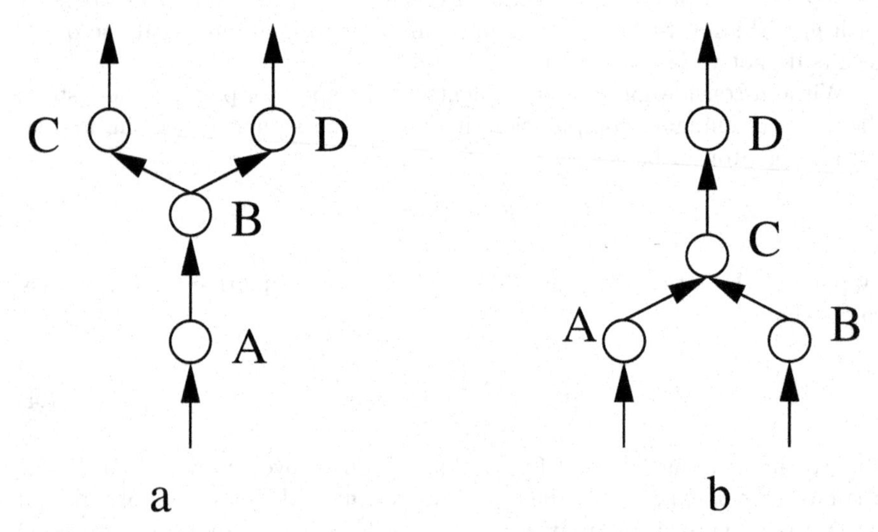

Fig. 7.3. A shared-Segment

In Equation (7.5), we have not considered sharing of segments by two or more operator paths. In a full-fledged DSMS, a shared-segment introduced by a common subexpression between two queries is a common way of performance optimization. For example, when two operator paths ABC, ABD share a segment AB, as illustrated in Figure 7.3–a, the total percentage of processing time units that we computed into Equation (7.5) for the shared-segment $\{AB\}$ is $P(AB)$ given by

$$P(AB) = \frac{l_{ABC}\bar{v}_{AB}}{C^S_{AB} l_{ABC}} + \frac{l_{ABD}\bar{v}_{AB}}{C^S_{AB} l_{ABD}} = 2\frac{\bar{v}_{AB}}{C^S_{AB}}$$

where C^S_{AB} is the processing capacity of the shared-segment AB. But the system actually spends only $\frac{\bar{v}_{AB}}{C^S_{AB}}$ portion of its computation time on the segment. Another $\frac{\bar{v}_{AB}}{C^S_{AB}}$ portion of computation time is overestimated.

Similarly, if k operator paths share a shared-segment, we have counted the processing time spent on that shared-segment k, $k \geq 2$ times in Equation (7.5), but the system only spends that processing time once, so we have overestimated it $k - 1$ times.

Assume that there are g shared-segments in the system, and that each of them is shared f_i times, where $f_i \geq 2$ and $1 \leq i \leq g$, the total percentage of computation time units overestimated due to those g sharing segments is $\mathcal{D}$, where

$$\mathcal{D} = \sum_{i=1}^{g} (f_i - 1) \frac{\bar{v}_i}{C^S_i} \tag{7.7}$$

and C^S_i is the processing capacity of the shared-segment which can be computed from Equation (6.2), and $\bar{v}_i$ is the mean input rate of the shared-segment.

Therefore, by taking the shared-segments into consideration, from Equation (7.5) and Equation (7.7), the total percentage of computation time units Φ:

$$\Phi \approx \sum_{i=1}^{k} \frac{\bar{v}_k}{C_i} - \sum_{j=1}^{g} (f_j - 1) \frac{\bar{v}_j}{C^S_j} \tag{7.8}$$

Equation (7.8) gives the approximate total percentage of the computation time units a query processing system requires given the input rates of its input data streams. From Equation (7.6), we know that the system will experience a query processing congestion if the estimated total percentage of computation time units is larger than 100%. The portion of the percentage of the computation time units exceeding 1.0 is what we have to shed in order to avoid a query processing congestion. Note that the total percentage of computation time units estimated here is the minimal total percentage needed by the system. The overhead incurred by other tasks in the system such as scheduling, monitoring or estimating the input rates of data streams, and so on, are not explicitly considered here. However, those costs actually are implicitly taken into consideration when we compute the processing capacity of an operator. The more time a system spends on processing other tasks, the less is the process rate of an operator.

Algorithm for Finding Shared-Segments

Each operator is identified by a unique label in a query processing system. As a result, an operator path is labeled by a sequence of operator labels

$\mathcal{X} = \{x_1, x_2, \cdots, x_n\}$, where $x_i, 1 \leq i \leq n$, is the label of ith operator along the path from the leaf node. Hereafter, we call $\mathcal{X}$ the **path string** of the operator path. In a general continuous query processing system over streaming data, a shared-segment between two or more operator paths exits due to query optimization through sharing of common sub-expressions among multiple queries. However, the sharing relationship between two or more operator paths may change dynamically or periodically in a DSMS because of (a) addition of newly registered query plans or deletion of currently active query plans; (b) periodic revision of an active query plan in order to adapt to the changes of input characteristics of input data streams, which further causes deletion and addition of a shared-segment. In order to handle the changes to the shared-segments, we propose an algorithm illustrated in Algorithm 4 which incrementally finds shared-segments and the number of times a shared-segment is shared in the system. We first present the data structure used in the algorithm and then present our algorithm.

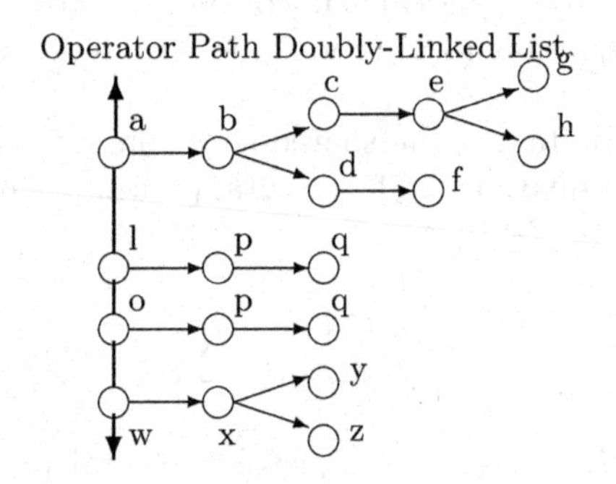

Fig. 7.4. The Global Operator Path

Data Structure

Each operator has two attributes $(label, frequency)$. The label attribute has its unique label in the system, and the frequency attribute maintains the number of times this operator is shared, which is initialized to zero. An operator path is represented as a linked list of its operator pointers starting from its leaf node. All operator paths are linked to a global doubly-linked path list illustrated in Figure 7.4 according to its path string. The operator paths in the global path link are sorted by the first label of its path string in order to find or delete an operator path efficiently. Once a new query plan is registered into the system, all its operator paths are inserted into the linked-list based on the first label of their path strings. For each operator path, if its first element does not exist in the list, all elements of that path are linked to the global list, and the frequency value of each operator along that path is set to one. If its first element is already in the list, it just increases the frequency value of the element by one, and then searches its second element along that branch; if found, increases its frequency value by one. Otherwise, its second element is linked to the global link list by creating another branch in the list. Its frequency value is set to one. Similarly, when an active query plan is deactivated, we have to delete the operator paths that are encompassed in it. To delete an operator path, we decrease the frequency value by one for each operator along that path. Whenever the value of frequency number of an operator is reduced to zero, the operator is deleted. Therefore, this global linked list maintains all operator paths and all operators of all active query plans in the system.

Algorithm 4: Sharing Segment Search Algorithm

```
  INPUT: PCLL - the global doubly linked list of operator path cluster;
  OUTPUT: SSLL - a set of shared-segments with their frequency value;
1 SSLL = NULL;
  /*the following algorithm to maintain all shared-segments and their
    frequencies.                                                      */
2 foreach (operator path cluster PC in PCLL) do
3 |  if (the frequency value of the first operator > 1) then
4 |  |  SSLL = SSLL UNION SEARCH(PC)
5 |  end
6 end
7 return SSLL;
```

The algorithm traverses the global doubly linked list for each operator path cluster. It calls procedure SEARCH($\mathcal{PC}$) to find all shared-segments of the operator path cluster $\mathcal{PC}$. If there exists shared-segments in an operator path cluster, the frequency value of the first operator of the operator cluster must greater than one since the shared common subexpressions of two queries must start from the leaf operator of an operator path. The procedure SEARCH($\mathcal{PC}$) finds shared-segments from a particular operator path cluster.

This algorithms is quite efficient. First, it has a linear time complexity of $O(n)$, where n is the number of active operators in the system. Second, the system does not need to execute the algorithm again until the global linked list is changed. In a continuous query system, it is unlikely that query plans are changed (addition, deletion, reoptimization) frequently due to the continuous computation requirement. Finally, only when a query addition or deletion happens, we need to execute the algorithm for changed path clusters, and not for all path clusters in the system.

Predicting the Input Rate of Each Input Stream

In order to estimate system load, we need to know the input rates of all input streams. Therefore, we design a stream property monitor to monitor not

Algorithm 5: SEARCH($\mathcal{PC}$)

```
   INPUT: PC – the global doubly linked list of operator path cluster;
   OUTPUT: C – a set of shared-segments;
   /*create a new set container for shared-segments;                          */
1  C = NULL;
2  if (PC− >FirstOperator− >Frequency > 1) then
       /* Create a new shared-segment S which consists of all elements before a
          fan-out element, including the fan-out element. The frequency value of
          the sharing segment is the frequency value of the elements.         */
3      Operator = PC− >FirstOperator;
4      while ((Operator != NULL)&&(Operator− >numberOfChildren > 1))
       do
5          S = S + Operator;
6          Operator = Operator− >next;
7      end
       /* Add the shared-segment S with its frequency value to the
          shared-segment set C.                                               */
8      C = C + S;
9  end
10 foreach (branch B of the fan-out element) do
       /*recursively CALL the search procedure SEARCH(B) and add the
          results to the set C.                                               */
11     C = C UNION SEARCH(B);
12 end
13 return the shared-segment set C.
```

only the arrival characteristics, but also the data properties of a data stream. By monitoring those properties in our system, we are able to: (*1*) choose the most suitable scheduling algorithm, (*2*) optimize a continuous query plan adaptively, and (*3*) predict the system load and to shed partial load when a system is overloaded in order to satisfy the predefined QoS requirements. Here we only discuss related techniques that we use to monitor input rate of an input stream.

The characteristics such as the input rate of a data stream are highly dynamic. Some of them change regularly while others change irregularly. Typically, sensors that monitor the temperature send data periodically; while the robot which is in charge of house cleaning emits data whenever it detects that the floor is dirty and when it has done the house cleaning. To monitor[4] the input rate of an input stream efficiently, we sample a series of time points over the time axis. If the input rates at the last n points have not changed too much (the change is measured by the variance of those input rates), we decrease the sample rate; otherwise, we increase the sample rate. This adaptive

[4] Due to the high cost of continuous and precise monitoring of the properties of a data stream, we monitor the properties periodically and approximately which is sufficient to make a decision in most cases.

algorithm makes it possible to monitor hundreds of data streams efficiently and effectively.

7.3.2 Placement of Load Shedders

As determined in Section 7.2, a load shedder is considered as part of the input queue of a normal operator to keep the load shedding overhead to a minimum. Since each active load shedder contributes to extra load on the system, it is logical to decrease the number of load shedders in the system. As an operator path is associated with an input stream, it should be sufficient to place at most one potential load shedder along an operator path, which motivates us to find its optimal place for each operator path in the system. Once a query processing congestion occurs, it is desirable to activate as few of load shedders as possible, that aids in allocating only the required load shedding to as few shedders as possible. In the following section, the location of each load shedder is assumed to be part of input queue functionality of an operator. The loss/gain concept used in the following section shares some common characteristics as those introduced in [93] and in [112]. However, the methods used to calculate the gain and loss differ. Also our shedders have a maximal capacity, which is used to prevent dropping too many tuples from violating the MTRE requirement of each operator path and this maximal capacity of a shedder is not present in any of them. Finally, we minimize the number of load shedders in the system through merging multiple shedders in query plans, which is not addressed in the other DSMSs either.

A load shedder can be placed at any location along an operator path. However, its location has a different impact on the accuracy of the final results, and on the amount of computation time units it releases. Specifically, placing a load shedder earlier in the query plan (i.e., before the leaf operator) is most effective in saving the amount of computation time units when a tuple is dropped, but its effect on accuracy may not be most effective. On the other hand, placing a load shedder after the operator which has biggest output rate in the query plan has the lowest impact on the accuracy when a tuple is dropped, but the amount of computation time units released may not be the largest. Therefore, the best candidate location for a load shedder along an operator path is the place where the shedder is capable of releasing maximal computational time units while introducing minimal relative errors in final query results by dropping one tuple.

Without considering the shared-segment among multiple operator paths, there are k candidate places to place a load shedder on an operator path $\mathcal{X}$ with k operators. Let $\{x_1, x_2, \ldots, x_k\}$ be its path label string, and v be the input rate of the data stream for this operator path. Let $b_1, b_2, \cdots, b_k$ be its k candidate places, where $b_i, 1 \leq i \leq k$ is the place right before the operator x_i.

We define the `place weight` W of a candidate place as the ratio of the amount of saved percentage of computation time units α to the relative error

ϵ in its final results introduced by a load shedder at that place by discarding one tuple. The place weight W of a shedder at a specific location along the operator path with its QoS requirements as $(MTTL = L_i)$ and $(MTRE = E_i)$ is defined as:

$$\mathcal{W} = \frac{\alpha}{\epsilon} \tag{7.9}$$

where

$$\alpha = \frac{v(d)}{C^S} - \frac{v_{shedder}}{C^O_{shedder}}$$

$$\epsilon = \begin{cases} \frac{v(d)}{v_{shedder}} & \text{for a random shedder;} \\ f\left(\frac{v(d)}{v_{shedder}}\right) & \text{for a semantic shedder;} \end{cases}$$

$$v(d) = \begin{cases} E_i * v_{shedder} & \text{for a random shedder;} \\ E_i * f(\frac{1}{v_{shedder}}) & \text{for a semantic shedder;} \end{cases}$$

$$v_{shedder} = v \prod_{i=x_1}^{x_n} (\sigma_i), \ x_1 \text{ to } x_n \text{ are operators before the shedder}$$

where C^S is the processing capacity of the segment staring from the operator right after the load shedder until the root node (excluding the root node) along the operator path.

If there is no operator after the shedder, C^S is defined as infinity and $(\frac{v(d)}{C^S} = 0)$. The computation time units that can be saved is zero and the shedder itself also introduces overhead in the amount $\frac{v_{shedder}}{C^O_{shedder}}$. $v(d)$ is the maximal drop rate by a shedder at this place without violating the MTRE E_i defined for the operator path. The total computation time units saved by dropping tuples at a rate of $v(d)$ is $\frac{v(d)}{C^S}$. However, a shedder also introduces additional overhead, which is $\frac{v_{shedder}}{C^O_{shedder}}$, to the system because it needs to determine whether a tuple should be dropped or not. $v_{shedder}$ is the input rate of the load shedder, and x_1 to x_n are the operators before the load shedder starting from leaf operator, and σ_i is the selectivity of the operator x_i. If there is no operator before the shedder, then $v_{shedder} = v$ and v is the input rate of the stream for the operator path $\mathcal{X}$. $C^O_{shedder}$ is the processing capacity of the load shedder. If the load shedder is a semantic one, $f(.)$ is a function mapping the selectivity of the shedder to the relative error in final query results.

In Equation (7.9), the input rate of an input stream is the only item that changes over time. All the other items[5] do not change over time until we revise the query plan. Therefore, for the operator path $\mathcal{X}$, it has k candidate places for a load shedder. We compute the place weight for each of those k candidate places. And their partial orders do not change as input rate changes because all of them have the same input rate of the input stream at any time instant. The place where the load shedder has the biggest place weight is the most effective one. We only need to compute these place weights *once* to find the

[5] Selectivity of an operator may be revised periodically. However, it is assumed that it does not change over a long period of time.

best place of a load shedder for an operator path. Let $\mathcal{W}(p_i)$ be the weight of the place that a load shedder locates along the operator path p_i,

$$\mathcal{W}(p_i) = max\{\mathcal{W}(b_1), \mathcal{W}(b_2), \cdots, \mathcal{W}(b_k), 0\} \tag{7.10}$$

where $b_1, b_2, \cdots,\ b_k$ are k candidate places along the path p_i. To prevent the case that a shedder introduces more overhead than it saves by dropping tuples at its maximal capacity, we add zero item in Equation (7.10). If zero is the maximal place weight along the operator path, it indicates that we cannot place a load shedder along this path because the additional overhead it introduces is bigger than what it saves.

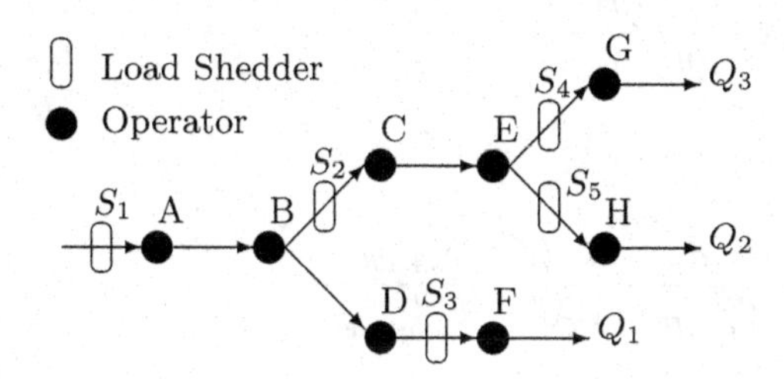

Fig. 7.5. Locations Of Load Shedders

For an operator path with a shared-segment with other operator paths, placing a load shedder before or along the shared-segment will not only impact the accuracy of the results of more than one query plan, but also likely to have a different impact on each query plan. For operator paths illustrated in Figure 7.5, the operator paths $\{ABDF\}$, which belongs to query Q_1, $\{ABCEH\}$, which belongs to query Q_2, and $\{ABCEG\}$, which belongs to query Q_3, share the segment $\{AB\}$, and the last two operator paths further share the segment $\{ABCE\}$. Placing a load shedder anywhere along the segment $\{AB\}$ will impact all three query plans, and placing a load shedder anywhere along the segment $\{CE\}$ will impact query plans Q_2, Q_3, but not Q_1.

We consider all operator paths that are connected with each other through `fan-out` operators such as operator B, E as an `operator path cluster`. To determine the location of a load shedder in such an operator path cluster, we partition each operator path in this cluster into a set of operator segments. For each path, the first segment consists of all operators from its leaf operator to its first fan-out operator. All other segments consist of all the operators between two fan-out operators plus the later fan-out operator. For example, the path cluster illustrated in Figure 7.5 is partitioned into a set of 5 segments $\{AB, CE, DF, G, H\}$. We compute the most effective position of a load shedder along each individual segment in the operator path cluster using Equation (7.9). When we compute the most effective position of a load shedder along a shared-segment such as $\{AB\}$, $\{CE\}$, the amount of percentage of computation time units saved is the sum of actual percentage of computation time units released by each segment starting from the operator right after the load shedder until the root operator. Similarly, the relative error introduced by the shedder is the sum of actual relative errors introduced in final query results of each path. For example, by placing a random shedder right before the operator A, the amount of percentage of computation time units released

$$\alpha = \frac{v(d)}{C^S_{ABDF}} + \frac{v(d)}{C^S_{ABCEG}} + \frac{v(d)}{C^S_{ABCDH}} - 2\frac{v(d)}{C^S_{AB}} - \frac{v_{shedder}}{C^O_{shedder}}$$

and

$$\epsilon = \frac{v(d)}{v_{shedder}}.$$

Similarly,

$$\alpha = \frac{v(d)}{C^S_{CEG}} + \frac{v(d)}{C^S_{CEH}} - \frac{v(d)}{C^S_{CE}} - \frac{v_{shedder}}{C^O_{shedder}}$$

and

$$\epsilon = f_{CEG}(\frac{v_d}{v_{shedder}}) + f_{CEH}(\frac{v_d}{v_{shedder}})$$

if a semantic shedder is placed right before the operator C.

We need to merge two or more load shedders along an operator path cluster into one. The reasons for merging are: (a) the most effective position of a load shedder along a segment does not mean it is the most effective position in its path cluster; (b) different queries have different maximal tolerable relative errors, which implies that different paths in an operator path cluster have different maximal tolerable relative errors. Therefore, a shedder in a shared-segment has different maximal capacity in terms of different paths; (c) the overhead introduced by shedders can be decreased by decreasing the number of shedders. We consider three load shedders S_2, S_4, S_5 along the segments connected directly to the first fan-out operator E in Figure 7.5. If the place weight of the load shedder S_2 is the biggest one among them, the load we have to shed from load shedders S_4 and S_5 can be moved forward to the load shedder S_2. However, the maximal load that the load shedder S_4, and S_5 can shed respectively are different if the queries to which the segment $\{G\}$, and $\{H\}$ belong have a different maximal tolerable relative error.

We define the `drop capacity` of load shedder s_i as $v(d) = D_i(e_i)$ such that $v(d)$ is maximized without violating its maximal tolerable relative error e_i. Before we merge load shedders of a path cluster, we have to initialize their maximal tolerable relative errors as follows. The load shedder along the segment which outputs final query results, has its maximal tolerable relative error and this error is equal to the maximal tolerable relative error E_i of the query plan to which it belongs. All the other load shedders of this path cluster has a drop capacity of zero.

We start the merge procedure backward. We first process the fan-out operators closest to the root node, then process the fan-out operators closer to any of those processed fan-out operators. For a fan-out operator with m ($m \geq 2$) fans, let $W(S_{Main})$ be the place weight of the load shedder along the segment on which the fan-out operator lies, and this load shedder is termed `main-shedder`. Let $S_1, S_2, \cdots, S_k$ be the place weights of its k load shedders, which are the first load shedders along all the segments originating from the fan-out operator to root operator. Note that there are k, instead of m, load shedders along its m branches because some branches may not have a shedder, i.e., its place weight is zero, or some branches have more than one shedders at its branches or the shedders on some branches are eliminated as a result of merging process. Those shedders are termed `branch-shedders`. Let S_i be the place weight of the branch-shedder with the smallest maximal tolerable relative error e_i among k branch-shedders. If $k * W(S_{Main}) <= \sum_{i=1}^{k} W(S_i)$, we eliminate the main-shedder since the total place weight that we gain at the Main shedders is no more than what we can get from branch shedders. Otherwise, considering each e_j of those k relative errors $e_1, e_2, \cdots, e_k$ associated with each branch-shedder, we maximize the drop rate $v(d_j)$ at the main-shedder such that the error introduced in final query results of the operator path at which S_i is located is no more than e_j. This maximized drop rate is limited such that the relative error introduced in final query results from each branch path is not more than the MTRE e_j of the branch. Notice, a drop rate at a main-shedder introduces a different relative error to each of its branch if some or all its branch-shedders are semantic shedders. Let $v(d)_s$ be the smallest of the maximal drop rate $v(d)_1, v(d)_2, \cdots, v(d)_k$ and $\acute{e}_1, \acute{e}_2, \cdots, \acute{e}_k$ be the relative errors introduced by $v(d)_s$ on the paths on which its k branch-shedders lie. For each branch-shedder S_i, we shift $\acute{e}_i$ of its load shedding capacity to the main-shedder, and the corresponding capacity of a branch-shedder S_i decreases to $e_i - \acute{e}_i$. If $e_i - \acute{e}_i = 0$, its corresponding branch-shedder is deleted. After merging, one operator path cluster may have more than one shedder, each of them having a different load shedding capacity. This capacity implicitly determines its maximal drop rate, which consequently determines the maximal load it can save.

Once the best location of a load shedder is determined, the load shedder function is incorporated into the input queue of an operator before we start to do load shedding. The shedder stays in non-active mode initially. All tuples bypass the shedder when it is in a non-active model, and there is no overhead during its non-active periods. Once it is activated, a tuple has to pass through the shedder before it can be processed by the next operator.

7.3.3 Allocation of Load for Shedding

From Equation (7.6) in Section 7.3.1, we know when to shed load. And the total load we need to shed is Δ in order not to violate the predefined QoS requirements of active queries in the system. The algorithms presented in Section 7.3.2 gives a list of non-active load shedders and their load shedding capacities. Now, the problem is how to allocate the total shedding load among all or some of these load shedders by activating them with a goal of minimizing the maximum total relative error introduced by load shedding.

Let $\mathcal{S} = \{S_1, S_2, \cdots, S_m\}$ be the set of non-active shedders in the system. The allocation of shedding load problem is formalized to find a subset of shedders $\acute{\mathcal{S}}$, where $\acute{\mathcal{S}} \subseteq \mathcal{S}$, and to activate them such that

$$\forall i, S_i \in \acute{\mathcal{S}} \quad \text{and} \quad \begin{cases} \sum_{i=1}^{k} \alpha_i & = \Delta \\ \sum_{i=1}^{k} \epsilon_i & \text{is minimized, and } \epsilon_i \leq e_i \end{cases}$$

where α_i is the percentage of computation time units released by the load shedder S_i with a dropping rate of $v(d)_i$, and ϵ_i is the relative error it introduces by that dropping rate. Both of them are defined in Equation (7.9).

The allocation problem is the well known `knapsack problem` by considering the total shedding percentage of computation time units Δ as the total capacity of a ship, and ϵ_i as the weight of the item, and α_i as the total value of the item. Although the 0-1 knapsack problem is a NP-hard problem, the fractional knapsack problem is solvable by a greedy strategy in $O(n \lg n)$ time. For the allocation problem, a load shedder does not have to shed load at its maximal dropping rate, but it can just shed part of its total capacity. Therefore, the allocation of load to be shed can be solved in $O(n \lg n)$, where n is the total number of non-active shedders in the system.

To solve the problem of allocation of shedding load among the shedders when we detect a query processing congestion, we first sort all non-active shedders in the system by their place weights $W(S_i)$. Without loss of generality, we assume that $W(S_1) \geq W(S_2) \geq \cdots \geq W(S_c)$ after sorting. Obeying a greedy strategy, we activate the shedder with the greatest place weight, i.e., S_1, and let it shed load at a drop rate such that its saved load $\alpha = \Delta$ if $\Delta \leq \alpha_1$, where α_1 is its saved load when it operates at that drop rate, then we stop the procedure. Otherwise, letting it work at its maximal drop rate without violating its capacity e_1, update the total shedding load to $\Delta = \Delta - \alpha_1$. If the updated total shedding load $\Delta > 0$, we then activate the non-active shedder with the next greatest place weight. We repeat this procedure until the updated total shedding load becomes zero or there are no non-active shedders available in the system. If the procedure ends with a non-zero Δ, it indicates that the load shedding cannot guarantee minimal required computation resources to satisfy all predefined QoS requirements in the system. In this case, we have to either violate some QoS requirements or choose some victim query plans to deactivate in order to meet QoS requirements of other query plans.

7.3.4 Load Shedding Overhead

The overhead introduced by load shedding mainly consists of two parts: 1) the overhead introduced by periodically estimating system load; and 2) the overhead of allocation of total shedding among all non-active shedders in the system. In order to decrease the overhead in 1), we can increase the length of period of estimating system load when the previous estimated system load is far away from system capacity or the monitored input rates have not changed dramatically. Therefore, the overhead due to estimation of system load is very small if the overall system load is light and/or the input rates of all data streams changes gradually.

The latter overhead is introduced by allocation of total shedding load among all non-active shedders. From Equation (7.9), we can see that the place weight of a load shedder changes as the input rate of a data stream changes. Although this change does not change the partial order of shedders along the same operator path, it can change the partial order of shedders of two different operator paths when the ratio of the current input rate to the input rate used to compute the place weight changes dramatically. Therefore, we have to reorder the non-active shedders in the system when we allocate the total shedding load among all non-active shedders. In a heavy loaded system with dynamic input rates, we may have to frequently activate non-active shedders or deactivate active shedders, and this overhead is not negligible.

In order to decrease the overhead of the $O(n \lg n)$ solution of allocation problem, we have to decrease the number of shedders in the system. Instead of maintaining all partial orders of the whole list of shedders in the system, we partition n shedders into m groups, where $m \ll n$, according to their place weights. One shedder may upgrade to its upper level or degrade to its lower level group only when its input rate changes by a factor of its standard input rate that was used to calculate the place weight. This factor can be calculated in advance as a property of a shedder. By maintaining those m groups of shedders in the system, we decrease the computation complexity of allocation problem to a constant. Namely, we activate the shedders in the first group and then shedders in the second group until the total saved load is no less than what is required. The shedders within a group is selected based on their maximal drop capacity. The shedder with a bigger drop capacity is activated first. To promote or degrade a shedder to/from a different group, we only need to compute the ratio of the input rate of an operator path to its standard input rate if the load shedding mechanism is active.

7.4 Experimental Validation

7.4.1 Prototype Implementation

Currently, the load shedding techniques proposed in this chapter have been implemented within our QoS framework of proposed QoS-aware DSMS, `MavStream` [127].

For load shedding, we have implemented both random and semantic shedders. Once a continuous query plan is registered with the system, the place weight of non-active shedders along each operator path of this query plan are computed, and then those shedders are classified into predefined groups according to their place weights in order to decrease the overhead introduced by allocation of total load shedding. The performance estimation subsystem estimates system load according to the input rate of each input stream from stream property monitor and then passes the estimated system load to load shedding module. The load shedding module works in either shedding-active mode, in which some shedders have been activated, or no-shedding-active mode, in which there is no active shedder in the system. If it works in no-shedding-active mode, it enters shedding-active mode once currently estimated load is bigger than system capacity. The load shedding module, in turn, enables non-active shedders in the highest-level group and/or next highest-level group until the total amount of saved percentages of computation time units is no less than what is required.

All active shedders are linked into a list according to their enabling orders. If it works in shedding-active mode and the current estimated system load is less than system capacity by a minimal threshold value, the load shedding system deactivates an active shedder in the list in the reverse order of enabling it until there are no more active shedders in the system. All deactivated shedders are returned to their corresponding groups. Although our load shedding approach guarantees the minimal computation of resources required to deliver predefined QoS requirements, it is possible to violate a particular QoS requirement because of the shortage of a QoS guaranteed scheduling strategy. The following scheduling strategies have been implemented in the prototype to allocate all available resource among queries: the PC scheduling strategy [131], which minimizes total tuple latency, the Chain strategy [111,128], which minimizes total queue size, and their hybrid – the threshold strategy [128, 131], and other general strategies such as various round-robin strategies. We also implemented a QoS guaranteed scheduling strategy – Earliest Deadline First (EDF), which is guaranteed to deliver QoS requirement given guaranteed total computation resources.

7.4.2 Experiment Setup

In this section, we briefly discuss the results of various experiments that we have carried out to validate our load shedding techniques, and to show how our load shedding techniques along with our scheduling strategies satisfy the tuple latency requirement of a query plan. The system consists of a source manager, a query processing engine, and a run-time scheduling module, and a load shedding module. The source manager is in charge of the meta information of the tuples from each data stream. It also monitors the input characteristics and stream properties of an input stream. The query processing engine is in charge of query plan generation and execution. A set of relational operators such as `project`, `select` and `window`-based `symmetric hash join` have been implemented in our query engine. The run-time scheduling model is used to determine which operator or operator path to execute in any time slot. The load shedding module in our proposed system consists of a load estimation subsystem and our load shedding allocation subsystem. The load shedding module with our run-time scheduling model is capable of delivering tuple latency requirements.

Input data streams

The input we have generated are highly bursty streams that have the so-called self-similar property, which we believe resembles the situation in real-life applications. Each input stream is a super imposition of 64 or 128 flows. Each flow alternates ON/OFF periods, and it only sends tuples during its ON periods. The tuple inter-arrival time follows an exponential distribution during its ON periods. The length of both the ON and the OFF periods are generated from a Pareto distribution which has a probability mass function $P(x) = ab^a x^{-(a+1)}, x \geq b$. We use $a = 1.4$ for the ON period and $a = 1.2$ for the OFF period. For more detailed information about self-similar traffic, please refer to [316, 324]. In our experiment, we use 5 such self-similar input data streams with different mean input rates.

Experimental query plans

All of our queries are continuous queries that consist of `select`, `project`, and `symmetric hash join` operators. To be more close to a real application, we run 16 actual continuous queries with 116 operators over 5 different data streams in our system. The selectivity of each operator is widely distributed ranging from 0 to 1. Both the selectivity and the processing capacity of each operator can be determined by collecting statistics periodically during run time. The list of queries used for experiments can be found in [128].

We group 16 queries into 3 groups with different QoS requirements in terms of maximal tolerable tuple latency and maximal tolerable relative error. The first group has QoS requirement of (tuple latency ≤ 0.6, relative error ≤ 0.15); the second and third group have a QoS requirement of (1.0, 0.25) and (1.5, 0.5) respectively. All the experiments were run on a dedicated dual processor Alpha machine with 2GB of RAM. One of the processors was used to collect experiment results while another processor was used for query processing.

7.4.3 Load Shedding with Path capacity strategy

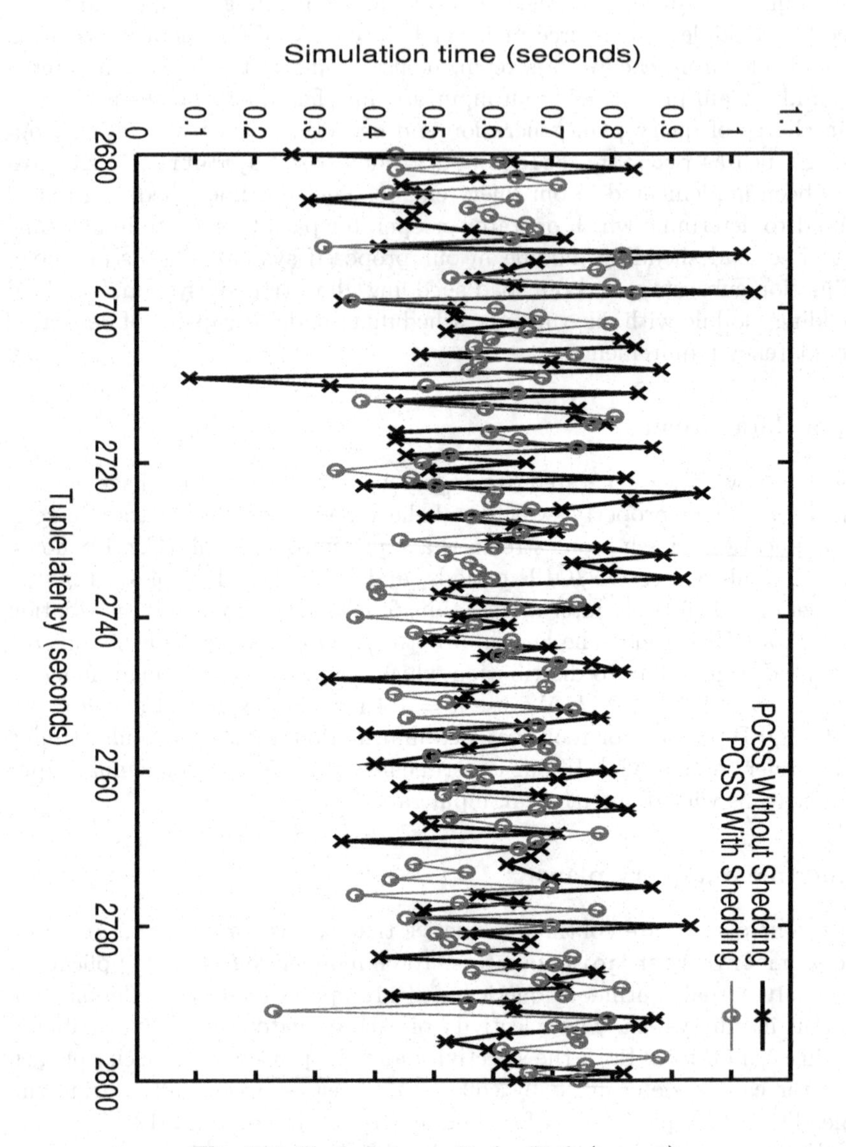

Fig. 7.6. Tuple Latency Under Path (group1)

This set of experiments shows the performance of system under load shedding techniques described in this chapter with PC scheduling strategy. Figures 7.6 and 7.7 show the tuple latency of all output tuples of a query in group 1 and group 3 respectively. The tuple latencies are larger than the maximal

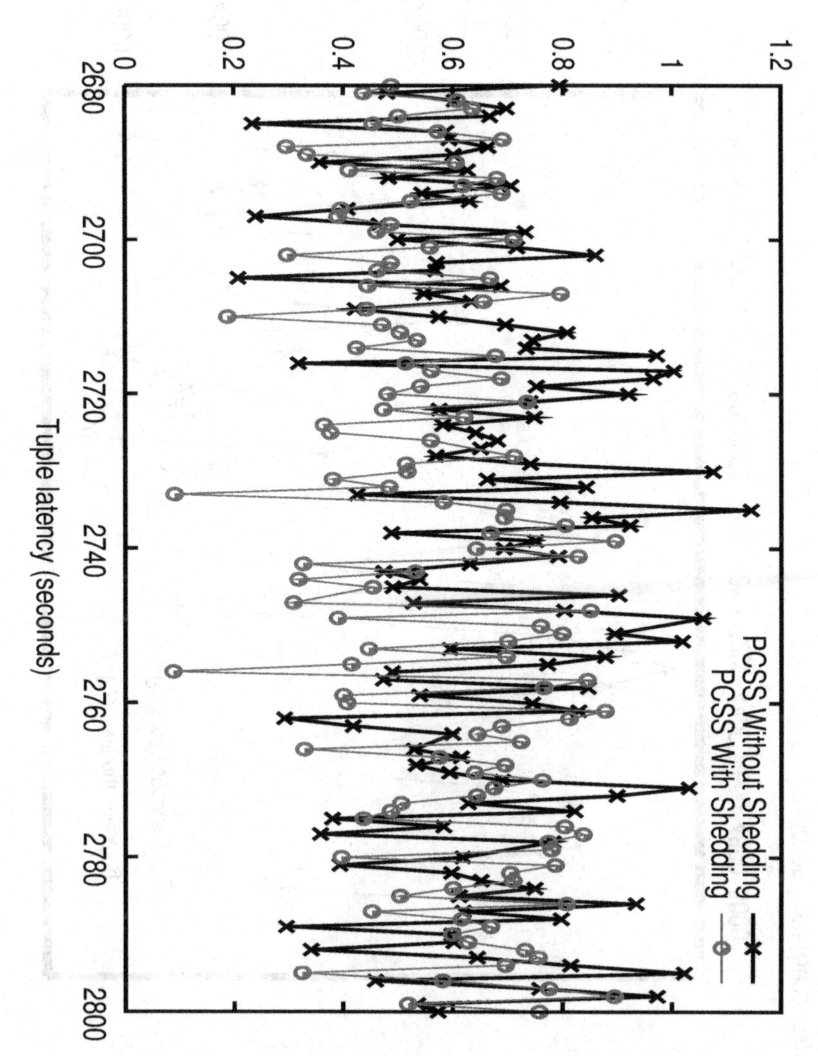

Fig. 7.7. Tuple Latency Under Path (group3)

tolerable tuple latency requirement in group 1; while those in Figure 7.7 are less than their maximal tolerable tuple latency requirement in group 3. This is because the path scheduling strategy is not a QoS guaranteed scheduling strategy though there are enough resources for all queries. However, the maximal tuple latencies under the PC strategy with load shedding are less than those without load shedding.

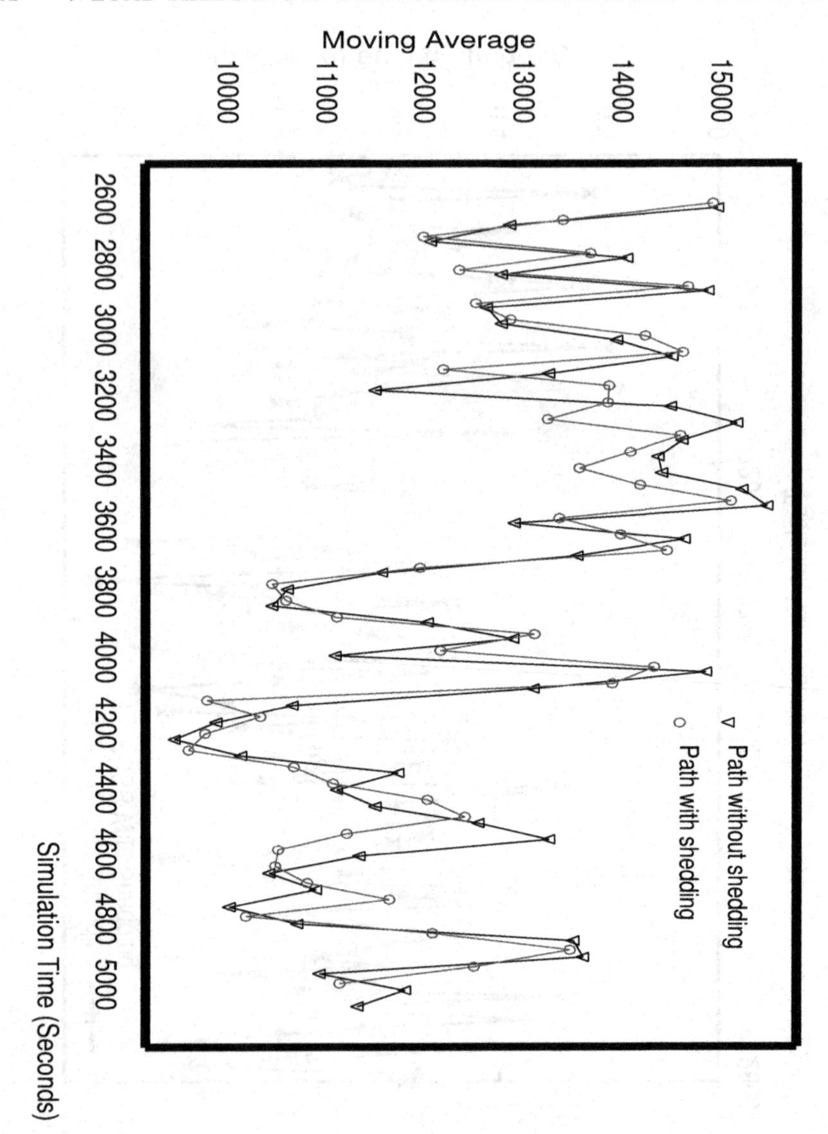

Fig. 7.8. Moving Average Under PC strategy

Figures 7.8 and 7.9 show the moving average of all tuples from a query in group 1 and the total internal queue size respectively in order to see the impacts on accuracy of final query results by load shedding. From both figures, we can see that the peak values of both the average value and the total memory requirement under load shedding are decreased when system experiences a query processing congestion. This shows our load shedding techniques detect congestion correctly and shed corresponding load effectively.

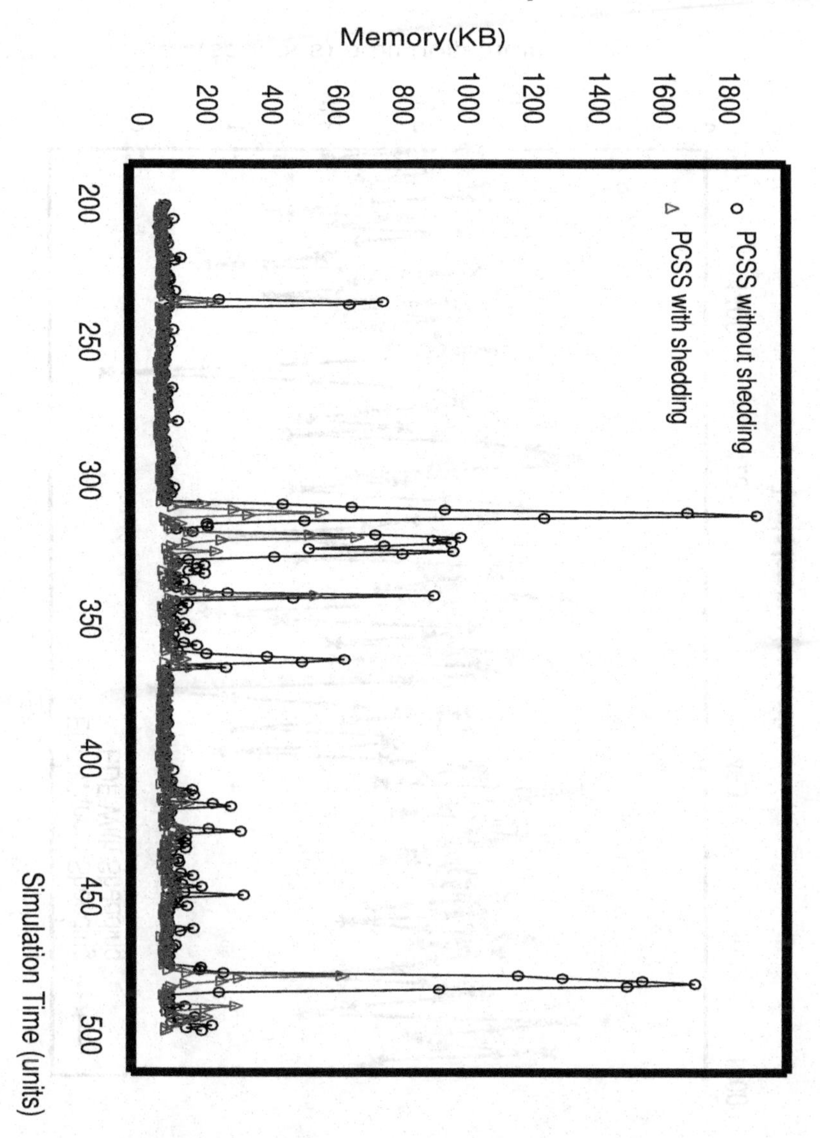

Fig. 7.9. Total Internal Queue Size Under PC strategy

7.4.4 Load Shedding with EDF scheduling strategy

This group of experiments shows the performance of our load shedding technique with Earliest Deadline First strategy. The EDF schedules the operator path with earliest deadline, the deadline of an operator path is defined as the age of the oldest tuple along the path plus its maximal tolerable tuple latency. The EDF is a QoS-guaranteed scheduling strategy in terms of tuple latency. Figure 7.10 clearly shows that the tuple latencies under EDF with load shed-

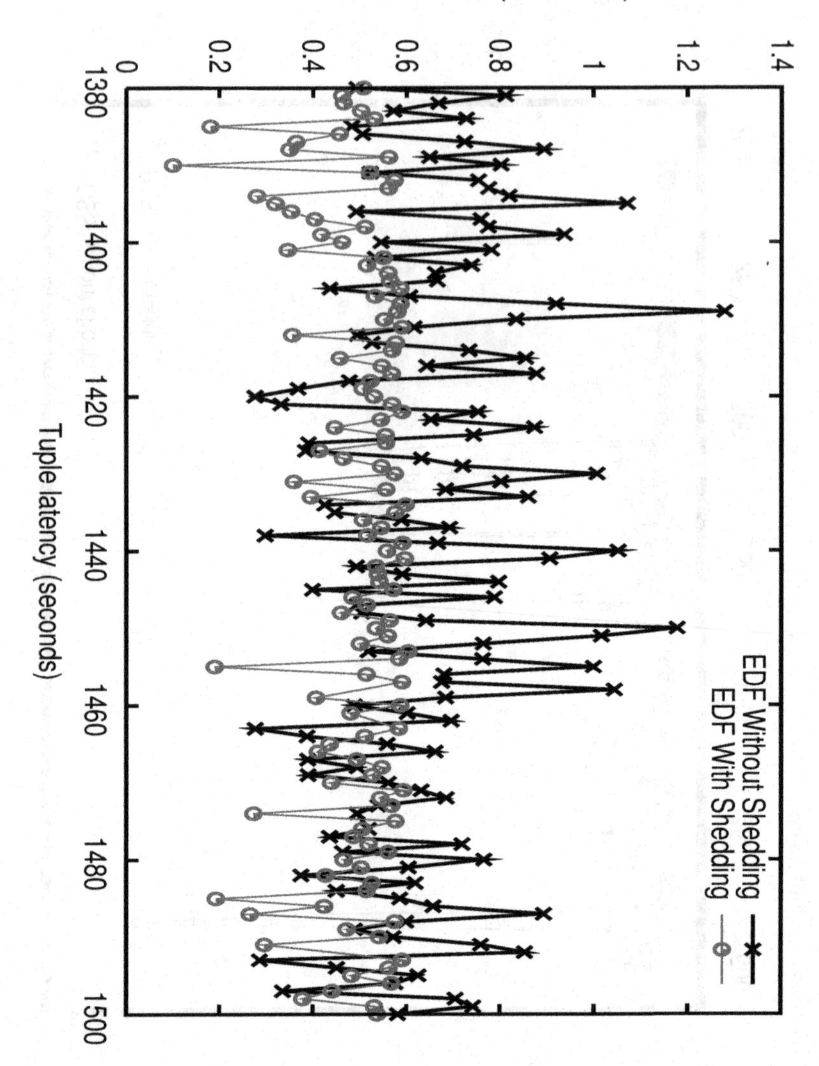

Fig. 7.10. Tuple Latency Under EDF (group1)

ding do not violate the predefined maximal tolerable tuple latency, and those latencies are less than those under EDF without load shedding. Figure 7.11 shows that the total internal queue size under EDF scheduling with/without load shedding. Both figures show that the query processing congestions under EDF come earlier than under PC strategy. This is because the overhead introduced by EDF itself is much bigger than that introduced by Path. This

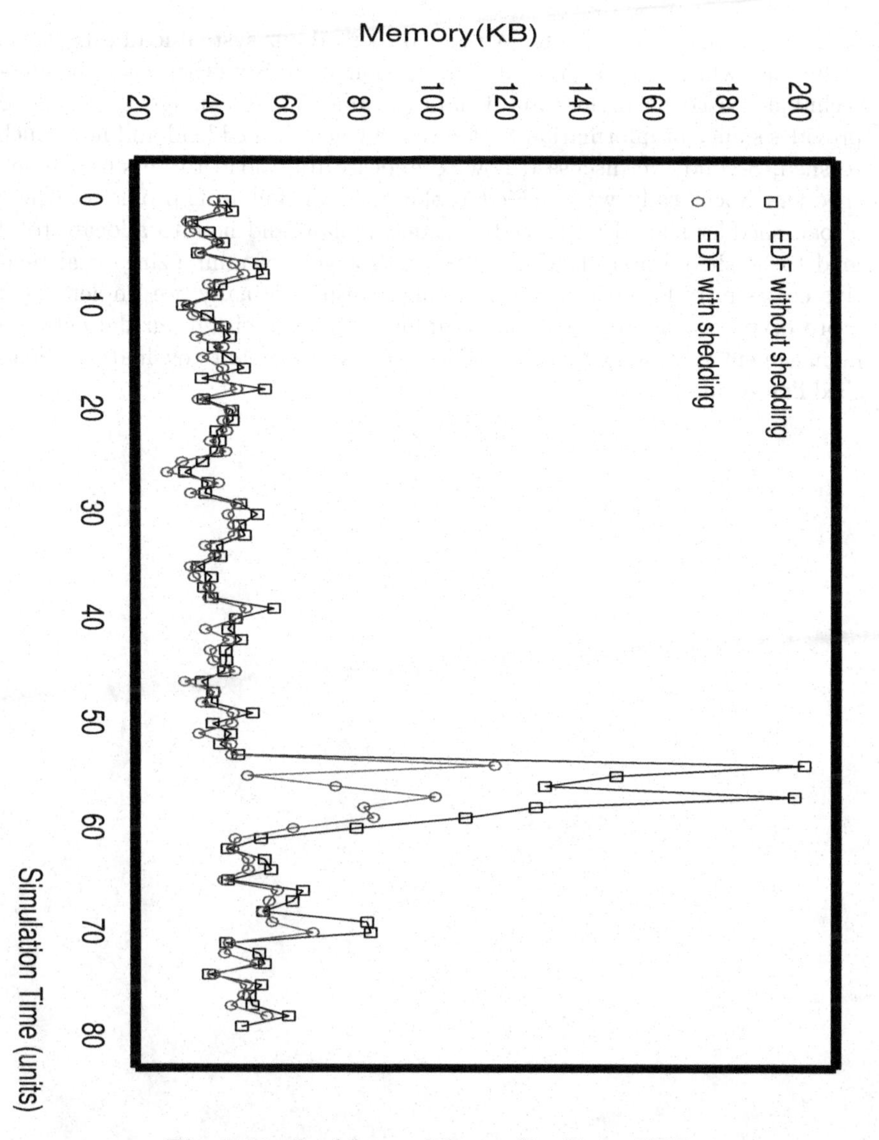

Fig. 7.11. Total Internal Queue Size Under EDF

means the system capacity decreases under EDF, and the number of tuples it can backlog without violating predefined QoS decreases as well.

7.5 Summary of Chapter 7

In this chapter, we have proposed a general purpose query processing congestion avoidance framework and load shedding techniques for a DSMS in order to meet all QoS requirements. We first presented our system load estimation technique, which can be used in conjunction with any other load shedding technique based on input rate of data streams. The estimated system load provides sufficient information to determine when to shed load and how much to shed. Second, we discussed how to allocate total load to be shed among shedders. Specifically, we provided a solution to the following problems: where a load shedder should be placed in a query plan, and how to allocate total load to be shed among load shedders with a goal of minimizing total relative errors introduced into the final query results. Finally, we implemented a prototype of our proposed load shedding approach within our data stream management system, and conducted various experiments to evaluate our load shedding techniques.

8

NFM^i: AN INTER-DOMAIN NETWORK FAULT MANAGEMENT SYSTEM

Automating network fault management has been an active area of research for a long period because of its complexity, and the return on investment it can generate for service providers. However, most fault management systems are currently custom-developed for specific service providers in specific domains. As service providers continuously add new capabilities and sophistication to their systems to meet the demands of growing user population, these systems have to manage a multi-layered network along with its built-in, legacy processing procedures. Our proposed approach is based on leveraging stream and complex event processing techniques to meet the needs of complex, real-word problems.

Various solutions for network fault management have been discussed in the literature. Proposed approaches [325–327] discuss domain-specific distributed architectures for network management. However, most of the telecommunication service providers employ a central fault management system because of the need for various types of experts and their effective collaboration to fix malfunctions. Medhi et al. [328] propose an architecture for a multi-layered network through various interfaces to exchange information between several domain managers and a single inter-domain manager; however, like other network fault management systems, it falls short on the aspect of flexibility. Babu et al. [329] propose an architecture for managing data traffic over the internet which is somewhat different from network fault management. The architecture proposed in this chapter takes a totally different approach by leveraging the advantages of stream and complex event processing to modularize the system, reduce its complexity, and improve its ease of use.

Specifically, we propose an integrated inter-domain network fault management system for such a multi-layered network based on data stream and event processing techniques. We discuss various components of our system and illustrate how data stream processing techniques can be adapted to build a flexible system for complex, real-world applications. We further identify a number of important extensions related to data stream and complex event processing during the course of our analysis of the application.

S. Chakravarthy and Q. Jiang, *Stream Data Processing: A Quality of Service Perspective*, Advances in Database Systems 36, DOI: 10.1007/978-0-387-71003-7_8,

8.1 Network Fault Management Problem

In telecommunication network management, Network Fault Management (NFM) is defined as the set of functions that (a) detect, isolate, and correct malfunctions in a telecommunication network, (b) compensate for environmental changes, and (c) maintain and examine error logs, accept and act on error detection notifications, trace and identify faults, carry out sequence of diagnostic tests, correct faults, report error conditions, and localize and trace faults by examining and manipulating database information.

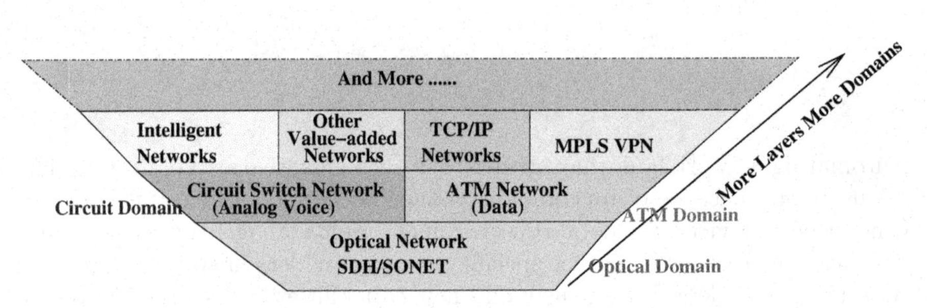

Fig. 8.1. A Typical Telecommunication Network

A typical telecommunication network, illustrated in Figure 8.1, is a multi-layered network, in which the bottom layer provides a transport service through SDH/SONET networks. Above that, a Public Switched Telephone Network (PSTN) circuit switch network with a Signaling System 7 (SS7) signaling network is used to provide traditional voice services, and an Asynchronous Transfer Mode (ATM) network is used to provide internet data service. Intelligent networks and other value-added networks can be added above the PSTN switch networks, and Border Gateway Protocol/Multiprotocol Label Switching (BGP/MPLS) Virtual Private Network (VPN) can be added above the ATM network. The NFM in such a multi-layered telecommunication network has been a challenging problem [325–328, 330–332], addressed by both industry and academia for a long time, because of its high cost and complexity. The recent convergence of data, voice, and cable networks has further compounded the scope of this problem.

Each network element (NE) in this multi-layered network reports the status of each of its components and the status of its environment (e.g., temperature) periodically (e.g., every 5 minutes). Some NEs have additional capabilities such as summarizing its status by processing the status message locally in order to reduce the number of messages reported or to identify trivial messages. Hence, these messages arrive in the form of a message stream, and each NE can be considered as a message stream source. These status and alarm messages from each NE, each Operation System (OS), and each network link are continuously collected in a Network Operations Center (NOC) to be further analyzed by experts to detect and to isolate faults. Once a fault is identified, sequence of actions need to be taken locally and remotely. Due to the complexity of the network and different interfaces of multiple-vendor's devices, each layer has one or more independent NFM systems [331,332]. For example, there is a SDH/SONET fault management system for the transport layer in the network as illustrated in Figure 8.1. There are also individual fault management systems for circuit switch and Transport Control Protocol/Internet Protocol (TCP/IP) networks. Similarly, each vendor has its own fault management systems even when multiple-vendors' devices are used. As a result, when a failure occurs at a lower level, it is propagated to all the components at the next level, and hence a large number of failure messages are reported to independent NFM systems. Moreover, there is demand for providing an integrated view of the whole network system and to process faults centrally.

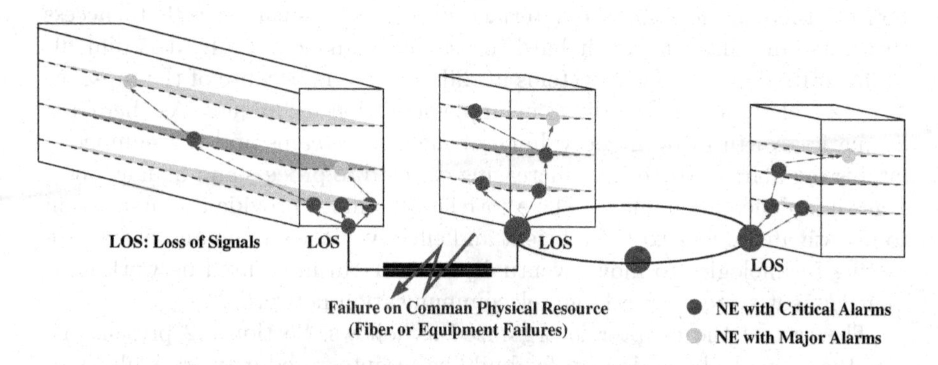

Fig. 8.2. A Fault Propagation Scenario

For example, when a failure occurs in a fiber link of the lower optical network as illustrated in Figure 8.2, all nodes involved in the fiber loop[1] report "SIGNAL LOST" alarms periodically until the fiber link is fixed. All virtual circuits also report "SIGNAL LOST" alarm periodically. Similarly all networks (above TCP/IP networks, VPNs) report "SIGNAL LOST" alarm. Some other components in the network may report a different alarm due to the failure of the fiber link. A SNMP agent in a router involved in the failure network will send SNMP traps to report that some destinations are unreachable.

Currently, due to the large volume of messages that are continuously reported by each NE and the complex message processing requirements, it is not possible to use a traditional DBMSs that supports triggers with each independent NFM system. Current NFM systems hard-code (or customize)

[1] In most cases, the underlying optical network is a loop network in order to achieve high reliability.

their data processing logic and specific monitoring rules (queries) in the system. As a result, various filters, pattern languages, regular expressions are employed to find interesting alarm messages and group these messages into subgroups based on various criteria. These subgroups are finally presented to experts to diagnose root causes or routed to an event correlation system to identify causes automatically. Once the causes are identified, a ticket is placed to a trouble ticket system to trace the problem and have it fixed by relevant engineers.

These legacy systems have several major shortcomings. First, current systems have difficulty adapting to new requirements from their customers because of the hard-coded queries. To add a new query or to add a new monitoring rule, the system has to be reconfigured partially. Second, current systems are very complicated and their performance is poor because there is almost no query optimization. Third, the scalability of the systems is limited because of the tight integration between query processing and other logical components. Fourth, there is no standard interface or language such as SQL to access these systems which makes it hard to use and manage. Finally, it is difficult to integrate different NFM systems at different layers because of the presence of hard-coded queries and different implementation techniques. As there is a dramatic growth in both the volume of message streams and the number of interesting alarms, there is an increasing demand to process and manage messages in an effective manner. The above shortcomings provide the motivation to investigate and to exploit efficient and effective data stream and event processing technologies to move eventually towards an integrated network fault management system for a large telecommunication network.

The rest of the chapter is organized as follows. Section 8.2 presents issues that need to be addressed for building an integrated network fault management system for a multi-layered telecommunications network. Section 8.3 elaborates on the architecture of our integrated inter-domain network fault management system, based on stream and event processing techniques, along with a discussion of its components. Our proposed three-phase model for applications such as these is presented in Section 8.4. Some transaction management and update issues relevant to these types of applications are discussed in Section 8.5. Finally, Section 8.6 contains the chapter summary.

8.2 Data Processing Challenges for Fault Management

As per the functional definition of a NFM system, it has to continuously collect and analyze (to detect, isolate, and trace faults) messages from different NEs and OSs to carry out sequences of actions (fix, report, and trace faults) in a near real-time manner. Although various aspects of data stream processing have been explored and some solutions have been proposed, there are still many challenges in building an integrated NFM system based on stream processing techniques.

8.2.1 Semi-structured Text Messages

Messages from NEs, OSs, and network links are semi-structured text messages. Each type of NE has its own format to report a particular kind of message and can report hundreds or even thousands of different kinds of messages. For the same type of NE or OS, different vendors have different message formats. Even for the same type of NE from the same vendor, different versions may have different formats for the same kind of message. In a typical telecommunication network, there are hundreds of different types of NEs and OSs and tens of devices from different vendors. The length of a message ranges from a few bytes to a few pages. Shown below is the message format and an actual formatted message taken from a circuit switch. It may be noted that all the upper case words indicate keywords and lower case characters indicate variables.

A sample message format:

```
REPT SM=a,b,c HWLVL=d SWLVL=e EVENT=j k
f g h i
HW-ERR FAIL-ADDR=m n-o DATA-BUS=p TIME=q
PROCESS: BG=r,s,t  CM=u,v  FG=w,x,y  z
ORIG-HW-STATUS:        a1: b1 c1 d1  a1: b1 c1 d1
FINAL-HW-STATUS:       a1: b1 c1 d1  a1: b1 c1 d1
PREVIOUS TYPE/COUNT:   e1 f1
SHADOW TYPE/COUNT:     g1 h1
AUX DATA:              i1 j1 k1 l1
ESCALATION-COUNTS:     m1 n1 o1 p1
```

An example message using the above message format:

```
+++ ARL-C H 01-01-16 17:47:20 LHL 3301 #000192 >
REPT SM=43,0,ACT HWLVL=0 SWLVL=RPI EVENT=57347 COMPLETED
CIO-1  PER-DET-BAD-PARITY
HW-ERR  FAIL-ADDR=H'8311 ROM-UNK  DATA-BUS=H'0 TIME=46:16.8
PROCESS:BG=64,0,RPI CM=NONE, FG=PC,LCNSCAN,RPI         NORMAL
ORIG-HW-STATUS:  MC0: ACT                         MC1: STBY
FINAL-HW-STATUS: MC0: ACT                         MC1: STBY
PREVIOUS TYPE/COUNT:  89    0
SHADOW TYPE/COUNT:    84    7
AUX DATA:          H'00000000 H'00000200 H'00000000 H'00000000
ESCALATION-COUNTS:H'00010000 H'00000000 H'00000000 H'00000000
END OF REPORT #000192 ++-
```

An example using a different message format:

```
S570-67 92-12-21 16:16:48 086901 MDIIMON BOZOVILL DSO

A  REPT MDII WSN  SIGTYPE DP  TKGMN 779-16     SZ 21    OOS 0
 SUPRVSN RB TIME 22:16:48 TEN=14-0-3-1 TRIAL 1 CARRFLAG NC ID
 OGT  NORMAL  CALL  CALLED-NO       CALLING-NO      DISCARD 0
```

8.2.2 Large Number of Messages

Multi-layered telecommunication networks produce a large number of messages. This is not only because each data source (e.g., a message channel of a NE) continuously reports a large number of messages in the form of a data stream, but also because the number of data sources in such a network is quite high. For example, a typical circuit switch produces around a 250 KB messages per hour, which is about 2,000 messages per hour. For a telecommunication network with approximately 400 circuit switches, the switch network can produce 100 MB message per hour. These messages do not include the messages from the transport network below it, the intelligent network layer above it, data networks, and other OSs.

8.2.3 Complex Data Processing

The primary role of a NFM system is to detect, isolate, and correct malfunctions in a telecommunication network. To detect malfunctions, a fault management system has to continuously monitor incoming messages and find "interesting" alarm messages. Once identified, NFM has to transform the interesting messages into `alarms` by stripping the unnecessary fields, adding additional fields, and applying various transformation functions to make the information meaningful and human-readable. To isolate malfunctions, a fault management system has to continuously process a large set of predefined rules over alarm streams. These rules are used to trace the root cause of the fault based on correlations, severity, and other properties of various alarms. Rules are usually defined based on the accumulated experience of experts over years. Of course, certain mining tools can also be used to help discover these rules which are beyond the scope of this book. Each rule can be considered as a continuous query over alarm streams. Once a fault is located, sequences of actions must be taken to rectify the faults. These actions have to be taken collaboratively by a team of experts at the NOC, the engineers onsite, and others. Some actions can be performed automatically while others have to be done under the supervision of experts.

8.2.4 Online Processing and Response Time

It is essential for a NFM system to respond quickly to critical alarms and minimize the effects of a fault that spreads over to other components in the network producing inconvenience/threat to the customers. Delayed response may result in suspension of important services to customers or even cause damage to the system. For example, a congestion problem on one trunk on Christmas day may block a large number of calls. This needs to be fixed as soon as possible by redefining the routing table to send a portion of blocked calls through different trunks. Therefore, a NFM system not only has to detect and isolate faults in a near real-time manner, but also fix critical problems as soon as possible in order to minimize the loss caused by these faults. Furthermore, a NFM system has to employ different strategies or priorities for handling different faults as there are a huge number of alarms in a large multi-layered network; this may entail discarding or delaying minor faults sometimes due to the shortage of system resources (i.e., CPU time, disk space) and/or human resources (i.e., experienced engineers and experts).

In a real fault management system, there are many more challenges, which are not listed or addressed here; they are: (*i*) building a collaborative alarm response interface for faults and an effective way to trace faults since it involves several expert and sometimes several days to fix some alarms and (*ii*) handling disparate hardware interfaces due to the use of devices from multiple vendors and multiple protocols in such a network. Here, we only focus on the challenges related to alarm processing outlined above.

Some of these challenges are unique and are different from the issues discussed in current data stream processing models. First, the input stream consists of semi-structured text messages that include numeric data, date/time, place, phone number, and other critical information. Second, the computation required to detect, isolate, and correct malfunctions in a fault management system is far more complicated than the operators discussed in current data stream management systems (mainly a set of traditional relational operators). Finally, the sequences of actions that need to be take when a fault is detected is complicated, involves experts, and can last for long periods of time. The above challenges make the design of these systems complicated even with the use of data stream processing techniques.

8.3 Stream- and Event-Based NFM^i Architecture

Inter-domain network fault management (NFM^i) architecture, illustrated in Figure 8.3, is based on stream and event processing techniques to provide an integrated NFM system for a multi-layered telecommunication network with online processing and near-real time response to faults. The system has many advantages compared to a traditional domain specific fault management system:

1. NFM^i provides an integrated view of the status of the entire network, and correlates alarms globally, which greatly decreases the number of alarms shown to network administrators.
2. NFM^i is more flexible than a traditional fault management system. In a traditional fault management system, the alarm processing is hard coded in the system, and as a result any change to the alarm processing (e.g., addition of new computations or rules to monitor) needs reconfiguration of the system. The stream- and event-based system proposed here can easily add new computations by developing new operators, and monitor new rules by issuing new continuous queries.

3. The system is easier to use and maintain because of the standardization of continuous queries (using extended SQL or another non-procedural language), and a clear separation between alarm processing and alarm formats.

On the other hand, the proposed system is quite different from a traditional data stream processing system as well, since:

1. NFM^i processes semi-structured messages in contrast to well-defined tuples assumed in most stream-based systems. Actually, the processing needed to convert a semi-structured message to a well-defined tuple can be done as part of stream processing, which usually takes at least one third or even more of total computation required.
2. The complicated processing requirements cannot be addressed using the basic `select-project-join` and `aggregation` operators. It requires computation of the correlations among alarms in an intelligent manner to decrease the number of alarms shown to the administrators.
3. NFM^i involves update operations, which are not usually discussed in the current data stream processing systems. For example, when an administrator takes some actions for an alarm, certain information (i.e., when and what kind of actions have been performed) has to be added to the alarm. In addition, when the problems related to that alarm have been fixed, the status of the alarm has to be updated for access by others.

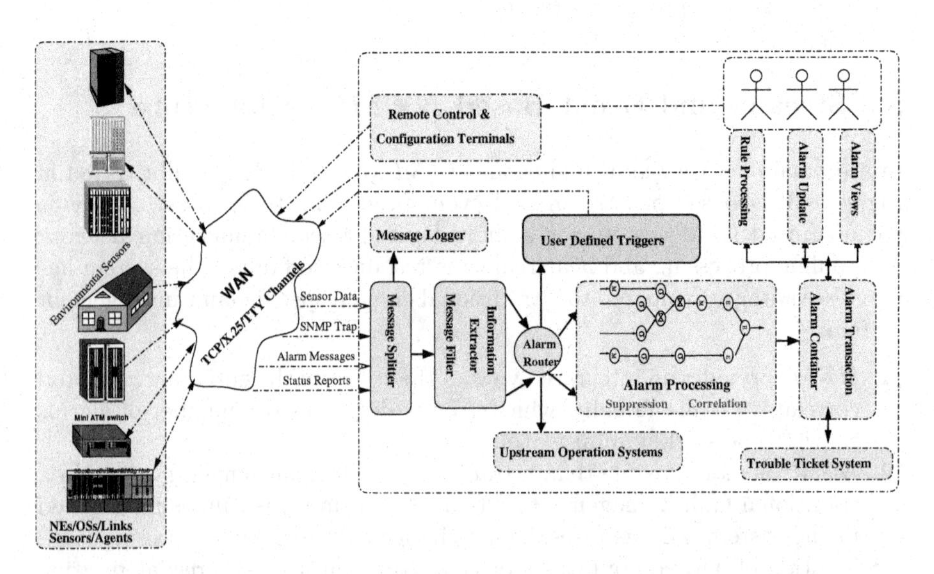

Fig. 8.3. Architecture of the Proposed Inter-Domain Network Fault Management System

In the following sections, we present a solution for each component in the architecture.

8.3.1 Message Splitter

Message splitting is the first function that is applied to the incoming alarm message streams. Each stream is a character stream, using which the messages are sent continuously. The message splitter processes this character stream, distinguishes and separates each message and converts a segment of consecutive characters into a message. Since messages come from different sources such as NEs, OSs, and agents, they have different message terminators. For example, a SNMP trap message consists of a one line message. Therefore, a new line can be used as a terminator for a SNMP trap message. For a message from a circuit switch, it is terminated by a specific set of characters such as `"\r\n\031"` or `"\r\n\033\005"`.

Therefore, a message splitter is defined as

$$splitter(\mathcal{T})\ over\ \mathcal{S}$$

where $\mathcal{T}$ is a string used to identify the end of a message and $\mathcal{S}$ corresponds to the input stream. The output is a message stream in which each message is a variable-length string.

When a new data source is added to the system, a terminating string is required and a message splitter is created automatically for this data source. The output message stream from the source is fed to the message filter and the information extractor module. A copy of the message stream is fed to the message logger. The message logger keeps messages for $\mathcal{N}$ days using a sliding `window`; it persists the most recent $\mathcal{N}$ days messages to be used as a reference information source for experts to further detect, isolate, and correct when they process the alarms.

8.3.2 Message Filter and Information Extractor

A large number of messages are generated from various components in a multi-layer telecommunication network and not all messages are of interest to the network administrators. Only a small portion of the messages are required for further processing in order to detect, isolate, and correct malfunctions. The message filter and information extractor modules provide a flexible and powerful computation to find interesting messages and extract required information from these messages. It takes the message streams from message splitters as its input and outputs formatted alarm messages which are similar to a tuple in a relation.

Each alarm consists of multiple fields extracted from messages along with the following common fields:

1. *timestamp*: time when the alarm was output from a NE, OS, or an agent.

2. *system_timestamp*: time when the alarm entered the fault management system.
3. *alarm_type*: defines the alarm type based on message format.
4. *data_source*: defines the source of the alarm.
5. *domain*: defines which domain the alarm comes from.
6. *data_source_type*: defines the data source type (e.g., File system, ATM switch) of the alarm data source.
7. *action*: defines how this alarm should be handled further. The value of this field can only be *New*, *Update*, *Clean*.
8. *severity*: defines the severity of this alarm.

As the messages are semi-structured, they are filtered based on keywords or patterns as well as their positions in the message. On the other hand, information extraction is not well supported by traditional filtering systems. Below, we propose a filtering system with information extraction based on keywords (or patterns) and their locations. No more than two passes are required to filter the incoming message and extract the required information, thus, achieving better performance.

A cursor is defined and used to trace the position within a message. The cursor points to the first character of the message. A set of operators are defined to move the cursor to a different position within the message. `c, w, f`, and `l` are used to move the cursor forward from its current location by one character, one word (which consists of only letters and hyphen), one field (separated by white space(s), (semi-) colon, period), or one line, respectively. When `w` is applied, the cursor is moved to the next non-whitespace character after the word. When `f` is applied, the cursor is moved to the beginning of next field. When `l` is applied, the cursor is moved to the begin of the next line. `bc, bw, bf`, and `bl` are used to move cursor backward one character, one word, one field, or one line, respectively. The end of a line can be reached through a `l` operation followed by a `bc` operation. These operators can be further extended to move multiple units using the format `c(n), w(n), f(n)`, and `l(n)`, where n is the number of units to be moved. `bm` and `em` are used to move the cursor either to the beginning or to the end of the message directly.

Once the cursor is moved to the correct position, `pattern(`$\mathcal{P}$`)` is used to match the specified pattern $\mathcal{P}$ from the current location of a cursor. If the pattern is matched, the cursor is moved to the first character to the right of the pattern, and the next operation can be performed. Otherwise, the filtering has failed and the message is not matched. $\mathcal{P}$ can be specified by a set of regular expressions with the OR operator (denoted by "|"). For example, a pattern can be specified as ("RMV " | "RST "), which is going to match "RMV" followed by a space or "RST" followed by a space.

The `find(`$\mathcal{P}$ $[, < \mathcal{S}(n) >]$`)` operator is proposed to search the specified pattern $\mathcal{P}$ from the current location of the cursor within the specified scope $\mathcal{S}(n)$, where $\mathcal{S}$ can be `line, message, section`, or `document`. Only `line` is used in this system; n is used to specify how many lines or sections to search.

If no scope is specified, search for the pattern is done in a global manner. In our message filter, the pattern is searched until the end of the message. Once the pattern is found, it moves the cursor to the first character following the pattern.

With a sequence of above operations, termed `filtering process`, a semi-structured message can be filtered (or matched) accurately and efficiently. In order to extract alarm information during the course of filtering, two operations are defined: `begin_field`(*field_name*) and `end_field`(*field_name*). The information between `begin_field` and `end_field` is marked for this field. Once the message is matched successfully, the information is extracted to the corresponding field; otherwise, no information is extracted. In addition, the operation `define_field`(field_name = value) can be used to add additional information to alarm information. For example, we have provided the following set of operations to filter (or match) the message given in Section 8.2 and to extract 6 fields of information discussed earlier (however, not all fields are shown). This filter process first tries to find the pattern ("REPT SM=") at the beginning of the message. If there is a match, then the SM# is extracted into field SM. It then searches for "HWLVL=" in this line, if "HWLVL=" is found then the following field is extracted into HWLVL field. if there is no match, the message is discarded. The filter process continues to work on the next message.

```
pattern("REPT SM=") begin_field(SM)    f end_field(SM)
find("HWLVL=", Line) begin_field(HWLVL) f end_field(HWLVL)
f pattern("SWLVL=") begin_field(SWLVL) f end_field(SWLVL)
f pattern("EVENT=") begin_field(EVENT) f end_field(EVENT)
l(2) f pattern("FAIL-ADD=") begin_field(ADD) f end_field(ADD)
find("TIME=", Line) begin-field(TIME) f end_field(TIME)
l(2) pattern("ORIG-HW-STATUS:") l pattern("FINAL-HW-STATUS:")
define_field(SOURCE="ARL-C") define_field(Date="01-01-16")
define_field(DOMAIN="PSTN") define_field(SOURCE_TYPE="SM")
define_field(ALARM_TYPE="REPT")
```

The alarm tuple output from this `filtering process` forms an alarm stream which has a schema formed by the 6 fields defined earlier preserving their order. Each filtering process is implemented as a super-operator, which may have to be split into a few simpler operators in order to optimize the system where multiple `filter processes` are registered to the system. these super-operators or operators can be treated as normal operators in data stream management systems. Various scheduling algorithms can be applied to schedule these operators in order to achieve required performance metrics (i.e., minimize memory requirement, tuple latency).

8.3.3 Alarm Processing

The main role of the alarm processing module is to detect and isolate the faults by analyzing the relationships between input alarm messages. In the multi-layered network shown in Figure 8.1, when the lower layer has a fault, it is usually propagated to all its upper components. This fault propagation dramatically increases the number of alarms reported by the entire network to increase dramatically.

A single NE or OS reports the same alarm periodically. For example, "SIGNAL LOST" alarms are reported periodically (i.e., every 5 seconds) until the problematic fiber link is fixed. Obviously, an administrator does not want to see the same problem repeatedly before the problem is solved. However, the administrator wants to increase the severity of the alarm if the problem is not fixed within a predefined time period in order to draw further attention to the alarms that persist (or are alive) in the system for a long time.

A fault in one component causes multiple NEs, OSs, and agents to report the same problem from their point of view. Some of these alarms have the same format and similar content; while the others may have significantly different formats and different content. However, there exists certain relationships among these alarms, and based on these relationships, an administrator wants the fault management system to automatically process (*not* discover) the relationships and decrease the number of alarms presented to the administrators.

There are additional issues involved in alarm processing. We only focus on the above two major problems in this section. Both problems require the fault management system to continuously monitor the alarm streams and evaluate the relationships of elements in these alarms. By considering each alarm as a primitive event[2], we propose a multi-phase model [333] to evaluate relationships among events in addition to generating them from CQs.

8.4 Three-Phase Processing Model for NFM^i

From the architecture presented in Figure 8.3, it is easy to observe that the generation of alarms, their correlation, and notification can be mapped to three distinct phases: processing of continuous queries, processing of event correlations (or compositions), and rule execution for notification and other purposes. Below, we elaborate on the three phases.

8.4.1 Continuous Query (CQ) Processing Phase

The first phase in our three-phase model (Figure 8.3) processes continuous queries. It takes the output streams from the message filters and information extractors as inputs and generates computed continuous streams to the

[2] In the remainder of this section, event and alarm are used interchangeably.

event detection phase. The scheduling algorithms and QoS delivery mechanisms (e.g., load shedding) along with other techniques developed for stream processing can be applied in this phase. In our NFM system, final results of stream computations are viewed as events for detecting faults and isolating faults that use multiple alarm streams and composite events. However, not all current stream processing models support complex event detection and rule processing. Also, in current stream processing systems, it is difficult to detect changes to one or more attributes on the same stream and to suppress the number of output alarms[3].

To overcome the above shortcomings, we enhance stream processing to support additional operators and in other ways to facilitate integration with event and rule processing. Although these enhancements are derived from the NFM application, their formulation has been generalized to make them relevant to any stream-based application:

1. The ability to define `computed` events on the results of CQs.
2. Addition of `stream modifiers` to detect expressive changes between tuples in a stream and `stream suppressors` based on a threshold value to decrease the number of alarms before they are sent to event processing.
3. Treat the results of CQs and event processing uniformly as streams so that they can be fed to each other without any restrictions.

The above seemingly simple enhancements significantly improve the ability of the alarm processing model to deal with complicated fault detection, isolation, and rectification. These enhancements further provide modularity and expressiveness to the specification of stream and event processing components. They also improve the ability to compute final results by using appropriate approaches and techniques developed for stream and complex event processing. At the same time, none of the enhancements affect the operator semantics, scheduling strategies, QoS delivery mechanisms, and other components proposed for stream data processing.

The ability to intersperse stream and complex event processing, using the above model, is very powerful. Event and stream processing can be composed in arbitrary ways to achieve desired processing and correlation using the proposed model.

Named Continuous Queries

The CQ name is analogous to the name of a table in a DBMS and it has the same scope and usage as that of a table. A named CQ is defined by using a CREATE CQ statement. This is further elaborated in Section 9.5.1.

[3] This, of course, depends on the operators supported in a system. We have not encountered, in the literature, operators for single stream computations presented in this chapter and Section 9.5.

Stream Modifiers

Intuitively, a stream modifier is defined as a function to compute the changes/aggregation (i.e., relative change of an attribute) between tuples (consecutive or in a `window`) of a data stream.

A family of stream modifiers [333] has been defined using the above definition of a stream modifier. They are capable of efficiently detecting the changes between tuples over a single stream. To illustrate the formulation of new stream modifier, we present two stream modifiers below that were driven by the analysis of the NFM application. Other stream modifiers can be similarly defined and a few more are presented in Section 9.5.2.

In order to reduce the number of alarms reported by the same NEs, OSs, and Agents for the same problem, we have defined the following `stream suppressors`. These suppressors are based on a threshold value, and they aggregate the same type of alarms within a `window`, rather than detecting the changes between two tuples. An alarm is produced only when the number of alarms accumulated exceeds the predefined threshold value.

RSuppressor

RSuppressor() is used to accumulate the same type of alarms. Once an alarm arrival rate exceeds the specified values, it outputs an alarm. It has the same usage as normal aggregation operators such as avg, max, etc. It is expressed as follows

$$RSuppressor(<\mathcal{R}> [, O|N < v_1, v_2, \cdots, v_j >])$$

It outputs the oldest or latest tuple with attributes $< v_1, v_2, \cdots, v_j >$ when the number of alarms in the `window` exceeds the threshold $\mathcal{R}$, and then the `window` is cleared. For example, the following continuous query can be used to accumulate the "SIGNAL LOST" alarms. It outputs the timestamp, alarm_id, alarm_type, data_source, and alarm_message of the first (or oldest) alarm in a two-hour sliding `window` when the number of alarms exceeds `10`.

```
SELECT    RSuppressor(<10>, N <timestamp, alarm_id,
          alarm_type, data_source, alarm_message>)
FROM      Lost_Signal_Stream [Range 2 hours]
GROUP BY  alarm_type, data_source, alarm_message
```

TSuppressor

TSuppressor() is used to accumulate alarms and take certain actions based on the value of the `action` field in the alarm. It is expressed as follows

$$TSuppressor(<\mathcal{T}>, O|N < v_1, v_2, \cdots, v_j >])$$

$\mathcal{T}$ is the threshold value for an alarm to stay on. $O|N < v_1, v_2, \cdots, v_j >]$ is used to specify the output fields. As we indicated earlier, each alarm has an `action` field, which can only have the value of `new` or `update` or `clean`. When an alarm with action field `new` is received, the newly arrived alarm is discarded if the alarm already exists, else, a new timer is started for this alarm. Only when the alarm stays there for more than T time units, it outputs an alarm and resets its timer. When an alarm with action field `update` is received, all fields of the old alarm is replaced with this newly arrived alarm and its timer is reset to zero. An alarm with the action field `clean` indicates that the problem has been fixed and no alarm should be reported hereafter to the administrator. Thus, once an alarm with action field `clean` is received, it clears the old alarm and no alarm is output.

```
SELECT     TSuppressor(<5 minutes>, N <timestamp, alarm_id,
           alarm_type, data_source, alarm_message>)
FROM       RmvRst_TRK_Stream [Range 2 hours]
GROUP BY   alarm_type, data_source, alarm_message
```

TSuppressor can be used, as shown above, to detect any problems that will be corrected within a planned time period. For a RMV TRK alarm, if the same alarm is reported again with the action field value of `clean` within 5 minutes, that means some actions have been taken and the problem has been fixed/corrected already, therefore, no alarm should be sent to administrators.

TSuppressor() is critical for alarms that are caused by a temporary action; once the action is taken, the alarm is automatically cleared. For example, when an administrator replaces an interface card for a NE, alarms are issued once he removes the card from the NE. After a few minutes, the administrator reinstalls a new card, and a restore alarm is issued once the NE detects that the interface starts functioning again. Similarly, when a patch is applied to a system, a few processes may have to be suspended temporarily, once the patch is installed successfully, these processes are restored, and corresponding alarms are issued. In both cases, no alarms should be reported to administrators through the system within a certain threshold T time units. Only when a threshold value is exceeded, an alarm should be presented to the administrators.

8.4.2 Complex Event Processing Phase

There is a large body of work on event processing, some of which have been discussed in Section 4.3.

Briefly, primitive or simple events are specific to a domain and are predefined. Primitive events are assumed to be detected by the underlying system along with the time of occurrence. On the other hand, composite events are composed of more than one primitive or composite event using event operators (Snoop event operators are described in [87, 285]). Some of the event operators proposed in the literature include: **and** (occurrence of two events in *any* order), `sequence` (occurrence of two events in *a particular* order), **not** (non-occurrence of an event within a well-defined interval or delimited by two events), `or` (occurrence of one of the two events), `aperiodic` (aperiodic occurrence of an event in an interval delimited by two events), `periodic` (periodic occurrence of a temporal event in an interval delimited by two events), `frequency` or `cardinality` (number of times an event occurs), and `plus` (event occurrence based on another event plus a temporal offset). Note that a complex[4] event can be used as one of the events in the above operators to facilitate construction of larger event expressions to deal with real-world situations.

The NFM application described in this chapter brings out the need for a `computed event` which can be the result of any arbitrary computation[5]. For example, an alarm is the result of a computation or a continuous query in our proposed model. An event processing engine needs to accept streams of different types of events and apply event detection. Note that the computation algorithm or the semantics of composite event operators do not change because of the `computed event`. In the three-phase model, `computed events`, defined on the output of continuous queries, act as primitive events of a complex event processing systems; `computed events` can be composed further using event operators as needed.

In order to combine complex event processing with stream processing in a seamless manner, one needs to take into account differences between the event processing model used to make sure it matches the stream processing model. For example, since stream processing models use data flow paradigm for processing, it would be appropriate to use an event processing model that also uses a data flow paradigm.

Detailed analysis of the two models (stream and complex event processing) and their integration using the three-phase model proposed here is the subject of Chapter 9.

8.4.3 Rule Processing Phase

Although limited human interventions are irreplaceable to correct some malfunctions identified by the alarms, the role of rule processing, nevertheless, is critical to automatically triggering sequence of actions for specific alarm types. Some malfunctions can be corrected without human interaction; some actions can be performed automatically but requires confirmation from an expert, while others require human intervention. For example, when a critical alarm is detected, an audio broadcast (in addition to sending an alarm to a group

[4] Composite and complex events are used interchangeable in this book.

[5] In this context, we are defining a `computed event` as the result of stream processing. As a matter of fact, this `computed event` can be the result of any arbitrary computation as the name suggests. In most domains, the events of interest are computed by processing raw data in various ways. `Computed` events play the role of primitive events and are composed using event operators. Hence, we use `computed` and primitive events interchangeably in the rest of the book.

of experts) may be necessary to get the attention of corresponding experts and administrators in order to respond to it as soon as possible. One alarm can trigger multiple sequences of actions and different alarms can trigger the same sequence of actions.

In order to improve the modularity, multiple rules (condition-action pairs) can be associated with an event in a complex event processing system. Whenever an event is raised (i.e., output as an alarm from continuous queries), it is propagated, as necessary, to detect complex events and corresponding conditions are checked to trigger actions (if the conditions evaluates to true). Components of Event-Condition-Action rules (ECA) are shown below:

`Event`	occurrence of a primitive or complex event
`Condition`	condition to be checked
`Action`	action sequence

Thus, whenever an alarm is detected (as an event), associated rules are triggered to evaluate the conditions based on the alarm attributes or temporal properties and associated actions are executed. In addition to the E, C, and A components, a rule may include coupling mode [31, 33, 182], consumption mode [86,87], and priority. In network fault management applications, most of the rules should be triggered immediately as the problem needs to be brought to the attention of various experts. The rule format is shown below:

```
Rule rule_name
    (event_name, condition_function, action_function
     [[,coupling_mode] [,priority] [,consumption_mode]])
```

Rules can be assigned priorities. In general, ECA rule processing goes through the following stages: (*i*) event detection, which is done by a complex event processing system using the alarms generated by continuous queries, (*ii*) condition evaluation and scheduling of actions, and (*iii*) execution of actions. In the first stage, alarm detection feeds into the event detection process. Once an event is detected, corresponding conditions are evaluated and actions are scheduled. In the final stage, all the scheduled actions are executed. Note that conditions and actions are arbitrary computations and can include triggering other events or starting continuous queries as well. `Consumption mode` is briefly discussed in Section 9.2.2. Coupling modes are summarized in Section 9.2.3.

8.4.4 Summary

From the analysis of NFM^i application, We have identified a number of issues that, in our opinion, have not received enough attention by the stream processing research community: (*i*) semi-structured message streams are becoming more common in stream-based applications, rather than the well-defined tuples assumed in current data stream processing, (*ii*) although data filtering can be done through current data stream processing computation, information extraction operators over streaming data are needed in order to form well-defined tuples, (*iii*) the real computation over streaming data is far more complex than what the current data stream systems provide, (*iv*) monitoring event (e.g., alarms) correlations in most applications (e.g., fault management systems) require expressive event composition and efficient detection, and (*v*) efficient rule processing is required to manage large number of rules and to trigger actions in a timely manner.

In addition to the above, support for other requirements such as transactions and views arise in the NFM^i application. We briefly discuss these requirements below.

8.5 Transactional Needs of Network Management Applications

Every alarm that is produced by the alarm processing phase should be processed scrupulously by the experts. These alarms need to be shared among experts and updated based on the action being taken, and the history of handling the alarm needs to be persisted for sharing and later analysis. This brings out the need for using a DSMS in conjunction with a system supporting transaction management. Some alarms also need to trigger sequences of actions to correct malfunctions. Issues that pertain to alarm processing are: (*i*) most alarms need to be processed by a team of experts consisting of those at NOC and onsite, (*ii*) processing time varies with alarms and can take from a few hours to a few weeks, (*iii*) alarms can be updated in multiple stages and used by other experts, (*iv*) more than one expert can process and view an alarm (each expert works on a subset of alarms), and (*v*) sequences of actions are triggered based on alarms. In order to trace each alarm effectively in the system, all the alarms produced are given a unique ticket number by the trouble ticket system. This number is used for keeping track of the updates, experts who are processing it, and the actions that are taken for that alarm.

As the alarm processing can take from a few hours to a few weeks, alarms should be available throughout that time period. In addition, alarms are also updated in multiple stages. An alarm container stores all the alarms so that they can be used by the experts over a period of time. As a single alarm can be accessed by more than one expert, alarm container need to be shared. Alarms should maintain the ACID properties of a transaction as the same alarm can be accessed concurrently by many experts. The alarm transaction addresses this issue so that an alarm can be accessed concurrently. Thus, an alarm transaction acts as the basic unit of operation for experts or expert programs.

Since alarm processing is a highly collaborative process among experts, an alarm container is proposed to contain all active alarms[6] output from the continuous query processing and complex event processing stages. This alarm container is implemented as a large block of shared memory with transaction support. Once an alarm is cleared, it is deleted from the container and archived. An alarm container can also be considered as a database of alarms, and various views can be defined over it to present alarms to experts and to update the status of alarms. Instead of building all the transactional features into a DSMS, an in-memory DBMS such as TimesTen [13,334] can readily be used for this purpose.

8.5.1 Updates and Views

Since different experts have different domain knowledge, they only monitor a small portion of alarms related to their knowledge and expertise. Therefore, various views have to be defined to select alarms and to project most useful fields of an alarm. Current fault management systems categorize alarms into small groups based on various fields. This grouping can be done by a `GROUP BY` clause in SQL allowing experts to subscribe to their groups of interest and defining fields that should be shown on their screens. Currently, this is done by defining various configuration files without a systematic thereby methodology making the process inflexible and difficult to manage and maintain. For example, when a new expert joins the team, the configuration files have to be updated to select alarms for his/her expertise. In our proposed system, rather than using various configuration files to select alarms and to select fields from alarms, we propose to use continuous queries to define multiple views for each expert, and the system can further optimize these CQs to achieve a better performance. The results of these CQs can be persisted using a traditional or in-memory DBMS.

This set of CQs can be defined to provide a set of snapshots of the alarm container. Once a new alarm is appended to the container, it is also shown on the screen of relevant experts. If *read* is the only operation over an alarm container, CQs work as intended. However, *update* and *delete* operations over the alarm container are necessary during the course of alarm processing. In order to maintain the ACID properties of an alarm, a simple lock mechanism is provided, which is transparent to the end-user. When an expert is trying to update a field of an alarm on his/her screen, a lock operation is triggered automatically to lock the corresponding field of that alarm in the alarm container. Once the update operation is done, a new alarm consisting of all touched fields of the updated alarm plus the updated field is generated and appended to the alarm container. The old alarm is deleted from the alarm container if there are no other locks on it. This updated alarm is processed as a new alarm and is processed by various continuous queries defined over

[6] Those waiting for further processing.

the alarm container. Since the updated alarm has the same alarm ID as the old one, it will automatically update the expert's screen by replacing the old alarm with the new alarm. The delete operation is done by changing the status of an alarm to "CLEAR" status, and the system automatically deletes those alarms with "CLEAR" status when their lifetime reaches a predefined threshold value. In addition, delete operation is automatically propagated to all the client sites (experts' screen displays) to delete those alarms from their screens. In summary, the degree of consistency supported is based on the domain semantics. The management of the alarm container is done outside of CQs either by an application or by a DBMS without affecting the performance of the continuous query or complex event processing systems.

8.6 Summary of Chapter 8

The goal of this chapter was to scrutinize a real-life, complex application to fully understand how it is being managed today and identify the technologies needed for improving the application along several dimensions: ease of management, modularity of specification, improving efficiency, ability to specify requirements at a higher level of abstraction, and provide transactional capabilities as needed.

We have been able to clearly quantify the need for stream as well as complex event processing, and rule-based handling of actions for this complex, real-world application. Based on the observed needs, we also proposed a model, a set of operators, and alarm processing techniques for an inter-domain network fault management system for a multi-layered telecommunication network. In order to do this, we had to make use of the unique capabilities of stream as well as complex event processing in a judicious manner.

We also developed solutions for the problems identified from the inter-domain network fault management system application. Most are general solutions and are applicable to other stream-based applications as well. For example, the three-phase model to process continuous queries and event processing is needed in most monitoring applications. However, some of the solutions illustrated in this chapter are specific to network fault management domain.

Finally we discussed the transactional needs of alarm management. In Chapter 9, we further analyze stream and event processing frameworks in detail and synthesize a general purpose architecture for integrating them synergistically.

9

INTEGRATING STREAM AND COMPLEX EVENT PROCESSING

In previous chapters, we discussed the requirements of stream processing, reviewed the techniques proposed in the literature and presented a number of techniques in detail. Our analysis of the Network Fault Management (NFM) system clearly indicated the need for complex event processing in addition to stream processing. We presented an architecture for stream processing detailing the functional components in Section 2.4. We extended that architecture in Figure 8.3 to include event processing. We also presented a three-phase general purpose model for integrating stream and complex event processing.

As reviewed in Section 4.3, event processing in the form of Event-Condition-Action (or ECA) rules has been researched extensively from the monitoring viewpoint to detect situations using complex events and to take appropriate actions in a timely manner. Several event specification languages and processing models have been developed, analyzed, and implemented. Event processing systems, typically, have concentrated primarily on complex events and rule processing either as part of a DBMS or in a standalone application environment, and have not supported stream processing (at least until recently). The inter-domain network fault management system (NFM^i) discussed in Chapter 8 clearly brings out the need for a symbiotic existence of stream and event processing in a single system. Another example is presented in Section 9.1 to further motivate this need.

Although researchers have addressed stream and event processing as two separate threads of research (mainly because of the chronology of their development), there are a number of similarities and differences between the two. We have established that for most stream processing applications, complex event detection and rule processing are also critical. In order to integrate Complex event Processing (CEP) into the stream processing architecture, we need to understand the semantics of event operators, computation models, and architectures developed for CEP over the years. Chapter 4 on literature review provided a bird's-eye view of the progress of CEP research and development (Section 4.3) to date. A short introduction to complex event processing is provided in Section 8.4.2.

S. Chakravarthy and Q. Jiang, *Stream Data Processing: A Quality of Service Perspective*, Advances in Database Systems 36, DOI: 10.1007/978-0-387-71003-7_9,

With the intention of adding an event processing component, many data stream processing systems have incorporated change detection and situation monitoring as well. However, most of the current data stream processing systems provide a limited repertoire of complex event specification (i.e., operators, event consumption modes, and rule association). The semantics of complex event detection are not always clear especially when an event stream consists of multiple occurrences of the same event. Also, as indicated in Section 4.3, the separation between stream and event processing (from a users' perspective) is not very clear. Some systems seem to be targeted mainly for event processing (e.g., RuleCore, Sentinel) and others towards stream processing (e.g., STREAM, `MavStream`) while a few indicate support for both stream and event processing (e.g., StreamBase, Coral8).

The rest of the chapter is organized as follows. Section 9.1 outlines the need for explicitly combining stream and event processing through another scenario which acts as a running example. Complex event processing is briefly explained in Section 9.2 to facilitate a comparison of stream and event processing models. Detailed comparison of stream and complex event processing models is presented in Section 9.3. An integrated architecture (based on the three-phase processing model introduced in Section 8.4) along with its advantages is the subject of Section 9.4. We present the stream- and event-side extensions needed for the proposed integrated architecture in Sections 9.5 and 9.6, respectively. Finally, we summarize this chapter in Section 9.7.

9.1 Motivation

Stream applications not only need computations on streams, but these computations often generate **`computed events`** that are domain specific (e.g., a car slowing down, car stopped, potential fire, and fault alarm) and several such events need to be composed or correlated, detected, and monitored for taking appropriate actions. Our view is that although each model, namely stream and complex event processing, is useful in its own right, their combined expressiveness and computational benefits far outweigh their individual capability.

Consider the car accident detection scenario from the linear road benchmark [335, 336] application. Our formulation is slightly different but easier to understand and brings out stream and event processing aspects elegantly. This application has received considerable attention and more information can be found at the following web sites: `www.cs.brandeis.edu/~linearroad`, `http://infolab.stanford.edu/stream/cql-benchmark.html`, and `http://www.cs.utexas.edu/~nav/SPC-LR`.

Example 9.1 (Car ADN). In a car accident detection and notification system, each express way in an urban area is modeled as a linear road, and is further divided into equal-length segments (e.g., 5 miles). Each registered vehicle is equipped with a sensor and reports its location and other relevant information (e.g., speed, car identification) periodically (say, every 30 seconds). Based on this stream data, the objective is to detect car accidents and slowing down of vehicles in a near-real time manner. If a car reports the same location (or with speed zero mph) for four consecutive times, `followed by` at least one car in the same segment and lane with a decrease in its speed by 30% during its four consecutive reports, then it is considered as a potential accident. Once an accident is detected, the following actions may have to be taken immediately: (*i*) notify the nearest police/ambulance control room about the accident, (*ii*) notify all the cars in k upstream segments about the accident, and (*iii*) notify toll stations, if any, so that cars that are blocked in the upstream for up to t minutes by the accident may not be tolled.

Every car in the express way is assumed to report its location every 30 seconds forming the primary input data stream for the above example. The schema of the car location data stream (i.e., `CarLocStr`) is given below:

```
CarLocStr(
     timestamp,     /* time stamp of this record   */
     carId,         /* unique car identifier       */
     speed,         /* speed of the car            */
     exp_way,       /* expressway: 0..10           */
     lane,          /* lane: 0, 1, 2, 3            */
     dir,           /* direction: 0(east), 1(west) */
     Xpos           /* car location coordinates    */
);
```

`CarSegStr` is another stream (derived from the `CarLocStr` stream) for grouping the cars from the same segment (e.g., 5 miles), in which the location of the car is replaced by the segment corresponding to the location. Assume that there is a direct relationship between Xpos[1] and the segment of the road. In general, given the location, it is possible to compute the road segment a car is in. The query shown below produces the `CarSegStr` stream from the `CarLocStr` stream.

```
SELECT timestamp, carId, speed, exp_way,
     lane, dir, (Xpos/5) as segmentId
     FROM   CarLocStr;
```

Detecting an accident in the above CAR ADN example has three requirements, and they are:

1. `Immobility` : checking whether a car is at the *same location* for four consecutive time units (i.e., over a 2 minutes `window`, in our example, as the car reports its location every 30 seconds).

[1] To make the discussion easy to follow, only one value is used for position.

2. `Speed Reduction` : finding whether there is at least one car that has reduced its speed by 30% or more during four consecutive time units.
3. `Correlation` : determining whether the car that has reduced its speed (i.e., car identified in `Speed Reduction`) is in the same segment (and the same lane) and it follows the car that is stationary (i.e., car identified in `Immobility`).

`Immobility` and `Speed Reduction` of a car can be computed using a CQ. Once the cars that satisfy the requirements (1) and (2) are identified, whether those cars form a temporal sequence along with the lane and segment constraints can be determined in an event processing model using a `sequence` event operator [86,228,337,338] with appropriate condition checking. As the same car (as well as different ones) can satisfy the `sequence` event many a times, checking for the condition identified in requirement (3) need to be carried out many a times. In addition, it is also important to avoid/minimize generating the same situation (or event) multiple times[2]. In other words, the number of times *the same* accident is reported should be kept to a minimum. Stream modifiers, proposed earlier, can be effectively used to reduce the number of primitive event notifications. Event generalization and extended consumption modes proposed in this chapter can be used effectively to improve the efficiency of detecting an accident. Although a `window`-based `join` can be used [3] to compute the `sequence` event, it will be difficult to control the number of events detected without using consumption modes.

We later illustrate how the above can be specified elegantly and computed efficiently using the architecture proposed in this chapter. Some of the earlier work on sequence processing [230], temporal aggregation [237], and trigger processing [214] address some computational and performance aspects that may be relevant to the extensions proposed in this chapter. However, they were not addressed in the context of streams and they primarily focused on event logs in the relational context without the notion of a `window`. In general, performance evaluation of event processing has not included either real-time aspects or QoS requirements.

---

[2] This requirement is similar to the suppression of alarms in the NFM^i application as discussed in Section 8.4.1.

[3] Although `sequence` event operator can be implemented as a join, other event operators (e.g., `not`, `aperiodic`) cannot be implemented using relational operators. If more than one sequence is involved, it also becomes harder to use relational operators, as the time of occurrence of the previous composite event is needed. Furthermore, event consumption modes cannot be simulated using the `window` concept. Hence the need for generalizing event specification proposed in Section 9.6.

9.2 Event Processing Model

Typically, ECA rules have been used to process event sequences (or streams) and to make the underlying system reactive for supporting situation monitoring, access control, and change detection. ECA Rule consists of three components:

1. Event: occurrence/happening of interest such as domain-specific events, clock-events, external events, and `computed events`.
2. Condition: can be a simple or a complex query; in general an arbitrary *side-effect free* computation.
3. Action: specifies a set of operations that are to be performed when an event occurs and the corresponding condition evaluates to `true`. Actions can raise events leading to cascaded rule processing.

ECA rules can be defined either at application level or at system level (as indicated in Section 4.3.2). Primitive or `computed` events are specific to a domain and are predefined. Composite or complex events, on the other hand, correspond to correlations and are composed, recursively, using primitive or composite events using event operators. A complex event is also termed an event expression. Event operators [86,218,228,285,339–342], used to compose events, can be unary (e.g., `frequency`, absolute temporal event), binary (e.g., `and`, `sequence`), or ternary (e.g., `not`, `aperiodic`).

Primitive events are detected (or `computed` using CQs) along with the time of occurrence. The time of occurrence of an event can either be the time at which a CQ finishes its computation or the timestamp of one of the tuples participating in the computation based on the application semantics. Composite events are detected using the event operator semantics which is based on the time of occurrence of its constituent events. The time of occurrence of a composite event is determined by the detection semantics [87,285,343].

Consider two primitive events `ES1` (event from sensor 1) and `ES2` (event from sensor 2), and a composite event `ES1 sequence ES2`. `ES1` and `ES2` are the constituent events of this event expression. A `ES1` occurrence starts the detection of the composite event and is termed the `initiator`. A `ES2` occurrence finishes the detection of the composite event and is termed the `terminator`. With the event occurrences of `ES1` at 10 a.m. and `ES2` at 11 a.m., this composite event is detected at 11 a.m. in point-based (or detection-based) semantics, i.e, at the time of occurrence of the `terminator`. The same composite event will be detected with an interval [10 a.m. - 11 a.m.] in interval-based (or occurrence-based) semantics, i.e., the interval formed by the time of occurrences of the `initiator` and `terminator`. For more details on point- or detection-based semantics, refer to [86,87] and for details on interval- or occurrence-based semantics, refer to [285,342–344].

Several computation models have been proposed for the detection of composite events in the literature: event detection graphs (EDGs) based on event algebra [86,211,337], extended finite state automaton [221,222], and colored

Petri nets [227,228,340]. EDGs are similar to operator trees used for relational queries. They can process sets of tuples, and can support both pull- and push-based computation semantics. In Snoop, EDGs use an event flow model very similar to the model used for the computation of continuous queries.

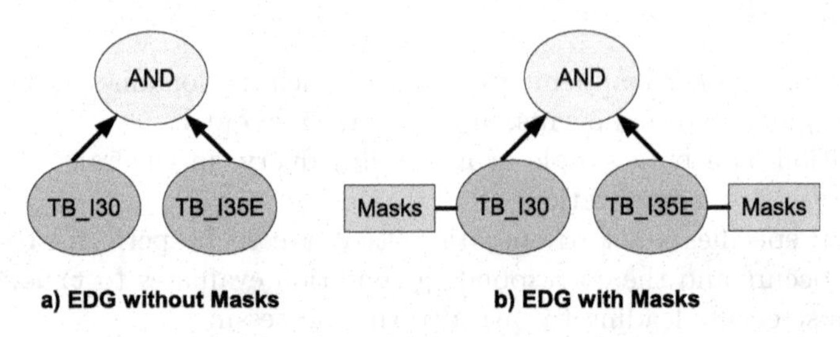

Fig. 9.1. A Simple Event Detection Graph (EDG)

9.2.1 Event Detection Graphs

In an EDG, leaf nodes represent primitive/`computed` events and internal nodes correspond to composite events (or event operators) and event occurrences flow in a bottom-up manner. Figure 9.1-a) shows a composite event `and` with two events `TB_I30` (*traffic block involving Interstate 30*) and `TB_I35E` (*traffic block involving Interstate I35E*). These two highways cross each other in the Dallas area. Whenever there is an occurrence of event `TB_I30` or `TB_I35E`, it is propagated to the `and` node. An `and` event is detected when both of its constituent events occur. Intuitively, in the absence of any other constraints (such as event consumption modes, explained below), the `and` operator can be modeled as `join` with a join condition on the timestamp attributes. In addition, as shown in Figure 9.1-b) EDGs can also support masks to filter event occurrences while events are propagated. For example, there can be a mask associated with event `TB_I30` which will only propagates events from 11 a.m. to 1 p.m.

We generalize the notion of mask introduced for primitive events in ODE [339]. This is done by allowing conditions to be specified on complex events. In addition, predicates from the condition part of the rule can be analyzed and pushed down the event detection graph as masks thereby reducing the number of events generated at every node of the EDG.

9.2.2 Event Consumption Modes

The `and` event shown in Figure 9.1-a) is detected when both events (`TB_I30`, `TB_I35E`) occur. All occurrences of events `TB_I30` and `TB_I35E` are combined, and none of them can be removed after they have taken part in event detection.

In general, multiple occurrences of the same event will continue to generate additional composite events although the occurrences are fairly old.

The event operator semantics indicated above has no constraints and hence is termed unrestricted (or general) parameter context (or event consumption mode). For some operators, this means that once an event occurs, it cannot be discarded at all. For example, for a `sequence` event operator, [87,228,337], *all* event occurrences that occur after a particular event occurrence will get paired with that event as per the unrestricted context semantics. In the absence of any mechanism for restricting event usage (or consumption), events need to be detected and parameters for those composite events computed using the unrestricted context definition of an event operator. However, the number of events produced (with unrestricted context) can be very large and more importantly, not all event occurrences and their combinations are meaningful for an application. In addition, detection of these events has substantial computation and space overhead to impact the QoS metrics. To alleviate this, event consumption modes (or contexts) were introduced and are supported by several complex event processing systems such as *ACOOD*, *SAMOS*, *Sentinel*, and *REACH* for restricting the generation of events – to reduce the number of events generated and to improve efficiency.

Consider the application in which the Texas Department of Transportation (TxDOT) wants to monitor "Whether there is a *traffic block involving Interstate 30 and Interstate 35E* in Dallas". This can be expressed as a complex event using the event operator `and` as shown in Figure 9.1-a). Whenever there is a traffic block[4] on I30 or I35E, the corresponding event is propagated to the `and` node. The complex event `and` is detected at the internal node whenever both the child nodes propagate corresponding events. Since an `and` event is detected whenever both its constituent events occur in any order, it intuitively represents the Cartesian product operation in a DSMS using only the timestamp attribute.

In real-world applications, all combinations (i.e., unrestricted context) of events may not be interesting or even meaningful. In order to restrict the detection to meaningful composite events, event consumption modes were introduced for *Snoop* [86,87]. Event consumption modes place restrictions on the pairing of events to detect a composite event and indicates when an event can be discarded. *Snoop* supports the following event consumption modes: *Recent*, *Proximal-Unique* [345], *Chronicle*, *Continuous*, and *Cumulative*. Relative computational effort needed along with storage requirements have been analyzed for the above consumption modes.

Briefly, in the *recent* event consumption mode, only the most recent occurrence of the `initiator` event (primitive or composite) that has started the detection of the complex event is used (useful for sensor class of applications). For the *chronicle* mode, the `initiator-terminator` pair that detects

[4] A traffic block can be detected using a continuous query as indicated in the CarADN example 9.1.

a complex event (recursively) is kept unique for the each complex event occurrence (useful for applications where there is a need to match events such as fault_report and fault_fix). In the *continuous* mode, each `initiator` of a participating event starts the detection of a new occurrence of the complex event (useful for applications requiring a moving/sliding window such as traffic monitoring). All participating occurrences of an event type (including the `initiator` and `terminator`) are accumulated as instances of the complex event until the event is detected in the *cumulative* mode (useful for applications such as a NFM where progress of accumulated active events are tracked at the end of the day). Finally, the *proximal-unique* mode is a variant of the *recent* mode with the additional constraint that the `terminator` is unique for each occurrence of the complex event (useful for detecting unique pairing of events that are closest to each other).

9.2.3 Event Detection and Rule Execution

Composite events are detected, by propagating primitive events as they occur, using an event detection graph. When an event is propagated, it is combined with the state information maintained by the event operator (similar to the synopsis used in CQ processing) to determine whether the composite event occurs. This depends on the semantics of the operator as well as the consumption mode associated with the event expression. If events are detected at a node, they are propagated to the parent nodes immediately. This is mainly due to lack of buffers and scheduling in event processing.

Any node in the event graph can be associated with a set of prioritized rules each with one or more conditions and actions. When an event is detected, conditions associated with the event are evaluated and corresponding rules are scheduled for execution based on the coupling mode associated with an event. A coupling mode indicates the temporal separation that can exist between an event detection, condition evaluation, and action execution. *Immediate* and *deferred* are commonly used coupling modes. *Immediate* coupling mode evaluates the conditions and triggers actions immediately (or within the same transaction) and *deferred* coupling mode postpones the evaluation of condition and action execution to a later point in time (or at the end of the transaction). Coupling modes and their effect on transactions are further elaborated in [182,346]. As we inferred from the NFM^i application (in Chapter 8), conditions need to be checked immediately for most of the response-sensitive monitoring applications and if they evaluate to `true`, actions need to be scheduled for execution immediately. Conditions can be a side-effect free function (or method) call to which all the event attributes are passed as parameters. Actions can be arbitrary computations to which event attributes are passed, as well, as parameters. A collection of event expressions is optimized in Sentinel by sharing common subexpressions among them (even if they belong to different parameter contexts) to save overall computation time and storage space.

9.3 Complex Event Vs. Stream Processing

Event processing [31, 187, 211–214, 222, 226, 228, 230, 235, 337, 338] and lately stream data processing [63, 106, 122, 127, 151, 181] have evolved independently based on situation monitoring application needs. Several event specification languages [86, 218, 228, 285, 339–342] for specifying composite events have been proposed and triggers have been successfully incorporated into relational databases. Different computation models [187, 211, 221, 222, 226–228, 337] for processing events such as Petri nets [227, 228], extended automata [221, 222, 339], and event graphs [187, 211, 337] have been proposed and implemented. Various event consumption modes [86, 187, 227, 228, 337] (or parameter contexts) have been explored and analyzed.

Similarly, data stream processing has received a lot of attention lately, and a number of issues – from architecture [63, 115, 122, 127, 151] to QoS [92, 93, 111, 112, 131, 180] – have been explored. Although both of these areas seem different at the outset, it is easy to identify the similarities between them. Not surprisingly, some of the computation model used for data stream processing is not dissimilar from the event processing models (e.g., event graph [86, 87]), but used with a different emphasis.

This section compares[5] complex event and stream processing models with respect to a number of important characteristics. This analysis forms the basis of our integrated architecture.

9.3.1 Inputs and Outputs

Inputs (or data sources) to an event processing model are a sequence of events (or event histories). Event sequences are ordered by their time of occurrence. Most event sequences considered by event processing models are generated by the underlying system (into which event processing is incorporated) such as an RDBMS (e.g., data manipulation operations `INSERT`, `UPDATE`, and `DELETE` act as events) or an application (e.g., method invocations act as events). The input rate of an event stream is not assumed to be very high. Also the attributes of an event object (a tuple) are assumed to be defined in terms of primitive data types. The outputs of event operators also form event sequences, which are ordered by their detection timestamp (may be an interval for composite events). Once events are detected, they are used to trigger a set of rules. Once the rules are triggered, necessary conditions are checked and actions are performed. Actions can include raising of (external) events requiring cascaded event detection and execution of rules. Condition evaluation and action execution can access stored repositories in addition to the parameters of the event.

[5] This analysis is based on the information available in the literature and may not include all commercial systems as their details are somewhat difficult to gather in the absence of published and/or accessible literature.

Primary inputs to a stream processing system are data streams. Input tuples in a data stream can be ordered by any attribute and not necessarily by the timestamp (e.g., sequence_id of a TCP packet in a TCP packet stream) as in the case of event sequences. In addition to streams, processing may also include stored relations. Furthermore, the input characteristics of data streams are highly unpredictable and dynamic (e.g., bursty). The data items from a data stream can be complex (e.g., semi-structured messages discussed in Section 8.2.1). The output of a data stream processing, if one of its input is a data stream, is a data stream as well. Thus, conceptually, both models have similar inputs and outputs. However, the data sources in the stream processing model are mostly external sources with high input rates and highly bursty input model, where as the input rates in the event processing model are assumed to be relatively low.

The above difference in input rate assumption can be clearly inferred from the techniques proposed for event detection. QoS was not considered critical (except for work on event showers [347]) and was not incorporated either in the specification or the computation model of any earlier complex event processing system.

9.3.2 Consumption Modes Vs. `Window` Types

Event consumption modes were introduced primarily to reduce the number of events detected without affecting the semantics of application groups. Event consumption modes, in turn, determined when to drop/discard event occurrences (both primitive and complex) from the system. The events that were used for detection depended solely on the context and the semantics of the operator. For example, for the **`sequence`** operator , one could not drop any event from the past if context was not specified (i.e., use of general or unrestricted context). However, with a *recent* context, for the same **`sequence`** operator, only the most recent occurrence of the initiator event is retained and the most recent occurrence of the terminator event is used for pairing. Event consumption modes indirectly helped in keeping a small portion of (the head of) an event sequence based solely on the value of timestamp and the context. Also, the set of event instances retained at an operator depended upon the dynamics of participating event sequences. For instance, if the completing/terminating event did not occur, instances of the other participating events would accumulate for some contexts such as *chronicle* and *continuous*. Event operators were considered **`non-blocking`** as there was no sorting or aggregate computations and complex events were detected continuously and incrementally.

In contrast, stream processing uses the notion of a `window` for each stream in a query and is independent of operator semantics. Also, a `window` is typically defined primarily in terms of time or number of tuples. The objectives of defining a `window` in stream processing are: (*i*) to convert **`blocking`** operators into a **`non-blocking`** computations, and (*ii*) to produce output in a continuous manner. The consumption mode used in event processing is not exactly the same as the `window` concept in streams. The relationship between `window` and consumption modes has not been investigated in the literature.

9.3.3 Event Operators Vs. CQ Operators

Event operators are quite different[6] from the operators supported by current stream processing systems. Event operators are mainly used to combine/correlate happenings along a time line using different event operators. Semantics of event operators, proposed in the literature, dictate only the use of the `timestamp` associated with an event (i.e., time of occurrence of that event) for detecting complex events (whether using point- or interval-based semantics). For example, a `sequence` operator is used to express and compute the ordering of two events (tuples) from its input event streams. Typically, there is no data manipulation or computation in event processing except as part of conditions and actions. On the other hand, current stream processing operators focus on how to express and define the computations including `join` and `aggregate` at the attribute and tuple level. Additionally, stream processing operators have input queues and `window` specification in order to deal with fluctuating input rates and `blocking` of inputs, respectively.

Event operators neither have input queues nor `window` specification, although consumption modes are used for a different purpose. Lack of queues is primarily due to the low input rate assumption, and best-effort optimization has been used instead of QoS satisfaction.

9.3.4 Best-Effort Vs. QoS

The notion of QoS is not present in the event processing literature. Although, there is some work on real-time events and event showers [347], none of the event processing models supports QoS requirements. Typically, in the event processing model, whenever an event occurs, it is detected and propagated to form a composite event as soon as possible. Thus, events are detected based on the best-effort method.

On the other hand, QoS support in a stream processing model is necessary and critical to the success of DSMSs for the following reasons: (*i*) inputs to a stream processing system are unpredictable and fluctuating in contrast to its fixed computation resources. During overload periods, some queries cannot get sufficient resources to compute their results, which can cause unexpectedly long delays in the results, (*ii*) many stream-based applications require real-time responses from a stream processing system. A delayed response may not be useful, and may even cause serious problems. Different applications may tolerate different response times or inaccuracy in the final query results, and (*iii*) queries with different QoS requirements must be treated differently

[6] Refer to footnote [3] on page 190.

with a goal to minimize the overall violation of predefined QoS specifications. Chapter 7 discussed the QoS delivery mechanisms for stream processing.

9.3.5 Optimization and Scheduling

Event expressions are transformed into event detection graphs or other models of computation. There has been some work on optimization, so that event detection can be made efficient by constructing smaller event detection graphs. Common event sub-expressions are grouped in order to reduce the overall response time, storage, and computation effort. In general, event processing does not deal with run-time optimizations (Ariel [214, 215] and RETE [348], and TREAT [349] has some run-time optimizations), nor does it address system capacity planning or detailed optimization. There is no framework or formalism for optimizing a given set of complex event expressions with respect to a well-defined set of QoS metrics. Recent work [271] has proposed a plan-based approach to optimizing complex event detection in distributed environments.

On the other hand, efficient approaches for processing CQs have been proposed. Optimizations in stream processing models include: (*i*) sharing of queues (inputs) among multiple operators, (*ii*) sharing of synopsis between overlapping `windows` (*iii*) sharing of operator computations, (*iv*) sharing of common sub-expressions, (*v*) approximate computation, and (*vi*) use of sketches and histograms.

Scheduling is also absent from event processing systems. Typically a dataflow architecture (implicitly, a First In First Out or FIFO scheduling strategy is employed in event processing models) is assumed as indicated earlier and memory usage or event-latency has not been addressed in the literature. On the other hand, optimizing memory capacity, tuple latency, and the combination of these two have prompted many scheduling algorithms [92, 111, 131] in stream processing. Chapter 6 discussed a number of scheduling strategies for continuous queries.

9.3.6 Buffer Management and Load Shedding

None of the event processing systems assumes the presence of queues/buffers between event operators. Events are assumed to be processed as soon as they arrive and partial results are maintained in event nodes (similar to synopsis). Most of the event processing models assume that the incoming events are not bursty and hence do not provide any kind of buffer management or explicit load shedding strategies. Event consumption modes can be loosely interpreted as load shedding, used from a semantics viewpoint rather than QoS viewpoint. On the other hand, load shedding is extremely important in a stream processing environment. Even with the choice of the best scheduling strategy, it is imperative to have load shedding strategies as the input rates can vary dynamically. Several load shedding strategies, placement of load shedders, and the amount of tuples to be shed (possibly limiting the error in query results) have been proposed [93, 112, 126, 132, 180].

9.3.7 Rule Execution Semantics

ECA Rules describe how the underlying system should respond when an event occurs, making the system reactive. Rules are considered important as they allow users to specify predefined actions to be executed when an event occurs and the corresponding conditions are satisfied. Existing event processing systems support dynamic enabling and disabling of rules or rule sets. Rule execution semantics specify how the set of rules should behave in the systems once they have been defined. A rich set of rule execution semantics [31,191–193,195] has been proposed in the literature to accurately define and execute rules in event processing models. The issues addressed include: rule processing granularity, instance/set oriented execution, iterative/recursive execution, conflict resolution, sequential/concurrent execution, coupling modes, observable determinism, confluence, and termination. Stream processing systems, typically, do not support high-level rule specification and processing. The rule execution model, even where rules are supported, is not explicit and rule analysis is lacking in stream processing work.

9.3.8 Summary

The above analysis clearly brings out the differences in assumptions and issues considered important in the two threads of work. This analysis also indicates that in order combine stream processing with complex event processing in a seamless manner, it is important to choose compatible processing architectures.

It will be difficult to combine incompatible execution models and obtain a synergistic and efficient system. Also, the above analysis indicates that there are significant differences in the event processing model that need to be addressed. For example, best-effort processing needs to be extended to QoS-driven processing so that one can reason about end-to-end QoS (tuple latency and memory usage) requirements. As another example, current complex event processing systems do not use any QoS-delivery mechanisms. In addition, both expressiveness and efficiency of event processing need to be extended by using the proposed generalized events and their evaluation. Finally, queueing/buffereing is needed in order to deal with bursty stream of events generated by CQs. Furthermore, it is necessary to reconcile with the notion of a `window` in stream processing with that of consumption modes in complex event processing. Our preliminary work indicates that the concept of a `window` is orthogonal to the notion of consumption modes. It makes sense to extend the `window` concept to event processing and to merge event consumption modes to obtain a common framework as well.

Based on our analysis, we argue that combining event processing with stream processing in an *ad hoc* manner without providing modularization and well-defined semantics will result in a system that is extremely difficult to use. Procedural approaches make it difficult to code an already complex problem; optimization will also be difficult as current techniques may not be applicable. This will lead to customization of the system for time-critical applications (which will not be much improvement over the current situation). Semantically as well as from an application modeling viewpoint, stream and event processing play different roles and hence need to be brought together in a symbiotic way by preserving their individuality and strengths. Furthermore, expressive event operators and the ability to compose complex events to define situations will become even more important as applications become more complex.

In conclusion, we draw upon EDGs for our integrated architecture as it corresponds to operator trees and matches processing of continuous queries whereas the other representations do not share these characteristics with continuous query processing.

9.4 MavEStream: An Integrated Architecture

The proposed integrated architecture is elaborated in Figure 9.2. Our architecture consists of four stages:

Continuous Query Processing (Stage 1): corresponds to the CQ processing of data streams. This stage represents the MavStream (or any other stream processing system) that accepts stream data as input, computes CQs, and produces output streams. In this discussion, we assume that CQs output data streams in the form of tuples. MavStream currently supports a number of stream operators: select, project, join, aggregation operators (sum, count, max, min, and average) and group by. Having functionality is implemented using a filter operator on the output of group by. Stream modifiers (discussed in Sections 8.4.1, 9.5.2, and 11.4) are also used as part of continuous queries. Output from a CQ can be consumed by an application; if needed, the output is also propagated to the event processing stage through the event generation interface.

Event Generation (Stage 2): This stage generates events based on the association of computed events (with or without masks) with CQs. Evaluation of masks is also performed in this stage. In addition to the extensions to both systems (further elaborated below), **stage 2** has been added to facilitate seamless integration of the two systems. This stage allows for stream output to be split to generate different event types from the same CQ.

Complex Event Processing (Stage 3): This stage represents the complex event processing component, where complex events are detected based on the definition of event expressions. Computed events generated by CQs act as primitive events. In the integrated architecture, computed events are raised by the event generation stage.

Rule Processing (Stage 4): Rule processing is a component of CEP system which processes rules that are associated with events. When events are detected, conditions (specified as methods) are evaluated and if they evaluate to `true`, corresponding actions are performed. Events and rules can be added at run-time. Rules can raise events resulting in cascaded execution of event detection and rule execution.

9.4.1 Strengths of the Architecture

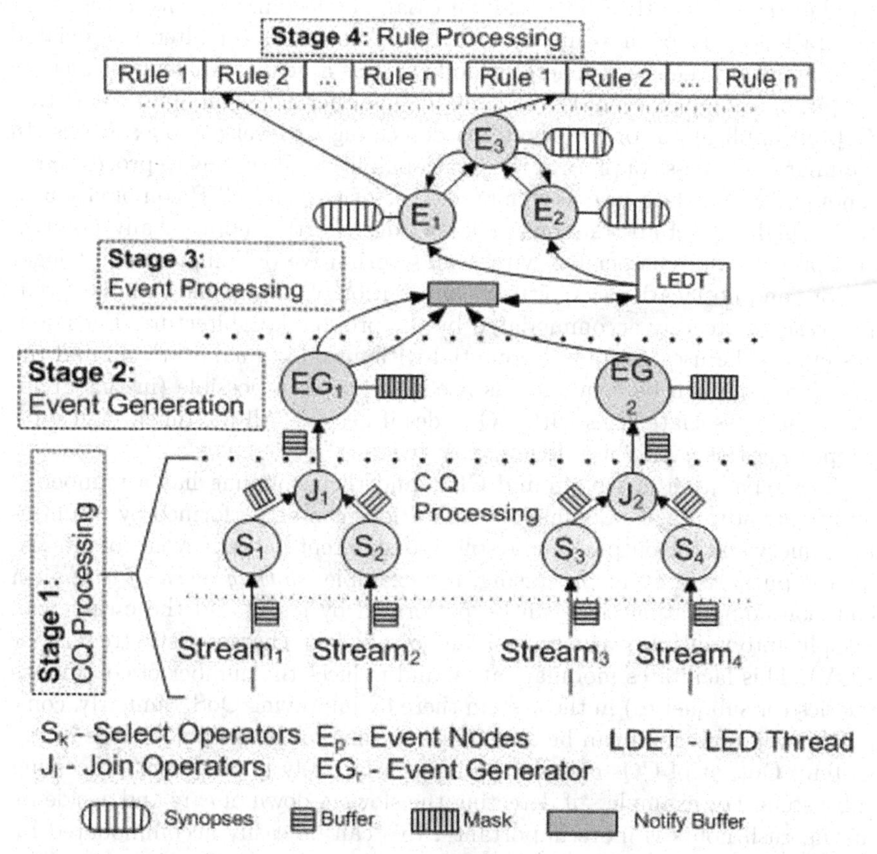

Fig. 9.2. EStreams: Four Stage Stream and Complex Event Integration Model

The architecture presented in Figure 9.2 is motivated by the separation of semantics and roles while preserving the expressiveness and efficiency of computation. Optimization of individual components will be much easier (and some work already exists in this direction) than optimizing the combined specification as a whole. Also, from the users' perspective, understandability and manageability of CQs and event specifications will be much easier than either a procedural approach or composing already overloaded constructs (or operators).

The seamless nature of our integrated architecture is due the compatibility of the chosen event processing model (i.e., an event detection graph) with that of the stream processing model used for stream processing.

We want to emphasize that the architecture shown above does not limit the applications to one stage of stream processing followed by one stage of complex event processing. We want to unequivocally indicate that there is no such arbitrary restriction in the proposed architecture. Incoming streams can be treated directly as events, if necessary, by feeding streams to the event generation operator in **stage 2**. If there are no masks (or filters) associated with an event, the event generator node acts as a `no-op`. Analogously, as the output of a complex event is a stream, it can either act as an input to another CQ, an application, or propagate to detect higher-level complex events. In summary, seamless coupling of the two capabilities allows one to process large amounts of raw data in one or more stages of CQ and CEP combination to derive higher-level abstractions or knowledge. Furthermore, at any point in this process, rules associated with events (primitive or complex) can trigger actions and notifications. Arbitrary composition of stream and complex event processing is readily accommodated by the proposed architecture. Each subsystem can be used to its full potential without additional overhead and the functionalities can be combined as needed. It is even possible (in this architecture) to associate rules with CQ nodes if needed. All the functionality for supporting this capability already exists.

The separation of stream and CEP, and their coupling has a number of additional advantages. Common computations can be performed by a continuous query and the output can be split into different types of events of interest for the purpose of event processing. For example, *slowing down of a car* is a common computation that can be performed by a CQ and the output can be split into multiple event types based on the lane characteristic (regular or HOV). This facilitates modularization and reduces the number of continuous queries (or subqueries) in the system there by improving QoS. Similarly, composite event detection can be added at any time to the output of CQs in the system. Output of CQs can also be input selectively to the event processing subsystem. For example, "if detecting the slowing down of cars and accidents during rush hours is more important", this can be easily accommodated by defining masks on an event for the same CQ.

Below, we discuss a number of stream- and event-side extensions that are useful for this architecture to attain its full potential. In addition to these extensions, some of the QoS-related differences in the models of the two systems, identified in the above analysis, need to be bridged as well. For example, it is important to investigate scheduling and QoS delivery mechanism for the complex event processing model to support end-to-end QoS requirements.

9.5 Stream-Side Extensions

In Section 8.4.1, we highlighted some of the extensions to make a DSMS compatible with the needs of complex, monitoring applications. Below, we continue with those extensions to provide additional operators and their role as part of CQs.

9.5.1 Named Continuous Queries

Many computations over stream data are difficult to express as a single CQ using SQL. In order to be able to compose computations and be able to use them for defining events, CQs need to be named. The name of a CQ is analogous to a table (stored or computed) and can act as input to another CQ or generate events. The queue (buffer) associated with the root operator in a CQ provides the output of a named CQ to be fed directly into another named CQ or generate `computed` events. A named CQ is defined by using the following CREATE CQ statement.

```
CREATE CQ CQ_Name AS (CQ definition)
```

However, the FROM clause in a named CQ can use any previously defined CQs or events (`computed` or complex) through their unique names. The meta information of a named CQ is maintained in a CQ_dictionary in the system. The meta information includes *query name*, its *input sources*, *output attributes* and their order in the output tuple, and its *output destination(s)*. If the output destination is an application, it can be in the form of a named pipe, socket, or an output queue/buffer. A default output destination is defined in the system simply as a sink if there is no destination associated with a CQ. A CQ with a sink as its destination can be disabled in the system until a meaningful destination is associated with it. For example, you can define a named CQ and register it with the system, and then use its name as part of another CQ definition. Once a named CQ is registered with the system, if it refers to other named CQs, the system will automatically associate them to the inputs of the registered CQ. In fact the starting of a CQ can be inferred from this dependency. A named CQ can output its final results to multiple destinations.

The following `CQ_Immobile` and `CQ_Decrease` named CQs can be used to find all cars that stay at the same location and the cars whose speed has decreased by 30% within the last 2 minutes for the car accident detection and notification example 9.1.

`Immobility` of a car can be computed using below CQ.

```
CREATE CQ CQ_Immobile AS (
   SELECT    carId, Xpos, count(*)
   FROM      CarLocStr [Range 2 minutes]
   GROUP BY  carId, Xpos
   HAVING    count(*) > 3
                                )
```

The above query will group the tuples based on the carId and position (Xpos). Since the cars produce tuples every 30 sec, this query will count the number of times for which a car is in the same position for at least four consecutive time points. Using the carId, other required attributes can be obtained.

`Speed Reduction` of a car can be computed using the following CQ. The first (lowest timestamp) and the last (highest timestamp) tuples of a partition are identified by their timestamp attribute values and the speed value from those two tuples is used for comparison. Other attributes can be obtained by making additional joins.

```
CREATE CQ CQ_Decrease AS (
       SELECT outer.carId
       FROM CarSegStr outer [Range 2 minutes]
       GROUP BY outer.carId
       HAVING (
           (SELECT speed as end_speed
            FROM CarSegStr last [Range 2 minutes]
            WHERE last.timestamp = MAX(outer.timestamp)
                  AND outer.carId = last.carId
           )
           <
           0.7*(SELECT speed as start_speed
            FROM CarSegStr first [Range 2 minutes]
            WHERE timestamp = MIN(outer.timestamp)
                  AND outer.carId = first.carId
            )
              )
```

The `Speed Reduction` is calculated by computing the difference in speed between the start and end tuples of the same car in a 2 minute `window` and applying the condition that each car's start speed is less than 30 percent of its end speed in that `window`. For the linear road benchmark application, this implies that the car is slowing down significantly.

The above queries can also be expressed using a partitioned `window` `[PARTITION by carId RANGE 2 minutes]` without using the `GROUP BY` as part of the main query.

9.5.2 Stream Modifiers

`Stream modifiers` are additional operators for expressing CQs. Stream modifiers are similar to aggregate functions and operate on partitions of a stream or a `window`. They can be used where an aggregate function can be used in SQL (i.e., in `SELECT` and `HAVING` clauses). Before we introduce the detailed semantics of a stream modifier, we define the state of a tuple in a data stream.

Definition 9.2 (State of a tuple). *The state of a tuple in a data stream is defined as the value of a tuple in that stream. The state of a tuple in a stream is denoted by* $s =< v_1, v_2, \cdots, v_n >$, *where* v_i *is the value corresponding to attribute* A_i *defined in the stream schema. The state of a tuple can also be defined in terms of a subset of attributes, analogously.*

Definition 9.3 (Stream Modifier). *A stream modifier is defined as a function that takes a partition or a window as input and computes a specified function. A stream modifier is denoted by*

$$M(< s_1, s_2, \cdots, s_i > [, P < pseudo >][, O|N < v_1, v_2, \cdots, v_j >]) \quad (9.1)$$

where M *is called the modifier function. The i-tuple* $< s_1, s_2, \cdots, s_i >$ *is the parameter required by the modifier function* M. *The* $P < pseudo >$ *defines a pseudo value for the* M *function in order to prevent underflow in arithmetic operations. The following j-tuple element is called the unused attributes output without any change. The* $O|N$ *part is called modifier profile, which determines whether the oldest or the latest values of the tuple used in the modifier function for j-tuple values. If* O *is specified, the oldest values are output and the latest values are output if* N *is specified. Both unused attributes and modifier profile are optional. The default is* N *and unused attributes are the ones not explicitly mentioned in the i-tuple. The output attributes can be renamed.*

A family of stream modifiers could be defined using the above definition. Currently, we have defined and implemented (details in Section 11.4) the following three stream modifiers in our system. In the following definitions, x^i and x^{i+1} are the values of attribute x from state i and $i+1$, respectively, and the parameters inside the brackets "[ ]" is optional. The **Diff()** and **RDiff()** stream modifiers produce k-1 new tuples if the partition contains k tuples.

Diff() is used to detect changes (difference) over two consecutive states of a tuple. It returns change of the values of attribute s_i, and the values of attributes given in $O|N <>$ profile. It is formally defined as follows:

$$Diff(< s_1 > [, N < v_1, v_2, \cdots, v_j >]) =< s_1^{i+1} - s_1^i [, v_1^{i+1}, v_2^{i+1}, \cdots, v_j^{i+1}] >$$

$$Diff(< s_1 > [, O < v_1, v_2, \cdots, v_j >]) =< s_1^{i+1} - s_1^i [, v_1^i, v_2^i, \cdots, v_j^i] >$$

RDiff() is used to detect the relative changes over two consecutive states of a tuple. It returns *relative* change of the values of each attribute s_i, and the values of attributes given in $O|N <>$ profile. It is formally defined as follows:

$$RDiff(< s_1 >, P < pseudo > [, N < v_1, v_2, \cdots, v_j >]) = \\ < \frac{s_1^{i+1} - s_1^i + pseudo}{s_1^{i+1} + pseudo}[, v_1^{i+1}, v_2^{i+1}, \cdots, v_j^{i+1}] >$$

$$RDiff(< s_1 > [, P < pseudo >][, O < v_1, v_2, \cdots, v_j >]) = \\ < \frac{s_1^{i+1} - s_1^i + pseudo}{s_1^{i+1} + pseudo}[, v_1^i, v_2^i, \cdots, v_j^i] >$$

Slope() is used to compute the slope of two attributes over two consecutive states. It returns the slope of pairs of attributes (e.g., s_1, s_2), and the values of attributes given in $O|N <>$ profile. It is formally defined as follows:

$$Slope(< s_1, s_2 >, P < pseudo > [, N < v_1, \cdots, v_j >]) = \\ < \frac{s_1^{i+1} - s_1^i + pseudo}{s_2^{i+1} - s_2^i + pseudo}[, v_1^{i+1}, v_2^{i+1}, \cdots, v_j^{i+1}] >$$

$$Slope(< s_1, s_2 > [, P < pseudo >][, O < v_1, \cdots, v_j >]) = \\ < \frac{s_1^{i+1} - s_1^i + pseudo}{s_2^{i+1} - s_2^i + pseudo}[, v_1^i, v_2^i, \cdots, v_j^i] >$$

Since we already have a `window` concept in current CQs, we can further extend the computation of a stream modifier to a `window` or a partition as **wDiff()**, **wRDiff()**, and **wSlope()**. When a `window` is specified, a stream modifier computes the function using the oldest (first) and latest (last) tuples of a partition instead of two consecutive tuples. Hence, **wDiff()**,**wRDiff()**, and **wSlope()** produce one output tuple per partition/window.

The following `CQ_Decrease` query can be used to find all cars whose speed has decreased by 30% or more within the last 2 minutes using the extensions described so far.

```
CREATE CQ DECREASE AS
   SELECT wRDiff(<speed> as C_speed, p<0.01>, N<car_id>)
   FROM  CarLocStr [Range 2 minutes]
   GROUP BY carId
   HAVING C_SPEED >= 0.3
```

9.6 Event-Side Extensions

In this section we discuss the extensions for the CEP system in terms of generalization of event specification, event specification using extended SQL, mask optimization, and enhanced event consumption modes.

9.6.1 Generalization of Event Specification

Event detection uses the time of occurrence always associated with an event. Both point-based [86] and interval-based [285] semantics have been developed for meeting the needs of applications. Other extensions are also needed to make the event specification and its usage more expressive.

Using the car accident detection and notification scenario (Example 9.1), we motivate the need for event generalization. Assume that *car location stream* and *car segment stream* are used as inputs to two continuous queries – CQ1 (checks every car for immobility) and CQ2 (checks every car for speed reduction). Primitive events `Eimm` and `Edec` are defined on CQ1 and CQ2, respectively. An accident is modeled using the *sequence* event operator as event `Eacc`, since an accident is detected when `Eimm` happens before `Edec`. In addition to the order of these two events, both cars should be from the *same segment* and from the same lane. CQ1 and CQ2 generate primitive events that do not differentiate segments and lanes and raise them as events `Eimm` and `Edec`, respectively. Attributes of the two events are:

```
Eimm: (timestamp, carId, speed, expWay, lane, dir, segmentId)

Edec: (timestamp, carId, speed, expWay, lane, dir, segmentId,
       decreaseInSpeed)
```

Consider the following event occurrences. Event `Eimm` occurs at 10:00 a.m. and `Edec` occurs at 10:03 a.m. and 10:04 a.m:

```
Eimm_1: (10:00 a.m., 1,  0 mph, I123, 3, NW, 104)

Edec_1: (10:03 a.m., 2, 40 mph, I123, 1, NW, 109, 45%)
Edec_2: (10:04 a.m., 5, 20 mph, I123, 4, NW, 104, 40%)
```

With current event processing, tuples with *carId 1* (10:00 am) and *carId 2* (10:03 am) trigger the event `Eacc`. Similarly tuples with *carId 1* and *carId 5* also trigger the event `Eacc`. The important condition that both the cars should be from the same segment and lane can only be checked in the condition part of the rule after the event `Eacc` is detected. As a result, a large number of unnecessary complex events are detected and eliminated after checking the condition (as it evaluates to `false` in most cases). This results in high overhead for the CEP subsystem. The above example illustrates the limitations of earlier event processing models. Although the above example can be modeled using instance level events of Snoop or by masks, all the instances need to be predefined which may be impossible in some cases.

Event generalization [286–288, 344, 350] overcomes the above and other problems by increasing the expressiveness of events. The basic idea is to allow for comparisons on any arbitrary attribute of participating events in addition to the use of timestamp attribute required for the event operator semantics. These conditions essentially filter unnecessary event detection as early as possible. We separate the attributes of an event into `implicit` attributes (e.g., timestamp, objectid) and `explicit` attributes (can be any attribute of an event). Along with the event operator, additional conditions can be specified either on the attributes (similar to `select` conditions) or across attributes of participating events (similar to `join` conditions). With event generalization, the *same segment and lane* problem described above as well as the matching of the *carId* can be easily solved by adding conditions on `Eimm` and `Edec` event attributes as part of the `Eacc` event definition. This is illustrated in the next section and elaborate further in Section 11.2.3.

9.6.2 Event Specification using Extended SQL

Event specification should be able to associate CQs for primitive events and other event streams for specifying complex events. Furthermore, the specification of masks (for both primitive and complex events) allow for the specification of events that are more expressive. Users can specify events based on CQs using the CREATE EVENT statement shown below:

`CREATE EVENT`	$\mathcal{E}_{name}$
`SELECT`	$\mathcal{A}_1,\ \mathcal{A}_2,\ \ldots,\ \mathcal{A}_n$
`FROM`	$\mathcal{E}_S \mid \mathcal{E}_X$
`MASK`	< *condition similar to a where clause* >

CREATE EVENT creates a named event $\mathcal{E}_{name}$, SELECT selects the attributes $\mathcal{A}_1, \mathcal{A}_2, \ldots, \mathcal{A}_n$ from either $\mathcal{E}_S$ or $\mathcal{E}_X$, where $\mathcal{E}_S$ is a named CQ or a stream name or a CREATE CQ statement and $\mathcal{E}_X$ is a complex event definition. MASK clause[7] specifies the conditions on the attributes of the participating events. Mask conditions are evaluated as early as possible in the event detection graph. This may entail pushing conditions down the event detection graph and to the event generation nodes of **stage 2** of the architecture shown in Figure 9.2. Remember that $\mathcal{E}_{name}$ corresponds to a node in the event graph.

The CREATE EVENT statement for a primitive event is shown below. `Eprim` selects all the cars that have segmentId less than fifteen from a named CQ `Estream` that is defined over the stream `CarSegStr`. As shown, MASK

[7] This can be done as part of the WHERE clause. The MASK clause has been used only for clarity.

specifies conditions (i.e., segmentId<15), and SELECT selects the carId and segmentId from the continuous query.

```
CREATE EVENT Eprim
      SELECT Estream.carId, Estream.segmentId
        FROM (CREATE CQ Estream as ...)
        MASK Estream.segmentId < 15;
```

Events for the Car ADN Example

Section 9.5.1 provides the CQs for the CAR ADN example. `Eimm` is the event created from the continuous query `CQ_Immobile`, and `Edec` is the event created from the continuous query `CQ_Decrease`. In both the events, additional attributes beyond those provided by the CQs created in Section 9.5.1 are used. As mentioned previously, required attributes can be obtained by making additional joins. Event `Eacc` represents an accident and is detected when an event `Eimm` happens before `Edec`, and the events corresponds to same segmentId and lane. Event expression $\mathcal{E}_X$ for the accident is "`Eacc = Eimm sequence Edec`" where `sequence` is an event operator. CREATE EVENT for the same is shown below:

```
CREATE EVENT Eacc
SELECT Eimm.carId as EIcarId, Edec.carId as EDcarId,
       Eimm.segmentId, Eimm.timestamp, Eimm.lane
  FROM (CREATE EVENT Eimm
              SELECT CQ_Immobile.carId, CQ_Immobile.segmentId
                     CQ_Immobile.lane, CQ_Immobile.timestamp
                FROM CQ_Immobile)
       sequence
       (CREATE EVENT Edec
              SELECT CQ_Decrease carId, CQ_Decrease.segmentId
                     CQ_Decrease.lane, CQ_Immobile.timestamp
                FROM CQ_Decrease)
  MASK Eimm.segmentId = Edec.segmentId
       AND Eimm.lane = Edec.lane
       AND Eimm.carId = Edec.carId
```

Event nodes are created in the EDGs based on the CREATE EVENT specifications. Output from the CQ is fed as inputs to the event nodes in the EDG as event streams. In the integrated architecture, input to the event nodes can be: from a named CQ, from a named event, directly from a named stream, and from a rule which raises that event. Once an event (e.g., `Eacc`) is detected, it is propagated to its parent event nodes and the rule processing stage.

9.6.3 Mask Optimization

Primitive events can be associated with one or more conditions on the attributes of events termed `masks`. Although these are associated with events, it is pushed down to **stage 2** of the architecture so that they are applied to the output of the CQ associated with that event for generating that event. As we have indicated earlier, a single CQ can produce multiple event types based on the filters/conditions specified by the masks. All masks that are relevant to the same CQ are grouped in one `event generating node` (e.g., EG1 and EG2 in Figure 9.2) even if they are specified by different event definitions. The masks need to be added to the event generating node at run-time when the events are specified. They also have to be deactivated/deleted when an event (primitive or composite) is deleted from the system.

9.6.4 Enhanced Event Consumption Modes

Analogous to the event operator semantics, current event consumption modes are also based on the timestamp and have similar drawbacks. In order to make the consumption modes more meaningful and consistent with stream processing, we introduce attribute-based event consumption. For example, the *recent* consumption mode from [87] can be viewed as a single tuple `window` and is used by applications that need the most recent value.

We will explain the limitation of the current consumption modes using the car accident detection and notification application (Example 9.1) and the *recent* consumption mode. Assume that event `Eimm` occurs at 10:00 a.m. with tuple *(carId 1, Time 10:00 a.m, segmentId 1, Speed 0)*. It is propagated to the `Eacc` node and it waits in the composite event node for the event `Edec` to occur, in order to detect `Eacc`. When the next instance of event `Eimm` occurs at 10:01 a.m. with the tuple *(carId 4, Time 10:01 a.m, segmentId 3, Speed 0)*, it replaces the previous instance with "carId as 1" even though they have different `carIds`. This is because the recent mode is based on a single tuple `window`, and the computation is based only on the timestamp where the instance with a latest timestamp replaces the previous instance.

It is useful to extend the event consumption modes to replace events based on implicit or explicit attributes thereby forming a set or a partition. Thus, when `carId` is used as an attribute for specifying the event consumption mode in the above example, only the event instance of "carId 1" that occurs at a later point in time can replace the "carId 1" that occurred at 10:00 a.m., and not "carId 4" (or any `carId` other than 1) that occurred at 10:01 a.m.

Currently, there is no notion of `window` and all the events are kept in the event node until a new instance occurs or until it is consumed. As the input rate is likely to be bursty in the integrated architecture (as it is fed by streams), there is a need for associating a buffer as well as a `window` with each event stream. Thus, by introducing the notion of a `window` along with the event consumption modes, the event processing system will provide additional mechanisms to enhance expressiveness.

Although consumption modes are associated with events, they are specified with rule definition (in *Snoop*) in order to be able to support different consumption modes for different rules on the same event. This is accomplished through the late binding of event consumption modes when the rules are specified. In the absence of a rule on an event or a participating event, there is no reason to detect that event. Events detected using the specified consumption mode are passed as arguments along with their attributes to the condition and action portions of the rule.

Specification of Enhanced Event Consumption Modes

In our integrated architecture, consumption modes have been enhanced to include attributes. Events can be unary, binary or ternary. Hence, it should be possible to specify consumption modes for each operand.

Enhanced event consumption modes are added to the specified as shown below: $\mathcal{CT}$ represents the context; `L`, `M`, and `R` represent the left, middle, and right event operands, respectively. `A` is specified when attribute-based partitioning is required by including partitioning attributes, and `E/T` is specified to indicate the number of tuples or the duration for which the tuples have to be stored in an event node. When an operator is binary, only `L` and `R` are specified. When an operator is ternary, any or all of `L`, `M` and `R` can be specified. Similarly, when it is a primitive event, only `L` is used.

```
CT [ ( L([A [, E|T]]), M([A [, E|T]]), R([A [, E|T]]) )]
```

A rule `Rsample` for an event `Esample` which uses the above notation is shown below. This event selects the cars with id ">1000" from a named CQ `Ssample` that is defined over the stream `CarLocStr`. In addition we want to partition the events for the mode specified based on the attribute carId. This rule should have immediate as $\mathcal{CM}$, recent as $\mathcal{CT}$ with attribute carId as `A` in the left event, and with highest priority value for $\mathcal{P}$ (i.e., 1). Conditions and actions are not shown. CREATE RULE statement for this rule is shown below:

```
CREATE RULE Rsample, IMMEDIATE, RECENT L(Esample.carId), 1
        ON (CREATE EVENT Esample
                        SELECT Ssample.carId, Ssample.timestamp
                         FROM (CREATE CQ as Ssample ...))
                         MASK Ssample.carId > 1000
```

9.6.5 Rule Processing

The rule system is responsible for evaluating conditions and triggering actions. A rule is used to trigger actions once its associated event is detected. In our integrated architecture, rules can be specified and created using the CREATE RULE statement as shown below.

```
CREATE RULE 𝓡name [ [, 𝓒𝓜 ] [, 𝓒𝓣 ] [, 𝓟 ] ]
         ON 𝓔name
 R_CONDITION Begin; (Simple or Complex Condition); End;
    R_ACTION Begin; (Simple or Complex Action); End;
```

As shown above, CREATE RULE creates the rule $\mathcal{R}_{name}$ along with its properties such as coupling mode $\mathcal{CM}$ (e.g., immediate, deferred), extended consumption mode or context $\mathcal{CT}$ (e.g., recent, continuous) and priority $\mathcal{P}$ (e.g., integer where 1 is the highest) as a positive integer indicating rule priority. ON specifies the event $\mathcal{E}_{name}$ associated with the rule and it can be replaced by the CREATE EVENT statement. In addition, a rule also contains conditions associated with the event and actions to be performed when conditions evaluate to `true`. Condition portion of the rule is analyzed to detect simple conditions on attributes that can be used as masks. These conditions are moved down in the EDG to the best possible node including the event generator node. Actions can be arbitrary computations (including SQL or PL/SQL).

Rule Creation for Car ADN Example

When an event corresponding to an accident `Eacc` is detected, various types of actions need to be performed. Creation of event `Eacc` is shown in Section 9.6.2. Rule corresponding to the CAR ADN can be expressed as shown below.

```
CREATE RULE AccidentNotify, IMMEDIATE,
            RECENT L(Eimm.carId), R(Edec.carId), 1
         ON EVENT Eacc
 R_CONDITION Begin; (true); End;
    R_ACTION Begin;
            //Notify Police Control Room (PCR)
            PCR(Eacc.segmentId, Eacc.EIcarId,
                   Eacc.EDcarId, Eacc.timestamp);
            //Notify Ambulance Control Room
            //Notify Upstream Cars
            //Notify Toll Station
            End;
```

Figure 9.3 shows the car accident detection and notification of Example 9.1 using the four-stage integrated event and stream processing architecture. It shows the named CQs, event generators, primitive and composite events, and rules.

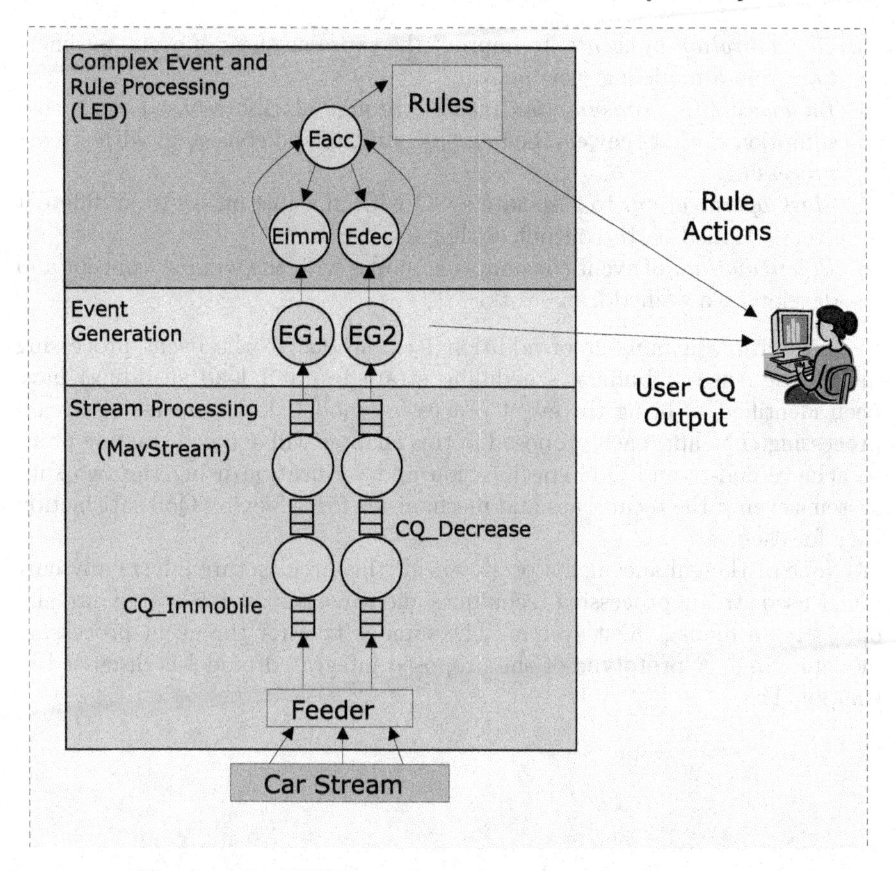

Fig. 9.3. CarADN Example using `MavEStream` Architecture

9.7 Summary of Chapter 9

In this chapter, we analyzed the similarities and differences between independently developed stream and complex event processing models. We proposed `MavEStream` as an integrated architecture that combines the strengths of stream and event processing synergistically.

Extensions to complex event and continuous query processing to enhance their individual as well as their combined expressive power, and computation efficiency are rarely discussed in the literature. Instead of trying to do both stream and event processing without clean separation, we proposed enhancements to stream and complex event and processing as well as their synergistic integration.

Some of the extensions identified for the integration are listed below:

1. *Named CQs:* to facilitate its use for defining events and other CQs.
2. *Stream modifiers:* to detect different kinds of changes in a stream.

3. *Generalization of events:* to improve the expressiveness of event specification from a modeling view point.
4. *Enhanced event consumption modes:* through attribute-based event consumption so that they can be more meaningful and consistent with stream processing.
5. *Mask optimization:* to associate a CQ with multiple masks from different events defined on the output of that CQ.
6. *Reconciliation:* of event consumption modes with the window concept and developing a unified framework.

In addition, a number of additional extensions to the event processing model (e.g., use of buffers, scheduling strategies, and load shedding) have been identified to bring the event processing model closer to that of stream processing. The approach proposed in this chapter will act as a starting point to achieve end-to-end QoS specification and verification using the two subsystems even if the techniques and mechanisms for achieving QoS satisfaction vary for each.

None of the enhancements proposed for this architecture affects any currently used stream processing techniques and can easily be integrated into any data stream management system. The same is true for the event processing model as well. A prototype of the proposed integrated model is discussed in Chapter 11.

10

MavStream: DEVELOPMENT OF A DSMS PROTOTYPE

MavStream is a data stream management system prototype developed at UTA. It is implemented in Java and supports most of the approaches and techniques elaborated in earlier chapters. It accepts input streams and continuous queries along with QoS requirements, processes them efficiently, and monitors the output to check for QoS satisfaction. A run-time optimizer is responsible for optimizing QoS requirements. If QoS requirements are not satisfied by the output, the current scheduling strategy is changed to a better one if possible; if the QoS requirements are still not met, load shedding is activated. Load shedding is deactivated by the run-time optimizer when it is no longer needed.

We first implemented an experimental testbed (in C language) which has been used for all the experimental validation presented in earlier chapters. This testbed does not have a run-time optimizer and does not support changing of scheduling strategies at run-time. As it was primarily developed for the purpose of validating our theoretical results, select features were implemented for evaluation.

The MavStream prototype presented in this chapter is a comprehensive system implemented with a view to keep the code base small and to facilitate incremental addition of functionality. As a prototype designed and implemented for internal usage, fancy features (e.g., Graphical User Interface or an Integrated Development Environment) were not included. Functional components of the MavStream system are shown in Figure 10.1.

There are a number of design decisions that affect the performance of a DSMS. As QoS is of primary concern, design decisions for every component of the system are important . For example, a schedulable unit can be an operator or an entire query or something in between such as an operator path. The granularity of execution (e.g., operators or queries) and the mechanism of execution (e.g., as a single process or as different processes or as threads) has an effect on the performance. The integration of load shedders into the system – whether as a separate operator or as part of an existing component – also has an impact on the performance of the overall system. Whether the data is archived and how it is accessed from secondary storage for processing continu-

S. Chakravarthy and Q. Jiang, *Stream Data Processing: A Quality of Service Perspective*, Advances in Database Systems 36, DOI: 10.1007/978-0-387-71003-7_10,

ous queries also has an impact on the system performance. As the tuples pass through a number of queues or buffers during their processing, optimization of buffer operations is critical. The individual algorithms for operators and the resulting size of synopsis has a bearing on the memory requirements of the system. Run-time monitoring of the output to change scheduling strategies or activate load shedding requires a design that needs to take the associated overhead into consideration. The ability to use different scheduling strategies for different queries, and changing the scheduling strategy for the same query at run-time need to be supported and requires a design that incurs minimal run-time overhead. Finally, the specification of QoS requirements needs to be intuitive and easy.

MavStream, being implemented in Java, has tried to strike a balance between the amount of functionality supported and the effort needed for its development. The rest of this chapter discusses a subset of the functionality supported by the prototype. For each functionality, the rationale and scope of the functionality along with design and implementation details are explained. In the last section, we present an evaluation of the run-time optimizer.

10.1 MavStream Architecture

10.1.1 Functionality

A client-server architecture is used for the prototype as the server has to interact with a number of users. Most of the effort was spent on the server to ensure that the functionality incorporated is indeed useful for a broad set of applications. Although we decided not to implement a fancy client, we wanted to make sure different types of clients could be developed and used with the server at a later stage. The communication between the client and the server is implemented in terms of a TCP/IP connection with commands and data sent over the socket. New commands can be added to extend current functionality. Currently, a CQ is sent to the server as a data object created by the input processor from a text file describing the CQ operators and their relationships. Each stream definition is similarly sent to the server as an object. The output of a CQ can be consumed by applications in multiple ways. The server can be gracefully shutdown by sending a command.

The server, being the main focus, has the modules needed for instantiating a CQ, processing a CQ, starting and terminating a CQ at a specified time (termed flexible CQs and discussed in Section 11.5), and supporting QoS delivery mechanisms (discussed in earlier chapters) such as scheduling and load shedding. Run-time monitoring of input and output is done by the *system monitor* module which interacts with the run-time optimizer (refer to Figure 10.1) responsible for applying appropriate strategies to satisfy QoS requirements.

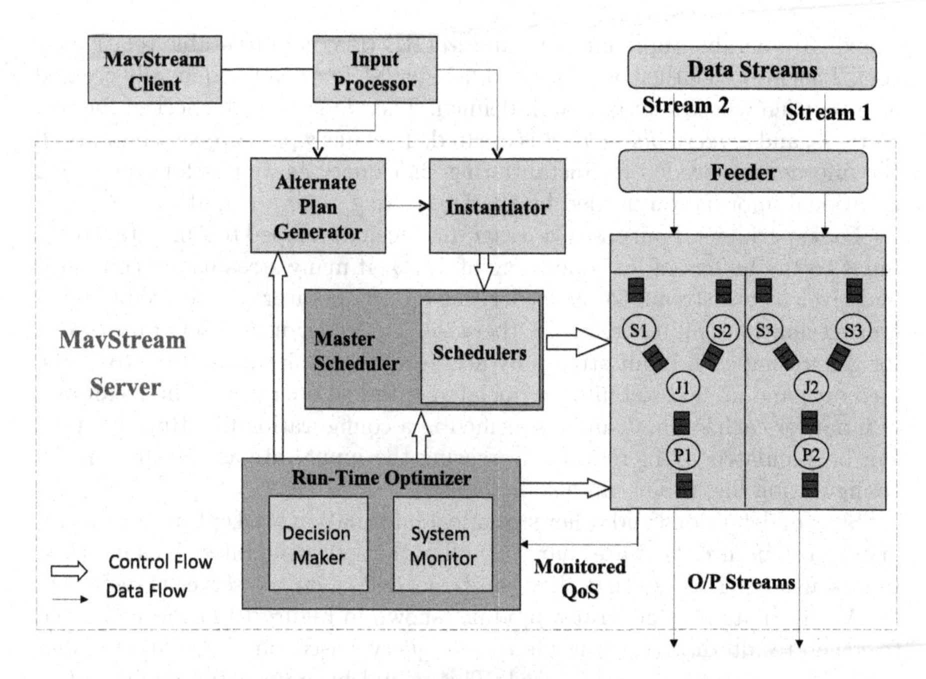

Fig. 10.1. Functional Components of MavStream System

Some of the commands currently supported by the server are: register a stream, send stream information to client, receive a query plan object, start query execution, output query results into a specified buffer, and stop query execution.

10.1.2 MavStream Server Design

The server registers data streams from the clients. The server provides details of available stream names and their schema definitions to clients for use in creating new continuous queries. The server initializes and instantiates all of the operators used in a continuous query. Query execution is started by scheduling query operators, operator paths, or segments depending on the scheduling strategy used. The server also stops a query, by stopping its scheduling and performing clean up. A query is stopped either explicitly or when the specified end query time is reached. A query is stopped only after all the tuples received before its end query time have been processed. A CQ name is mapped to a unique identifier for internal use by the system.

Currently, continuous queries are defined in a text file, by specifying the stream operators and other relevant information such as window type, query start time, streams used as input etc. The CQ specification also requires the user to provide the input/output association among operators to form a query tree. Specification of a CQ can also include: QoS expected values, MTTL (maximal tolerable tuple latency) and MTRE (maximal tolerable relative error). This file can either be generated using a GUI or can be manually created as a text file whose syntax is well-defined. The file is parsed, checked for correctness, and a *query plan object* is created. The query plan object contains all the information needed for instantiating that query as well as for computing additional information needed by the DSMS (e.g., operator path).

For experimental purposes, a *feeder* has been developed to simulate stream input to the buffers of leaf operators of a CQ. If many streams are combined and given as one stream to the feeder, the `split` operator can be used for generating multiple input streams. Otherwise, the feeder uses a separate thread for generating each input stream by accessing the tuples from a file (or main memory) and are fed to buffers associated with leaf operators. The mean rate of input for each stream can be specified in a configuration file. Bursty inputs can be simulated by increasing/decreasing the input rate as specified in the configuration file. Input can also be paused.

Stream definitions and other statistical information are kept in main memory data structures that are shared by all of the server modules. This information is also persisted so that they can be loaded when the server is restarted.

An alternate plan generator module (shown in Figure 10.1) was conceived to generate alternative plans for a user query based on the characteristics of the streams and operators used. This would have been the equivalent of static query optimizer for generating a good plan as we do not perform any structural changes to the query at run-time. In fact, if multiple plans are generated and associated with input and operator characteristics, it is possible to swap plans at run-time if the input stream characteristics were to change drastically. This component has not been implemented in the current version. This functionality will also be useful for merging CQs to exploit common subexpressions.

Instantiator

Instantiator has the responsibility of initializing and instantiating stream operators and their associated buffers on accepting user queries from the client. A CQ is instantiated based on its start time. If the query is registered for a future time, a temporal event is set to instantiate and start the CQ at the specified time. The event mechanism itself is used internally for starting and stopping queries – currently based on time. When a query is sent to the server, appropriate temporal events along with their actions (for the start and termination of a CQ) are created in the server. This can be further extended to start queries based on any user-defined event (e.g., when a traffic accident is detected on I30).

The *Instantiator* creates an instance of each operator in the query and initializes it. It then associates input and output queues (or buffers) for consuming and producing tuples. Every operator is an independent object and expects predicates associated with that operator in a predefined form. *Instantiator* extracts the predicate information from the input and converts it into the form required by each operator. *Instantiator* also initializes the query operators with `window` information. The *Instantiator* also creates also computes additional query characteristics (e.g., operators, paths) needed for scheduling and run-time optimization. Some of this information is inserted into the ready queue used by the scheduler. *Instantiator* does all the necessary initialization without actually scheduling the operators.

10.1.3 MavStream Server Implementation

Input Processor

The input processor (not part of the server) extracts the information of operators of the query from the user input. Each operator definition is populated in a data structure called *OperatorData*. The *OperatorData* is wrapped in an *OperatorNode* that has references to its parent and child operators. The query plan object is processed by the *Instantiator*. The query tree is constructed in a bottom-up manner to ensure that the child operators are defined prior to their parent operators. A reference to the root operator is kept in the query plan object.

Instantiator

In order to instantiate operators, the tree in the query plan object is traversed in post order. For each *OperatorNode*, the type of the operator is identified and instantiated. Each operator's output buffer is used as an input buffer to its parent operator. Buffers of leaf operator are associated input streams. As the operator design requires the input conditions to be in a specified format, the conditions given by the user are converted, by the *Instantiator*, to the format used by the operator algorithms. For example, the parameters for the `project` operator is a list of attribute names to be projected. The list of attributes is converted into a positional notation as expected by the operator. As the schema can change over the course of processing a continuous query, conditions and attribute lists are adjusted by the *Instantiator* while instantiating a query plan object.

Once the operators are instantiated, the query tree is processed again to extract operators, operator paths, segments, and simplified segments. The processing capacity and memory release capacity of paths are computed using individual operator processing and memory release capacities. They are sorted separately on processing and memory release capacities for use by the run-time optimizer. A reference to these data structures is maintained in the query plan object (see Figure 10.2). The references to these data structures are used during query processing by the run-time optimizer. Furthermore, the input processor module processes the QoS parameters and stores them in the

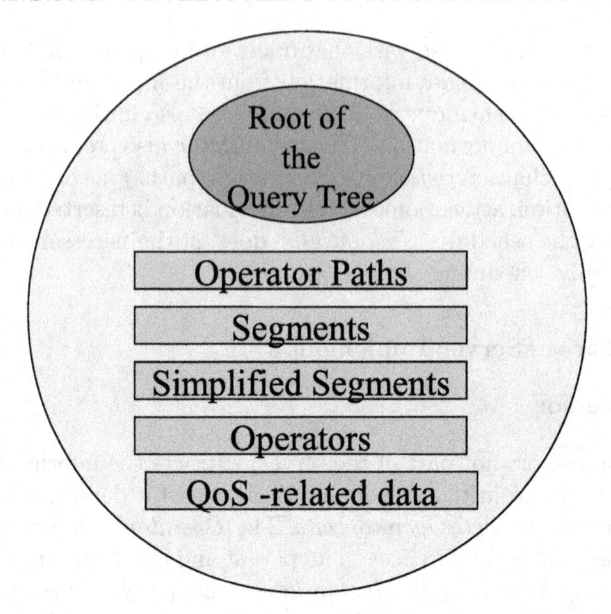

Fig. 10.2. Query Plan Object With Data Structures

appropriate data structures for later use by the *system monitor*. In addition, the server stores the query plan object of each query during its lifetime and also maintains information required for book keeping and statistics.

10.2 Window Types

10.2.1 Functionality

The blocking nature of the `join` and some `aggregate` operators necessitates the use of a `window` to allow stream processing operators to produce continuous output. A brief discussion of the `window` concept and `window` types can be found in Section 2.3. `MavStream` supports basic `time-` and `tuple-based` `window` types along with their variants. We decided to support only those `window` types whose computation does not require accessing past (stored) data items of the stream. Hence reverse `landmark` and reverse `window` types are not currently supported. Also, `ad hoc` SQL queries are currently not supported as we did not want to build a traditional query processing engine.

10.2.2 Design

The temporal aspects of a continuous query along with `window` parameters can be specified by the following four pieces of information. This information is sufficient to define basic `window` types along with their reverse versions.

Begin query: defines the starting time (including date, if needed) of the query (can be `Now` or a later time.

Window size: defines the size of the *first* `window` with respect to the begin query time.

Window movement as (move_start, move_end): represents the amount by which the current `window` endpoints will be moving (in either direction). Negative movements define reverse `window` queries. Positive movements indicate forward movement of a `window`. A value of 0 for both defines a fixed (or snapshot) window. A value of 0 for the first and a non-zero value for the second defines landmark queries. `Window` movement essentially determines the type of a query.

End Query: defines the end time (or termination time) of a query.

Special keywords, `Now` and `Infinity` are used to represent the current time and forever, respectively. Begin and end query values are always specified as time. For time-based (or physical) `window` representation, the window size and movement are specified in terms of time values, whereas for logical (or tuple-based) `window`, they are specified in terms of number of tuples. For example, the continuous query, "compute the hourly average temperature of Room A every 10 minutes from 10 am to 10 pm", from the `MavHome` project has the following `window` specification:

```
Begin window = 10 am
Window size = 11 am
Window movement = (10 minutes, 10 minutes)
End query = 10 pm
```

The query will start execution at the next 10 am and will execute until 10pm.

As another example, if every person entering a store generates a tuple, then the query "Compute the time it takes for 100 customers to enter the Walmart store for a month starting immediately", can be represented using the following logical `window` specification:

```
Begin window = Now
Window size = 100              // tuples
Window movement = (100, 100) // tuples; non-overlapping
End query = Now + 1 month
```

The type of the `window` is determined by the sign and the value of the window movement. The following `window` types can be specified by varying the move_start and move_end values:

- Forward only `window`: both the start and end move values are positive.
- Reverse only `window`: negative values for both the start and end move values.

- Landmark window: move_start is set to zero and the move_end is a non-zero value. A positive value of move_end gives a forward landmark window whereas a negative value gives a reverse landmark window.
- Sliding window: here both the move_start and move_end values of window movement are non-zero. If both values are positive (and same), it is a forward sliding window whereas same negative values move the window in the reverse direction. Whether a window is overlapping or not is determined by the values of the start_move value in conjunction with the window size.

Note that, of the four components, begin query and end query is applicable to a query. The other components can be specified individually for each stream used in a query (although the window is likely to be the same for all stream inputs of a query).

10.2.3 Implementation

All continuous queries need to include values for the following: `begin query`, `end query`, `window movement` as (move_start and move_end) and `window size`. An operator that needs a `window` for its computation will be initialized with the values from the input. Operators make use of this information for their computation. Whether a sliding `window` is overlapping or disjoint is determined by the operator. For sliding `window` queries, this information is used to determine whether to reuse any part of the result computed for the previous window (termed reuse). The other alternative is to recompute the results from scratch for each window and not use any previously computed results. Both reuse and recompute are supported in `MavStream`. For `non-blocking` operators such as `select`, tuples are consumed from the buffer and are not stored in the synopsis. On the other hand, for `blocking` operators such as `join`, it is important to store the tuples until both the streams have moved to the next `window`. Input tuples and intermediate computed values are stored in the synopsis for that operator. To accommodate all the parameters of a `window` and its operation, a separate `window` class is defined. An object of this class is used in `window`-based operators to provide controlled access to `window` parameters.

10.3 Stream Operators and CQs

10.3.1 Functionality

`MavStream` currently supports the following operators:

- `select` – relational `select` operator on a stream; includes a condition.
- `split` – splits a stream into one or more streams based on conditions on attributes. The conditions are analogous to `select` conditions.

- project – projects a subset of the attributes of a tuple. The attributes are specified by their names.
- join (window-based symmetric hash and nested-loop versions) – performs join on two streams.
- group by – creates partitions of a stream window based on the values of attributes specified.
- GFilter – serves the purpose of applying a select on the output of group by to simulate the effect of the having clause.
- aggregate operators (sum, average, max, min, and count).
- Stream modifiers – Diff, RDiff, Slope, and their window versions.

In addition, a stream schema is specified with a name, attributes of the schema by their names along with their types. Currently, only primitive data type are supported in MavStream. Stream modifiers have been discussed in Section 9.5 and their implementation is further elaborated in Section 11.4. MavStream also supports an event generator stream operator that will be discussed in Section 11.2.4.

Continuous queries are constructed from the above set of operators. In the absence of a GUI-based client, CQs and stream definitions are input from a text file and parsed. From this, a query plan object is generated and sent to the server. Specification of CQ includes QoS specifications, and other selectivity information of operators, if available. QoS specification is discussed in Section 10.5.

10.3.2 Design of Operators

The varying nature of an input stream is handled with data flow architecture for processing input tuples. Hence, it entails that the operators be scheduled and perform computations only when data is available. An operator processes tuples present in its input buffers when it is allocated time by the scheduler. Furthermore, the operator should suspend itself when there are no more tuples in the input buffer.

Based on the requirements of the stream operators, it is evident that there are certain properties, data structures and methods that are common to all operators. Each operator is a schedulable entity. Each operator interacts with a number of components of the server: buffer manager, scheduler, as well as the optimizer. Hence, it is necessary to present a common view for all operators rather than viewing them as individual operators. If all other components view operators as an abstraction, then the interaction among them can be simplified. Moreover, new operators can be added without changing other modules. All these requirements lead to combining the common attributes and functionality of operators into a common (generic) operator.

Every operator is inherited from a generic operator and specialized as needed. This abstraction allows the specification of properties common to all operators such as state, priority, output queues, and also provides an interface for other modules to start, stop, suspend, and resume the operator. Throughout its lifetime, an operator can be in one of the four states: ready, running, suspended, and stopped depending on the availability of data and the scheduling policy. All operators get a specified time quantum which is dependent on the scheduling strategy and the priority or processing capacity of the operator. Each operator reads a tuple (or a set of tuples) from its input buffer, processes it, and delivers the results to the output buffer.

Join – nested loop and symmetric hash

We briefly discuss some of the issues associated with the design of a symmetric hash join operator. For more details on other operators, please refer to [136, 137]. The symmetric hash join operation includes the task of reading one tuple (or a finite number) at a time from its input queue, hashing it to its corresponding hash table based on the value of the join attribute and probing the other hash table to find the tuples that satisfy the join condition and are in the desired window. If two tuples named 'x' and 'y' are considered for processing at the same time then the output would be two 'xy' tuples if they satisfy the join criteria. In order to avoid duplicates in the result, every tuple has to be processed atomically. An atomic action ensures that the next tuple is not considered until the current tuple is completely processed. Due to the atomicity requirements, a single thread implementation was preferred; even if two threads are used, they cannot be executed asynchronously as they would interfere with each other.

For both joins (nested loop and symmetric hash), we support computation with reuse and without reuse (or recompute). Computation with reuse is beneficial for an overlapping sliding window as the computations performed in the previous window can be reused partially for the next window (depending upon the amount of overlap). Whereas recompute will start the computation for a new window from scratch. Reuse, as expected, has a slight increase in memory usage and book-keeping overhead but avoids recomputation thereby saving CPU cycles.

Group By and Having

Group by is implemented as a window-based aggregate operator which supports the standard SQL aggregate operations on the groups or partitions formed by group by attributes and produces output incrementally. This operator supports all the window types used in MavStream.

The group by operator accepts as input, a list of attributes over which grouping is done, and one or more aggregate operators along with their attributes.

In our system having is simulated using a separate operator on the output of a group by and is implemented as a GFilter operator. This design saves the complexity of processing complex subqueries as part of the having condition.

Being a separate operator, this does not provide the same expressiveness as the general `having` clause. The use of this operator is illustrated with an example:

The query represented below in SQL for computing the immobility of a car uses the `group by` and the `having` clause with a condition.

```
SELECT   CarId, Xpos, count(*)
FROM     CarLocStr [Range 2 minutes]
GROUP BY CarId, Xpos
HAVING   count(*) > 3
```

The query given below computes the same result as the above query with the `having` clause replaced by the `GFilter` operator.

```
SELECT *
FROM
    ( SELECT   CarId, Xpos, count(*) as tot_count
      FROM     CarLocStr [Range 2 minutes]
      GROUP BY CarId,Xpos
    ) as tempTable
GFilter  tot_count > 3;
```

`GFilter` operator can evaluate any complex condition on the attributes of the stream. This operator does not change the input schema but outputs tuples which satisfy the condition. The input to this operator is an attribute-based condition (similar to the `select` condition). This operator uses the Free Ecma Script Interpreter (FESI) condition evaluator for the evaluation of the condition. `GFilter` maps the attributes over which the condition is defined, to the position in the input stream to evaluates arbitrary conditions. The tuple is output or filtered depending on whether the condition evaluates to true or not. It is important that aggregates are computed and projected by the `group by` query for this to work correctly. Although it behaves like a `select` operator, it is given a separate name to distinguish their usage. This operator should be used on the output of a `group by` computation.

10.3.3 Implementation

The `select` operator checks whether each input tuple satisfies a given condition. Instead of building an efficient condition evaluator that can evaluate any arbitrary condition, we decided to use an existing condition evaluator. FESI, a powerful `Java`-based utility that can perform many functions in `Java` (condition evaluation is one of them), was selected for the purpose of condition evaluation.

`Project` operator expects a list of attributes that need to be projected. The actual operation is done using the position of attributes in the tuples. The user submits a list of attributes to be projected. This list is converted to a position list by the query *Instantiator*. In our design it was decided to convert the operand list to position list by the query *Instantiator* and pass only the position list to the `project`. The algorithm for `project` assumes that the position list is already set before starting the `project` operation. Schema information of each stream is stored in two hash tables, one organized by attribute name and the other by attribute position. These hash tables are used for converting attribute names to their positional value. This is done only once at the time of query instantiation. This information is also used for creating the schema for the output stream as well. The output stream schema is computed from the query specification while condition names and positions are adjusted during instantiation.

`Window`-based operators maintain a synopsis of tuples based on `window` definition. For the `join` (symmetric hash and nested loop versions) operator, the synopsis will contain the input tuples that belong to a `window` from both the streams. The `join` operator consumes a tuple from the input buffer, joins the tuple with all the tuples of the other stream maintained in the synopsis that belong to the current `window` and satisfy the `join` condition.

There are two variants for the `join` computation based on whether common computations are exploited for an overlapping `window`. In the case of a disjoint `window`, there is no overlap between two consecutive `windows` and hence join over each `windows` is computed independently. In an overlapping `window` (shown in Figure 2.4), there is overlap between consecutive `windows` as computations between `new ws` (start of new window) and `old we` (end of old window) are common and can be reused for the next `window`. Based on this, `join` is classified as `join` using reuse or recompute (i.e., without reuse). In the former case, common computations between two successive `windows` are not computed again. Common computations are kept track of and stored and used for the computation of the next `window`. During the processing of the first `window`, tuples falling in the overlapping `window` are identified. In Figure 2.4, common computation involves processing tuples between `new ws` and `old we`. Those tuples that fall between `new ws` and `old we` and satisfy the join condition are produced not only as output but are marked and stored. This approach avoids re-computation of an overlapping region, which can be substantial if the overlap is significant with respect to the `window` size.

In the latter (recompute) case, there is no additional storage involved since the results of current `window` are not stored. The performance difference in these two variants increases as the `window` size and overlap increase. This variant of `join` can be used when memory is critical. However, where response time is critical, `join` with reuse is likely to be a better alternative. The timestamp of the resulting tuple is set to the maximum of the two participating timestamps. This is the earliest time at which this `join` can take place. This also produces the output of a `join` in proper timestamp order.

The `split` operator has been introduced to partition a single heterogeneous stream into multiple homogeneous streams based on application logic. This operator expects a list of conditions that are evaluated against a stream of tuples. FESI evaluator is used for evaluating the conditions. Multiple output buffers are associated with the `split` operator.

`Group By` operator

The `group by` operator is created by extending the operator class. It supports various aggregate functions of `sum, aggregate, count`, etc., implemented as methods within the operator. We discuss the algorithm for `group by` operation and the issues encountered in using a `Java` HashTable.

Algorithm

The operator maintains groups/partitions for each `window` in a hash table called *GHashTable.* Each group of the *GHashTable* has a *GroupHandle* (GH) attached to it. First we describe the data structures and then the algorithm.

1. GHashTable: Stores all the tuples in the current `window` hashed by the values of their grouping attributes. Each bucket in HashTable stores the tuple in the following form. $(< T_1, t_1 >), (< T_2, t_2 >) \cdots (< T_n, t_n >)$, where T_i represents the i_th tuple and t_i represents the tuple timestamps associated with the tuple T_i. This operator uses two GHashTables:
   - currentGHashTable: this `Java` HashTable is used to construct the groups for the current `window`.
   - overlapGHashTable: this HashTable is used to temporarily store the tuples while the groups are constructed for the overlap part of the next `window`. For a disjoint `window` specification, this HashTable will be empty.
2. GroupHandle, GH (one for each group): Stores the output tuple of each group and the maximum timestamp (GH.maxTS) among all the tuples in the group.

Algorithm 6 computes the `Group By` clause and applies the aggregate functions on each partition.

Issues in using Java HashTable:

To implement the `group by` operator using the `Java` HashTable class, each bucket in the table should represent *a* group. If two key value pairs with the same key are inserted into the HashTable then they are hashed to the same bucket. If the bucket already contains some value for the same key then `Java` overwrites the old value with the new value associated with the last key value hashed. Hence, if we have multiple tuples in a `window` with the same values for attributes on which we are performing `Group By`, then only the last tuple will be stored as the rest of them will be overwritten. To avoid this problem, we have implemented a HashTable in which if the same key is inserted for different tuples then all the tuples associated with the key get stored in a

Algorithm 6: Group By Computation

1: **if** current tuple timestamp $<$ End Query **then**
2:   **if** current tuple timestamp is within current window bounds **then**
3:     Group the tuple in *currentGHashTable*
4:     **if** current tuple timestamp $>$ next begin window time **then**
5:       Group tuple in *overlapGHashTable*
6:     **end if**
7:   **else**
8:     Apply aggregate operators on groups in *currentGHashTable.*
9:     Sort GH obtained for each group based on timestamp.
10:     Output the sorted GH List.
11:     Reorganize the *currentGHashTable* and *overlapGHashTable* appropriately.
12:   **end if**
13: **else**
14:   stop the operator; wake up the scheduler
15: **end if**

vector inside the bucket (essentially support multiple groups for each bucket) to which they are hashed. It is also possible that more than one key gets hashed to the same bucket. This is handled by associating each bucket with a list of vectors representing different groups being hashed to the same bucket. Each vector in the list contains tuples for only one group. In Figure 10.3, group by is done on first two attributes of the stream. Two tuples are hashed to the same bucket as they have the same key. In GHashTable the first two tuples are inserted in the vector for Group1. We assume that third tuple also hashes to the same bucket. Although the bucket is the same, the key is not the same, so a new group (Group 2) is created to insert the third tuple. Aggregations without a Group By use the same algorithm without performing any hashing.

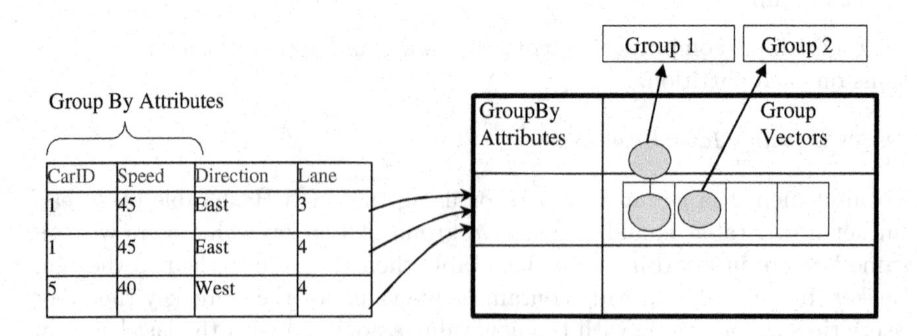

Fig. 10.3. GHashTable Details

The `group by` operator class has a separate method for each aggregate operator supported. These methods compute the aggregate values for each group/partition when the `window` for the `group by` is elapsed.

10.4 Buffers and Archiving

10.4.1 Functionality

The purpose of buffers (or queues) for CQ processing is to provide a mechanism for handling the mismatch between input rates and the processing capacity of an operator or the system. Buffers are the primary in-memory storage structure of a DSMS. Buffers are used for storing tuples that flow from the input streams to the application (destination) through a sequence of operators. Buffers are the non-processing components of a DSMS. That is, the state of tuples is not changed while they are in buffers. Typically, tuples flow in a First In First Out (FIFO) manner through the buffers[1]. Hence buffers are implemented as a FIFO queue.

The number of buffers associated with each operator in a CQ depends on the number of operands used by the operator. Each operator outputs its result into one or more buffers (e.g., `split`) each of which acts as an input to another operator or application. It is possible that the output of a result from an operator is consumed by more than one operator. This is mainly due to sharing subexpressions in a multiple CQ processing environment.

As the amount of physical memory is limited, there is an upper limit on the number of tuples that can be stored in main memory buffers and synopsis. If the number of tuples in the system exceed this limit, there is no other alternative but to drop them or store them on secondary storage.

In `MavStream`, a shared buffer is used if multiple operators read from the same buffer. The logic of its implementation is slightly complicated for deleting tuples from the buffer, but the amount of memory saved is significant which is important in a DSMS environment. Also, as our load shedding mechanism is incorporated into buffers, this adds additional complexity in determining the maximum load to be shed as the QoS requirements may be different for queries involved in a shared buffer. Load shedding may be unavoidable in a main memory-only configuration.

`MavStream` also provides an alternative in which the secondary storage also acts as a temporary buffer for those tuples that cannot fit in main memory. The system can be configured to run in main memory-only mode or to make use of disk when the specified memory limit is reached. The buffer manager handles the storage of tuples on disk and feeds the operator as if they were stored in a main memory buffer. The management of main memory buffers

---

[1] For dealing with out of order arrivals, tuples in a buffer can be processed slightly differently.

and secondary storage for tuples is totally transparent to the operator as well as the user.

10.4.2 Buffer Manager Design

In MavStream, buffers are the intermediate storage structures used by the operators. All operators in a query tree are connected using buffers. Buffers are implemented as queues. Buffers are of two types: *bounded* and *unbounded.* An unbounded buffer has no limit and continues to grow until main memory is used up. This makes it a main memory stream processing system. Buffers support two operations: dequeue and enqueue. Enqueue and dequeue operations must be synchronized to ensure correctness as the same location may be accessed by multiple operators at the same time.

A bounded buffer has an upper limit on the number of elements it can hold, which can be specified while instantiating a buffer. When the specified limit is reached, successive elements are stored on disk preventing any loss of data. As buffers can be shared among operators. every buffer internally maintains a common pointer for all operators (in addition to individual pointers) which points to the latest element consumed by all operators. All elements including and prior to the common element consumed can be safely discarded freeing main memory. These buffer spaces can be filled by reading elements, in the order in which they arrived, from the disk. To accomplish this, buffer incorporates minimal persistence logic to store and retrieve elements to and from the secondary storage as and when needed.

Each buffer is associated with two secondary storage files (called buffer log files). Tuples are inserted into these files when the buffer limit is exceeded. Tuples from the disk are read in the order of their arrival. To avoid sequential scan of these files, we use an indexed file and read objects from the appropriate position. Tuples in the buffer log file are stored as serialized byte stream objects. In order to retrieve a tuple (or a sequence of tuples) from the buffer log file, the starting position and the size of the byte stream for the tuple (or sequence of tuples) are needed. This information is stored in a main memory index table[2]. Each entry in the index table consists of a sequence number, the byte size of the tuple and its offset into the log file. For each buffer log file there is an associated index table. The size of an index entry is assumed to be much smaller than the tuple itself.

In order to avoid the overhead of indexing into larger files, two files are used whose sizes are configurable. Once a file reaches its maximum size, a new log file is started. Enqueue and dequeue operations transparently handle unbounded or bounded buffers.

---

[2] If the size of each tuple is the same, there is no need for an index. The offset from where to read from the file can easily be maintained in the buffer itself. The two- or multi-file approach is still useful.

10.4.3 Buffer Manager Implementation

In order to make the deletion of tuples from a file efficient, the concept of two buffer log files is introduced. We keep appending the tuples into the first buffer log file until a predefined limit is reached. Once that limit is reached, the tuples are stored in the other buffer log file. The buffer manager starts reading tuples from the first buffer log file as soon as enough memory is available in the main memory buffer. Then the buffer manager switches the retrieval to the next log file once all tuples are read from the first file. After this, the first can be cleared by reopening it in write mode. This way we can delete all tuples from the file with negligible cost. Also, the corresponding main memory index is cleared when a buffer log file are cleared.

A batch of tuples is retrieved from a buffer log file. This process is invoked when the main memory buffer is empty by x% (where x is a configurable parameter) of its allotted limit. This minimizes the number of accesses to the buffer log file and increases the overall efficiency of the system. Buffer log files are switched as needed as part of the retrieval. The buffer log files are switched only after all the tuples from the file is consumed.

10.5 Run-time Optimizer

Run-time optimizer (see Figure 10.1) is the central component of `MavStream`. It consists of a *system monitor* to measure various characteristics of the input streams as well as the outputs generated by a DSMS. The *system monitor* can also direct operators to recompute selectivity, memory release capacity, and processing capacity periodically. Run-time optimizer includes a *decision maker* that, based on the measured values, makes a number of decisions to optimize the execution of CQs in the system.

10.5.1 Functionality

Analogous to the inputs used in *Aurora* [63], the QoS specifications (tuple latency, memory used, and throughput) are input to the `MavStream` system as piecewise linear approximation of their functions. An example of a function and its approximation are shown in Figures 10.4 and 10.5, respectively. In `MavStream`, each QoS measure of interest is specified using a two dimensional graph. The QoS graphs are approximated as piecewise linear functions and contain the values of the QoS measures as shown in Figure 10.5. The X values of a QoS graph represent relative time from the start of a query. The Y values specify the expected value of a specific QoS parameter at a time point. For tuple latency, memory utilization, and throughput, Y values specified are in time, size (in byte), and tuples/sec, respectively. As QoS measures are approximated as piecewise linear functions, for each interval in a piecewise function, only the start and end *(x,y)* values need to be specified. The usage

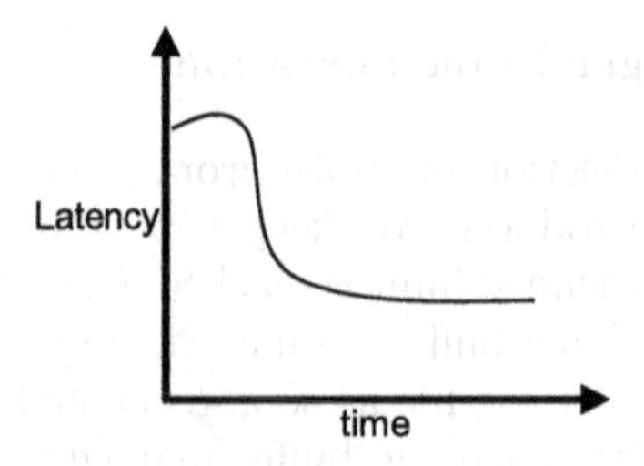

Fig. 10.4. Latency Graph

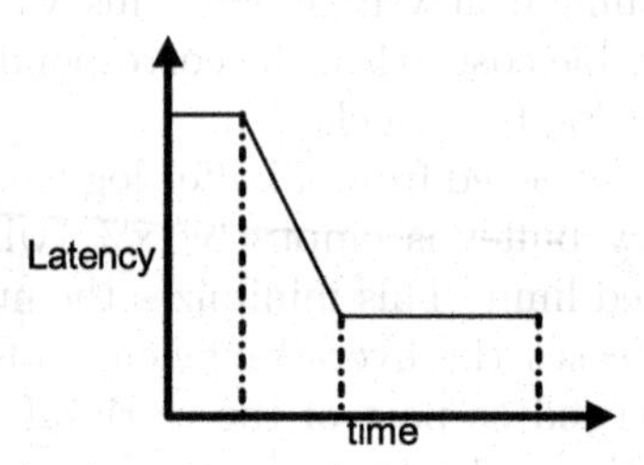

Fig. 10.5. Latency Graph: Piecewise Approximation

of two dimensional graph and piecewise approximation provides the flexibility to specify either exact values or relaxed values for any QoS measure.

The expected QoS values for any specified interval is computed using the slope and boundary values of that interval. For a continuous query, it may be difficult to provide the QoS values for the entire lifetime of query. Hence we assume that the user provides a few intervals. The number of intervals specified is presumed to be at least one. The expected QoS values for time periods between given intervals are extrapolated from the boundary values of the preceding and succeeding intervals. For time periods that lie outside all the intervals provided, QoS value of the end time of the last interval specified or the beginning time of the first interval specified is extrapolated to obtain the expected value. This allows the run-time optimizer to have an expected value for comparison at any point in the lifetime of a query.

Each QoS measure has a priority associated with it. The priority of a QoS measure indicates the severity of its violation and determines how that violation is handled. The run-time optimizer is responsible for monitoring QoS measures of a query, make decisions to alter the scheduling strategy of a query and to invoke load shedders to drop tuples when it cannot meet the QoS requirements by changing scheduling strategies.

10.5.2 Run-time Optimizer Design

The primary goal of the run-time optimizer is to monitor QoS measures to ensure meeting user-specified QoS values to the best extent possible. Based on the monitoring, the best (or optimal) scheduling strategy is chosen for a query. In `MavStream`, the run-time optimizer acts like the decision making component of a closed loop feedback control system, where *expected* QoS values of the reference output and *measured* QoS values representing the actual output are used. The run-time optimizer consists of a *system monitor*, which monitors the values of QoS measures for a query (in addition to input stream and operator characteristics) and a *decision maker*, which chooses the best scheduling strategy for a query and controls the load shedders. In this section, we discuss the details of the *decision maker*.

Inputs to Run-time Optimizer

The goal is to match the user requirements with the resources available to the system and to make optimal use of available resources. Application requirements, typically, determine QoS requirements and as the resources available to a system vary, user-specified QoS requirements will have to be diligently mapped to available resources on the system. This calls for the prioritization of QoS measures (first from application viewpoint followed by available system resources viewpoint) so that the right decision is made by the run-time optimizer to match the QoS requirements of a query. Rather than specifying priority for queries explicitly, the priority of a query in `MavStream` is inferred from its QoS specifications.

Priority of QoS Measures

Each QoS measure is given a priority for each query which is translated into a weight used for computing a score used for selecting a scheduling strategy. The run-time optimizer may choose from several different available strategies to be used over the lifetime of a query. We have categorized the QoS measures into three priority classes:

1. **Must Satisfy:** this is an extremely important QoS measure for the query/application. Internally, this priority class has the highest weight associated with it. If QoS measures with this specification are violated for any query, run-time optimizer tries to find a better scheduling strategy and if no better scheduling strategy is available, it activates load shedders for that query.
2. **Best Effort:** this class has medium weight. The run-time optimizer does not invoke load shedders for this priority class. This class of priority can be used for applications that do not tolerate errors in results (hence the decision not to use load shedding). The scheduling strategy with the highest score is chosen for the QoS measures that are violated.
3. **Don't Care:** this class has the lowest weight. The actions taken by the run-time optimizer are similar to the Best Effort class except that when

more than one better strategy is available any one of the scheduling strategies which has a higher score than the current can be chosen. This priority class is a candidate for using secondary storage if the available memory is not sufficient.

The algorithm used by the run-time optimizer can be extended to handle any number of priority classes. The actual weights for each priority class need to be specified and the values of weights are normalized based on the number of priority classes used while selecting a scheduling strategy for a query.

10.5.3 Run-time Optimizer Implementation

The performance of QoS measures of a query depends predominantly on the scheduling strategy chosen for that query and the arrival rates of input streams. If the arrival rates of input streams exceed the processing capacity, tuple latency and memory utilization are bound to increase. The processing capacity of any system is fixed and can be computed by monitoring query characteristics such as selectivity and system characteristics such as memory release capacity and operator processing capacity (explained and formalized in Section 6.1.2). The run-time optimizer therefore can carry out decisions based on the arrival rate of streams. As the input rates of streams are bursty, any change in the arrival rates of input streams can potentially trigger a change in scheduling strategy for queries using that stream. This approach, although very useful, does not take into account the **actual** QoS requirements of the query and may end up taking decisions to change scheduling strategy when it may not be necessary. Hence, we are using the feedback mechanism which measures the **actual** QoS values and takes appropriate actions to rectify undesirable situations. This approach uses a static table called the decision table to make decisions. Decisions based on changes to the input stream characteristics are pro-active whereas decisions based on the feedback mechanism are reactive in nature (and will lag the actual changes).

Decision Table

Research in DSMS has proposed many scheduling strategies – each with its own characteristics and each deals with QoS measures in different ways. For example, the *Chain* scheduling [85] is an optimal strategy to minimize the memory requirement whereas the Path Capacity Scheduling [131] is optimal for tuple latency. The decision table encompasses and represents this information, in the form of ranking, as the relative appropriateness of a strategy for a QoS measure. Each row in the decision table holds a relative rank of a strategy for a particular QoS measure. The information about the rank can be easily obtained by analyzing the performance characteristics of each strategy for the measure being considered. The run-time optimizer uses this *static* information from the decision table along with some heuristics to choose the best scheduling strategy for a query violating one or more of its QoS measures. An example decision table is shown in Table 10.1. The rank value in the table is derived from the analysis of available scheduling strategies (as shown in Chapter 6).

QoS/Strategy	Round Robin	PC	Segment	Simplified Segment
Tuple Latency	2	4	1	3
Memory Utilization	2	1	4	3
Throughput	2	4	1	3

Table 10.1. Decision Table (Showing Relative Strategy Rank)

Since four scheduling strategies are considered in the above table, the ranking is from 1 to 4. As additional strategies are added, the table can be expanded. The motivation behind using ranks for scheduling strategies is that by knowing the relative appropriateness of scheduling strategies for various QoS measures, better results can be obtained by choosing a favorable scheduling strategy when that measure is violated. A static decision table provides a low run-time overhead for deciding the scheduling strategy for a query. In a continuous query processing environment, the impact of changing a favorable scheduling strategy at run-time will be significant for that measure. An alternative approach considered for ranking strategies was to use binary values for the table where a value of one representing a favorable strategy for the QoS measure and zero representing a non-favorable strategy. The run-time optimizer can then choose a strategy that is favorable for a majority of QoS measures. Unfortunately, this alternative does not capture relative appropriateness and results in a sub-optimal decision. Also, this approach can lead to more strategies getting the same score and hence may not be distinguishable from one another.

System Monitor

The *system monitor* continuously (over intervals determined by the run-time optimizer) monitors the output of a query for QoS measures of interest. The monitored QoS measures are compared against expected values obtained from the QoS input graph. The run-time optimizer keeps track of the QoS measures that are being violated and the percentage by which the measures fall short or exceed the expected value. Based on the QoS measures violated and their priority class (given by the user), a score is computed for each scheduling strategy available in the system using the decision table. The rank used in the decision table are normalized with respect to the number of scheduling strategies when scores for strategies are computed. The weight of the priority class to which a QoS measures belongs is also considered when computing the score of a strategy for a particular QoS measures as shown in Equation (10.1).

The score of a strategy for a query is computed by adding the score obtained from Equation (10.1) for each of the QoS measures that are violated by that query. If several scheduling strategies have a higher score for the violating measure than the current strategy, the run-time optimizer chooses the one with the highest score and initiates action to change to that scheduling strategy. If several scheduling strategies have the same score, any one of them can be chosen.

$$Score\ of\ a\ strategy\ for\ a\ query = Weight\ of\ Priority\ Class \times \frac{Rank\ in\ Decision\ Table}{Total\ Number\ of\ Strategies} \quad (10.1)$$

Since there is an overhead associated with changing the scheduling strategy of a query, the algorithm used by the run-time optimizer tries to balance between the number of times the scheduling strategy is considered for switched and the overhead incurred. If the strategy is re-computed often and results in changing strategies, the overhead will be high. On the other hand, if the strategy is not changed for a long period of time, the overhead will be low but if a QoS measure is being violated, it will continue to be violated for a longer period. Also, when a strategy is changed, its effect becomes visible only after a period of time (as the operators have to be scheduled sufficient number of times to make a difference in the QoS values at the output). This necessitates the run-time optimizer to consider the time it takes to effect changes to QoS measures as a result of switching. The algorithm also includes measures to deal with decisions when multiple measures are violated at the same time.

Choosing the Best Strategy

We illustrate the possible transitions and actions taken by the run-time optimizer with an example. The strategy chosen uses the rank given in Table 10.1. The numbers *1, 0.5, 0.01*, respectively, denote the weights used for *must satisfy*, *best effort* and *don't care* priority classes described earlier. A continuous query may have multiple QoS measures associated with it. At any point in time, some QoS measures may be satisfied and others not. As violated QoS measures can fall into the same priority class or different priority classes, the following two scenarios needs to be handled: (*i*) violated measures belong to same priority class and (*ii*) violated measures belong to different priority classes.

Violated measures belong to the same priority class: the actions taken when violated measures belong to the same priority class depend on the priority class of QoS measures. When only one of the measures is violated, the run-time optimizer tries to find a better strategy for the violated measure. As shown in Table 10.2, when only memory utilization is violated (and its priority is *best effort*), SS (or segment strategy) gets the highest score (of 0.5) and is, hence, chosen by the run-time optimizer. The scores obtained (for each strategy) when multiple measures are violated are shown in Table 10.3. All measures are assumed to belong to the *must satisfy* class for this example. Hence the use of weight of 1 in the computation of scores. Using the scores in Table 10.3 either PCS or SS can be chosen when all QoS measures are violated. If the QoS measures are still violated even after choosing the best strategy, the *decision maker* starts activating load shedders if the measures belong to the *must satisfy* class. Load shedding is always chosen as a last resort when the optimizer has exhausted all available scheduling alternatives. If the measures belong to either *best effort* or *don't care* priority class, the run-time optimizer takes no further action and continues monitoring.

Memory Utilization Violated	**Score**
Round Robin	0.5*(2/4) = 0.25
PCS	0.5*(1/4) = 0 .125
Segment	0.5*(4/4) = 0.5
Simplified Segment	0.5*(3/4) = 0.275

Table 10.2. Single QoS Measure Violated

All Measures Violated	**Score**
Round Robin	1*(2/4) + 1*(2/4) + 1*(2/4) = 1.5
PCS	1*(4/4) + 1*(1/4) + 1*(4/4) = 2 .25
Segment	1*(1/4) + 1*(4/4) + 1*(1/4) = 1.5
Simplified Segment	1*(3/4) + 1*(3/4) + 1*(3/4) = 2.25

Table 10.3. Multiple QoS Measures Violated

Violated measures belong to different priority classes: when violated QoS measures belong to multiple priority classes, the run-time optimizer takes actions for lower priority measures only after higher priority measures are satisfied. This is accomplished by introducing priority classes. Therefore the run-time optimizer tries to satisfy the QoS measures in the order of their priority. In other words, if higher priority measures are not satisfied, the system first tries to satisfy the critical intent of the user and then worry about others, if possible.

The priority-wise decision making scheme proposed avoids switching to satisfy lower priority measures until higher priority measures are satisfied. When strategies are chosen based only on violation of QoS measures belonging to lower priority measures (even when the higher priority QoS measures are satisfied), the selection made may not be good for the higher priority measures. This can lead to higher priority measures getting violated immediately.

For example, if tuple latency belongs to the *must satisfy* class and memory utilization belongs to the *best effort* class, run-time optimizer will choose SS scheduling when tuple latency is satisfied and memory utilization is violated. However, this can lead to degradation of tuple latency and result in a *must satisfy* class being violated again. To prevent these situations, higher priority measures are also taken into account when decisions are taken for lower priority measures. The disadvantages of this approach is that the best strategy for lower priority measures may never be chosen. Because of the nature of priorities, this approach is better than choosing strategies that are unfavorable for higher priority QoS measures. The basic idea is to prevent priority inversion from happening which has been considered in real-time scheduling.

QoS Measure	Priority class	Weight
Tuple Latency	must satisfy	1
Memory Utilization	best effort	0.5
Throughput	don't care	0.01

Table 10.4. QoS Measure, Priority Class, and Weight

The weights can be customized to reflect the relative priority of the three classes. We illustrate the use of weights and the *extent of violation* used for determining the strategy with an example. When a QoS measure is violated, the weights are used to compute the score. However, when some of the QoS measures are satisfied, the weight is adjusted based on the margin by which the QoS measure is satisfied. Table 10.4 depicts a scenario where QoS measures fall into different priority classes. As mentioned above, memory utilization will be considered only after satisfying tuple latency. For example, if the expected value for tuple latency is *2 seconds* and the observed value is *1 second* the reduction in the percentage for the weight will be *0.5* (computed as (2 - 1)/2) using Equation (10.2). The reduction percentage is multiplied with the range of reduction (1 - 0.5 in this case) to obtain the reduced weight of *0.75* using the Equation 10.3. This reduced weight is used to compute the scores for strategies as shown in Table 10.5 assuming tuple latency satisfaction and memory utilization violation. The intuition behind this is to change the weight (decrease) used based upon the extent by which a particular QoS measure is satisfied. The formula gives a reduced weight of 1 for *must satisfy* if the measure is satisfied exactly. If the measure is satisfied with some room to spare, it decreases the weight thereby increasing the contribution of the lesser priority measures for determining the score. Although a simplistic linear formula is used here to illustrate the concept, adaptive approaches (e.g., exponential mean) for tuning the weight using history can be developed.

$$Reduction\ Percentage = \frac{Expected\ Value - Observed\ Value}{Expected\ Value} \quad (10.2)$$

$$\begin{aligned} \textit{Reduced weight} &= \textit{Initial Weight} \\ &- (\textit{Reduction Percentage} * \textit{Weight Range}) \end{aligned} \tag{10.3}$$

Latency satisfied and Memory violated	**Scores**
Round Robin	0.75*(2/4) + 0.5*(2/4) = 0.625
PCS	0.75*(4/4) + 0.5*(1/4) = 0.875
Segment	0.75*(1/4) + 0.5*(4/4) = 0.6875
Simplified Segment	0.75*(3/4) + 0.5*(3/4) = 0.9375

Table 10.5. Violation of Measures with Different Priority Classes

Impact of Strategy Switching

The run-time optimizer, after selecting a strategy based on monitored measures, changes the scheduling strategy of a query by removing schedulable objects (operators, paths, and segments) from the ready queue of the current scheduler and placing them in the ready queue of the selected scheduler and initiating the new scheduler. The new scheduler starts scheduling them. To avoid unnecessary switches and to ensure that the right strategy is chosen we use the *lookahead factor*. *Lookahead factor* specifies the future time point at which the expected values (from the input) are used for the switch. By comparing the measured values to expected future values, the run-time optimizer ensures that it is ready to meet the QoS requirements as expected. The usage of *lookahead factor* avoids unwanted switches and makes sure that the right strategy is chosen thereby reducing the effect of switching delays. *Lookahead factor* should be chosen as a value greater than the time required to schedule all operators at least once and should be less than the interval used to monitor the output of a query. The monitoring interval need not be the same over the life of a query. In fact, it is determined from the input graph of expected QoS measures.

Avoiding Cycles Using the Same Strategies

As a consequence of the fluctuations in the arrival rates of streams and conflicting requirements of QoS measures, there is a possibility that the run-time optimizer will cycle through the same sequence of strategies. This cycling through the same sequence of strategies can occur for two or more strategies. For example, the run-time optimizer might choose the Path Capacity and the Segment strategies alternatively for a query to satisfy latency and memory requirements if both measures are of the same priority. This may lead to unnecessary switches that needs to be prevented.

The run-time optimizer handles the above by remembering the history. Whenever the run-time optimizer changes the strategy, it keeps track of the QoS measures that were violated and those that were satisfied. Before making a change in the scheduling strategy, the run-time optimizer verifies whether it is changing to a strategy that was used earlier. If it is, the run-time optimizer compares the measures that were violated previously to measures that are satisfied currently and vice versa. If they turn out to be the same (for more than 2 repetitions), the run-time optimizer assumes it as a potential indication of a cycle. To avoid cycles, the run-time optimizer tries to find a new strategy by taking into consideration previously violated and currently violating measures. Although this method prevents cycles, it can also sometimes prevent a genuine change to an older strategy.

The above technique can be easily extended to check for cycles involving more than two strategies or include additional parameters. But this process will incur some additional overhead for keeping track of multiple strategies, parameters, and incurs more comparisons. The addition of parameters and keeping track of k repetitions (where k is at most the number of strategies) also increase the probability of preventing genuine changes.

It is entirely possible that strategies alternate (or cycle) due to changes in expected QoS values. This should not be prevented as these are genuine changes of scheduling strategies dictated by the QoS requirements. To overcome this, cycle checking is done within a piece-wise segment of the QoS input. When the segment is crossed, checking for cycles will start afresh.

Overhead

The addition of a run-time optimizer results in some overhead in the form of monitoring, decision making, and switching strategies. The monitoring overhead includes the computation of QoS measures. The overhead for *decision maker* consists of computing expected measures from the QoS graph, comparing expected values to monitored values and the decision making process itself. Since the number of QoS measures and priority classes are small and finite, the time taken for making decisions can be considered as small and constant. The number of times a query changes its scheduling strategy will be, in the worst case, the number of times the query output is monitored. Hence, the overhead is directly proportional to the frequency of monitoring which can be reduced by: (*i*) minimizing the frequency of monitoring and (*ii*) minimizing the number of strategy switches.

Decision Maker

The algorithm for making decisions is shown in Algorithm 7. For each query, the details about the current strategy, previous strategy and QoS graphs are

Algorithm 7: Run-time Optimizer Algorithm

```
    INPUT: current time, monitored QoS values
    OUTPUT: next time to monitor, decision for QoS delivery
 1  foreach query do
 2      foreach QoS measure do
 3          Compare monitored and expected values using the lookahead factor;
 4          if violated then add to violated measures list;
 5          else
 6              Compute reduced weight using current expected values;
 7              add to satisfied measures list;
 8          end
 9      end
10      if violated measures list ≠ NULL then
11      new strategy ← get strategy using
        violated and satisfied measures list;
12      cycle ← check with history for detecting cycles;
13      if cycle == false then
14      current strategy ← new strategy;
15      Record current strategy details and switch to new strategy;
16      else
17          continue with the current strategy;
18          consider load shedding, if appropriate;
19      end
20  end
21  return get next time to monitor ;
```

tracked by the run-time optimizer. The *system monitor* provides the monitored values. The *decision maker* considers each priority class and finds violating measures for the current priority class using the *lookahead factor*. The *decision maker* chooses the best strategy for remedying the violated measures by taking into consideration the reduced weights of satisfied measures. The *decision maker* also conducts some checks to ensure that a query does not cycle through strategies. The flow chart of the sequence of checks made by the *decision maker* is shown in Figure 10.6

System Monitor

System monitor computes QoS measures of queries and arrival rates of input streams as directed by the run-time optimizer. It can also update selectivity and other parameters (e.g., memory release capacity), if requested. The *system monitor* keeps an ordered list of times at which it needs to collect output information for a query. It obtains QoS values and provides it to the *decision maker*. The *decision maker* compares measured QoS values with that of expected values and takes appropriate actions. It also determines the time the query needs to be monitored next. Based on the next time point for moni-

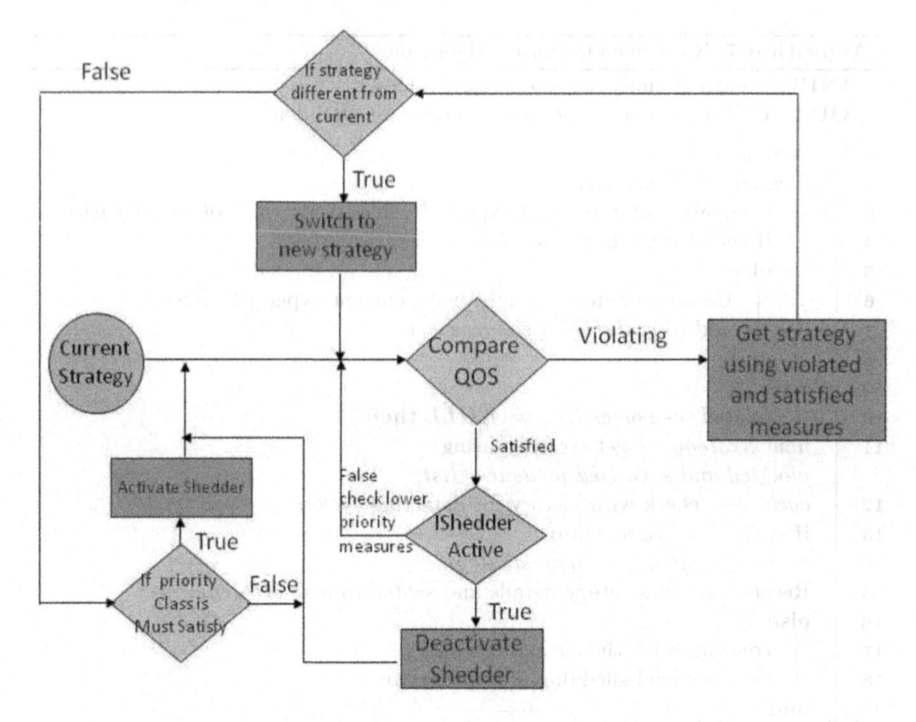

Fig. 10.6. Run-time Optimizer Flow Chart

toring output, *system monitor* determines the amount of time for which it should sleep. The algorithm for the *system monitor* is given in Algorithm 8.

Algorithm 8: *System Monitor* Algorithm

```
1  while true do
2      if no queries to monitor then
3      wait;
4      else
5          foreach query to be monitored do
6              if current time == time to monitor then get
               current QoS values;
7              provide current QoS values to the Decision Maker;
8              get next time to monitor;
9              if (next time to monitor < min_next time to monitor) then
               min_next time to monitor = next time to monitor;
10         end
11         wait min_next time to monitor − current time;
12     end
13 end
```

10.6 QoS-Delivery Mechanisms

10.6.1 Functionality

Operating systems schedule tasks using their own priority schemes and hence are not very useful when scheduling needs differ from the prioritization used by the operating systems. Granularity of scheduling plays a major role in the performance of a DSMS. We discussed some issues regarding process-level scheduling versus operator-level scheduling in Section 5.1. It is not realistic to schedule at a tuple level as the total number of tuples in the system is unbounded and context switching has some cost associated with it. In order to get finer control of various scheduling strategies, `MavStream` keeps control of scheduling at the operator level as it forms the basic building block for all schedulable objects (e.g., operator, operator path, segment) in our system. Either an exhaustive or a threshold strategy (see Sections 5.1.3 and 6.1.1 for their descriptions) is used for computation. This decision is also based on the assumption that the thread switching cost is extremely small in current architectures. The design and implementation is somewhat easier and modular as operator paths and segments can be grouped into sequence of operators for scheduling and all schedulable objects are composed of operators. `MavStream` currently supports the following scheduling strategies: *data flow*, *round-robin*, *weighted round-robin*, *path capacity*, *segment* and *simplified segment*.

The load shedding approach discussed in Chapter 7 has been implemented in `MavStream`. The run-time optimizer measures QoS violations by comparing monitored values to expected values. If the run-time optimizer does not find a better scheduling strategy that reduces QoS violations, it can invoke load shedders (already built into the buffers and are not activated by default) to save computation time depending on the priority class of the violated measures. Load can continue to be shed as long as the error introduced is within the tolerable limits specified by MTRE (maximum tolerable relative error). As soon as QoS measures start meeting the expected values, load shedding is deactivated. The use of feedback from the *system monitor* module provides a reliable measure of the actual performance of a query in the system. Hence, this feedback is used to control the operation (activation/deactivation) of load shedders.

Load shedding is a configurable parameter to the server and can either be enabled or disabled. Similarly, a single (or a set) of scheduling strategies can be specified as part of the configuration.

10.6.2 Scheduler Design

The run-time optimizer (explained in Section 10.5) requires a different approach to scheduling as not all queries use the same scheduling strategy at any point in time. Ability to change the scheduling strategy of a query at run-time entails that the system have multiple schedulers (one for each scheduling strategy) that can be activated as needed. At any time instant, a particular scheduling strategy may or may not have objects in its ready queue for scheduling. Therefore, the run-time optimizer must notify the scheduler when it decides to use the selected scheduling strategy for a query. Since potentially all the schedulers can be active, each of them competes for CPU cycles. Multiple schedulers need only to be active when they have objects in their ready queue; therefore, we need a mechanism native to MavStream to control the various schedulers.

The Master Scheduler (MS) used in MavStream is similar to the hierarchical scheduling discussed in Section 5.4.4. However, in MavStream, the first level selects the scheduler and the second level schedules objects (e.g., operators, paths). Each scheduler in MavStream is modeled as an independent thread of execution. Master scheduler runs as a separate thread allocating time for each scheduler to execute. The master scheduler currently follows a fair scheduling scheme by using a weighted round robin approach for all the schedulers. The weight can be changed based on the priority of the queries determined by the priority classes of QoS measures and the closeness of expected values to the predicted values (based on the estimated QoS values using the model presented in Chapter 5). Currently, the time allocated for each scheduler is determined by the number of objects (note that each schedulable object consists of one or more operators) in the ready queue of each scheduler. Since each operator (in an object) gets a fixed quantum of time for execution, the master scheduler allocates enough time for all the objects in the ready queue to execute at least once. The master scheduler does not get involved in the way objects get scheduled by each scheduler. Further each scheduler notifies the master scheduler if it finishes processing before the allocated time quantum. In case the scheduler has not completed processing the operators, it is preempted by the master only after the object (operator path or segment) being scheduled currently completes its execution. The algorithm for master scheduler is shown in Algorithm 9.

Algorithm 9: Master Scheduler Algorithm

1 **while** *true* **do**
2 process strategy change requests
3 **if** *all scheduler queues empty* **then**
4 wait; **else**
5   **foreach** *scheduler* **do**
6   **if** *ready queue* $\neq$ *empty* **then** resume *scheduler*;
7   wait for: object *time quantum* * number of objects in *ready queue*;
8   suspend *scheduler*;
9   **end**
10 **end**
11 **end**

10.6.3 Scheduler Implementation

In order for an operator (from a path or segment) to be scheduled, it has to be instantiated and be ready to execute. When a query plan object is received by the `MavStream` server, the operators associated with the query tree are not instantiated. However, it may not be possible to create paths (that have instantiated operators) when the server receives a query plan which is not instantiated right away (because it is set to be executed at a later time). Hence, operator paths of the query plan containing empty operator nodes are created and inserted into the query plan object. Each empty operator node has a pointer to the instantiated operator, which is populated whenever the operator is instantiated. At the start time, the query tree is instantiated, and the operator paths, with correct pointers to the instantiated nodes, are inserted into the scheduler's ready queue. This reduces the time for instantiating a query.

The ready queue of each scheduler is sorted in the descending order of the appropriate measure (e.g., processing capacity or memory release capacity of operator paths). The operator path with maximum value will be first in the queue. The scheduler removes the first object from the ready queue and schedules the operators of the object in the appropriate sequence and assigns the time quantum. Scheduler starts the operator thread and waits. Consider round robin scheduling in which every operator is assigned the same time quantum. If an operator finishes its operation early, it wakes up the master scheduler thread immediately.

Data structures for paths are implemented using `Java` Vector class as they are synchronized (i.e., only one thread can handle an operator at any given time). For sorting the paths, we use the `Java` Collections API which sorts using the modified merge sort (with worst case complexity O(nlogn)). Paths implement `Java` Comparable class as they must be mutually compared for sorting. All scheduling strategies extend an abstract class *Scheduler* which has the general functionality. A scheduler is implemented as a *runnable* class. The scheduler class supports methods to add and remove an object (e.g., operator or path) to the ready queue. All are abstract methods and are implemented in specialized schedulers. Their implementation differs from one scheduler to another based on the specific scheduling policy and properties used for ordering schedulable objects.

The Master Scheduler encapsulates various schedulers. All schedulers are inherited from the base class *Scheduler*. The *Scheduler* class also provide the Master Scheduler with a uniform interface used by all schedulers. Schedulers include a variable *blnThreadSuspended* that indicates the state of scheduler. This variable is set to true when a scheduler is suspended. Scheduler class also supports methods to start a scheduler thread in a suspended state, suspend the execution of scheduler by setting *blnThreadSuspended* to true, and resume the execution of scheduler by setting *blnThreadSuspended* to false.The *Scheduler* class also defines an abstract method, *runScheduler*, that must be implemented by each subclass. This method has facilities to notify the Master Scheduler when a scheduler's ready queue is empty. The Master Scheduler has its own ready queue *timeSlicerQueue* where it receives requests to start queries and change strategies. Master scheduler checks its ready queue and processes the requests before allocating time to schedulers.

10.6.4 Load Shedder Design

The premise of load shedding is that if a sufficient number of tuples are discarded, the processing capacity will match the load and is likely to satisfy QoS measures. When tuples are dropped, accuracy of computed results will suffer. As discussed in Chapter 7, load shedding is an optimization problem and consists of the following subproblems: (*i*) when to shed load, (*ii*) how much load to shed, (*iii*) where to shed, and (*iv*) how to shed.

In this section, we present the feedback-based load shedding approach. The overhead for the whole approach is kept low by performing as many decisions as possible before the query is started. The predefined QoS requirements considered also include the maximal tolerable relative error (MTRE) of a continuous query for its final query results. Where to shed load and how much to shed is determined using the formulae presented in Chapter 7. However, when to shed is determined by the actual QoS values measured by the *system monitor* and is further elaborated in the implementation section. Some experimental results are also included in the evaluation section (Section 10.7).

10.6.5 Load Shedder Implementation

The location of shedders is determined before the query starts executing. Since the number of active shedders has to be kept to a minimum to minimize the overhead, we have to ensure that maximum amount of computation (and storage) is achieved by activating any shedder. Hence, the shedders are initialized at positions having the highest place weight which are also calculated before the query starts. Maximum amount of resources are freed when the shedder with the highest place weight (as discussed in Section 7.3.2) is activated. Therefore, when the run-time optimizer detects that a query is likely to violate QoS requirements, it takes a greedy approach and activates the shedder with the highest place weight from the list of non-active shedders.

The list of load shedders are kept sorted by their place weights. The list is sorted when locations of shedders are determined statically at the time of query instantiation and hence does not involve any run-time overhead. When activated, the load shedder starts dropping tuples at the maximum allowed drop rate. The run-time optimizer keeps the load shedder active until either the QoS requirements are met or when it finds a better strategy for the query after dropping some tuples based on the measured output values. The load shedders are deactivated when a new strategy is found so that the results produced by the query are closer to the actual. Furthermore, the availability of a new strategy can denote potential availability of resources to meet QoS requirements without dropping load.

The load shedders are implemented as part of the input queues of operators as they incur the least overhead (as determined in Section 7.2) and drop tuples at the earliest possible time. Load shedding is implemented as a function in the *Buffer* class. The approach of making load shedding a function of the buffer is straightforward and efficient. The state of shedders is inactive initially in all the buffers. The state of the load shedder is checked when a tuple is enqueued (involves a simple `test` function). If the shedder is inactive, tuples are enqueued into the buffer, else the function to determine whether a tuple has to be dropped is invoked. The *QoSData* object in the run-time optimizer maintains, for each query, a list of load shedders with references to buffers where load shedders are kept sorted on their place weight. When QoS requirements begin to get violated, the *Decision Maker* starts activating load shedders using *activateShedder* method of the *QoSData* object. The activation of shedders only involve setting the state of load shedders inside the input queues to true. Once activated every tuple enqueued into the buffer is subject to an additional check for determining whether it needs to be dropped using the *checkDropCondition* function. This function determines the type of load shedder and calls the appropriate function.

Random Load Shedder

The random load shedder drops tuples at random based on a probability value. The run-time optimizer has the option of setting the drop probability, with an upper limit that is determined by the maximum drop rate. The maximum drop rate is computed when the location of load shedders is computed using the arrival rates and maximal tolerant relative error (MTRE). The maximum drop rate specifies the highest percentage of tuples that can be dropped without possibly violating the tolerable error limits. When a load shedder is activated to drop tuples randomly, *checkRandomDropCondition* method is called. A random value between 0 and 1 is generated for each tuple enqueued. If the value generated is greater than the drop probability of the shedder the tuple is enqueued else it is dropped. For example, if the maximum drop rate is 10%, the drop probability value set is 0.1.

Semantic Load Shedder

Semantic load shedders drop tuples based on the semantics specified for dropping a tuple. A tuple is dropped based on the value of an attribute in that tuple. Currently, a tuples can be dropped based on the *highest*, *lowest* or *center* (or mean) value of an attribute in that tuple. A buffer is added to the list of load shedders only if the input stream of that path contains the attribute that will be used for load shedding. Once the semantic shedder is initialized by the Input Processor using the *initializeSemanticLoadShedder* function, the *monitorSemanticShedderRange* function is called every time a tuple is enqueued into the buffer. This function keeps track of the highest, lowest, and mean values for the attribute specified. On activation by the run-time optimizer, the semantic shedder uses the values seen so far and uses them to drop tuples based on the property specified. For example, the center first shedder will drop all the tuples that fall within a fixed percentage around the mean. The percentage of tuples to be dropped around the range of interest can be specified as an option. The *checkSemanticDropCondition*, and *checkCondition* methods of the *Buffer* class performs the check for semantic shedding.

10.7 System Evaluation

Experiments have been conducted to evaluate the run-time optimizer of the `MavStream` system. Experiments have been conducted using synthetically generated streams and each stream is input using the feeder module. Each feeder thread runs on a separate processor and the input rate follows a Poisson distribution with pauses and increase in input rates to simulate a bursty input stream. The experiments were conducted on an unloaded machine running Red Hat Enterprise Linux Application Server 4 with four dual core AMD Opteron 2GHz processors and 16GB of RAM. The maximum allowed heap for `Java` run-time was kept at 8GB. The `Java` version used is 1.5. The feeder threads and the run-time optimizer were bound to separate cores. All the query processing and scheduling was performed on a single core.

10.7.1 Single QoS Measure Violation

The query used in this experiment has eight operators including two `hash join` operators and three input streams. The `window` used for the `hash join` was a tuple-based `window` of 500 tuples. For evaluation purposes, the QoS measure considered was tuple latency and a single interval was specified with start and end values of 1 second. When a single interval, with the same values for the start and end of an interval, is given, that value is used throughout the lifetime of a query. The priority was set to *Best Effort* class. The three scheduling strategies considered were path capacity (PC), segment and simplified segment. The mean input rates for the Poisson distribution was set to 2000, 1800 and 2200 tuples/sec. Each input stream consisted of two million tuples.

Experiments were conducted by using several scheduling strategies individually first without enabling the run-time optimizer and an experiment was conducted using the run-time optimizer with a starting strategy different from the best strategy for satisfying the QoS to verify whether the *decision maker* converges to the correct strategy. These experiments are plotted on the same graph to compare their effect on the QoS measure. Among the three strategies, the PC strategy provides the best performance for tuple latency; hence, the run-time optimizer should choose PC as the scheduling strategy. Initially segment strategy was chosen as it provides relatively the worst tuple latency. The monitoring interval of the run-time optimizer for all strategies was fixed to 3 seconds. When a single QoS measure is provided, the run-time optimizer chooses the best strategy for the QoS measure. The run-time optimizer cannot perform better than the best scheduling strategy for a QoS measure when load shedding is not allowed.

As shown in Figure 10.7 the tuple latency is high as the segment strategy was used at the start of the experiment. The segment strategy schedules the operators that lie in the segment with the highest memory release capacity first, hence it does not produce any output initially. When output is produced, the run-time optimizer determines that tuple latency is higher than the expected value and therefore changes the scheduling strategy of query to PC. The run-time optimizer does not make any further changes as it does not find any better strategy to improve tuple latency. Figure 10.8 shows the latency of the query for a smaller period of time over the lifetime of query. From Figure 10.8, it can be observed that the strategy chosen by the run-time optimizer (i.e., PC) provides tuple latency equivalent to the best strategy (which is also PC). This experiment shows that the run-time optimizer converges to the best strategy for tuple latency in spite of starting with an adverse strategy.

10.7.2 Multiple QoS Measures Violation

The query used in this experiment also has eight operators which includes two `hash join` operators and three input streams. The `window` used for the `hash join` was a tuple based `window` of 500 tuples. The QoS measures considered were tuple latency and memory utilization. The three scheduling strategies considered were PC, segment and simplified segment. Load shedding was disabled for this set of experiments.

QoS Measures With Different Priority

For this experiment the QoS measures were given different priorities. Tuple latency belonged to the *Must Satisfy* priority class and a single interval was specified with a constant value of 500 ms. Memory utilization belonged to the *Don't Care* class and the expected values were 10MB for the first 500 seconds and 1MB for the remaining time. The mean input rates for the Poisson distribution was set to 800, 950 and 500 tuples/sec. Each input stream consisted of two million tuples and the mean rates for the Poisson distribution was doubled at different points in time to simulate bursty nature of input. As tuple latency has higher priority than memory utilization, run-time optimizer chooses PC when tuple latency is violated as shown in Figure 10.9. Due to the low weight associated with the *Don't Care* priority class, the specification of memory utilization does not make any difference in the scores computed using the decision table.

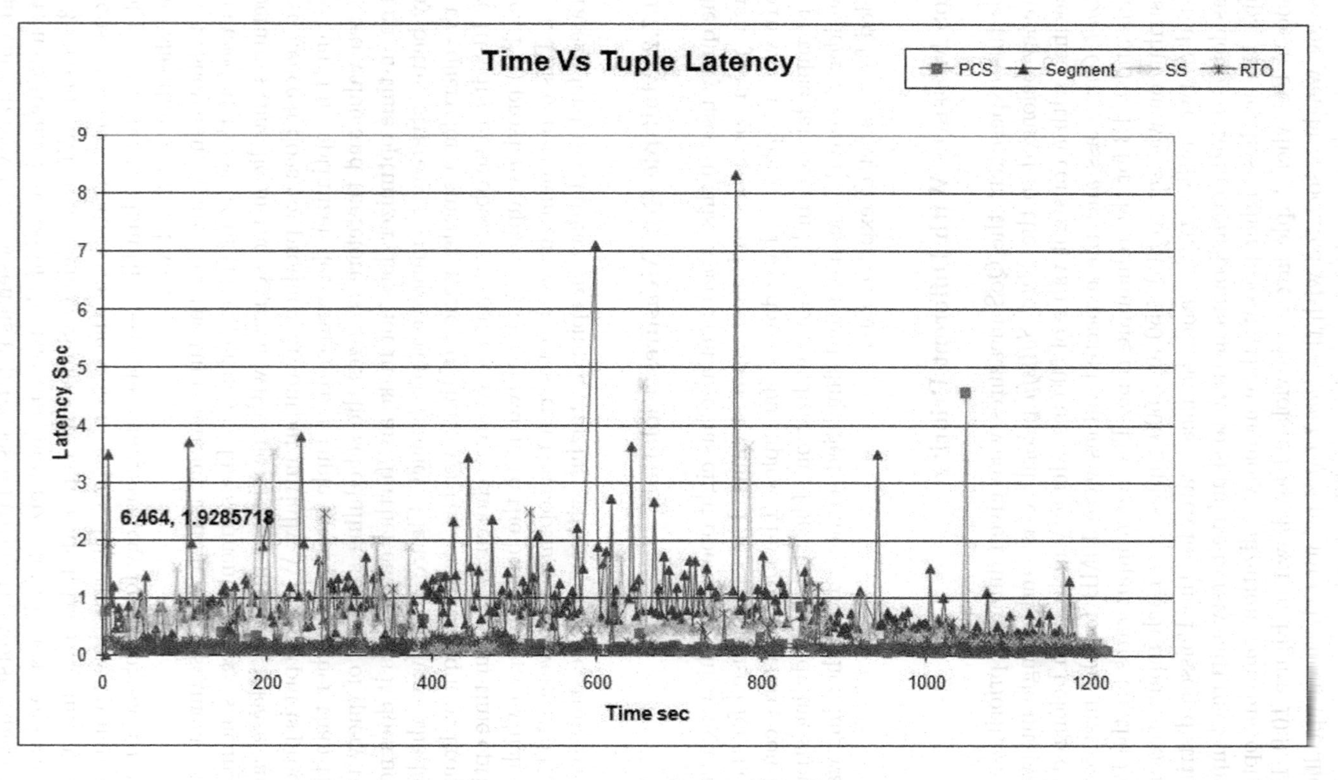

Fig. 10.7. Latency: Single QoS Measure

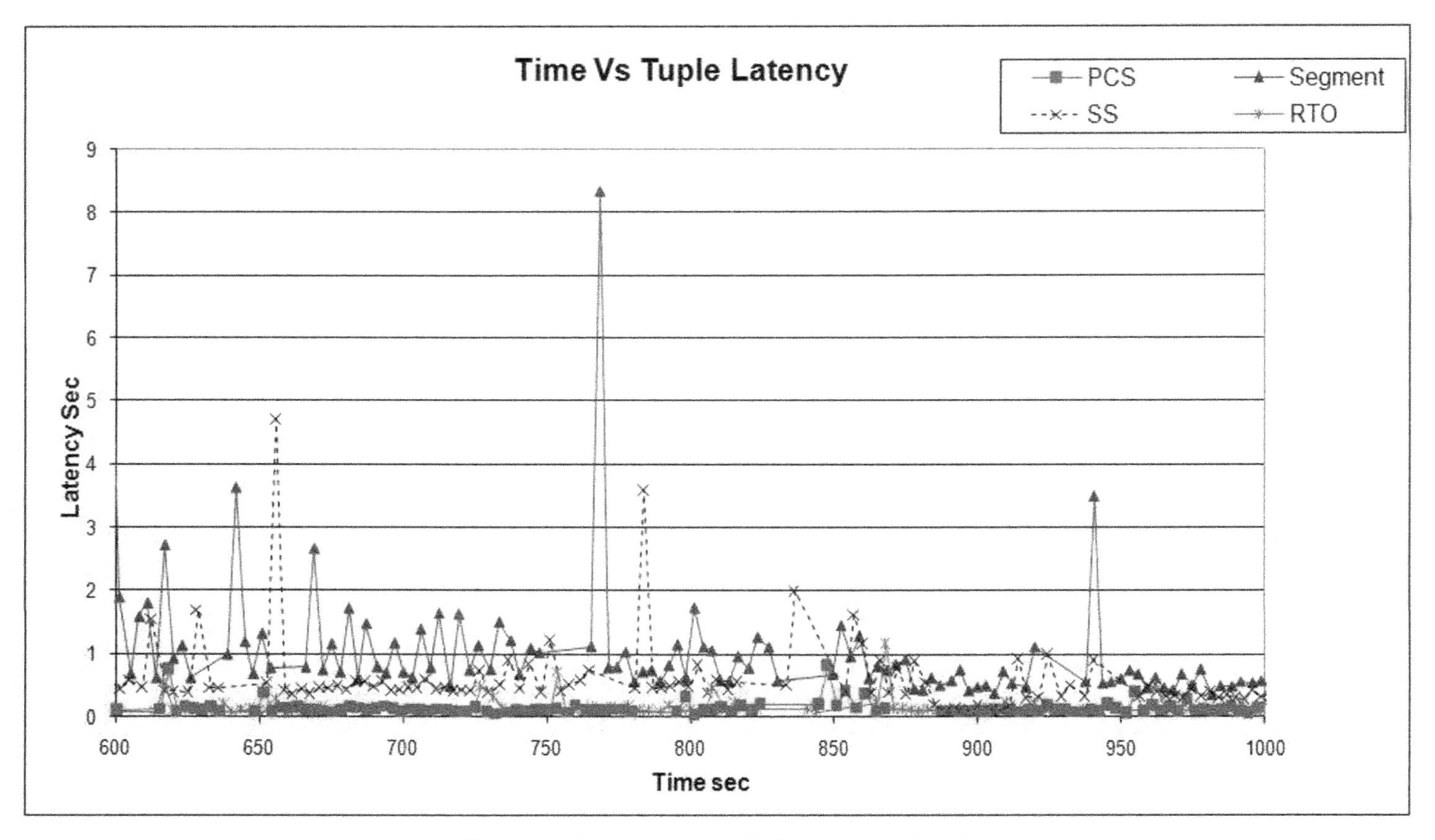

Fig. 10.8. Latency: Single QoS Measure – Details

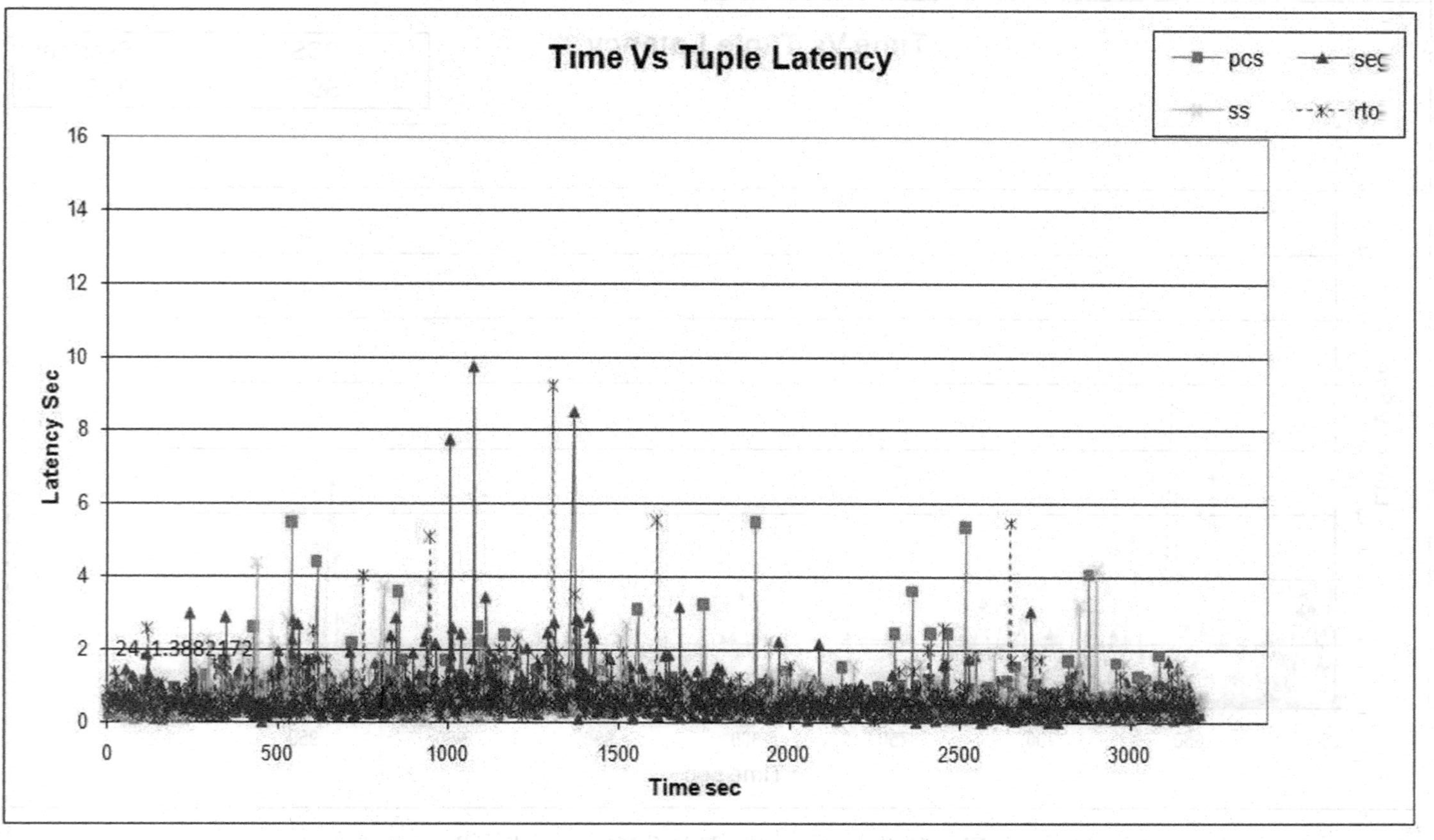

Fig. 10.9. Latency: Different Measures with Different Priorities

QoS Measures with the Same Priority

The QoS intervals specified for this experiment was same as that of the previous experiment. Both QoS measures belonged to the *Must Satisfy* class. The mean input rates for the Poisson distribution was set to 2000, 1800, and 2200 tuples/sec. The initial strategy chosen was the segment strategy as it provides the worst tuple latency. The memory requirement was kept high for an initial time period of 500 seconds. As shown in Figure 10.11 the memory requirement is satisfied *initially* and hence the run-time optimizer chooses PC strategy to improve latency.

After 500 seconds, the expected memory utilization reduces drastically and hence memory usage gets violated. The run-time optimizer chooses the simplified segment strategy when both tuple latency and memory utilization are violated and segment strategy if only memory utilization is violated. Since both QoS measures of interest have the same priority, the run-time optimizer favors both measures that are being violated equally and chooses the appropriate strategy. As shown in Figure 10.10 and Figure 10.11 the tuple latency and memory utilization provided initially by the run-time optimizer is near to that provided by PC strategy. When memory utilization starts getting violated at time point 539, run-time optimizer chooses the segment strategy where the memory utilized decreases noticeably as shown in Figure 10.11. As the tuple latency provided is within the QoS limits the run-time optimizer continues execution in segment strategy. Hence by choosing a strategy to improve the performance of violating QoS measures, the run-time optimizer is able to provide better performance for both measures of the query than by executing the query using a single scheduling strategy.

10.7.3 Effect of Load Shedding on QoS Measures

These experiments were conducted to observe the effect of load shedding on QoS measures. The performance of QoS measures without shedding was compared to the performance of QoS measures with various error tolerance limits for shedding. The higher error tolerance limits translate to higher drop probability for the random load shedders. This will lead to more tuples being dropped from the system decreasing the tuple latency and memory utilization. The query used for these experiments consisted of eight operators with two `hash joins` and three input streams, each stream containing 2 Million tuples.

For the first experiment, a tuple-based `window` of 1000 tuples was used. The streams were fed using Poisson distribution with a mean rate of 1000, 750, and 500 tuples/second. The mean for the Poisson distribution was doubled at different points in time to simulate bursty nature of streams. The QoS measure considered was tuple latency and a single value was specified with start and end values of 1 second. Memory utilization was set to *Don't Care* priority and hence did not affect the decisions made by run-time optimizer. The error

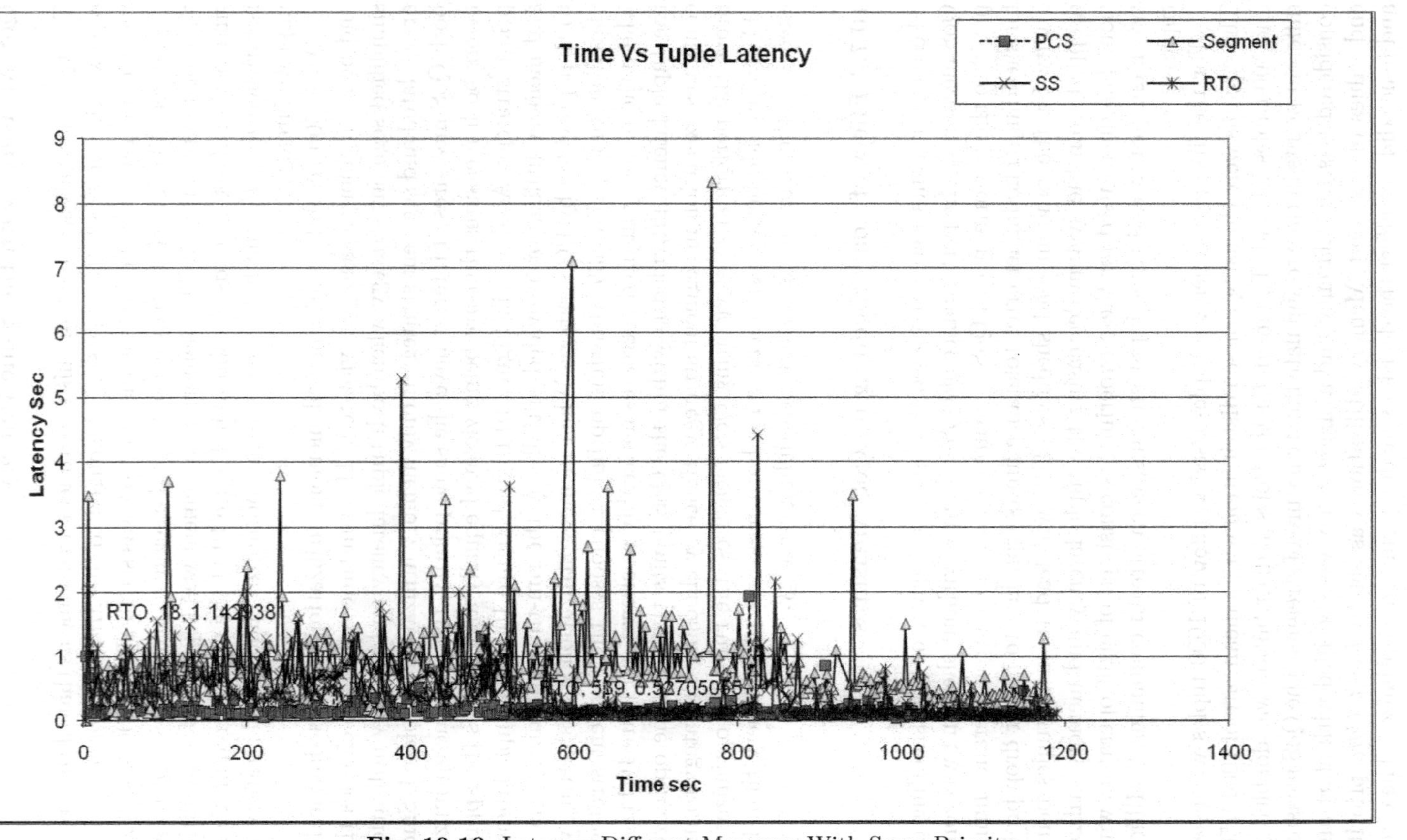

Fig. 10.10. Latency: Different Measures With Same Priority

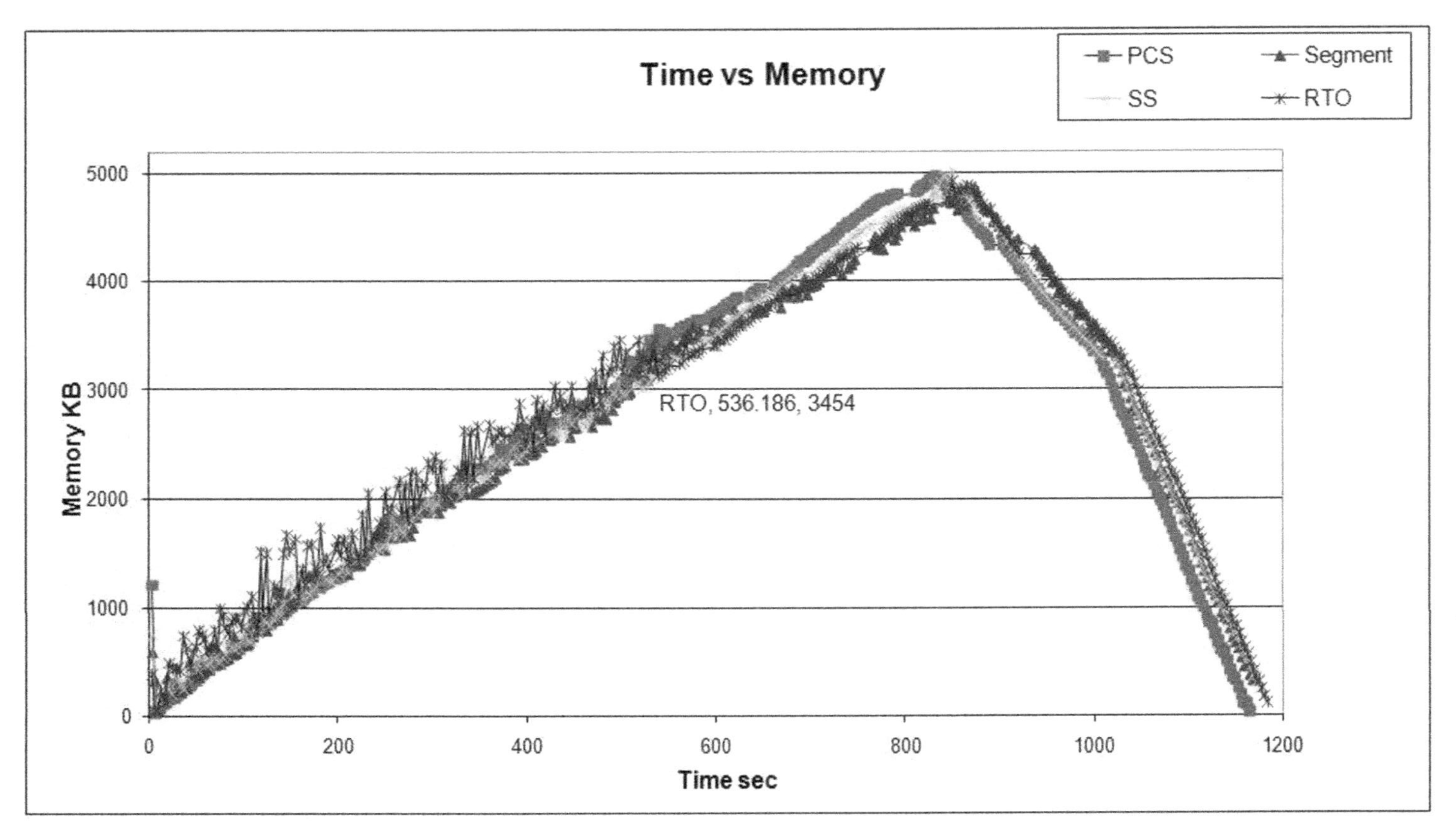

Fig. 10.11. Memory Utilization: Different Measures with Same Priority

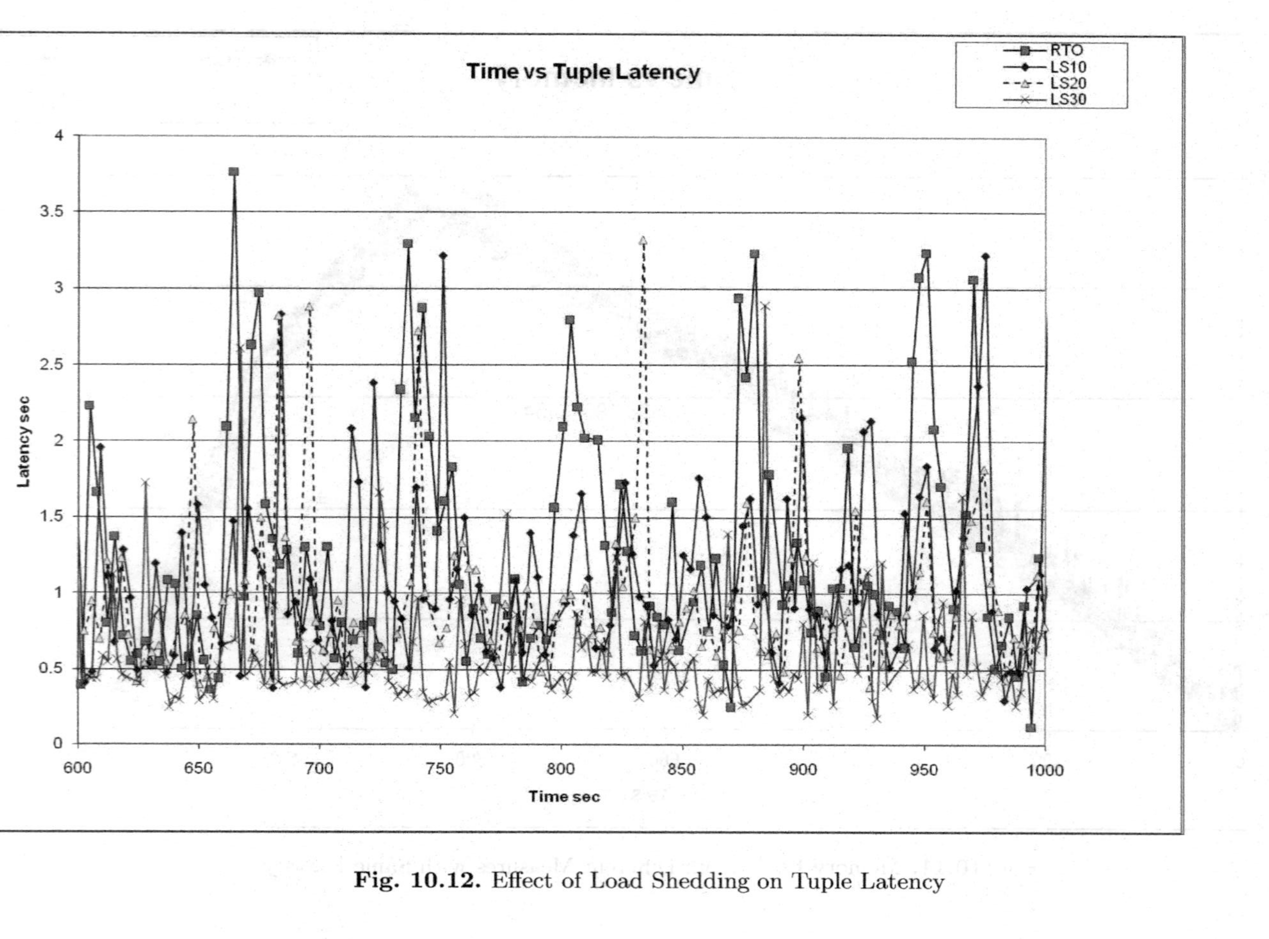

Fig. 10.12. Effect of Load Shedding on Tuple Latency

tolerance in the results of the query was varied from 0 to 30 percent in steps of 10. The run-time optimizer chose PC strategy, the optimal strategy for tuple latency. The run-time optimizer, after changing the scheduling strategy of the query to PC strategy, determines that the latency is still being violated and hence starts activating load shedders. As seen from the Figure 10.12, the higher the error tolerance limit, the lower is the tuple latency. This is as expected. As the load shedders are part of the input queues of operators, tuples are dropped immediately and hence they provide lower memory utilization which can be seen from Figure 10.13. In the figures, LSn corresponds to load shedding of n% of tuples.

10.7.4 Effect of Load Shedding on Error in Results

This experiment was conducted to observe the error introduced in the result by the load shedders. The query consisted of two operators: `select` and an `aggregate`. The data set used was a modified version of Linear Road Benchmark [335, 336] data set. The input rate of the stream followed a Poisson distribution with the mean set to 2000 tuples/sec. The mean was doubled at different points in time. A time-based `window` of 20 seconds was used for this experiment. The average speed of cars was calculated for each `window` without shedding and with various error tolerance levels for random load shedding. The error tolerance limits translate to the maximum allowed drop probability for random shedders. The error introduced in the average speed of car was much lower than the tolerant limits as indicated in Figure 10.14.

The same experiment was carried out for the three variants of semantic shedding. The *center first* shedder introduces a higher error as the values at center affect the results most (in this application) by dropping more tuples near the mean. The lowest and the highest first shedders introduce very small amounts of errors as shown in Figure 10.15. As the query used in semantic shedders calculates the average, the impact of highest and lowest first shedders are minimal due to outliers in the data. These results emphasize the importance of the application knowledge about the distribution of data while using semantic shedders.

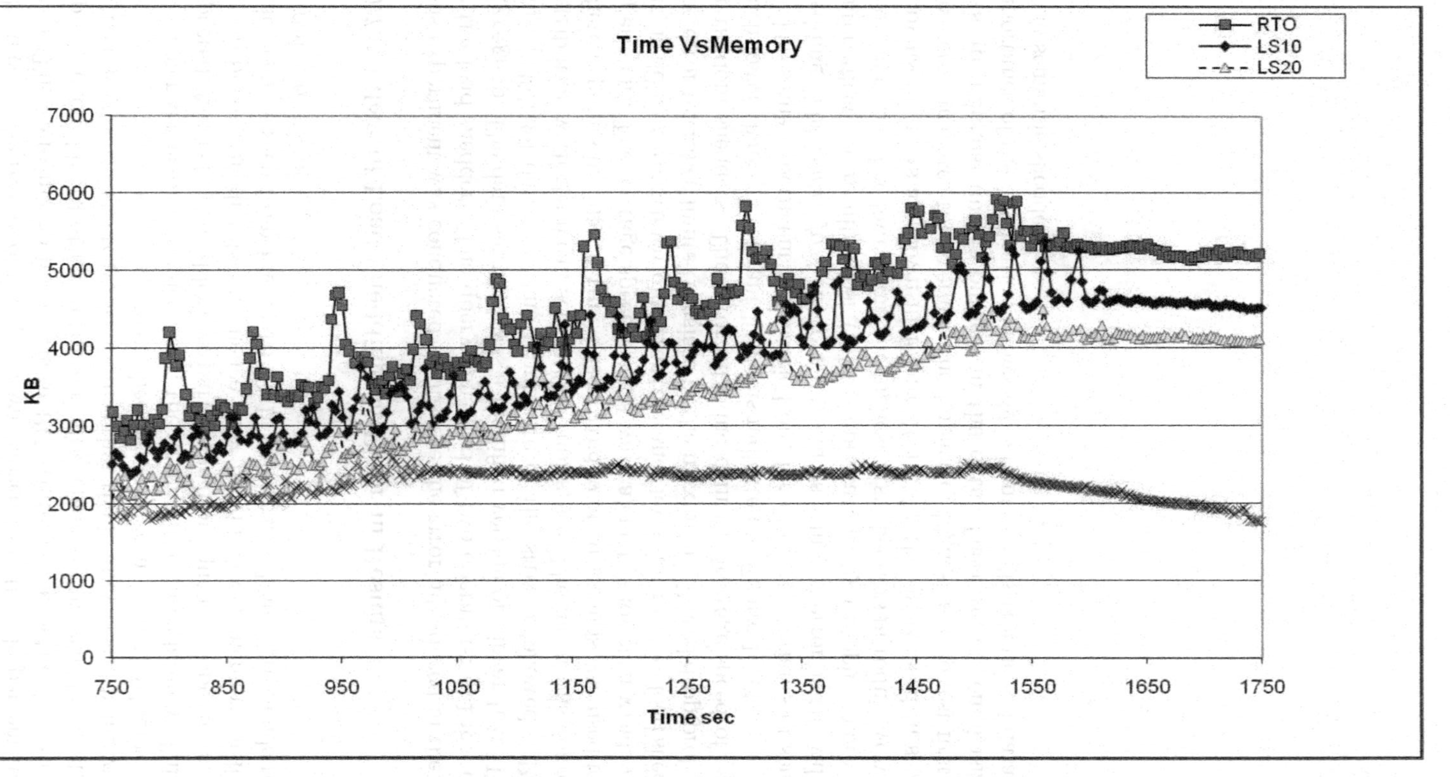

Fig. 10.13. Effect of Load Shedding on Memory Utilization

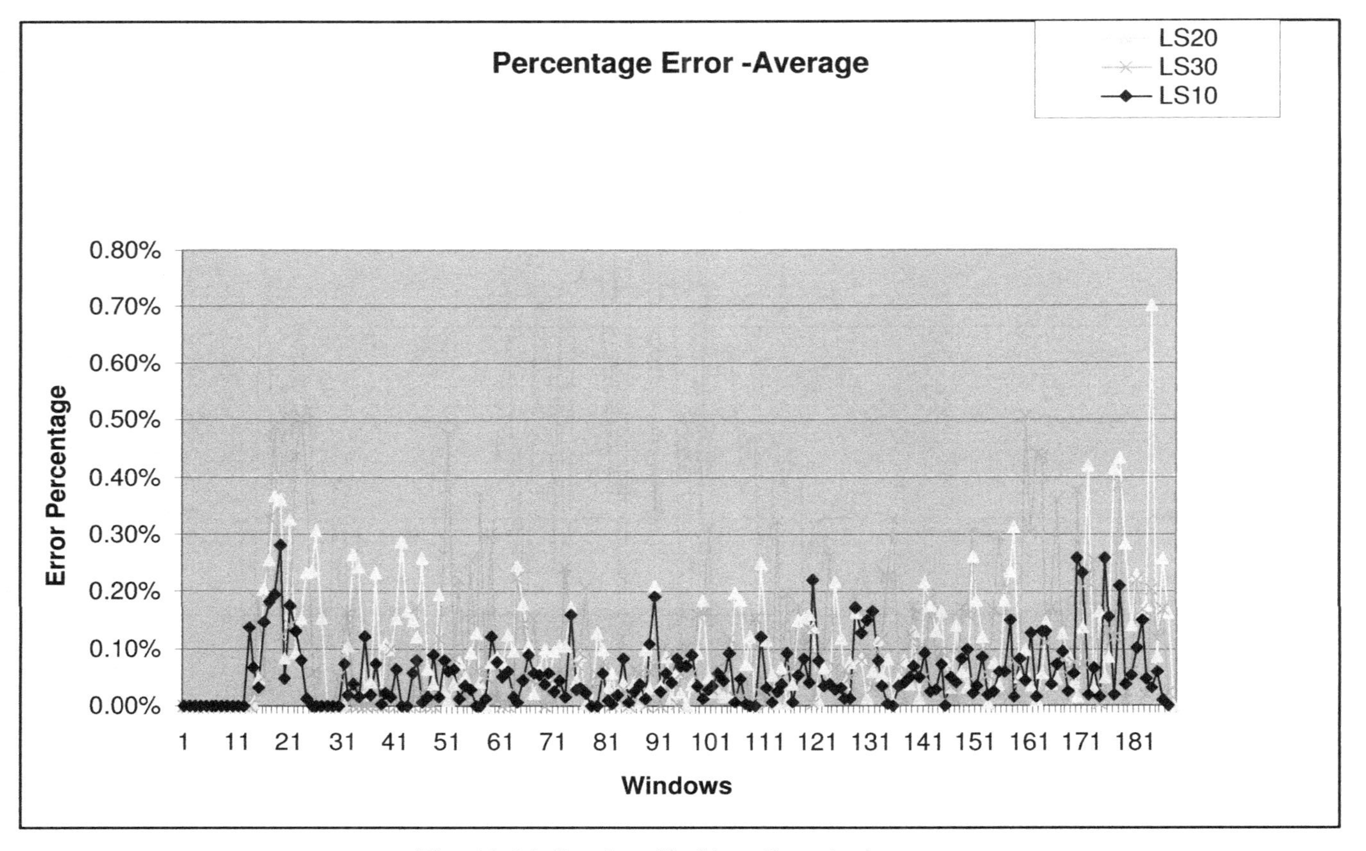

Fig. 10.14. Random Shedders: Error in Average

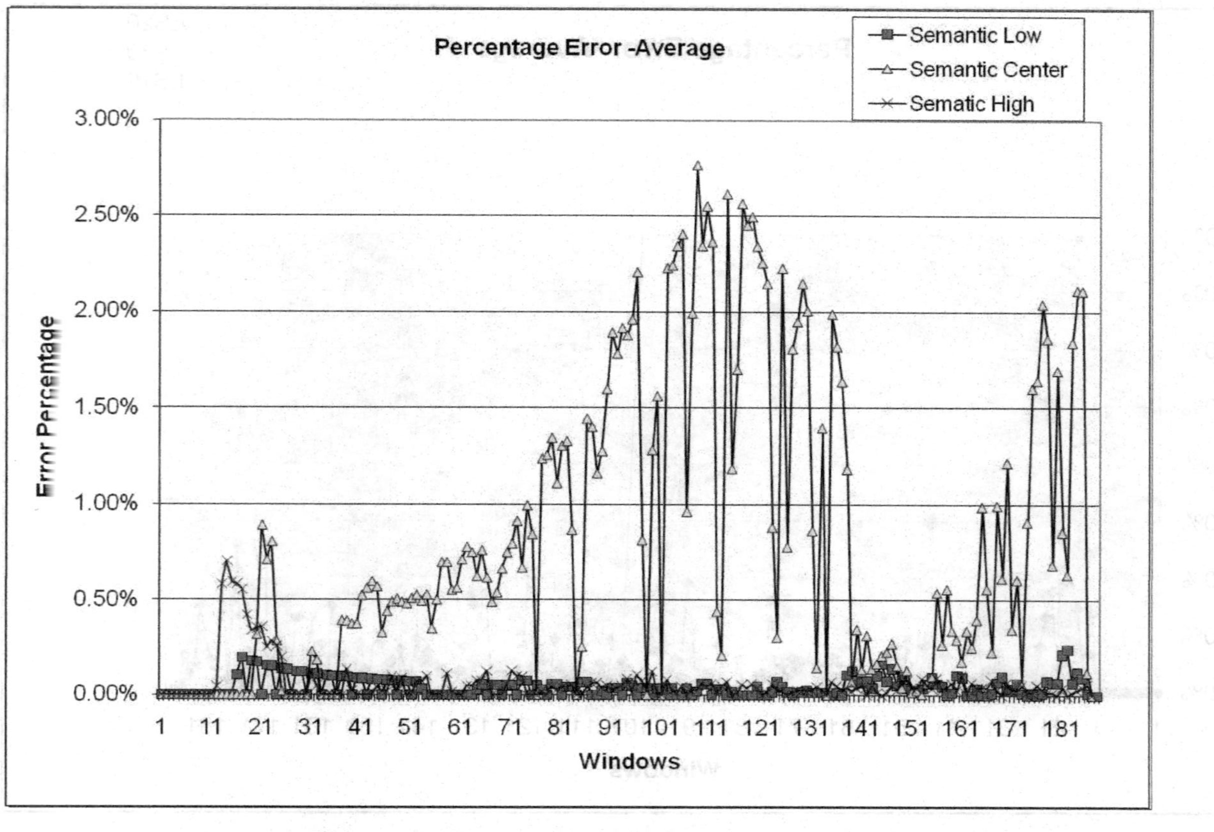

Fig. 10.15. Semantic Shedders: Error in Average

11

INTEGRATING CEP WITH A DSMS

In this chapter, we discuss the design and implementation of integrating complex event processing with a stream processing system. In Chapter 8, we derived the need for this integration and proposed a three-phase processing model (shown in Figure 8.4). For this synergistic integration, the stages, relevance, as well as the significance of each stage has been discussed in Section 9.4 and illustrated in Figure 9.2. In addition, meaningful extensions, of stream and complex event processing for enhancing the functionality of the overall system, have been elaborated in Sections 8.4.1, 9.5, and 9.6.

In Figure 9.2, **stage 1** corresponds to a general purpose DSMS (whose implementation has been discussed in Chapter 10), and **stage 3** corresponds to a CEP. Usually, rule processing (**stage 4**) is part of the CEP system. **Stage 2** is the interface that bridges the two and creates a system that can be used in multiple ways – as a stream processing system, a CEP system, and a combination thereof – with capabilities to associate CQs with events and vice versa in a flexible manner. Complex applications with multiple stages of stream and event processing can be readily accommodated using the architecture presented in Figure 9.2. Hence, in this chapter we focus on **stage 2** and extensions of CEP.

Rather than integrating complex event processing into `MavStream` from scratch, we adapt an existing, complex event processing subsystem to obtain a versatile system that can be used in multiple ways as indicated above. Although this chapter discusses the integration of two specific, independently developed systems – `Snoop`-based Local Event Detector (or LED[1] described in [88, 187, 253, 258, 351]) and the `MavStream` stream processing system described in Chapter 10, we believe that the integration approach presented here is applicable to arbitrary stream and CEP systems provided both use the same computation model (dataflow in this case).

[1] In the rest of the book, the LED, which uses the Snoop event specification language, is used interchangeably with a generic complex event processing system or CEP.

S. Chakravarthy and Q. Jiang, *Stream Data Processing: A Quality of Service Perspective*,
Advances in Database Systems 36, DOI: 10.1007/978-0-387-71003-7_11,

To recapitulate, `computed events` from continuous queries act as primitive events. Event operators supported by the LED include: `and` (occurrence of two events in any order), `sequence` (occurrence of two events in a particular order), `not` (non-occurrence of an event within a well-defined time interval or within a time interval defined by two arbitrary events), `or` (occurrence of one of the two events), `temporal` (a clock-based event which occurs at a specified, future time), `aperiodic` (non-periodic occurrence of an event within a well-defined time interval or within a time interval defined by two arbitrary events), `periodic` (repeated occurrence of a temporal event with constant and regular time interval within a well-defined time interval or within a time interval defined by two arbitrary events), `frequency` or `cardinality` (minimum number of times an event should occur), and `plus` (a temporal event based on another event with a time offset). Complex events can be composed using `computed events` (used as primitive events) and any of the above operators recursively. LED also supports event consumption modes (`recent`, `chronicle`, `continuous`, `cumulative`, and `proximal-unique`) briefly discussed in Section 9.2.2. LED also supports a prioritized rule execution model in `immediate` or `deferred` coupling modes briefly introduced in Section 9.2.3. Cascaded event and rule processing are also supported in the LED.

This chapter starts with the integration issues in Section 11.1. We then present the design and implementation of the integrated system in Sections 11.2 and 11.3. Implementation of stream modifiers introduced in Sections 8.4.1 and 9.5.2 is continued in Section 11.4. Finally, we present some of the additional benefits (e.g., starting and stopping continuous queries based on time or event occurrences) by using the available CEP component in Section 11.5. We conclude in Section 11.6 and outline features that are being added currently.

11.1 `MavEStream`: Integration Issues

We use the car accident detection and notification (Example 9.1 discussed in Section 9.1) to highlight the issues that arise during the integration of stream and complex event processing systems. As explained in the example, an accident is detected when `Immobility`, `Speed Reduction` are computed and their `Correlation` is detected.

The CQ that detects whether the car has stopped (i.e., `Immobility`) from Section 9.1 is repeated below.

```
CREATE CQ CQ_Immobile AS (
  SELECT     carId, Xpos, count(*)
  FROM       CarLocStr [Range 2 minutes]
  GROUP BY   carId, Xpos
  HAVING     count(*) > 3
                         )
```

The CQ that detects whether the car has reduced its speed (i.e., `Speed Reduction`) using stream modifiers from Section 9.5.2 is given below.

```
CREATE CQ DECREASE AS
   SELECT wRDiff(<speed> as C_speed, p<0.01>, N<car_id>)
   FROM  CarLocStr [Range 2 minutes]
   GROUP BY carID
   HAVING C_SPEED >= 0.3
```

The events generated by the above two CQs need to be `Correlated` in order to detect an accident. This can be done by the `sequence` event operator[2]. The event operator will perform the sequence correlation, but the condition (on same segment and lane) evaluation is not done efficiently in current event processing systems. Once a car is detected to have lowered its speed significantly following another car that has stopped, a `sequence` event gets raised and the check for "whether both cars are in the same segment and lane" is done in the condition part of the rule associated with the event. Event generalization (discussed in Section 9.6) is proposed as a solution to this problem. Also, it is important to limit the number of times the same accident is raised or notified. Stream modifiers (discussed in Sections 8.4.1 and 9.5.2) are proposed as a solution to this problem. Both will be illustrated in Section 11.2.3 below.

11.1.1 Event Generation

Due to the nature of input streams, the number of output tuples generated by a CQ can be large. Events can be generated from CQs either for each tuple or for a group of tuples. Event processing assumes that each event (primitive or complex) has a timestamp associated with it which is treated as the time of occurrence of that event. LED assumes that each event is an object with a timestamp. There can be an arbitrary number of constituent events in a composite event, each having a predefined number of attributes that act as parameters. The event operators are defined using temporal semantics.

Each stream tuple has an ordering attribute (either a timestamp or another designated attribute). For the purposes of computing QoS values, a timestamp is usually added by the system for each input tuple and this timestamp is carried over through the operators. This timestamp can also be used for implementing time-based `window` specifications. Tuples in the output stream are also ordered either on timestamp or some attribute value. In order to process stream output as events, a timestamp needs to be identified when output tuples are generated as events. Usually, the timestamp already associated for computing QoS values is used for this purpose. When an event is generated for a single tuple, the timestamp associated for computing the QoS can be

[2] Refer to footnote [3] on page 190.

used. On the other hand, when an event is generated for a group of tuples, either the maximum or the minimum timestamp of the tuples in the group can be used.

11.1.2 Continuous Event Query (CEQ) Specification

For the integrated system, in addition to CQs, events need to be specified along with a flexible way to associate a CQ with multiple events and vice versa. It is indeed possible for a single CQ to generate multiple types of events. For example, detection of speeding on an interstate highway is the same for all lanes. Once speeding is detected, it may be useful to separate speeding on the HOV lane versus the others. Although a CQ output can be split into multiple streams as part of stream computation, the above specification of defining an event type based on a CQ need to be, preferably, part of the event specification. Although computation will be transparent to the user, clarity of understanding will be better. The system is responsible for accepting event specifications and optimizing the generation of events. With this approach, new events can be specified on existing CQs at any point in time. It is also possible that multiple CQs generate the same event (e.g., slowing down of a car irrespective of the input stream).

This entails extending the language constructs to specify continuous queries, events and rules, and a combination thereof. It should be possible to define both a CQ and its associated event together (termed a Continuous Event Query or CEQ) or independently as well as in a temporally disconnected manner. If CEQ allows for the independent specification of events and continuous queries along with a mechanism to associate events with predefined continuous queries, we then have maximum flexibility. This way the CEQ specification can be used for (*i*) defining CQs and associated events, (*ii*) defining only events (both primitive and composite) and their mapping with or without predefined CQs, and (*iii*) defining only CQs without event specification.

11.1.3 Events and Masks

As CQs can produce a large number of output tuples, we need to improve the efficiency of the integrated system by exploiting the information associated with an event specification. Specifically, it should be possible to avoid generating events from CQs that will go unprocessed in the CEP stage. In addition, it should be possible to generate multiple events efficiently from a CQ.

In rules associated with events, conditions are typically specified as part of the rule to check for event attribute values (or parameter) that are passed from the event. Events are detected based on the event operator semantics and using consumption modes acting as constraints. Thus, in the absence of masks[3] on events, the conditions are checked *after* the event is generated or detected in the conditions part of the rule. This approach leads to excessive generation of events from CQs, and waste of processing to filter events in the rule condition using event parameters. Masks provide a mechanism using which attribute-based constraints can be applied to the generation of events from the output of CQs for reducing uninteresting events.

Event generalization (discussed in Section 9.6) provides a mechanism that generalizes and subsumes the notion of masks. Support for masks and its optimization can have a significant effect on the performance of the integrated system. Since events can be both primitive and composite, it should be possible to specify masks for both types of events. In other words, optimal processing of generalized events needs to be addressed.

11.1.4 Address Space Issues

As **stage 1** and **stages 3 & 4** correspond to standalone systems, each currently executes in its own address space. The issue is whether to keep them in their own address spaces or bring them together into a single address space. Additionally, depending upon the choice made for the above, **stage 2** can be developed either as a separate system (as a middleware) or can be included in either of the two address spaces. If multiple stages of continuous query and event processing are involved, large amounts of data need to be passed between address spaces multiple times. In the integrated system, data structures need to be shared, EDGs need to be constructed for event processing, query plans need to be instantiated for continuous query processing, and event objects need to be passed from a CQ to the event processing stage. Also, as event specification will initiate CQs to start generating events, run-time communication between the two systems needs to be taken into account. In the absence of a single address space, end-to-end QoS satisfaction will be harder to accomplish.

If each system is in a separate address space then Inter Process Communication (IPC) is required for passing data and for invoking Remote Procedure Calls (RPC). For the amount of data to be passed across the systems, the overhead introduced by the use of IPC and RPC needs to be considered.

11.1.5 Summary

To support general monitoring applications without sacrificing declarative nature of specification to preserve encapsulation, and management of large number of CQs, events, and rules in the system, the following are incorporated:

1. Flexible generation of events either for each tuple or for a group of tuples.

[3] Masks were first proposed in Ode [221, 222] for primitive events. The concept of instance-level events (in addition to class-level events in an object-oriented environment) supported in the LED [187,352] serves the purpose of simple masks.

2. A mechanism for specifying CQs and events individually as well as combine them in a flexible manner.
3. Improve the expressiveness and efficiency of the integrated system by improving the expressiveness and efficiency of the stream and event processing components.
4. An interface (**Stage 2**) that can take advantage of specifications on either side.
5. End-to-end QoS support for the integrated system.

11.2 Design of the Integrated System

In this section we elaborate on the design of the integration of `MavEStream`, an integrated event and stream processing system. Most of the issues discussed below relate to the design of **stage 2** in Figure 9.2.

11.2.1 Address Space

It is clear that all the processing of CQs, event detection, and rule execution should happen in the same address space to reduce tuple latency. The cost of sending tuples across address spaces (using IPC) and making remote procedure calls is significant and is not conducive to the QoS needs of monitoring applications. Hence, the `MavEStream` system includes all the components in a single address. Within an address space, common data structures can be shared, objects can be passed efficiently, and invocation of APIs does not incur additional overhead. Furthermore, to bring the event computation model closer to the continuous query processing model, buffers and operators can be specialized from the same class hierarchy. Scheduling can also be extended to include event operators and concepts such as operator paths can be relatively easily extended to include both continuous query and event operators. A single QoS monitor can be used to measure end-to-end QoS values, and a single run-time optimizer can handle QoS optimization (even if the optimization itself is slightly different for the two components) in an effective manner. Hence, the rest of the discussion in this chapter assumes a single address space for the integrated system.

11.2.2 Continuous Event Queries

For ease of understanding, we use an extended form of SQL to demonstrate the proposed constructs. In a CEQ specification, either the continuous query name or its specification can be used as part of the event specification. The Car ADN (Example 9.1 illustrated in Section 9.1) problem can be represented by a generic CEQ specification as shown below:

```
CREATE EVENT EImmobile
       SELECT CQ_Immobile.carId as carId,
              CQ_Immobile.segmentId as segmentId
         FROM CQ_Immobile

CREATE EVENT EDecrease
       SELECT CQ_Decrease.carId as carId,
              CQ_Decrease.segmentId as segmentId
         FROM CQ_Decrease

CREATE EVENT EAccident
       SELECT *
         FROM EImmobile  sequence  EDecrease

CREATE RULE AccidentNotify, IMMEDIATE
         ON EAccident
R_CONDITION Begin;
            EImmobile.segmentId == EDecrease.segmentId;
            End;
   R_ACTION Begin;
            //Notify all cars in upstream
            End;
```

The above query can also be expressed as a single CEQ where individual events are not named. Below, the continuous event query has been defined independently using previously defined CQs and primitive events. Continuous queries are named (as `CQ_Immobile` and `CQ_Decrease`, defined in Section 9.5.1), and the query name has been used as the query identifier. The Events `EImmobile`, `EDecrease` are defined on the queries by using query names `CQ_Immobile` and CQ_Decrease. The composite event `EAccident` is defined using named primitive events `EImmobile` and `EDecrease`. The rule `AccidentNotify` is associated with the composite event `EAccident`. The condition associated with the rule checks whether the pair of cars that were output from the event `EAccident` are from the same segment (more conditions can be added). In this example, we have associated conditions with the rule and masks have not been used. In the next section we show how we can model the same using event generalization.

```
CREATE EVENT EAccident
      SELECT *
        FROM (CREATE    CQ CQ_Immobile AS (
              SELECT    carId, Xpos, count(*)
                FROM    CarLocStr [Range 2 minutes]
            GROUP BY    carId, Xpos
              HAVING    count(*) > 3
                                                )
             )
             sequence
             (CREATE   CQ CQ_Decrease AS (
              SELECT   outer.carid
                FROM   CarSegStr outer [Range 2 minutes]
            GROUP BY   outer.carid
            HAVING (
              (SELECT speed as end_speed
                 FROM CarSegStr last [Range 2 minutes]
                WHERE last.timestamp = MAX(outer.timestamp)
                  AND outer.carid = last.carid
              )
              <
              0.7*(SELECT speed as start_speed
                     FROM CarSegStr first [Range 2 minutes]
                    WHERE timestamp = MIN(outer.timestamp)
                      AND outer.carId = first.carid
                  )
                 )
```

11.2.3 Events and Masks

In MavEStream, as events are generated by a CQ and passed on to the event processing system, it should be possible to apply masks to filter a generic event into different types of events. Masks on primitive events, when pushed to the event generation phase, provide a powerful mechanism in reducing the number of events generated. Although masks can be evaluated as part of event nodes, pushing them as low as possible in the EDG is preferred (very similar to pushing selections down the operator tree for relational queries).

Definition 11.1 (Mask). *is a Boolean condition on the attributes of an event (primitive or composite).*

Mask, as defined above, corresponds to the event generalization discussed in Section 9.6. A Mask can either be conditions on the attributes of a single event or conditions that span events when used with event expressions.

Specification of a condition as a mask instead of specifying the same as part of a rule allows for the evaluation of masks *before* the event is detected. Below we show the CREATE EVENT statement that includes masks. Below, ES is either a stream name or a named CQ or a CREATE CQ statement. Similarly EX represents an event name or an event expression. *Mask_condition* is analogous to the condition expressed in a WHERE clause.

```
CREATE EVENT Event_name
      SELECT attributes
        FROM ES | EX
        MASK <mask_condition>
```

Evaluation of Masks

The effectiveness of masks depends on where they are evaluated. By applying masks *before* an event is raised, the number of events raised and processed can be significantly reduced.

Hence, masks are analyzed and are pushed down the EDG (including the event generator operator) to the extent possible. Before an event is generated as the output of a CQ, any associated mask is evaluated. Tuples that do not satisfy the mask conditions do not generate an event whereas those that satisfy the condition are raised and processed further. Tuples/objects that correspond to events are converted into event objects and passed to the LED for event composition. Note that an event is not propagated up the event detection graph in the LED unless additional complex events need to be detected using that event.

Masks that are applicable to a composite event (equivalent of `join` condition) are evaluated at the composite event node in conjunction with the detection of the complex event. Composite masks cannot be checked until the corresponding constituent events are detected. Masks on primitive events are supported and evaluated on the stream side as described later in this chapter. The LED is being extended to handle generalized event specification that will have the ability to handle masks on event expressions.

For the Car ADN (Example 9.1 illustrated in Section 9.1) example, we illustrate the specification of an event (car slowing down on HOV lanes) with and without the use of masks.

In the approach that does not use masks, conditions are defined on the rule – one for the HOV lane detection and one for checking the segmentID. In this approach, each event raised by the participating CQs is composed using the `sequence` operator semantics. If the `sequence` event is detected, the conditions of the rule are evaluated. This adds significant computation overhead for detecting the `EAccident` event, not to mention the number of unnecessary events raised and discarded after condition evaluation. For example, the composite event needs to be detected for each pair of cars from different segments, several functions need to be invoked for checking conditions in rules, and parameters need to be retrieved and used to determine whether the condition is satisfied. The rule *AccidentNotify* on the complex event *EAccident* for this approach is shown below:

```
CREATE RULE AccidentNotify, IMMEDIATE
         ON EAccident
R_CONDITION Begin;
            EImmobile.segmentId = EDecrease.segmentId AND
            EDecrease.lane = "HOV" AND EImmobile.Lane = "HOV"
            End;
   R_ACTION Begin;
            //Actions
            End;
```

In the above rule, we have used the lane attribute in the rule condition even though the CQ_Immobile and CQ_Decrease CQs and events EImmobile, EDecrease and EAccident are not shown to output it. It is straightforward to generate them by modifying the continuous queries.

In the approach that uses masks, the system determines the best place to evaluate the mask conditions and pushes them down the EDG as far as possible (up to the event generator operator). With masks, the conditions in the rule essentially check for conditions that could not be separated and pushed down. For example, in the rule AccidentNotify shown above, all the rule conditions will be pushed down as masks and the rule condition becomes empty. Although an action is executed, in principle, after evaluating a rule-condition, rules are triggered significantly less number of times. The event EAccident definition is shown below using masks.

```
CREATE EVENT EAccident
      SELECT *
        FROM EImmobile  sequence  EDecrease
        MASK EImmobile.segmentId = EDecrease.segmentId
             AND EDecrease.lane = 'HOV'
             AND EImmobile.lane = 'HOV'
```

The above event EAccident can also be expressed as three separate create events with appropriate masks. The specification of the composite event remains the same. Specification of additional mask conditions – on the two primitive events and on the composite event – allows the system to optimize the evaluation of this event both on the event processing side and on the stream processing side. Some of the conditions are evaluated on the stream side even before the events are raised and some are evaluated on the event side as an extension of the operator semantics.

The event generalization explained in Section 9.6 forms the basis of the above specifications and their efficient translation. Event generalization provides a powerful specification mechanism for *augmenting* the semantics of event operators which can also be exploited by the system for significantly improving the efficiency of event detection. These extensions are critical for the integration of the two computation models from the QoS perspective. For more information on event generalization, refer to [286, 287].

11.2.4 Event Generator Interface

The Event Generator Interface (or EGI), shown as **Stage 2** in Figure 9.2, deals with the transformation of a CQ output into an event object for use by the event processing component. EGI is responsible for generating event objects from tuples produced by CQs. EGI keeps track of the mapping of events to CQs. EGI also applies the masks inferred from event definitions and generates event objects for only those tuples that satisfy masks.

The design for the EGI also facilitates the consumption of a CQ output by an application directly prior to the generation of events. In other words, the output of a CQ can be: (*i*) consumed by an application, (*ii*) used to generate different types of events, or (*iii*) input to another CQ for further processing. Functions of the EGI are summarized below:

- Populating attribute values of event objects with attribute values of a CQ output.
- Generating event objects from CQ output along with an appropriate timestamp.
- Passing the event object to the event detector for processing.

Event Generator as an Operator

The choice of a single address space implies that the EGI bridges the gap between the two systems in terms of object formats used by the two. However, this interface needs to access data structures created by both CQ and event specifications. When events are registered, it is important to make sure that the CQ's that act as input to any of those events are properly enabled to generate event objects. Furthermore, when a CQ is registered it is also necessary to make sure that it feeds the event nodes, if any, that are dependent on its output.

Based on the above considerations, the event generator interface is modeled as an operator termed Event Generator Operator (or EGO). Specifically, it is a unique stream operator that is instantiated by the system. However, the scheduling of this operator is determined dynamically by the system depending upon whether there is a consumer on the event processing side for the events produced by this operator.

The EGO is scheduled by the scheduler of the DSMS (this operator becomes part of a continuous query although instantiated by the system) and is not scheduled unless there is an event definition on that CQ. An EGO is attached to each CQ as the root operator. There is only one EGO for each named CQ. Also, the buffer between the last operator of a CQ and the EGO act as the output buffer for that CQ. Applications consume the CQ output directly from that buffer. The EGO input buffer always receives the tuples produced by the CQ but is not consumed by the EGO unless an event is defined on that CQ. With this design of the interface, the mask evaluation is best done at the event generator operator of each query as tuples can be dropped if they do not satisfy the mask. This also happens to be the earliest place where CQ output that does not contribute to events can be dropped. Note that multiple masks can be associated with an event generator operator in order to generate multiple event types from the same CQ.

The design of the EGO is as follows:

1. Each CQ has an event generator operator as its root operator. Tuples from the CQ are inserted into the input buffer of the event generator operator. An event generator operator consumes these tuples *only if* events are defined on the query. This operator is not scheduled unless the operator is enabled, i.e., there is at least one event type to be generated by this CQ for a consumer.
2. The output of the CQ can also be directly used by an application, bypassing the event generator operator. This avoids any increase in tuple latency for those applications which directly want to consume the output of the CQ.
3. This operator is capable of managing masks (i.e., modifying, deleting, or adding a new mask) at run-time (i.e., when a CQ is executing). This functionality is needed as events can be added or deleted at any time.
4. This operator stores the mapping of the mask to event names. Thus, whenever any mask is evaluated to be true the corresponding event name is used to create the appropriate event object.
5. One of the major components of event generator is the mask evaluator. This is very similar to the condition evaluation in the `split` operator (discussed in Section 10.3) except for the generation of event objects as output. Multiple event streams are generated as output.

Figure 11.1 shows the event generator operator EG1 as the root operator of a continuous query, mappings maintained at EG1, and the propagation of events to the LED buffer discussed below.

11.2.5 Need for a Common Buffer for All Events

Once an event object is created from a CQ output, the event object is propagated to the LED for further processing. This propagation can be carried out in two ways: (*i*) send the event object directly to the appropriate primitive event node or (*ii*) place the event object in a common buffer used by the LED.

Currently, the LED used for this integration has a global buffer into which primitive events are inserted by the application as well as the LED (in case

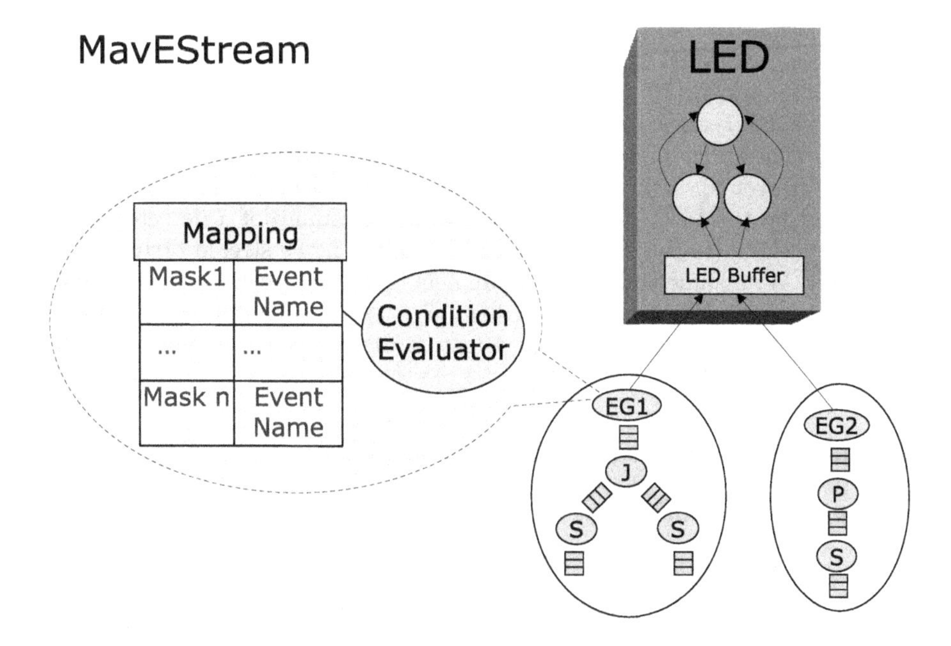

Fig. 11.1. Event Generation and Propagation

of events raised by the action part of a rule). It uses a single, global buffer for all primitive events as the order of processing of events is critical for detecting complex events. If events (even if they belong to multiple event types) are not consumed by the LED in the order of their occurrence times, they will get accumulated at the event nodes waiting for events that have occurred earlier. If a single buffer is not used, composite events detected may be out of order.

Although it is possible, in principle, to associate a different buffer (or queue) with each leaf event node, the event detection may not be correct in the presence of event consumption modes (or parameter contexts briefly discussed in Section 9.2.1), because the order of event consumption cannot be determined when multiple buffers are present. For example, in the *recent context*, if two events are consumed from the same buffer, the second one will replace the first. If there is an event in between the two that forms a composite event, then the event detection will not be correct for the recent context specified. In other words, the order in which the events are consumed have to be the same as event generation.

Although events are generated from separate CQs, correlation between them is primarily through the timestamp. In the Car ADN example (Section 9.1), if two streams are being processed from two lanes (or from two sides) of the same highway, slowing down of traffic in one direction (or lane) can be correlated with the other only if they are happening around the same time, otherwise they would correspond to independent happenings, which have no correlation. Hence, the timestamp order of event consumption is critical even in the integrated system. Thus, we do not consider the multiple buffer approach for the `MavEStream` system.

The `MavEStream` architecture has a single LED buffer as shown in Figure 11.1. The order in which the event generator operators enqueue event objects (or events) in the LED buffer will be the order in which they will be consumed by the LED. We assume that the timestamp of a detected event is closely related to the time at which the tuples in the stream arrive at the processor. We assume that QoS requirements produce the same kind of delay (or lag) in the events produced. If there is a considerable difference between the arrival time of tuples and the detection of the events, it will affect the overall accuracy of the system.

11.2.6 Complex Events and Rule Management

Complex Event Instantiation

In a standalone complex event processing system, events (primitive or complex) are created when they are defined (or registered). In the integrated system, there can be a temporal separation between the creation of a CQ and a primitive or complex event based on that CQ. Also, CQs can be registered to execute at a later time using *flexible queries* (described in Section 11.5). These features require a different approach to how event and CQ registrations are managed.

The late binding approach for event creation is taken in `MavEStream`. That is, events (primitive or complex) are created only when inputs to these events are being generated. This will prevent the creation of events and accumulation of event occurrences when other constituent events are not yet available for event detection. Consider a complex event CE1 defined in terms of primitive events PE1 and PE2. Let PE1 be associated with a continuous query CQ1 that is already registered and executing, and PE2 be associated with a flexible continuous query fCQ2 that is set to start at a future time.

If the complex event CE1 and associated primitive events PE1 and PE2 are instantiated at the time of CE1 registration, there will be events generated for PE1 (as CQ1 is generating output), but there will be no events for PE2 (as fCQ2 is not yet started). In this approach, CQ1 event occurrences that are propagated may accumulate at PE1 depending on the event expression). The complex event CE1 cannot start processing until the continuous query fCQ2 starts (for all operators except `or`). This can be determined for an arbitrary event expression as well. Not using late binding can waste system resources (such as memory, CPU cycles) and can adversely affect QoS values of other CEQs.

If the late binding approach is used and the creation of CE1 as well as PE1 and PE2 are postponed to the start of the continuous query fCQ2, the above problem is avoided. In `MavEStream`, events that are associated with continuous queries are always instantiated when the associated continuous queries are instantiated. The mapping is created and managed by the EGI when the inputs are processed. Analogously, when a continuous query is terminated, associated events are deleted if they are no longer needed.

Rule Instantiation

ECA rules associate events with conditions and actions. A rule consists of a condition and action methods as described in [88, 253, 258]. Rule processing component of LED has not been modified for the integration. MavEStream associates rules to already defined primitive or complex events.

11.3 Implementation Details of Integration

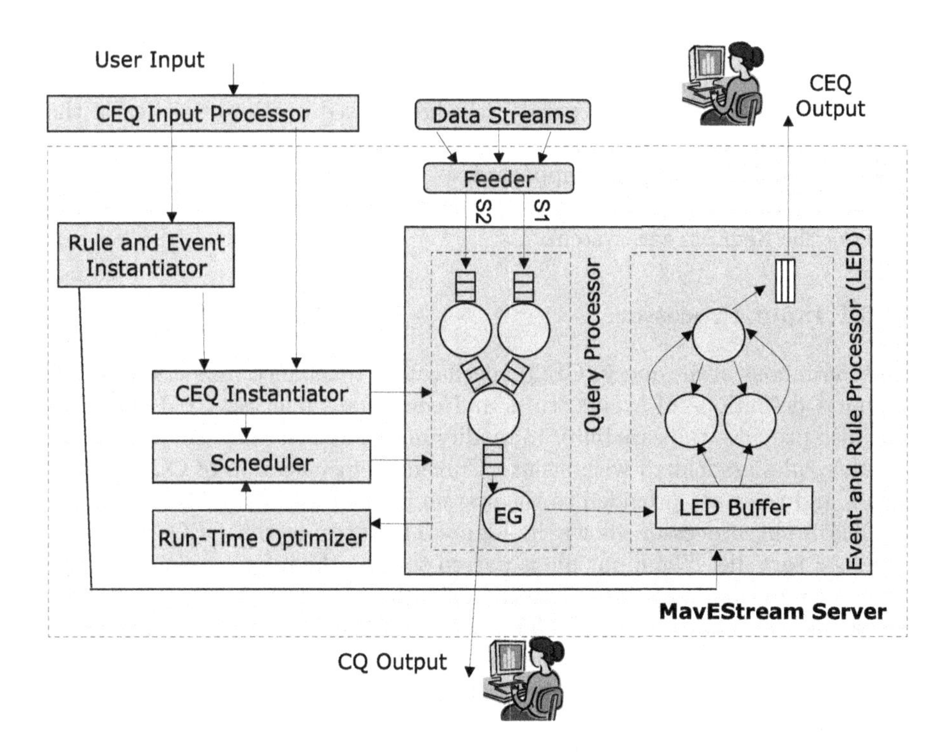

Fig. 11.2. MavEStream Architecture

MavEStream, shown in Figure 11.2, is implemented by integrating the Local Event Detector (LED) into the MavStream server. Both systems are homegrown, implemented in Java, and run in the same address space. In addition to the components shown in Figure 10.1, `MavEStream` consists of an event and rule *Instantiator*, the event generator interface, and a local event detector.

The system accepts CQs, CEQs, event definitions, rule definitions, or combinations thereof. The CQ part is processed by the CQ *Instantiator* as described in Chapter 10. The ECA part of CEQ is given to the rule and event *Instantiator* (shown as CEQ *Instantiator* in Figure 10.1 which generates the appropriate event generator operators of the event detection graph. The rule *Instantiator* then associates rules to the event nodes. Events and rules needed for instantiating flexible queries are generated when a query plan object is received by the server.

The master scheduler schedules the continuous queries including the event generator operator which is responsible for raising events which are enqueued in the LED buffer as event objects. Currently, the LED runs as a separate thread based on the presence of objects in the LED buffer; event operators are not scheduled either. The local event detector consumes event objects from the buffer and detects events using a FIFO computation model and pushes the consumed event as far up the event graph as possible. For each detected event, the conditions defined on it are evaluated and actions are scheduled for execution if the corresponding conditions evaluate to true. Rule processing is done using a separate scheduler based on the priorities of the rules. Cascaded event and rule processing are supported. Both immediate and deferred coupling modes are supported.

Below, we briefly explain the implementation of some of the new components of the `MavEStream` system.

11.3.1 Input Processor

The continuous event query (CEQ) specification (explained in Section 11.2.2) supports definitions of events, rules and continuous queries. CEQ specification also provides the capability to modify masks associated with events, and deleting rules associated with events. Currently, specification of CQs, events, masks and rules are provided to the system in the form of an ASCII file.

The input processor shown in Figure 11.3 accepts the CEQs from the user as a text file. The input file is parsed to split the information into CQs, ECA part and the mappings. The CQ definitions are used by the query plan generator to generate a query plan objet, and the ECA part is parsed and stored in the event container along with mappings to the CQs. When a query plan is instantiated (based on its start time), the ECA part is instantiated including the event generator operator.

Query plan generator

Query plan generator is responsible for generating a query plan object from the text input of CEQ specifications. Each operator definition is populated

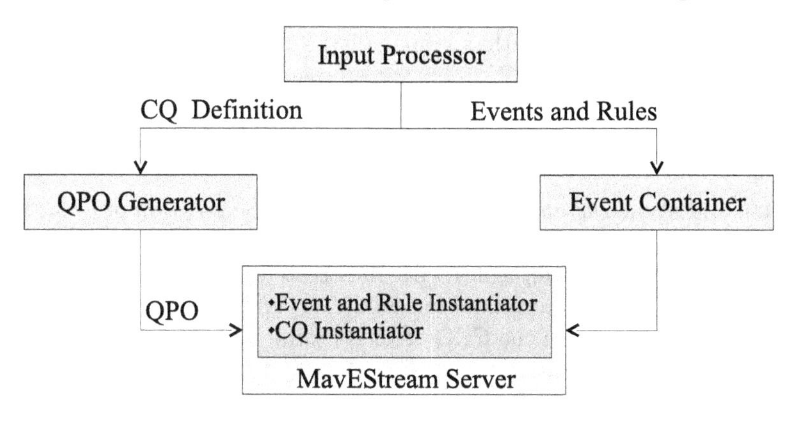

Fig. 11.3. Input Processor

in a data structure called *operatorData* which is wrapped in an *OperatorNode* that has references to the parent and child operators. The query plan is stored in the *OperatorNode* and given to the server for instantiation. *OperatorNode* encapsulates all the information about a query – for scheduling, for QoS monitoring, and output consumption.

The query plan generator is implemented as the QueryPlanGenerator class. The methods that are used to create the query plan are as follows:

1. *CreateOperatorDataInfo*: Used for creating the operator data information from the user input.
2. *CreateOperatorNodeInfo*: Used for creating the operator node by wrapping the operatorData and for associating the parent and child operators.
3. *CreateQueryPlan*: This method calls the above two methods for creating the query plan.

Event container

The event container stores the information regarding events and rules until they can be created, following the creation of the CQ. This is implemented in the `ECADefinitionContainer` data structure. This data structure consists of:

1. *CompositeEventInfo*: a Java *HashTable* that stores the information of composite events defined by the user.
2. *PrimitiveEventInfo*: a *HashTable* that stores the information of primitive events defined by the user. Optimization is done by mapping the primitive event definitions based on the query name on which the events have to be defined. This design avoids the event generator operator to be locked multiple times when more than one event is defined on a query which is already executing.

3. *Rule info*: a *HashTable* that stores all the rule definitions given by the user.

11.3.2 Event and Rule *Instantiator*

The rule and event *Instantiator* is responsible for the creation of event nodes and rule objects. The *Instantiator* invokes the APIs of the LED for creating event nodes and associating rules with the created event nodes. The *Instantiator* accesses the event container for definitions and rules to create the event nodes for the ECA part of the CEQ defined by the user. Creation of the EDG is done by creating primitive events first, followed by composite events, and finally associating rules with event nodes.

Primitive event definition contain event name, event type ("primitive"), CQ_name, and masks. Composite event definitions contain event name, event type, operator, and constituent events. Primitive and composite events, as well as rules are instantiated in the `MavEStream` server. The event detection algorithms used in the LED [87,285] are not modified. The event object contains all the parameters of an event and can be accessed by the condition and action portion of the rule. The event definition has a unique name assigned to each event. The EventType is "Composite" and the operator can be any operator supported by the LED.

A new rule is created using the following information: rule name, event name, full name of the condition method in Java, and full name of the action method in Java. Each rule is created with a unique name given by the user. In the car ADN example, the rule called `AccidentNotify` is created. The event name is used to obtain the event node to which rules are associated using the APIs. The rule has the condition and action specified by the class name and the method signature. Currently, `MavEStream` does not allow dynamic modification of rules.

11.3.3 Event Generator Interface

After a CQ is instantiated, an event generator operator is attached as the root operator. Output tuples of a CQ are inserted into the event generator operator buffer. If the event generator operator is *enabled* (it is *enabled* if there is an event node instantiated to consume the events generated by this operator), it is scheduled to consume the tuples, and evaluates them against available masks and then converts them into event objects. Attributes of the stream tuples are inserted as event attributes, an event occurrence timestamp is added and the event object is propagated to the LED buffer. This interface is implemented by extending the *Instantiator* to create the event generator operator and the server to schedule the operator, respectively.

Event Generator Operator and Masks

It is clear that the handling of the event generator operator needs to be somewhat different from handling the rest of the continuous query operators. As the events are associated with the CQs, the event generator operator has to generate event objects with appropriate event names for further processing. Also, masks need to be added and deleted dynamically unlike other continuous operators. The mapping between the CQs, masks, and event names need to be managed by the event generator operator as shown in Figure 11.1.

Adding Events and Masks

It should be noted that in the `MavEStream` system, a named primitive or complex event is instantiated only once. This is because event nodes can be shared by other events by exploiting named common event subexpressions.

There may be various reasons for the addition of events, masks, and rules. If a new event is created on an existing CQ using a new mask, the mask and the mapping need to be added to the event generator interface. If new conditions and actions are to be added for an existing event, they are added dynamically. When a CQ is terminated, it will have a bearing on many events that are using the events generated by this CQ. Analogously, when an event is deleted, it has to be propagated to the event interface to adjust the mask and mapping appropriately.

Mapping between a mask and an associated event (or eventHandle) is stored as a key value pair in the HashTable *MaskAndEventHandle*. This table is accessed to obtain the reference of the event nodes for a mask. When an event is defined without a mask, the eventHandle associated with the event is added to the *MaskAndEventHandle* HashTable with `true` as the mask. The mapping allows the user to modify or add masks while the event generator operator is being executed, by giving the event name and a new mask. When such a request is made by the user, the event generator operator will access the mask for the corresponding event name and update the HashTable appropriately.

Algorithm 10 outlines the implementation of the event generator operator. The condition evaluator evaluates the masks on each incoming tuple and drops the tuple if the mask evaluates to `false`. If a mask condition evaluation is successful then the corresponding event associated with the mask is raised. Since the tuples here are assumed to be ordered by timestamp or a sequence number, we check if the ordering attribute of the tuples is greater than the end query, and if it evaluates to true, the operator is stopped from being scheduled. Evaluating masks before event generation significantly reduces the number of events generated. The more the selectivity of the mask, the greater the number of events filtered. The effectiveness of masks has been validated experimentally as well. Please refer to [140, 284] for additional information.

Several classes have been extended and new classes created for the implementation of EGI. Some of the major classes and their methods are:

Algorithm 10: Event Generator Operator

```
1  if enabled then
2  if mask is to be added or modified then
3  use Semaphore to add/delete mask
4  Lock the operator; perform update; unlock
5  if no tuples in input buffer then
6  Suspend operator and Notify scheduler
7  else
8      if tuple timestamp > endQuery then
9      stop operator
10     else
11         foreach mask do
12             evaluate the mask condition
13             if mask is true then
14             Raise the corresponding event
15         end
16     end
17 end
```

1. **EventGenerator:** This class is used for accessing *MaskAndEventHandle* hash table and storing masks and event handles. Following are the methods supported by this class.
   a) *addMaskAndEventHandle*: This method is responsible for populating the HashTable. This method accepts the mask and the eventHandle that is associated with the mask as inputs.
   b) *runOperator*: This method implements the abstract method for super class Operator. This method is executed by the scheduler whenever the event generator operator is scheduled. In this method masks are checked, event objects are created, and corresponding events are raised. As explained in Section 11.2.4, FESI condition evaluator has been used for evaluating mask conditions.
2. **EventOperatorLock:** This class is responsible for locking the event generator operator. It is essential to lock the event generator in case masks have to be modified or new events have to be added if the operator is running.
   a) *getLockToAddMask:* This synchronized method sets the semaphores in the EventGenerator.
   b) *releaseLock:* This method releases the lock of the EventGenerator.
3. **GenerateEvent:** This class makes API calls to the LED for creating events. Once generated events have an eventHandle with which they can be referenced.
   a) *generatePrimitiveEvent:* This method generates a primitive event and returns the event handle associated with the event.

b) *generateCompositeEvent:* This method generates a composite event and returns an event handle. It accepts the event name, constituent event names and an event operator as inputs.

11.4 Stream Modifiers

Below, we discuss the implementation of stream modifiers introduced in Section 9.5. Stream modifiers are stream operators and are defined as part of a CQ. These modifiers are typically used in conjunction with `GROUP BY` and `GFilter` (for simulating simple `HAVING` clause as discussed in Section 10.3.2) and are usually the top operators of a CQ plan.

To recall, `stream modifiers` were introduced in order to capture changes of interest in a data stream and applying conditions on them. For example, as shown in Section 9.5.2, the CQ for Speed reduction in the example 9.1 which uses the wRDiff stream modifier is repeated below:

```
CREATE CQ DECREASE AS
    SELECT   wRDiff(<speed> as C_speed, p<0.01>, N<car_id>)
      FROM   CarLocStr [Range 2 minutes]
  GROUP BY   carID
    HAVING   C_SPEED >= 0.3
```

For each window of 2 minutes which is already grouped by carID, the wRDiff calculates the relative difference in speed between the first and the last tuple of each partition and checks whether it has changed by more than 30%. The output of this operator can be consumed by the event generator operator to generate events (for different lanes for example) using masks. The output of this node can also be used by another stream modifier, TSupressor (discussed in Section 8.4.1) for example, to limit the same events being generated within a specified time period. For example, if these events are being generated for more than `t` minutes, then you can infer the occurrence of the event `Speed Reduction` to avoid false generation of events or handling of large number of events of the same type with in a short period of time.

Events are generated from a CQ (by the event generator operator as explained in Section 11.2.4) with or without using stream modifiers. The definition and explanation of stream modifiers (both tuple- and window-based) were presented in Section 9.5.2. Implementation of both tuple- as well as window-based modifiers is explained below.

11.4.1 Tuple-Based Stream Modifiers

A tuple-based stream modifier is useful to calculate changes (or any other function) to consecutive tuples in a partition/window without having to change the window definition of the entire query. These modifiers produce specified change between two consecutive tuples. These modifiers can be placed anywhere in a CQ. Synopsis consists of single tuple which is updated whenever an output is produced. Algorithm 11 outlines the implementation of tuple-based stream modifiers.

Algorithm 11: Tuple-based Stream Modifier

```
1  prev_tuple is set to null
2  while current tuple timestamp ≤ endQuery do
3      if current tuple is the first tuple of the partition/window then
4          prev_tuple is set to current tuple
5      else
6          compute change between prev_tuple and current tuple
7          using the appropriate modifier (provided prev_tuple is not null)
8          output the new tuple
9          prev_tuple is set to current tuple
10     end
11     stop operator
12 end
```

11.4.2 Window-Based Stream Modifiers

Window-based stream modifiers compute the changes between the first tuple and the last tuple of a partition/window. A window-based stream modifier can be placed anywhere in the continuous query. One tuple is output for each partition/window. Algorithm 12 outlines the implementation of window-based stream modifiers. The current tuple timestamp is compared with the end time of the query and the operator continues if the former is less than or equal to the latter. The first tuple for each partition/window is stored in *first-tuple* and the *last-tuple* is replaced by every other tuple. When the tuple in the next partition/window arrives, the change is computed using the *first-tuple* and the *last-tuple*. In order to handle overlapping windows, tuples of the overlapping window needs to be stored in the synopsis until the start of the next window and the same algorithm is applied to the next window.

11.4.3 Implementation

Stream modifiers are implemented as stream operators. All the operators extend from the abstract class *Operator*. In addition to implementing these operators as classes, they need to be integrated into the query plan. This entails extensions to the *Instantiator* for instantiating these operators as part of a CQ as well as the data structure that stores the parameters of the operator used for creating the query plan. Furthermore, these operators need

Algorithm 12: Window-Based Stream Modifier

```
1  first-tuple and last_tuple are set to null
2  while current tuple timestamp ≤ endQuery do
3      if current tuple is the first tuple of partition/window then
4      compute change for current partition/window using the first_tuple and
       the last_tuple (provided both are non-null)
5      output new tuple
6      update first_tuple with current tuple
7      else
8          replace the last_tuple with the current tuple
9          if current tuple timestamp ≥ next begin window time then
10         store the tuple in synopsis (for next overlapping window)
11     end
12 end
13 stop operator
```

to be taken into account while computing an operator paths or its segments. The processing and memory release capacity of these operators needs to be computed as well. Load shedders are also installed into the queues associated with these operators. Extensions done to the data structure and *Instantiator* are summarized below.

Instantiator *extensions*

The *Instantiator* has been extended for implementing these operators. Additional methods have been developed to instantiate each operator. These methods create an object of the operator and populate the operator object with the parameters given by the user. The methods are: *instantiateDiff, instantiatewDiff, instantiateRdiff, instantiatewRdiff, instantiateSlope, and instantiatewSlope.*

Operator Data extensions

The *OperatorData* data structure is extended with the following constructs to store the user input before the operators are instantiated:

1. *GroupByAttributes*: This is a vector of the attributes on which `Group By` operator is to be applied.
2. *GFilterAttributes*: This stores the attributes as a vector on which GFilter evaluates the condition.
3. *ModifierAttributes*: This stores attributes of the stream modifier in a vector.
4. *ModifierProfile*: This stores the stream modifier profile as an integer to determine whether the subtuple should contain the old or the new state.

11.5 Additional Benefits of CEP Integration

The presence of an event processing component that supports temporal and composite events along with actions in the form of rules can be leveraged for supporting other features elegantly. For example, in `MavEStream`, we are able to instantiate, start, and stop continuous queries using the event mechanism.

Continuous queries can be specified to `MavEStream` to be started at a later time or even specified to be executed periodically. It is also possible to start the execution of a registered CQ when a specified event occurs. For example, in the linear road benchmark scenario (Example 9.1 in Section 9.1), it is *possible* to start a number of predefined continuous queries automatically only when an accident is detected in order to monitor specific roads and road segments that are not usually monitored. The goal of monitoring may change to assessing the extent of slowing down to provide a better indication for routing traffic. We term these `flexible queries.`

Flexible queries are readily implemented using the event operators supported by the CEP component. Currently, CQs that need to start at a later time (than registered) are implemented by creating temporal events for the start and end time of the query. A user query is checked before it is instantiated to determine whether it is defined as a flexible query. If it is a flexible query, then the instantiation is delayed until the temporal event for start time of the query is raised.

The temporal event operators (absolute and relative temporal events) supported by the LED are used for starting the instantiation and execution of a CQ. When a flexible CQ definition is received by the `MavEStream` server, temporal events are created using the LED. Temporal events are created with the start and end times of the flexible query and the query is stored in the `MavEStream` server. At the start time, an event is generated which notifies the `MavEStream` server that the flexible query should start. The query is then instantiated and started.

When the end query event is raised, the query needs to be stopped and the server has to delete the nodes and other data structures used by the query. In continuous query processing, tuples that are buffered at the intermediate queues of operators need to be processed before terminating the query. To address this, when a query stop time is reached, an *endQuery* tuple is input to all leaf operators of a that query. This tuple is recognized by each operator and when it reaches the root operator, all the tuples that arrived prior to the end time of the query would have been processed. In case of subquery sharing, a count is kept at each operator and the count is used to determine whether to propagate the *endQuery* tuple. When the root operator receives the *endQuery* tuple, it notifies the server to delete the information stored for the query. For removing the objects of the query from the scheduler, the scheduler thread is locked before removing the operators. The class below sketches the implementation of such a query.

1. **FlexibleQueryGenerateEvent:** This class calls the API of the LED for generating the event for the flexible query.
   - *SetStartEvent:* this method accepts a time (including an optional date) at which the query is to be scheduled along with the unique query identifier. It sets the temporal event for the start of the query. The action part of the rule defined for the event calls the method for instantiating and scheduling the query at the query start time.
   - *SetEndEvent:* this method accepts a time (including an optional date) at which the query is stopped and the query name as query identifier. It sets the temporal event for stopping the query. The action part of the rule defined for the event calls the method for stopping the query and deleting query constructs.

11.6 Summary of Chapter 11

In this chapter, we discussed the design and implementation of an integrated system to synergistically support complex event and stream processing. We discussed the implementation of the event generator interface as well as stream modifiers introduced earlier. Finally, additional benefits of CEP integration to support flexible queries were discussed.

The computation model of LED does not match the CQ model in many respects. Event processing need to be enhanced to include buffers or queues between operators. Scheduling needs to be extended to include event operators, and QoS delivery mechanisms need to be incorporated on the event processing side. These extensions are being investigated both from a theoretical and system viewpoints.

12

CONCLUSIONS AND FUTURE DIRECTIONS

What is an effective architecture for situation monitoring applications? How do we progress towards a flexible, composable architecture for analyzing large volumes of data? These questions certainly need to be answered as we move towards pervasive devices and just-in-time monitoring requirements. The amount of data that will be generated, and hence need to be processed is only going to increase dramatically as the technology improves. Application requirements will grow to include distributed data handling, handling of errors, privacy issues, security as well as collaboration/cooperation among applications. Filtering, fusion, aggregation, and correlation (to name a few) will become preferred mechanisms for dealing with vast amounts of disparate raw data to extract nuggets meaningful and useful knowledge.

12.1 Looking Ahead

As an answer to the above questions, the general architecture of situation monitoring applications is depicted in Figure 12.1. Ability to convert very large amounts of raw data into actionable knowledge and in real-time (or near real-time) will form the cornerstones of these architectures. Figure 12.1 shows the components at the subsystem level. The inverted triangle is symbolic of the data reduction/aggregation/fusion/correlation process through a multi-stage process using which nuggets of actionable knowledge are extracted.

There may be several layers of data reduction and correlation. The initial reduction of raw data is likely to come from a computation-intensive process (whether it is stream processing, fusion, mining, or some other mechanism is not so critical) which gives rise to a number of high-level, domain/application-specific "interesting events". The results from this stage can be used directly or stored for later analysis. These "interesting events" are further composed as dictated by the application semantics to detect higher-level "situations". This process of generation of "interesting events" and correlation may be repeated several times until the desired level of abstraction is reached.

S. Chakravarthy and Q. Jiang, *Stream Data Processing: A Quality of Service Perspective*,
Advances in Database Systems 36, DOI: 10.1007/978-0-387-71003-7_12,

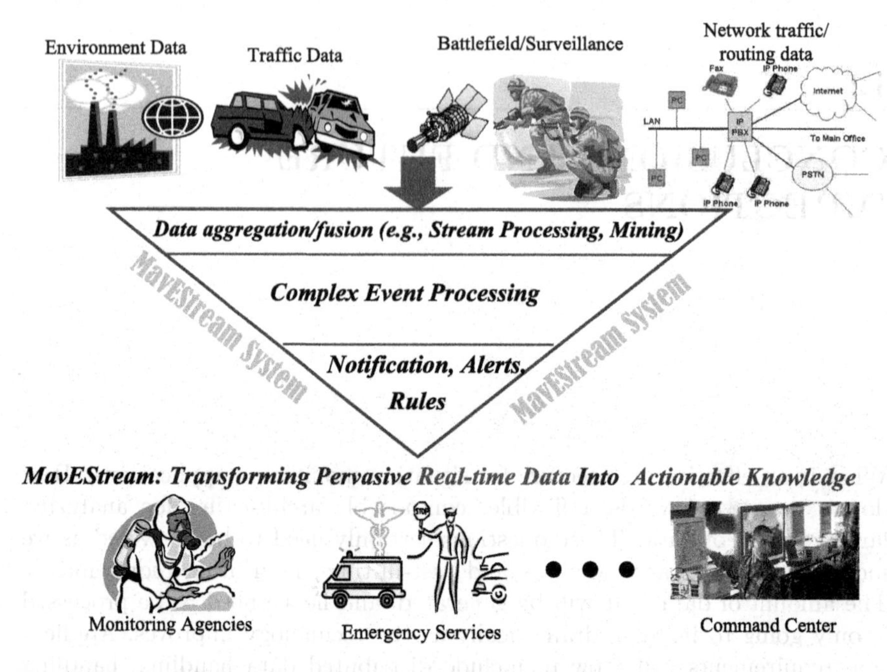

Fig. 12.1. General Architecture of Situation Monitoring Applications

It is important to understand that stream processing is only one approach for converting large amounts of raw data into "interesting events" or results that are useful in their own right. This layer can change/evolve, in a number of ways including newer techniques, over time. The complex event processing layer is also likely to undergo changes (as we have already witnessed over the course of 20+ years). Together, the components indicated Figure 12.1, will provide the functionality needed for situation monitoring applications for a long time.

In the rest of this chapter, we provide future research directions for the topics covered in this book.

12.2 Stream Processing

The functionality of a DSMS can be further improved by addressing the following:

1. Generation of alternative query plans and their optimization with respect to QoS requirements.
2. Dynamically adding a continuous query (i.e., at run-time) in a multiple continuous query processing environment with sharing of subexpressions.

3. Distribution of queries to multiple available DSMS processors for load balancing purposes. This could include minimizing the number of distinct streams used by each processor.

12.2.1 Continuous Query Modeling

Continuous query modeling discussed in this book provides a formal mechanism for estimating QoS requirements and also for verifying given QoS requirements. Our approach provides a closed-form solution to estimate various QoS parameters using queueing theory. The queueing model approach can be used as a formal basis for developing system capacity planning and QoS verification tools. Various "what-if" scenarios can be explored to understand the resource requirements as well as the impact of resources on the QoS metrics.

In addition, the estimation of QoS parameters provide sufficient quantitative information for use at run-time. Based on the input rates measured at run-time and the QoS prediction of the model, it is possible for DSMSs to dynamically choose suitable QoS deliver mechanisms. For example, switching from a memory-favorable scheduling strategy to a tuple-latency favorable scheduling strategy, dynamically activating and deactivating load shedding, and admission control (if all else fails) can be beneficially applied. Additionally, the estimated QoS parameters provide an effective way to verify whether defined QoS requirements of a continuous query can indeed be satisfied.

There are several additional problems that can be explored:

1. Although we have demonstrated the modeling of a few widely-used operators, this approach can be applied to other operators and query plans with those operators. The approach remains the same with specifics (e.g., service time computation) changing based on the operator semantics.
2. Our analysis is based on Poisson arrival rates for input data streams. Although the results of our analysis, based on this class of input streams, are useful for most applications, it would be meaningful to extend this analysis self-similar data streams with Long-Range Dependence (LRD) process [353], and others as well. It would also be interesting to study how bursty behavior of input data streams impacts the performance of different query plans of a query and the overall performance of a DSMS.
3. In our study, we have used a one-server queueing model. However, in a multi-processor (or multi-core) architecture, several servers are available for processing. This analysis can be extended to a multi-server queueing model as well.

12.2.2 Scheduling

The family of scheduling strategies proposed in the literature satisfies the requirements of many stream-based applications. The PC strategy is useful for applications that consider tuple latency as the most critical requirement.

The MOS strategy is useful for applications that favor minimization of the total memory requirement. The segment strategy and the simplified segment strategy provide trades-offs between tuple latency and total memory requirement for those applications that are sensitive to both. The threshold strategy – a dynamic hybrid of the PC and the MOS strategy – is pragmatic as it inherits the advantages of both strategies. The strategies discussed and their characteristics cover a wide spectrum of requirements and together with other strategies such as chain provide a rich set of strategies for a DSMS to work with.

Further work on scheduling can address the following:

1. Mostly, event-driven, preemptive scheduling models have been developed and analyzed in the literature. It would be useful to develop alternative scheduling models such as non-preemptive ones and analyze their applicability to a DSMS.
2. Further study is needed to determine the (optimal) size of a batch – either in terms of CPU time or the number of tuples – during a schedule as it is important and necessary to decrease the scheduling overhead and to be adaptive to application characteristics.
3. Operator internal scheduling has not been studied in the literature for two or multi-way operators. As we have shown in Section 6.1.1, different operator-internal-scheduling strategies have different impact on the total memory requirement of a DSMS. Appropriate operator-internal-scheduling strategies can further decrease the total memory requirement of a DSMS.

12.2.3 Load Shedding

In a continuous query processing system, load shedding provides a mechanism for freeing up resources to reduce QoS violations, to the extent possible. The formula we have developed for estimating system load is in closed-form and hence can be calculated efficiently based on current input rates and characteristics of continuous queries. The system load estimation component is not dependent on the load shedding component or other components in our QoS framework, and can be integrated into other load shedding mechanisms. Our algorithms for load shedding and load distribution are applicable to any DSMS. The combination of load estimation and run-time QoS monitoring and optimization, together, provides a robust approach for satisfying application requirements.

Additional problems to be addressed in load shedding are:

1. Reducing the high-overhead of load shedding (at the tuple level): each shedder, whether random or semantic, introduces a minimal cost (that of a `test` operator to check whether load shedding is activated or not). In a DSMS with hundreds of continuous queries, the number of load shedders

can be quite large. As a result, the total cost of shedders can be high. The load shedding mechanisms based on dropping tuples using shedders have their limitations in practical DSMSs. It is necessary and important to exploit other load shedding mechanisms as well.

2. `Approximate` algorithms: as an alternative to load shedding, it may be useful to develop `approximate` algorithms for expensive operators such as two or multiple-way join operators. There has been some initial work in the literature on this [75, 115, 180, 354, 355]; however, further research on this problem is required to make it practically useful.
3. `Anytime` (contract) algorithms [160–162]: `anytime` algorithms are extensively studied in real-time systems and artificial intelligence systems. An `anytime` algorithm is an algorithm that can be interrupted at any time and will still produce results of a certain quality which is a function of allocated computation time. Therefore, `anytime` algorithms are ideal choices in lieu of load shedding in DSMSs if each operator (at least each expensive operator) can be implemented as an `anytime` algorithm. Once the system is deemed short of resources, it can limit the computation time allocated for each operator implemented using an `anytime` algorithm.The algorithm can determine the optimal results based on allocated computation time. Implementation of operators using an efficient `anytime` algorithm needs further attention.
4. Admission control: instead of dropping tuples, it may be possible and may even be more effective to temporarily suspend some continuous queries (based on the continuous query mix and QoS requirements) in the system to obtain the effect of shedding load. Admission control may be used for load balancing as well by dynamically adding resources for processing new continuous queries submitted to the system.

12.3 Integration of Stream and Event Processing

Our analysis of complex, real-life network fault management application vividly brought out the need for the integration of data stream processing with complex event (and rule) processing. Based on the analysis, we proposed a three-phase processing model, which was translated into a architecture with four distinct stages. This architecture was used for the integration of two existing systems (`MavStream` and LED) for developing an integrated system. We also presented stream modifiers, reduction of events generated by early processing of masks, and a versatile way to build monitoring applications by composing stream and event processing stages arbitrarily. On the event side, event generalization is seen as one of the important extensions needed for making the system versatile.

A list of open problems and future work in event and rule processing include:

1. Extending the event processing model: use of queues for event processing along with the modeling of operators and estimation of various QoS metrics.
2. Scheduling algorithms for complex event processing and their analysis for latency and memory requirements. Relationship between scheduling and the event consumption modes need to be explored as well.
3. Load shedding mechanisms for event processing: here, the relationship between accuracy and latency is not straightforward as the semantics of event operators is mainly dependent on the time of occurrence of events (or timestamp). A linear relationship between drop percentage and error introduced in the result may not be appropriate in this case.
4. Currently, the concept of a `window` is not used for complex event processing. Events are detected incrementally and there is no notion of `blocking` although the distance between an initiator (an event that starts the detection of a complex event) and a terminator event (an event that concludes the detection of a complex event) for some operators (e.g., **`sequence`**, **`not`** from Snoop [86, 87]) can be arbitrarily large. Instead, the notion of event consumption modes (or parameter contexts) have been proposed and used. There is a need to understand the relationship between the `window` concept of a continuous query and the consumption modes of event processing to reconcile the two to establish a uniform computation model.
5. Most of the earlier work on complex event processing has not addressed QoS requirements. Benchmarks (except for Beast [247,248]) have not been developed to measure the performance of complex event and rule processing systems. Benchmarks for stream processing (in addition to the linear road benchmark) are also needed.
6. Although a large number of operators have been developed and supported for stream processing, completeness of operators has not been investigated. New operators are added by each system based on the needs of the domain for which it is targeted. The notion of a host language into which both stream and complex event processing expressions can be embedded may be a solution to achieve Turing completeness. The proposal of StreamSQL as a language is perhaps a step in that direction.

The other issue that has not been convincingly deliberated in the literature is the differences between event and stream operators – from the semantics as well as computation aspects. Their interchangeability has not been established. Considerable work exists for the execution semantics (in terms of termination, observable determinism, and confluence) of events and triggers [191, 192, 195]. No such analysis exists for stream processing especially when it is combined with event processing as well. The approach we have taken in this book is to keep the distinction between the two as they serve different roles and purposes in expressing application semantics, and provide mechanisms to combine them in arbitrary ways. This approach also supports modularity and facilitates sharing of subexpressions for both stream and event processing.

12.4 Epilogue

The purpose of this book has been to take motivated readers through the journey of identifying, formulating, and developing solutions to a new problem. This journey involves the following exciting steps: (*i*) gather application requirements, (*ii*) identify problems, (*iii*) develop theories, their analysis, and algorithms for solving the identified problems, and (*iv*) develop architecture, design, and implement a system or a prototype to demonstrate the feasibility of solutions developed.

References

1. C. J. Date: An Introduction to Database Systems, Volume 1, Sixth Edition. Addison Wesley, Reading (1995)
2. C. J. Date: An Introduction to Database Systems, Volume 2, Sixth Edition. Addison-Wesley, Reading (1995)
3. Abraham Silberschatz and Henry F. Korth and S. Sudarshan: Database System Concepts, 3rd Edition. McGraw-Hill Book Company (1997)
4. M. Stonebraker, ed.: Readings in Database Systems. Morgan Kaufman Inc. (1988)
5. J. D. Ullman: Principles of Database and Knowledge-Base Systems, Vol. I. Computer Science Press International, Inc., MD 20850 (1988)
6. J. D. Ullman: Principles of Database and Knowledge-Base Systems, Vol. II. Computer Science Press International, Inc., MD 20850 (1989)
7. M. T. Ozsu and P. Valduriez: Principles of Distributed Database Systems. Prentice Hall, Englewood Cliffs, New Jersey (1991)
8. Ahmed K. Elmagarmid: Database Transaction Models for Advanced Applications. Morgan Kaufmann Publishers Inc. (1992)
9. Ramez Elmasri and Shamkant B. Navathe: Fundamentals of Database Systems, 2nd Edition. Benjamin/Cummings (1994)
10. Ramakrishnan, R.: Database Management Systems. WCB/McGraw-Hill (1998)
11. Stonebraker, M., Çetintemel, U., Zdonik, S.B.: The 8 requirements of real-time stream processing. SIGMOD Record **34**(4) (2005) 42–47
12. Garcia-Molina, H., Salem, K.: Main Memory Database Systems: An Overview. IEEE Transactions on Knowledge and Data Engineering **4**(6) (1992) 509–516
13. TimesTen: Oracle TimesTen Homepage (2005) `http://www.oracle.com/timesten/index.html`.
14. Baulier, J., Bohannon, P., Gogate, S., Gupta, C., Haldar, S., Joshi, S., Khivesera, A., Seshadri, S., Silberschatz, A., Sudarshan, S., Wilder, M., Wei, C.: DataBlitz Storage Manager: Main Memory Database Performance for Critical Applications. In: In ACM SIGMOD - Industrial Session: Database Storage Management. (1999) 519–520
15. Teanovic, A., Nystrm, D., Hansson, J., Norstrm, C.: Embedded Databases for Embedded Real-Time Systems: A Component-Based Approach. Technical

report, Linkoping University (2002) http://www.mrtc.mdh.se/publications/0366.pdf.
16. Boncz, P., Grust, T., Keulen, M., Manegold, S., Rittinger, J., Teubner, J.: MonetDB/XQuery: a fast XQuery processor powered by a relational engine. In: Proceedings of the ACM SIGMOD International Conference on Management of Data. (2006) 479–490
17. Altibase: Altibase Home Page (2004) http://www.altibase.com/english/.
18. SolidDB: IBM SolidDB Home Page (2007) http://www.ibm.com/software/data/soliddb/.
19. BerkeleyDB: Bekeley DB and Oracle Embedded Databases (1996) http://www.oracle.com/database/berkeley-db/index.html.
20. Olson, M.A., Bostic, K., Seltzer, M.I.: Berkeley db. In: USENIX Annual Technical Conference, FREENIX Track. (1999) 183–191
21. Empress Embedded Database: Empress Software Inc. (2004) http://www.empress.com/.
22. eXtremeDB: McObject Precision Data Management, eXtremDB home page (2008) http://www.mcobject.com/.
23. SIAD/SQL6: Trace Mode, Industrial Real-Time DBMS SIAD/SQL 6 (1988) http://www.tracemode.com/products/overview/database/.
24. Abbott, R., Garcia-Molina, H.: Scheduling Real-time Transactions: A Performance Evaluation. In: Proceedings of the Fourteenth International Conference on Very Large Data Bases. (1988) 1–12
25. Abbott, R., Garcia-Molina, H.: Scheduling Real-time Transactions. SIGMOD RECORD **17**(1) (1988) 71–81
26. S. H. Son, ed.: Sigmod Record: Special Issue on Real-Time Database Systems. Volume 17:(1). SIGMOD (1988)
27. Abbott, R., Garcia-Molina, H.: Scheduling Real-time Transactions with Disk Resident Data. In: Proceedings of the Fifteenth International Conference on Very Large Data Bases. (1989) 385–396
28. Buchmann, A., McCarthy, D., Hsu, M.: Time-Critical Database Scheduling: A Framework for Integrating Real-time Scheduling and Concurrency Control. In: Proceedings of the Fifth International Conference on Data Engineering. (1989) 470–480
29. Abbott, R., Garcia-Molina, H.: Scheduling I/O Requests with Deadlines: A Performance Evaluation. In: Proceedings of the Eleventh Real-Time Systems Symposium. (1990) 113–124
30. Carey, M.J., Jauhari, R., Livny, M.: On Transaction Boundaries in Active Databases: A Performance Perspective. IEEE Transactions on Knowledge and Data Engineering **7**(1) (1991) 78–84
31. Chakravarthy, S., Blaustein, B., Buchmann, A., Carey, M., Dayal, U., Goldhirsch, D., Hsu, M., Jauhari, R., Ladin, R., Livny, M., McCarthy, D., McKee, R., Rosenthal, A.: HiPAC: A Research Project in Active, Time-Constrained Database Management. Technical report, Xerox Advanced Information Technology, Cambridge (1989)
32. Chen, S., Stankovic, J., Kurose, J., Towsley, D.: Performance Evaluation of Two New Disk Scheduling Algorithms for Real-time Systems. Journal of Real-Time Systems **3**(3) (1991) 307–336
33. Dayal, U., Blaustein, B.T., Buchmann, A.P., Chakravarthy, U.S., Hsu, M., Ledin, R., McCarthy, D.R., Rosenthal, A., Sarin, S.K., Carey, M.J., Livny, M.,

Jauhari, R.: The HiPAC Project: Combining Active Databases and Timing Constraints. SIGMOD Record **17**(1) (1988) 51–70
34. Abbott, R., Garcia-Molina, H.: Scheduling Real-Time Transaction: Performance Evaluation. ACM Transactions on Database Systems **17**(3) (1992) 513–560
35. DeWitt, D.J., Katz, R.H., Olken, F., Shapiro, L.D., Stonebraker, M.R., Wood, D.: Implementation Techniques for Main Memory Database Systems. In: Proceedings of the ACM SIGMOD International Conference on Management of Data. (1984) 1–8
36. Franaszek, P., Robinson, J., Thomasian, A.: Concurrency Control for High Contention Environments. ACM Transactions on Database Systems **10**(1) (1992) 304–345
37. Graham, M.H.: Issues in Real-time Data Management. Journal of Real-Time Systems **4**(3) (1992) 185–202
38. Gray, J., Good, B., Gawlick, D., Homan, P., Sammer, H.: One Thousand Transactions per Second. In: Proceedings of the Thirtieth IEEE Computer Society International Conference. (1985) 96–101
39. Haritsa, J.R., Carey, M.J., Livny, M.: On Being Optimistic about Real-time Constraints. In: Proceedings of the ninth ACM SIGACT-SIGMOD-SIGART symposium on Principles of database systems. (1990) 331–343
40. Haritsa, J.R., Carey, M.J., Livny, M.: Dynamic Real-Time Optimistic Concurrency Control. In: Proceedings of Eleventh Real-Time System Symposium. (1990) 94–103
41. Haritsa, J.R., Livny, M., Carey, M.J.: Earliest Deadline Scheduling for Real-Time Database Systems. In: Proceedings of Twelfth Real-Time System Symposium. (1991) 232–242
42. Haritsa, J.R.: Transaction Scheduling in Firm Real-time Database Systems. PhD thesis, University of Wisconsin-Madison (1991)
43. Hong, D., Johnson, T., Chakravarthy, S.: Real-Time Transaction Scheduling: A Cost Conscious Approach. In: Proceedings, International Conference on Management of Data (SIGMOD). (1993) 197–206
44. Hong, D.: Real-Time Transaction Scheduling: Synthesizing Static and Dynamic Factors. PhD thesis, The University of Florida at Gainesville (1995) `http://itlab.uta.edu/sharma/People/ThesisWeb/hong_phd_thesis.pdf`.
45. Hong, D., Chakravarthy, S., Johnson, T.: Locking Based Concurrency Control for Integrated Real-Time Database Systems. In: Proceedings, International Workshop on Real-Time Databases (RTDB). (1996) 138–143
46. Chakravarthy, S., Hong, D.K., Johnson, T.: Real-Time Transaction Scheduling: A Framework for Synthesizing Static and Dynamic Factors. Real-Time Systems Journal **14**(2) (1998) 135–170
47. Hong, D.K., Chakravarthy, S., Johnson, T.: Incorporating Load Factor into the scheduling of Soft real-time transactions for main memory databases. Information Systems **25**(3) (2000) 309–322
48. Huang, J., Stankovic, J.A., Towsley, D., Ramamritham, K.: Experimental Evaluation of Real-Time Transaction Processing. In: Proceedings of Tenth Real-Time Systems Symposium. (1989) 144–153
49. Huang, J., Stankovic, J.A., Ramamritham, K., Towsley, D.: Experimental Evaluation of Real-time Optimistic Concurrency Control schemes. In: Proceedings of the Seventeenth International Conference on Very Large Data Bases. (1991) 35–46

50. Johnson, T., Shasha, D.: The performance of concurrent B-tree Algorithm. ACM Transactions on Computer Systems **18**(1) (1993) 51–101
51. Kim, W., Srivastava, J.: Enhancing Real-Time DBMS Performance with Multiversion Data and Priority Based Disk scheduling. In: Proceedings of Twelfth Real-Time Systems Symposium. (1991) 222–231
52. Lee, J., Son, S.H.: Using dynamic adjustment of serialization order for real-time database systems. In: Proceedings of Fourteenth Real-Time Systems Symposium. (1993) 66–75
53. Lin, Y., Son, S.H.: Concurrency Control in Real-time Databases by Dynamic Adjustment of Serialization Order. In: Proceedings of Tenth Real-Time Systems Symposium. (1990) 104–112
54. Sivasankaran, R., B.Purimetla, Stankovic, J., Ramamritham, K.: Network services database - a Distributed Active Real-Time Database (DARTDB) application. In: Proceedings of First IEEE Workshop on Real-Time Applications. (1993) 184–187
55. Purimetla, B., Sivasankaran, R., Ramamritham, K., Stankovic, J.: Real-Time Databases: Issues and Applications. In: Advances in Real-Time Systems, Prentice-Hall (1995) 487–507
56. Sha, L.: Concurrency control for distributed real-time databases. SIGMOD RECORD **17**(1) (1988) 82–98
57. Ramamrithm, K.: Real-Time Databases. International Journal of Distributed and Parallel Databases **1**(2) (1993) 1–30
58. Stankovic, J.A., Zhao, W.: On real-time transactions. SIGMOD RECORD **17**(1) (1988) 4–18
59. Singhal, M.: Issues and approaches to design of real-time database systems. SIGMOD RECORD **17**(1) (1988)
60. Hansson, J., Berndtsson, M.: Active real-time database systems. In: Active Rules in Database Systems. Springer (1999) 405–426
61. A. Buchmann and M. T. Ozsu and M. Hornick and D. Georgakopoulos and F. Manola: A Transaction Model for Active Distributed Object Systems. Morgan Kaufmann Publishers Inc. (1992)
62. MavHome: MavHome Project Home Page, University of Texas at Arlington (2001) `http://cygnus.uta.edu/mavhome/`.
63. Carney, D., Çetintemel, U., Cherniack, M., Convey, C., Lee, S., Seidman, G., Stonebraker, M., Tatbul, N., Zdonik, S.B.: Monitoring Streams - A New Class of Data Management Applications. In: Proceedings of the International Conference on Very Large Data Bases. (2002) 215–226
64. Cook, D.J., Youngblood, M., Heierman, E., Gopalratnam, K., Rao, S., Litvin, A., Khawaja, F.: Mavhome: An agent-based smart home. In: Proceedings of the First IEEE International Conference on Pervasive Computing and Communications. (2003) 521–524
65. iPolicy Networks: iPolicy Networks Homepage (2006) `http://www.ipolicynetworks.com`.
66. ebay: ebay Inc. (1995) `http://www.ebay.com`.
67. Yahoo: Yahoo Inc. (1995) `http://www.yahoo.com`.
68. Google: Google Inc. (1998) `http://www.google.com`.
69. Leland, W.E., Taqq, M.S., Willinger, W., Wilson, D.V.: On the self-similar nature of ethernet traffic. In: Proceedings of the Eight International ACM Conference on Communications Architectures, Protocols and Applications. (1993) 183–193

70. Crovella, M.E., Bestavros, A.: Self-similarity in World Wide Web traffic: evidence and possible causes. IEEE /ACM Transactions on Networking **5**(6) (1997) 835–846
71. Jagadish, H., Faloutsos, C.: Data reduction - a tutorial. In: Proceedings of Fourth International Conference on Knowledge Discovery and Data Mining. (1998)
72. StreamSQL: StreamSQL Home page (2006) `http://blogs.streamsql.org`.
73. Wang, S., Rundensteiner, E.A., Ganguly, S., Bhatnagar, S.: State-Slice: New Paradigm of Multi-query Optimization of Window-based Stream Queries. In: Proceedings of International Conference on Very Large Data Bases. (2006) 619–630
74. Hammad, M.A., Franklin, M.J., Aref, W.G., Elmagarmid, A.K.: Scheduling for shared window joins over data streams. In: Proceedings of International Conference on Very Large Data Bases. (2003) 297–308
75. Golab, L., Özsu, T.: Processing Sliding Window Multi-Joins in Continuous Queries over Data Streams. In: Proceedings of International Conference on Very Large Data Bases. (2003) 500–511
76. Wilschut, N., Apers, P.M.G.: Pipelining in query execution. In: IEEE International Conference on Databases, Parallel Architectures and their Applications. (1991) 562–573
77. Arasu, A., Babu, S., Widom, J.: The CQL continuous query language: semantic foundations and query execution. VLDB Journal **15**(2) (2006) 121–142
78. Ghanem, T.M., Aref, W.G., Elmagarmid, A.K.: Exploiting predicate-window semantics over data streams. SIGMOD Record **35**(1) (2006) 3–8
79. Jiang, Q., Adaikkalavan, R., Chakravarthy, S.: NFM^i: An Inter-domain Network Fault Management System. In: ICDE. (2005) 1036–1047
80. Urhan, T., Franklin, M.: Xjoin: A reactively-scheduled pipelined join operator. IEEE Data Engineering Bulletin **23**(2) (2000) 27–33
81. Urhan, T., Franklin, M.: Dynamic pipeline scheduling for improving interactive performance of online queries. In: Proceedings of International Conference on Very Large Data Bases. (2001) 501–510
82. Babcock, B., Babu, S., Datar, M., Motwani, R., Widom, J.: Models and issues in data stream systems. In: Proceedings of the Twenty-first ACM SIGACT-SIGMOD-SIGART Symposium on Principles of Database Systems. (2002) 1–16
83. Kleinrock, L.: Queueing Systems. Volume 1. John Wiley, New York (1975)
84. Kleinrock, L.: Queueing Systems. Volume 2. John Wiley, New York (1976)
85. Babcock, B., Babu, S., Datar, M., Motwani, R., Thomas, D.: Operator scheduling in data stream systems. The VLDB Journal **13**(4) (2004) 333–353
86. Chakravarthy, S., Mishra, D.: Snoop: An expressive event specification language for active databases. Transactions of Data Knowledge and Engineering **14**(1) (1994) 1–26
87. Chakravarthy, S., Krishnaprasad, V., Anwar, E., Kim, S.: Composite Events for Active Databases: Semantics, Contexts and Detection. In: VLDB. (1994) 606–617
88. Dasari, R.: Events and Rules for Java: Design and Implementation of a Seamless Approach. Master's thesis, The University of Florida at Gainesville (1999) `http://itlab.uta.edu/sharma/People/ThesisWeb/rajesh_thesis.pdf`.
89. Balakrishnan, H., Balazinska, M., Carney, D., Cetintemel, U., Cherniack, M., Convey, C., Galvez, E., Salz, J., Stonebraker, M., Tatbul, N., Tibbetts, R.,

Zdonik, S.: Retrospective on aurora. VLDB Journal: Special Issue on Data Stream Processing **13**(4) (2004) 370–383

90. Abadi, D., et al.: Aurora: A New Model and Architecture for Data Stream Management. The VLDB Journal **12**(2) (2003) 120–139
91. Zdonik, S.B., Stonebraker, M., Cherniack, M., Çetintemel, U., Balazinska, M., Balakrishnan, H.: The aurora and medusa projects. IEEE Data Eng. Bull. **26**(1) (2003) 3–10
92. Carney, D., etintemel, U., Rasin, A., Zdonik, S., Cherniack, M., Stonebraker, M.: Operator scheduling in a data stream manager. Proceedings Of the International Conference On Very Large Data Bases (2003) 838–849
93. Tatbul, N., Çetintemel, U., Zdonik, S.B., Cherniack, M., Stonebraker, M.: Load Shedding in a Data Stream Manager. In: Proceedings of International Conference on Very Large Data Bases. (2003) 309–320
94. Cherniack, M., Balakrishnan, H., Balazinska, M., Carney, D., Çetintemel, U., Xing, Y., Zdonik, S.B.: Scalable distributed stream processing. In: CIDR. (2003)
95. Borealis: Second Generation Stream Processing Engine (2003) `http://nms.lcs.mit.edu/projects/borealis/`.
96. Xing, Y., Zdonik, S.B., Hwang, J.H.: Dynamic Load Distribution in the Borealis Stream Processor. In: Proceedings of International Conference on Data Engineering. (2005) 791–802
97. Abadi, D.J., Ahmad, Y., Balazinska, M., Çetintemel, U., Cherniack, M., Hwang, J.H., Lindner, W., Maskey, A., Rasin, A., Ryvkina, E., Tatbul, N., Xing, Y., Zdonik, S.B.: The Design of the Borealis Stream Processing Engine. In: Conference on Innovations in Data Research. (2005) 277–289
98. Ahmad, Y., Berg, B., Çetintemel, U., Humphrey, M., Hwang, J.H., Jhingran, A., Maskey, A., Papaemmanouil, O., Rasin, A., Tatbul, N., Xing, W., Xing, Y., Zdonik, S.B.: Distributed operation in the borealis stream processing engine. In: SIGMOD Conference. (2005) 882–884
99. Hwang, J.H., Balazinska, M., Rasin, A., Çetintemel, U., Stonebraker, M., Zdonik, S.B.: High-Availability Algorithms for Distributed Stream Processing. In: Proceedings of International Conference on Data Engineering. (2005) 779–790
100. Hwang, J.H., Cha, S., Çetintemel, U., Zdonik, S.B.: Borealis-r: a replication-transparent stream processing system for wide-area monitoring applications. In: SIGMOD Conference. (2008) 1303–1306
101. Tatbul, N., Zdonik, S.B.: Dealing with overload in distributed stream processing systems. In: ICDE Workshops. (2006) 24–24
102. Xing, Y., Hwang, J.H., Çetintemel, U., Zdonik, S.B.: Providing resiliency to load variations in distributed stream processing. In: VLDB. (2006) 775–786
103. Tatbul, N., Çetintemel, U., Zdonik, S.B.: Staying fit: Efficient load shedding techniques for distributed stream processing. In: VLDB. (2007) 159–170
104. StreamBase: StreamBase Home Page (2004) `http://www.streambase.com`.
105. STREAM: Stanford Stream Data Management (STREAM) Project (2003) `http://www-db.stanford.edu/stream`.
106. Babu, S., Widom, J.: Continuous queries over data streams. In: Proceedings of the ACM-SIGMOD International Conference on Management of Data. (2001) 109–120

107. Arasu, A., Babcock, B., Babu, S., McAlister, J., Widom, J.: Characterizing memory requirements for queries over continuous data streams. ACM Transactions of Database Systems **29** (2004) 162–194
108. Babu, S., Srivastava, U., Widom, J.: Exploiting k-constraints to reduce memory overhead in continuous queries over data streams. ACM Transactions of Database Systems **29**(3) (2004) 545–580
109. Arasu, A., Widom, J.: A Denotational Semantics for Continuous Queries over Streams and Relations. SIGMOD Record **33**(3) (2004) 6–12
110. Arasu, A., Babu, S., Widom, J.: Cql: A language for continuous queries over streams and relations. In: Database Programming Languages, 9th International Workshop. (2003) 1–19
111. Babcock, B., Babu, S., Motwani, R., Datar, M.: Chain: operator scheduling for memory minimization in data stream systems. In: Proceedings of the 2003 ACM SIGMOD international conference on Management of data. (2003) 253–264
112. Babcock, B., Datar, M., Motwani, R.: Load shedding for aggregation queries over data streams. In: Proceedings of International Conference on Data Engineering. (2004) 350–361
113. Olston, C., Jiang, J., Widom, J.: Adaptive filters for continuous queries over distributed data streams. In: Proceedings of the ACM-SIGMOD International Conference on Management of Data. (2003) 563–574
114. Arasu, A., Widom, J.: Resource sharing in continuous sliding-window aggregates. In: Proceedings of the Thirtieth International Conference on Very Large Data Bases. (2004) 336–347
115. Motwani, R., Widom, J., Arasu, A., Babcock, B., Babu, S., Datar, M., Manku, G.S., Olston, C., Rosenstein, J., Varma, R.: Query processing, approximation, and resource management in a data stream management system. In: Conference on Innovations in Database Research. (2003)
116. Babu, S., Munagala, K., Widom, J., Motwani, R.: Adaptive caching for continuous queries. In: Proceedings of the 21st International Conference on Data Engineering. (2005) 118–129
117. Coral8: Coral8 Homepage (2005) `http://www.coral8.com/`.
118. Chandrasekaran, S., Cooper, O., Deshpande, A., Franklin, M.J., Hellerstein, J.M., Hong, W., Krishnamurthy, S., Madden, S., Reiss, F., Shah, M.A.: TelegraphCQ: Continuous Dataflow Processing. In: Proceedings of ACM-SIGMOD International Conference on Management of Data. (2003) 668
119. Chandrasekaran, S., Cooper, O., Deshpande, A., Franklin, M.J., Hellerstein, J.M., Hong, W., Krishnamurthy, S., Madden, S., Raman, V., Reiss, F., Shah, M.A.: Telegraphcq: Continuous dataflow processing for an uncertain world. In: Conference on Innovations in Database Research (CIDR). (2003)
120. Shah, M.A., Hellerstein, J.M., Chandrasekaran, S., Franklin, M.J.: Flux: An Adaptive Partitioning Operator for Continuous Query Systems. In: Proceedings of International Conference on Data Engineering. (2003) 25–36
121. Krishnamurthy, S., Chandrasekaran, S., Cooper, O., Deshpande, A., Franklin, M.J., Hellerstein, J.M., Hong, W., Madden, S., Reiss, F., Shah, M.A.: TelegraphCQ: An Architectural Status Report. IEEE Data Engineering Bulletin **26**(1) (2003) 11–18
122. Madden, S., Franklin, M.J.: Fjording the stream: An architecture for queries over streaming sensor data. In: Proceedings of International Conference on Data Engineering. (2002) 05–55

123. Avnur, R., Hellerstein, J.: Eddies: Continuously Adaptive Query Processing. Proceedings of the ACM SIGMOD International Conference on Management of Data (2000) 261–272
124. Chandrasekaran, S., Franklin, M.J.: Streaming Queries over Streaming Data. In: Proceedings of International Conference on Very Large Data Bases. (2002) 203–214
125. Truviso: Truviso Home Page (2004) http://www.truviso.com/.
126. Jiang, Q., Chakravarthy, S.: Anatomy of a Data Stream Management System. In: ADBIS Research Communications. (2006)
127. Jiang, Q., Chakravarthy, S.: Data stream management system for MavHome. In: Proceedings, Annual ACM SIG Symposium On Applied Computing. (2004) 654–655
128. Jiang, Q.: A Framework for Supporting Quality of Service Requirements in a Data Stream Management System. PhD thesis, The University of Texas at Arlington (2005) http://itlab.uta.edu/ITLABWEB/Students/sharma/theses/Jia05PHD.pdf.
129. Jiang, Q., Adaikkalavan, R., Chakravarthy, S.: MavEStream: Synergistic Integration of Stream and Event Processing. In: International Conference on Digital Communications. (2007) 29–29
130. Jiang, Q., Chakravarthy, S.: Queueing analysis of relational operators for continuous data streams. In: CIKM. (2003) 271–278
131. Jiang, Q., Chakravarthy, S.: Scheduling Strategies for Processing Continuous Queries over Streams. In: Proceedings of the Annual British National Conference on Databases. (2004) 16–30
132. Jiang, Q., Chakravarthy, S.: A framework for supporting load shedding in data stream management systems. TR CSE-2004-19, UT Arlington (2004) http://www.cse.uta.edu/research/publications/Downloads/CSE-2004-19.pdf.
133. Kendai, B., Chakravarthy, S.: Load Shedding in MavStream: Analysis, Implementation, and Evaluation. In: British National Conference on Databases (BNCOD). (2008) 100–112
134. Gilani, A., Sonune, S., Kendai, B., Chakravarthy, S.: The Anatomy of a Stream Processing System. In: BNCOD. (2006) 232–239
135. Chakravarthy, S., Pajjuri, V.: Scheduling Strategies and Their Evaluation in a Data Stream Management System. In: BNCOD. (2006) 220–231
136. Gilani, A.: Design and Implementation of Stream Operators, Query Instantiator and Stream Buffer Manager. Master's thesis, The University of Texas at Arlington (2003) http://itlab.uta.edu/ITLABWEB/Students/sharma/theses/Gil03MS.pdf.
137. Sonune, S.: Design and Implementation of Windowed Operators and Scheduler for Stream Data. Master's thesis, The University of Texas at Arlington (2003) http://itlab.uta.edu/ITLABWEB/Students/sharma/theses/Son03MS.pdf.
138. Pajjuri, V.K.: Design and Implementation of Scheduling Strategies and their Evaluation in MavStream. Master's thesis, The University of Texas at Arlington (2004) http://itlab.uta.edu/ITLABWEB/Students/sharma/theses/Paj04MS.pdf.
139. Kendai, B.: Runtime Optimization and Load Shedding in MavStream: Design and Implementation. Master's thesis, The University of Texas at Arlington (2006) http://itlab.uta.edu/ITLABWEB/Students/sharma/theses/Ken06MS.pdf.

140. Garg, V.: MavEStream: An Integration and Event and Stream Processing. Master's thesis, The University of Texas at Arlington (2005) `http://itlab.uta.edu/ITLABWEB/Students/sharma/theses/Gar05MS.pdf`.
141. Cranor, C.D., Johnson, T., Spatscheck, O., Shkapenyuk, V.: The Gigascope Stream Database. IEEE Data Engineering Bulletin **26**(1) (2003) 27–32
142. Cranor, C.D., Johnson, T., Spatscheck, O., Shkapenyuk, V.: Gigascope: A Stream Database for Network Applications. In: Proceedings of ACM-SIGMOD International Conference on Management of Data. (2003) 647–651
143. Zhu, Y., Shasha, D.: StatStream: Statistical Monitoring of Thousands of Data Streams in Real Time. In: Proceedings of International Conference on Very Large Data Bases. (2002) 358–369
144. Madden, S.R., et al.: The design of an acquisitional query processor for sensor networks. In: Proceedings of ACM SIGMOD International Conference on Management of Data. (2003)
145. Madden, S.R., et al.: Tag: a tiny aggregation service for ad-hoc sensor networks. Proceedings of the 5th symposium on Operating systems design and implementation (2002) 131–146
146. Bonnet, P., Gerhke, J.E., Seshadri, P.: Towards sensor database systems. In: Proceedings of the Second International Conference on Mobile Data Management. (2001) 3–14
147. Yao, Y., Gehrke, J.E.: Query processing in sensor networks. In: Proceedings of International Conference on Innovations in Database Research. (2003) `http://www-db.cs.wisc.edu/cidr/cidr2003/program/p21.pdf`.
148. Hammad, M.A., Mokbel, M.F., Ali, M.H., Aref, W.G., Catlin, A.C., Elmagarmid, A.K., Eltabakh, M.Y., Elfeky, M.G., Ghanem, T.M., Gwadera, R., Ilyas, I.F., Marzouk, M.S., Xiong, X.: Nile: A Query Processing Engine for Data Streams. In: Proceedings of International Conference on Data Engineering. (2004) 851
149. Seshadri, P.: Predator: A Resource for Database Research. SIGMOD Record **27**(1) (1998) 16–20
150. Liu, L., Pu, C., Tang, W.: Continual queries for internet scale event-driven information delivery. Trasactions of Knowledge and Data Engineering **11**(4) (1999) 610–628
151. Chen, J., Dewitt, D., Tian, F., Wang, Y.: Niagaracq: A scalable continuous query system for internet databases. In: Proceedings of the ACM-SIGMOD International Conference on Management of Data. (2000) 379–390
152. Sullivan, M., Heybey, A.: Tribeca: A system for managing large databases of network traffic. In: usenix. (1998) 13–24
153. Sullivan, M.: Tribeca: A stream database manager for network traffic analysis. Proceedings of the International Conference on Very Large Data Bases (1996) 594–605
154. Cortes, C., Fisher, K., Pregibon, D., Rogers, A., Smith, F.: Hancock: A language for extracting signatures from data streams. In: In Proc. of the 2000 ACM SIGKDD Intl. Conf. on Knowledge Discovery and Data Mining. (2000) 9–17
155. Terry, D.B., Goldberg, D., Nichols, D., Oki, B.M.: Continuous queries over append-only databases. In: Proceedings of the ACM SIGMOD International Conference on Management of Data, ACM Press (1992) 321–330
156. Goldberg, D., Nichols, D., Oki, B.M., Terry, D.B.: Using collaborative filtering to weave an information tapestry. ACM Communications **35**(12) (1992) 61–70

157. Bai, Y., Thakkar, H., Wang, H., Luo, C., Zaniolo, C.: A data stream language and system designed for power and extensibility. In: CIKM '06: Proceedings of the 15th ACM international conference on Information and knowledge management, New York, NY, USA, ACM (2006) 337–346
158. Das, G., Gunopulos, D., Koudas, N., Sarkas, N.: Ad-hoc top-k query answering for data streams. In: VLDB. (2007) 183–194
159. Golab, L., Özsu, M.T.: Issues in data stream management. SIGMOD Record **32**(2) (2003) 5–14
160. Zilberstein, S., Russell, S.: Optimal composition of real-time systems. Artificial Intelligence **82**(1–2) (1996) 181–213
161. Larson, K., Sandholm, T.: Bargaining with limited computation: deliberation equilibrium. Artificial Intelligence **132**(2) (2001) 183–217
162. Horvitz, E., Zilberstein, S.: Computational tradeoffs under bounded resources. Artificial Intelligence **126**(1-2) (2001) 1–4
163. Menasce, D.A., Almeida, V., Dowdy, L.W.: Capacity Planning and Performance Modeling: from mainframes to client-server systems. Prentice Hall (1994)
164. Menasce, D.A., Almeida, V.: Capacity Planning for Web Performance: Metrics, Models, and Methods. Prentice Hall (1998)
165. Kang, J., Naughton, J.F., Viglas, S.: Evaluating window joins over unbounded streams. In: Proceedings of International Conference on Data Engineering. (2003) 341–352
166. Viglas, S., Naughton, J.F., Burger, J.: Maximizing the Output Rate of Multi-Way Join Queries over Streaming Information Sources. In: Proceedings of International Conference on Very Large Data Bases. (2003) 285–296
167. Viglas, S.D., Naughton, J.F.: Rate-based query optimization for streaming information sources. In: Proceedings of the ACM-SIGMOD International Conference on Management of Data. (2002) 37–48
168. Arasu, A., Babcock, B., Babu, S., McAlister, J., Widom, J.: Characterizing memory requirements for queries over continuous data streams. In: Proceedings of the Twenty-Seventh ACM SIGMOD-SIGACT-SIGART Symposium on Principles of Database Systems. (2002) 221–232
169. Henzinger, M.R., Raghavan, P., Rajagopalan, S.: Computing on data streams. TR-1998-011, Compaq Systems Research Center, Palo Alto, CA (1998)
170. Guha, S., Koudas, N., Shim, K.: Data-streams and histograms. In: Proceedings of the Annual ACM Symposium on Theory of Computing. (2001) 471–475
171. Babcock, B., Datar, M., Motwani, R.: Sampling from a moving window over streaming data. In: Proceedings of the Annual ACM-SIAM Symp. on Discrete Algorithms. (2002) 633–634
172. Rubin, I., Wu, J.C.H.: Analysis of an M/G/1/N queue with vacations and its iterative application to FDDI timed-token rings. IEEE/ACM Transactions on Networking **3** (1995) 842–856
173. Lee, T.: M/G/1/N queue with vacation time and limited service discipline. Performance Evaluation archive **9** (1989) 180–190
174. Takagi, H.: Queuing analysis of polling models. In: ACM Computing Surveys. Volume 20. (1988) 5–28
175. J.Daigle, M.Roughan: Queue-length distributions for multi-priority queueing systems. In: Proceedings of Eighteenth Annual Joint Conference of the IEEE Computer and Communications Societies. (1999) 641–648

176. Amsaleg, L., Franklin, M., Tomasic, A.: Dynamic query operator scheduling for wide-area remote access. Journal of Distributed and Parallel Databases **3**(6) (1998) 217–246
177. Hellerstein, J., Franklin, M., et al: Adaptive query processing: Technology in evolution. IEEE Data Engineering Bulletin **23**(2) (2000) 7–18
178. Hellerstein, J., Madden, S., Raman, V., Shah, M.: Continuously adaptive continuous queries over streams. Proceedings of the ACM SIGMOD International Conference on Management of Data (2002) 49–60
179. Tatbul, N., Zdonik, S.B.: Window-aware load shedding for aggregation queries over data streams. In: VLDB. (2006) 799–810
180. Das, A., Gehrke, J., Riedewald, M.: Approximate join processing over data streams. In: Proceedings of the ACM-SIGMOD International Conference on Management of Data. (2003) 40–51
181. Mokbel, M.F., et al.: Place: A query processor for handling real-time spatio-temporal data streams. In: Proceedings of International Conference on Very Large Data Bases. (2004) 1377–1380
182. Dayal, U., Buchmann, A.P., Chakravarthy, S.: The hipac project. In: Active Database Systems: Triggers and Rules For Advanced Database Processing. Morgan Kaufmann (1996) 177–206
183. Stonebraker, M., Hanson, E., Potamianos, S.: A rule manager for relational database systems. Technical Report UCB/ERL M87/38, EECS Department, University of California, Berkeley (1987) http://www.eecs.berkeley.edu/Pubs/TechRpts/1987/892.html.
184. Stonebraker, M., Hanson, E., Potamianos, S.: The POSTGRES rule manager. IEEE Transactions on Software Engineering **14**(7) (1988) 897–907
185. Dittrich, K.R., Kotz, A.M., Mulle., J.A.: An Event/Trigger Mechanism to Enforce Complex Consistency Constraints in Design Databases. SIGMOD Record **15**(3) (1986) 22–36
186. InterBase Software Corporation Bedford, MA: InterBase DDL Reference Manual, InterBase Version 3.0. (1990)
187. Chakravarthy, S., et al.: Design of Sentinel: An Object-Oriented DBMS with Event-Based Rules. Information and Software Technology **36**(9) (1994) 559–568
188. Li, L., Chakravarthy, S.: An Agent-Based Approach to Extending the Native Active Capability of Relational Database Systems. In: ICDE. (1999) 384–391
189. Kim, Y.H.: A Generalized ECA Agent for Extending Active Capability of RDBMS. Master's thesis, The University of Florida at Gainesville (2000) http://itlab.uta.edu/sharma/People/ThesisWeb/ykim_thesis.pdf.
190. Chakravarthy, S., Nesson, S.: Making an Object-Oriented DBMS Active: Design, Implementation, and Evaluation of a Prototype. In: EDBT. (1990) 393–406
191. Aiken, A., Widom, J., Hellerstein, J.M.: Behavior of Database Production Rules: Termination, Confluence, and Observable Determinism. In: SIGMOD RECORD. (1992) 59–68
192. Aiken, A., Hellerstein, J.M., Widom, J.: Static analysis techniques for predicting the behavior of active database rules. ACM Trans. Database Syst. **20**(1) (1995) 3–41
193. Widom, J., Ceri, S.: Active Database Systems: Triggers and Rules. Morgan Kaufmann Publishers, Inc. (1996)

194. Baralis, E., Ceri, S., Paraboschi, S.: Improving rule analysis by means of triggering and activation graphs. In: Rules in Database Systems. (1995) 165–181
195. Kim, S.K., Chakravarthy, S.: A Practical Approach to Static Analysis and Execution of Rules in Active Databases. In: CIKM. (1997) 161–168
196. Baralis, E., Ceri, S., Widom, J.: Better termination analysis for active databases. In: Rules in Database Systems. (1993) 163–179
197. van der Voort, L., Siebes, A.: Enforcing confluence of rule execution. In: Rules in Database Systems. (1993) 194–207
198. Baralis, E., Widom, J.: An algebraic approach to static analysis of active database rules. ACM Transactions of Database Systems **25**(3) (2000) 269–332
199. Dinn, A., Paton, N.W., Williams, M.H., Fernandes, A.: An Active Rule Language for ROCK & ROLL. In: In Proceedings of British National Conference on Databases (BNCOD). (1996) 36–55
200. Fernandes, A., Williams, M.H., Paton, N.W.: A Logic-Based Integration of Active and Deductive Databases. New Generation Computing **15**(2) (1997) 205–244
201. Ceri, S., Manthey, R.: Chimera: a model and language for active DOOD Systems. In: Proceedings of East-West Database Workshop, Workshops in Computing. (1994) 3–16
202. Zaniolo, C.: A unified semantics for active and deductive databases. In: Rules in Database Systems. (1993) 271–287
203. Harrison, J.V., Dietrich, S.W.: Integrating active and deductive rules. In: Rules in Database Systems. (1993) 288–305
204. Widom, J.: Deductive and active databases: Two paradigms or ends of a spectrum? In: Rules in Database Systems. (1993) 306–315
205. Bayer, P., Jonker, W.: A framework for supporting triggers in deductive databases. In: Rules in Database Systems. (1993) 316–330
206. Simon, E., Kiernan, J.: The A-RDL System. In: Active Database Systems: Triggers and Rules For Advanced Database Processing. Morgan Kaufmann (1996) 111–149
207. Coupaye, T., Collet, C.: Denotational semantics for an active rule execution model. In: Rules in Database Systems. (1995) 36–50
208. Reddi, S., Poulovassilis, A., Small, C.: Extending a Functional DBPL with ECA-rules. In: Rules in Database Systems. (1995) 101–118
209. Jaeger, U., Obermaier, J.K.: Parallel Event Detection in Active Database Systems: The Heart of the Matter. In: Proceedings of Second International Workshop on Active, Real-Time, and Temporal Database Systems. (1997) 159–175
210. Dittrich, K.R., Gatziu, S., Geppert, A.: The Active Database Management System Manifesto: A Rulebase of ADBMS Features. In: Rules in Database Systems. (1995) 3–20
211. Engstrom, H., Berndtsson, M., Lings, B.: ACOOD Essentials. Technical report, University of Skovde (1997) `http://www.ida.his.se/ida/research/tech_reports/reports/tr97/HS-IDA-TR-97-010.ps`.
212. Diaz, O., Paton, N., Gray, P.: Rule Management in Object-Oriented Databases: A Unified Approach. In: Proceedings of International Conference on Very Large Data Bases. (1991) 317–326

213. Schreier, U., et al.: Alert: An Architecture for Transforming a Passive DBMS into an Active DBMS. In: Proceedings of International Conference on Very Large Data Bases. (1991) 469–478
214. Hanson, E.N.: The Design and Implementation of the Ariel Active Database Rule System. Transactions of Knowledge and Data Engineering **8**(1) (1996) 157–172
215. Hanson, E.N.: Active Rules in Database Systems. In W.Paton, N., ed.: Ariel. Springer (1999) 221–232
216. Meo, R., Psaila, G., Ceri, S.: Composite Events in Chimera. In: Proceedings of Internation Conference on Extending Database Technology. (1996) 56–76
217. Ceri, S., Fraternali, P., Paraboschi, S., Branca, L.: Active rule management in chimera. In: Active Database Systems - Triggers and Rules For Advanced Database Processing. Morgan Kaufman Publishers Inc. (1996) 151–176
218. Gehani, N.H., Jagadish, H.V., Shmueli, O.: Composite Event Specification in Active Databases: Model & Implementation. In: Proceedings of International Conference on Very Large Data Bases. (1992) 327–338
219. Díaz, O., Jaime, A.: EXACT: An Extensible Approach to Active Object-Oriented Databases. VLDB Journal **6**(4) (1997) 282–295
220. Collet, C., Coupaye, T., Svensen, T.: NAOS efficient and modular reactive capabilities in an object-oriented database system. In: Proceedings of the International Conference on Very Large Data Bases. (1994) 132–143
221. Gehani, N.H., Jagadish, H.V.: ODE as an Active Database: Constraints and Triggers. In: Proceedings of International Conference on Very Large Data Bases. (1991) 327–336
222. Lieuwen, D.L., Gehani, N.H., Arlein, R.: The Ode Active Database: Trigger Semantics and Implementation. In: Proceedings of International Conference on Data Engineering. (1996) 412–420
223. Stonebraker, M., Jhingran, A., Goh, J., Potamianos, S.: On rules, procedures, caching and views in data base systems. In: SIGMOD Conference. (1990) 281–290
224. Buchman, A., Branding, H., Kudrass, T., Zimmermann, J.: Rules in an open system: The REACH rule system. In: Rules in Database Systems. (1993) 111–126
225. Buchmann, A.P., Zimmermann, J., Blakeley, J.A., Wells, D.L.: Building an integrated active oodbms: Requirements, architecture, and design decisions. In: In Proceedings of the 11th International Conference on Data Engineering, IEEE Computer Society Press (1995) 117–128
226. Dinn, A., Williams, M.H., Paton, N.W.: ROCK & ROLL: A Deductive Object-Oriented Database with Active and Spatial Extensions. In: Proceedings of International Conference of Data Engineering. (1997) 491–502
227. Gatziu, S., Dittrich, K.R.: SAMOS: An Active, Object-Oriented Database System. IEEE Quarterly Bulletin on Data Engineering **15**(1-4) (1992) 23–26
228. Gatziu, S., Dittrich, K.R.: Events in an Object-Oriented Database System. In: Proceedings of Rules in Database Systems. (1993) 23–39
229. Anwar, E., Maugis, L., Chakravarthy, S.: A New Perspective on Rule Support for Object-Oriented Databases. In: SIGMOD Conference. (1993) 99–108
230. Seshadri, P., Livny, M., Ramakrishnan, R.: The Design and Implementation of a Sequence Database System. In: Proceedings of International Conference on Very Large Data Bases. (1996) 99–110

231. Widom, J.: The Starburst Rule System: Language Design, Implementation, and Applications. IEEE Quarterly Bulletin on Data Engineering **15**(1-4) (1992) 15–18
232. Widom, J., Cochrane, R.J., B, G, .L.: Implemented Set-Oriented Production Rules as an Extension of Starburst. In: Proceedings 17th International Conference on Very Large Data Bases, Barcelona (Catalonia, Spain) (1991) 275–286
233. Kappel, G., Retschitzegger, W.: The TriGS Active Object-Oriented Database System - An Overview. ACM SIGMOD Record **27** (1998) 36–41
234. Retschitzegger, W.: Composite Event Management in TriGS - Concepts and Implementation. In: Proceedings of International Conference on Database and Expert Systems Applications. (1998) 1–15
235. Kotz-Dittrich, A.: Adding Active Functionality to an Object-Oriented Database System - a Layered Approach. In: Proceedings of the Conference on Database Systems in Office, Technique and Science. (1993) 54–73
236. Motakis, I., Zaniolo, C.: Formal Semantics for Composite Temporal Events in Active Database Rules. Journal of System Integration **7**(3-4) (1997) 291–325
237. Motakis, I., Zaniolo, C.: Temporal Aggregation in Active Database Rules. In: Proceedings of ACM-SIGMOD International Conference on Management of Data. (1997) 440–451
238. Paton, N.W.: Active Rules in Database Systems. Springer (1999)
239. Jaeger, U., Freytag, J.C.: An Annotated Bibliography on Active Databases. SIGMOD Record **24**(1) (1995) 58–69
240. Vinoski, S.: Distributed Object Computing With Corba. C++ Report (1993) 33–38
241. TIBCO: TIBCO Business Events Homepage Homepage (2001) `http://www.tibco.com/software/complex_event_processing/businessevents/default.jsp`.
242. WebLogic - BEA Systems, Inc.: WebLogic Events Architecture (1999) `http://www.weblogic.com/docs/techoverview/em.html`.
243. ILOG JRules: ILOG, Inc. (2002) `http://www.ilog.com/products/jrules/whitepapers/index.cfm?filename=WPJRules4.0.pdf`.
244. Vitria BusinessWare: Vitria Technology, Inc. (1999) `http://www.vitria.com`.
245. J. Melton (Editor): (ISO/ANSI) working draft database language SQL (SQL3) (1993)
246. Dittrich, A.K., Simon, E.: Active database systems: Expectations, commercial experience, and beyond. In: Active Rules in Database Systems. Springer (1999) 367–404
247. Gatziu, S., Dittrich, K.R.: A Designer's Benchmark for Active Database Management Systems: OO7 meets the Beast. In: In Timos Sellis, editor, Rules in Database Systems, Second International Workshop, RIDS '95, Springer Verlag (1995) 309–323
248. Geppert, A., Berndtsson, M., Lieuwen, D., Roncancio, C.: Performance evaluation of object-oriented active database management systems using the beast benchmark. Theory and Practice of Object Systems (TAPOS) **4**(3) (1998) 135–149
249. Transaction Processing Council: TPC Homepage (2001) `http://www.tpc.org/`.
250. Schwiderski, S., Herbert, A., Moody, K.: Composite events for detecting behavior patterns in distributed environments. In: TAPOS Distributed Object Management. (1995)

251. Yang, S., Chakravarthy, S.: Formal Semantics of Composite Events for Distributed Environments. In: ICDE. (1999) 400–407
252. Chakravarthy, S., Liao, H.: Asynchronous Monitoring of Events for Distributed Cooperative Environments. In: CODAS. (2001) 25–32
253. Tanpisuth, W.: Design and Implementation of Event-based Subscription/Notification Paradigm for Distributed Environments. Master's thesis, The University of Texas at Arlington (2001) http://itlab.uta.edu/ITLABWEB/Students/sharma/theses/Tan01MS.pdf.
254. Kalantery, N.: A distributed event processing method for general purpose computation. J. Syst. Archit. **44**(6-7) (1998) 547–558
255. Chakravarthy, S., Yang, S.: Architecture and Implementation of an Interactive Tool for the Design and Visualization of Active Capability. In: VDB. (2002) 111–125
256. Díaz, O., Jaime, A., Paton, N.W.: Dear: a debugger for active rules in an object-oriented context. In: Rules in Database Systems. (1993) 180–193
257. Chu, H.: A Flexible Dynamic ECA Rule Editor for Sentinel: Design and Implementation. Master's thesis, The University of Florida at Gainesville (1998) http://itlab.uta.edu/sharma/People/ThesisWeb/hungju-thesis.pdf.
258. Chakravarthy, S., Dasari, R., Varkala, S.R., Adaikkalavan, R. In: Events and Rules for Java: Using a Seamless and Dynamic Approach. Volume 155. IOS Press (2006) 3–17
259. Anwar, E.: An Extensible Approach to Realizing Extended Transaction Models. PhD thesis, The University of Florida at Gainesville (1996) http://itlab.uta.edu/sharma/People/ThesisWeb/emsa_phd_thesis.pdf.
260. Anwar, E., Chakravarthy, S., Viveros, M.: An extensible approach to realizing advanced transaction models. In: Proceedings of the workshop on Advanced Transaction Models and Architecture. (1996) 176–188
261. Geppert, A., Dittrich, K.R.: Rule-based implementation of transaction model specifications. In: Rules in Database Systems. (1993) 127–142
262. Berndtsson, M., Chakravarthy, S., Lings, B.: Task sharing among agents using reactive rules. In: CoopIS. (1997) 56–65
263. Berndtsson, M., Chakravarthy, S., Lings, B.: Result sharing among agents using reactive rules. In: CIA. (1997) 126–137
264. Berndtsson, M., Chakravarthy, S., Lings, B.: Extending database support for coordination among agents. Int. J. Cooperative Inf. Syst. **6**(3-4) (1997) 315–340
265. Berndtsson, M.: Active Capability Support for Cooperation Strategies in Cooperative Information Systems. PhD thesis, University of Exeter (1998) http://www.his.se/upload/22381/phd-thesis.pdf.
266. Berndtsson, M., Hansson, J.: Workshop report: The first international workshop on active and real-time database systems (artdb-95). SIGMOD Record **25**(1) (1996) 64–66
267. Andler, S., Hansson, J., Eriksson, J., Mellin, J., Berndtsson, M., Eftring, B.: Deeds towards a distributed and active real-time database system. SIGMOD Record **25**(1) (1996) 38–40
268. Buchmann, A., Chakravarthy, S., Dittrich, K.: Dagstuhl Active Database Seminar Home Page (1994) http://www.dagstuhl.de/en/program/calendar/semhp/?semnr=199412.
269. Zaniolo, C., Ceri, S., Faloutsos, C., Snodgrass, R.T., Subrahmanian, V.S., Zicari, R.: Advanced Database Systems. Morgan Kaufmann (1997)

270. N. W. Paton: Active Rules in Database Systems. Springer (1999)
271. Akdere, M., Çetintemel, U., Tatbul, N.: Plan-based complex event detection across distributed sources. Proc. VLDB Endow. **1**(1) (2008) 66–77
272. Pietzuch, P.R., Shand, B., Bacon, J.: Composite event detection as a generic middleware extension. IEEE Network **18**(1) (2004) 44–55
273. Pietzuch, P.: A Scalable Event-Based Middleware. PhD thesis, Cambridge University (2004) `http://www.cl.cam.ac.uk/techreports/UCAM-CL-TR-590.pdf`.
274. Luckham, D.C.: The Power of Events: An Introduction to Complex Event Processing in Distributed Enterprise Systems. Addison-Wesley Longman Publishing Co., Inc., Boston, MA, USA (2001)
275. Adi, A., Etzion, O.: AMiT - The Situation Manager. VLDB Journal **13**(2) (2004) 177–203
276. Rizvi, S., Jeffery, S.R., Krishnamurthy, S., Franklin, M.J., Burkhart, N., Edakkunni, A., Liang, L.: Events on the Edge. In: Proceedings of the ACM SIGMOD International Conference on Management of Data. (2005) 885–887
277. Cooper, O., Edakkunni, A., Franklin, M.J., Hong, W., Jeffery, S.R., Krishnamurthy, S., Reiss, F., Rizvi, S., Wu, E.: HiFi: A Unified Architecture for High Fan-in Systems. In: Proceedings of the Thirtieth international conference on Very Large Data Bases. (2004) 1357–1360
278. Zaniolo, C., et al.: Stream Mill (2001) `http://wis.cs.ucla.edu/stream-mill/index.html`.
279. Barga, R.S., Goldstein, J., Ali, M.H., Hong, M.: Consistent streaming through time: A vision for event stream processing. In: CIDR. (2007) 363–374
280. White, W.M., Riedewald, M., Gehrke, J., Demers, A.J.: What is "next" in event processing? In: PODS. (2007) 263–272
281. Demers, A.J., Gehrke, J., Panda, B., Riedewald, M., Sharma, V., White, W.M.: Cayuga: A general purpose event monitoring system. In: CIDR. (2007) 412–422
282. Brenna, L., Demers, A.J., Gehrke, J., Hong, M., Ossher, J., Panda, B., Riedewald, M., Thatte, M., White, W.M.: Cayuga: a high-performance event processing engine. In: SIGMOD Conference. (2007) 1100–1102
283. Wu, E., Diao, Y., Rizvi, S.: High-performance complex event processing over streams. In: SIGMOD Conference. (2006) 407–418
284. Garg, V., Adaikkalavan, R., Chakravarthy, S.: Extensions to Stream Processing Architecture for Supporting Event Processing. In: DEXA. (2006) 945–955
285. Adaikkalavan, R., Chakravarthy, S.: SnoopIB: Interval-based event specification and detection for active databases. Transactions of Data Knowledge and Engineering **59**(1) (2006) 139–165
286. Adaikkalavan, R.: Generalization and Enforcement of Role-Based Access Control using a Novel Event-based Approach. PhD thesis, The University of Texas at Arlington (2006) `http://itlab.uta.edu/ITLABWEB/Students/sharma/theses/Ada06PHD.pdf`.
287. Adaikkalavan, R., Chakravarthy, S.: Event Specification and Processing for Advanced Applications: Generalization and Formalization. In: DEXA. (2007) 369–379
288. Adaikkalavan, R., Chakravarthy, S.: Events must be complete in event processing! In: Proceedings, Annual ACM SIG Symposium On Applied Computing. (2008) 1038–1039

289. Chakravarthy, S., Adaikkalavan, R.: Event and Streams: Harnessing and Unleashing Their Synergy. In: International Conference on Distributed Event-based Systems. (2008) 1–12
290. Baldoni, R., ed.: Proceedings of the Second International Conference on Distributed Event-Based Systems, DEBS 2008, Rome, Italy, July 1-4, 2008. In Baldoni, R., ed.: DEBS. Volume 332 of ACM International Conference Proceeding Series., ACM (2008)
291. Event Processing Technology Society: EPTS Home Page (2008) http://www.ep-ts.com/.
292. Event-based.org: Event-Based Org Homepage (2007) www.event-based.org.
293. Chandy, M., Etzion, O., von Ammon, R., Niblett, P.: 07191 Summary – Event Processing. In Chandy, M., Etzion, O., von Ammon, R., eds.: Event Processing. Number 07191 in Dagstuhl Seminar Proceedings (2007)
294. Shatsky, Y., Gudes, E., Gudes, E.: Tops: a new design for transactions in publish/subscribe middleware. In: DEBS. (2008) 201–210
295. White, S., Alves, A., Rorke, D.: Weblogic event server: a lightweight, modular application server for event processing. In: DEBS. (2008) 193–200
296. Aleri: Aleri Home Page (2004) http://www.aleri.com/products/aleri-streaming-platform/.
297. Apama: Progress Software Home Page (2004) http://www.progress.com/index.ssp.
298. AMiT: IBM, AMiT Home Page (2004) http://www.haifa.ibm.com/dept/services/stes.html.
299. Corona Enterprise Suite: Red Rabbit Software Home Page (2004) http://www.redrabbitsoftware.com/.
300. Esper: Esper Home Page (2004) http://esper.codehaus.org/.
301. GemFire Real-Time Events: GemFire Real-Time Events Homepage. http://www.gemstone.com/products/gemfire/rte.php (2008)
302. INETCO: INETCO Homepage. http://www.inetco.com/ (2008)
303. Oracle CEP: Oracle CEP Homepage. http://www.oracle.com/technologies/soa/complex-event-processing.html (2008)
304. RuleCore: RuleCore Homepage (2007) http://www.rulecore.com/.
305. Seirio, M., Berndtssons, M.: Design and Implementation of a ECA Rule Markup Language. In: Proceedings of the International RuleML Conference. (2005) 98–112
306. SENACTIVE EventAnalyzer: SENACTIVE EventAnalyzer Homepage. http://www.senactive.com/index.php?id=eventanalyzer&L=1 (2008)
307. SL Real-Time Visibility: SL Real-Time Visibility Homepage. http://www.sl.com/solutions/cep.shtml (2008)
308. WestGlobal: WestGlobal Vantify Experience Centre Homepage. http://www.westglobal.com/index.php?option=com_content&view=article&id=35&Itemid=62 (2008)
309. Jain, N., et al.: Towards a Streaming SQL Standard. In: VLDB. (2008)
310. Medhi, J.: Stochastic Models in Queueing Theory. Academic Press (1999)
311. Takagi, H.: Analysis of Polling system. MIT, Cambridge, MS (1986)
312. Takagi, H.: Queueing Analysis – Foundation of Performance Evaluation, Volume 1: Vacation and Priority Systems, Part 1. North Hollan (1991)
313. Stallings, W.: High-speed networks and Internets. Second Edition. Prentice Hall (2002)

314. C.Fricker, Jaibi, M.: Monotonicity and stability of polling models. Queueing systems **15** (1994)
315. Kendall, D.G.: Some problems in the theory of queues. Journal of the Royal Statistical Society **B 13** (1951) 151–185
316. Leland, W., Taqqu, M., Willinger, W., Wilson, D.: On the self-similar nature of ethernet traffic. IEEE/ACM Transactions on Networking **2** (1994) 1–15
317. Bischof, W.: Analysis of M/G/1-Queues with Setup Times and Vacations under Six Different Service Disciplines. Queueing systems **39** (2001)
318. Zhou, J., Ross, K.A.: Buffering database operations for enhanced instruction cache performance. In: Proceedings of the ACM SIGMOD International Conference on Management of Data. (2004) 191–202
319. Deshpande, A.: An initial study of overheads of eddies. SIGMOD Record **33**(1) (2004) 44–49
320. Jiang, Q., Chakravarthy, S.: Analysis and Validation of Continuous Queries over Data Streams. TR CSE-2003-7, UT Arlington (2003) `http://www.cse.uta.edu/research/publications/Downloads/CSE-2003-7.pdf`.
321. Ramakrishnan, K.K., Jain, R.: A binary feedback scheme for congestion avoidance in computer networks. ACM Transactions on Computer Systems **8(2)** (1990) 158–181
322. Yang, C., Reddy, A.: A taxonomy for congestion control algorithms in packet switching networks. IEEE Network **9** (1995) 34–45
323. Jacobson, V.: Congestion avoidance and control. In: ACM Computer Communication Review. (1988) 314–329
324. Beran, J.: Statistics for Long-Memory Processes. New York: Chapman and Hall (1994)
325. Bjerring, L.H., Lewis, D., Thorarensen, I.: Inter-domain service management of broadband virtual private networks. Journal of Network and Systems Management **4**(4) (1996) 355–373
326. Diaz-Caldera, R., Serrat-Fernandez, J., Berdekas, K., Karayannis, F.: An approach to the cooperative management of multitechnology networks. Communications Magazine, IEEE **37**(5) (1999) 119–125
327. Mountzia, M.A., Rodosek, G.D.: Using the concept of intelligent agents in fault management of distributed services. Journal of Network and Systems Management **7**(4) (1999) 425–446
328. Medhi, D., et al.: A network management framework for multi-layered network survivability: An overview. In: IEEE/IFIP Conference on Integrated Network Management. (2001) 293–296
329. Babu, S., Subramanian, L., Widom, J.: A data stream management system for network traffic management. In: Proceedings of the Workshop on Network-Related Data Management (NRDM 2001). (2001) 685–686
330. Baras, J., Li, H., Mykoniatis, G.: Integrated, distributed fault management for communication networks. Technical Report CS-TR 98-10, University of Maryland, University of Maryland (1998)
331. Gambhir, D., Post, M., Frisch, I.: A Framework for Adding Real-Time Distributed Software Fault Detection and Isolation to SNMP-based Systems Management. Journal of Network and Systems Management **2**(3) (1994) 257–282
332. Frohlich, P., Nejdl, W.: Model-based alarm correlation in cellular phone networks. In: Proceeding of the International Symposium on Modeling, Analysis, and Simulation of Computer and Telecommunications Systems (MASCOTS). (1997) 197–204

333. Jiang, Q., Adaikkalavan, R., Chakravarthy, S.: Estreams: Towards an integrated model for event and stream processing. TR CSE-2004-3, UT Arlington (2004) http://www.cse.uta.edu/research/publications/Downloads/CSE-2004-3.pdf.
334. TimesTen Team: In-memory data management for consumer transactions the timesten approach. In: Proceedings of the ACM-SIGMOD International Conference on Management of Data. (1999) 528–529
335. Arasu, A., et al.: Linear road: A stream data management benchmark. In: Proceedings of the International Conference on Very Large Data Bases. (2004) 480–491
336. Jain, N., Amini, L., Andrade, H., King, R., Park, Y., Selo, P., Venkatramani, C.: Design, implementation, and evaluation of the linear road benchmark on the stream processing core. In: 25th ACM SIGMOD International Conference on Management of Data (SIGMOD 2006). (2006)
337. Branding, H., Buchmann, A.P., Kudrass, T., Zimmermann, J.: Rules in an Open System: The REACH Rule System. In: Rules in Database Systems. (1993) 111–126
338. Gehani, N.H., Jagadish, H.V., Shmueli, O.: COMPOSE: A System For Composite Event Specification and Detection. Technical report, AT&T Bell Laboratories (1992) ftp://ftp.research.att.com/dist/db/att-db-93-14.ps.Z.
339. Gehani, N.H., Jagadish, H.V., Shmueli, O.: Event Specification in an Object-Oriented Database. In: Proceedings of ACM-SIGMOD International Conference on Management of Data. (1992) 81–90
340. Gatziu, S., Dittrich, K.R.: Detecting Composite Events in Active Databases using Petri Nets. In: Proceedings of Workshop on Research Issues in Data Engineering. (1994)
341. Roncancio, C.: Toward Duration-Based, Constrained and Dynamic Event Types. In: Active, Real-Time, and Temporal Database Systems. (1997) 176–193
342. Adaikkalavan, R., Chakravarthy, S.: SnoopIB: Interval-Based Event Specification and Detection for Active Databases. In: ADBIS. (2003) 190–204
343. Galton, A., Augusto, J.C.: Two Approaches to Event Definition. In: Proceedings of the 13th International Conference on Database and Expert Systems Applications. (2002) 547–556
344. Adaikkalavan, R., Chakravarthy, S.: Formalization and Detection of Events over a Sliding Window in Active Databases Using Interval-Based Semantics. In: ADBIS (Local Proceedings). (2004)
345. Elkhalifa, L.: InfoFilter: Complex Pattern Specification and Detection over Text Streams. Master's thesis, The University of Texas at Arlington (2004) http://itlab.uta.edu/ITLABWEB/Students/sharma/theses/Elk04MS.pdf.
346. Dayal, U., Blaustein, B., Buchmann, A., Chakravarthy, S., et al.: HiPAC: A Research Project in Active, Time-Constrained Database Management. Technical Report CCA-88-02, Xerox Advanced Information Technology, Cambridge (1988)
347. Birgisson, R., Mellin, J., Andler, S.F.: Bounds on Test Effort for Event-Triggered Real-Time Systems. In: International Workshop on Real-Time Computing and Applications Symposium. (1999) 212–215
348. Forgy, C.L.: RETE: A Fast Algorithm for the Many Pattern/Many Object Pattern Matching Problem. Artificial Intelligence 19 (1982) 17–37

349. Miranker, D.P.: TREAT: A better match algorithm for AI production systems. In: Proceedings of AAAI 87 Conference on Artificial Intelligence. (1987) 42–47
350. Adaikkalavan, R., Chakravarthy, S.: How to Use Events and Rules for Supporting Role-Based Security? (Invited Paper). In: DEXA Workshops. (2006) 698–702
351. Chakravarthy, S., Krishnaprasad, V., Tamizuddin, Z., Badani, R.H.: ECA Rule Integration into an OODBMS: Architecture and Implementation. In: ICDE. (1995) 341–348
352. Lee, H.S.: Support for Temporal Events in Sentinel: Design Implementation and Preprocessing. Master's thesis, The University of Florida at Gainesville (1996) http://itlab.uta.edu/sharma/People/ThesisWeb/hsl_thesis.pdf.
353. Grossglauser, M., Bolot, J.: On the relevance of long-range dependence in network traffic. IEEE/ACM transactions on Networking (1999) 15–24
354. Feigenbaum, J., Kannan, S., Strauss, M., Viswanathan, M.: An Approximate L1-Difference Algorithm for Massive Data Streams. In: Proceedings of the Annual Symposium on Foundations of Computer Science. (1999) 501–511
355. Srivastava, U., Widom, J.: Memory-limited execution of windowed stream joins. In: Proceedings of the International Conference on Very Large Data Bases. (2004) 324–335

Index